BY THE AUTHOR

Introduction to Contemporary Music
Music: Adventures in Listening

OPERAS IN ENGLISH *(singing versions)*
Beethoven: *Fidelio*
Falla: *Atlantida*
Leoncavallo: *Pagliacci*
Mascagni: *Cavalleria rusticana*
Montemezzi: *L'Amore dei tre re* (The Loves of Three Kings)
Musorgsky: *Boris Godunov*
Poulenc: *Dialogues des Carmélites; La Voix humaine* (The Human Voice)
Prokofiev: *The Flaming Angel; War and Peace*
Puccini: *La Bohème; Il Tabarro* (The Cloak); *Tosca*
Tcherepnin: *The Farmer and the Nymph*
Verdi: *Rigoletto; La Traviata*

Joseph Machlis

Professor of Music, Queens College of the City University of New York

The Enjoyment of Music

An Introduction to Perceptive Listening

FOURTH EDITION SHORTER

W · W · NORTON & COMPANY · INC · NEW YORK

Acknowledgments: Photographs reproduced in this volume have been supplied by the following, whose courtesy is gratefully acknowledged.

F. A. Ackermanns Kunstverlag: pp. 102, 131.
Alinari-Art Reference Bureau, Inc.: pp. 229, 243, 247.
Archiv für Kunst und Geschichte: pp. 169, 172.
ASCAP: p. 377.
The Bettmann Archive: pp. 126, 226, 266, 268, 277, 326, 361.
Bibliothèque et Musée de l'Opéra: p. 116.
Bibliothèque Nationale: pp. 213, 233.
Bruckmann-Art Reference Bureau, Inc.: p. 240.
Photographie Bulloz: pp. 79, 86, 95, 111, 163, 244, 299, 304.
Margaret Carson: p. 37 (Barry Tuckwell, photo by Morrie Lawrence).
CBS Records: pp. 35 (Benny Goodman), 37 (J. J. Johnson), 392, 395, 401.
Columbia-Princeton Electronic Music Center, New York: p. 416 (photo by Manny Warman).
Culver Pictures: p. 237.
Czechoslovak Government Committee for Tourism: p. 97.
Lee Edmundson: p. 40 (Jacqueline Meyer).
Johan Elbers: p. 37 (Gerard Schwartz).
El Escorial: p. 219.
Fantasy/Prestige/Milestone Records: p. 399.
Alison Frantz: p. 161.
German National Tourist Office: p. 257.
Photographie Giraudon: pp. 62, 298.
Peter Gravina: p. 32 (Gary Karr).
Jane Hamborsky: p. 37 (Steven Johns).
The Heather Professor of Music, Oxford University: p. 281.
Historisches Museum der Stadt Wien: pp. 71, 191.
Hurok Concerts, Inc.: pp. 32 (Mstislav Rostropovich), 42 (Van Cliburn).
Instituto Centrale del Restauro: p. 28.

Jenco, Decatur, Illinois: p. 40 (celesta).
Kazuko Hillyer International, Inc.: p. 35 (Paula Robison).
John F. Kennedy Center for the Performing Arts: pp. 5, 138.
Mrs. Annie Knize, New York: p. 337 (owner).
Kupferstichkabinett des Germanischen Nationalmuseums: p. 68.
Kupferstichkabinett der Öffentlichen Kunstsammlung, Kunstmuseum, Basle: pp. 4, 9.
Lincoln Center for the Performing Arts: p. 42 (André Marchal).
Ludwig Industries: p. 40 (Bobby Christian, Al Payson, gong).
Lyra Management, Inc., New York: p. 35 (Lady Barbirolli).
Mannes College of Music: p. 35 (Mary Ellis).
The Metropolitan Museum of Art: pp. 161, 252.
Musser, Division of Ludwig Industries: p. 40 (chimes, glockenspiel).
Nationalhistoriske Museum Frederiksborg: p. 251.
Österreichische Nationalbibliothek: p. 259.
C. F. Peters Corporation: p. 423.
RCA Records: pp. 32 (Walter Trampler), 389.
Rijksmuseum, Amsterdam: pp. 8, 245.
Scala Fine Arts Publishers, Inc.: p. 232.
Adrian Siegel/The Philadelphia Orchestra: p. 35 (Bernard Garfield).
Soprintendenza alle Gallerie, Florence: p. 249.
Christian Steiner: p. 32 (Itzhak Perlman).
TASS from Sovfoto: p. 90.
Trans World Airlines: p. 221.
Universitätsbibliothek, Tübingen: p. 136.
University of Virginia: p. 165.

Poetry on p. 423 from Federico García Lorca, *Selected Poems*. Copyright 1955 by New Directions Publishing Corporation. Reprinted by permission of New Directions Publishing Corporation.

Library of Congress Cataloging in Publication Data

Machlis, Joseph, 1906-
The enjoyment of music. Fourth Edition, shorter.
Bibliography: p.
Includes index.
1. Music—Analysis, appreciation.   I. Title.
MT6.M134   1977b   780'.15   76-52482

ISBN 0-393-09125-2

3 4 5 6 7 8 9 0

FOR EARLE FENTON PALMER

Contents

Preface to the Fourth Edition

In preparing this new edition of *The Enjoyment of Music,* I adhered to the philosophy of the original book, which was based on my conviction that teaching a student how to enjoy an art is not quite the same as teaching him its history. Early in my own teaching, I abandoned chronological order in favor of a psychological approach, just as, in teaching freshmen how to appreciate literature, I would have begun with Mailer and Vonnegut or the great novels of the nineteenth century and worked my way back to *Piers the Plowman* and *Beowulf,* rather than the other way around. By beginning with works either familiar to students or easily accessible to them, we build up their confidence in their ability to enjoy music, which is half the battle; and by proceeding gradually from the simplest level to a more advanced, we expand their horizons and foster their growth in the most natural way. For this reason, once the materials of music have been explained, the book moves to nineteenth-century Romanticism, the style that is apt to be most accessible to a beginner. From there I move back to late eighteenth-century Classicism, then back to the older music, and finally forward to the twentieth century. As a result Tchaikovsky, Beethoven, Bach, Debussy, and Stravinsky are encountered in a sequence that bears some relationship to their music, rather than in a sequence depending solely on the order in which they happened to be born.

This edition introduces a number of changes that were made in the light of classroom experience and changing tastes. Among the nineteenth-century works I added are Schumann's *Mondnacht* and the Verdi *Requiem,* the latter concluding a new chapter on choral music. I rewrote the first two chapters and replaced a number of works with others that will, I believe, make for a more effective presentation in class. Thus, in the chapter on Schubert, *To Sylvia* replaced *Heidenröslein;* in the chapter on Chopin, I substituted the *Mazurka in C-sharp minor* for the *Polonaise in A flat.*

In accordance with the ever-growing interest in old music, I expanded the chapters on the Middle Ages and Renaissance, and made a number of substitutions that will render this music more interesting to young people. Among the newcomers are the Introit *Gaudeamus omnes,* the Kyrie from Machaut's *Notre Dame Mass,* and Dufay's motet *Alma redemptoris mater.* An entire chapter is devoted to Josquin; included are the beautiful *Lament on the Death of Ockeghem* and his delightful nonsense song *Scaramella.* Weelkes's *As Vesta Was Descending* is included as one of the supreme examples of the Elizabethan madrigal. In the section on Baroque music I expanded the chapters on Monteverdi and Purcell.

In the section on twentieth-century music, the excerpts from Stravinsky's *Le Sacre du printemps* now include the *Danse sacrale;* and the shattering *A Survivor from Warsaw* of Schoenberg has also been added. I greatly expanded the section on American music, especially in reference to the first and second New England Schools and the unjustifiably forgotten figures who came between. The discussion of twentieth-century Americans is now much longer, and Martin Williams has contributed a chapter on Duke Ellington. Among the new titles are the *String Quartet* of Ruth Crawford, a pioneering figure now receiving long overdue recognition.

The list of contemporary works includes a number of newcomers, among them George Crumb's powerful setting of Garcia Lorca's *Ancient Voices of Children,* Elliott Carter's *Eight Etudes and a Fantasy,* and—an unusually witty example of electronic music—Mario Davidovsky's *Synchronisms No. 1.* To keep the book from becoming too unwieldy, these additions had to be balanced by a number of deletions. The appendices have been revised, especially the Reading List, which emphasizes recent and easily available books; and the Chronological List was brought up to date. I hope that these and similar changes will make the text more useful for both student and teacher.

I have not gone along with the practice, currently the fashion in books of this nature, of devoting a brief chapter or two to non-Western music. The musics of Asia and Africa represent a diversity of ancient cultures with an extraordinarily rich and complex literature, any adequate discussion of which would carry us far beyond the confines of this book. To attempt to cover so vast a subject in a few pages is as pointless as would be, in a book on African or Asian music, for the author to dismiss the musical heritage of the West in six or seven pages. Such a procedure can have no educational value whatever.

For those who are using the Norton set of records that go with the book, references have been added, in the margin, to the location of the recording of the particular work being discussed at that point. It is not suggested that the text cannot be taught with other recordings of the same work if the instructor so prefers. The sole advantage of the Norton records is that they bring together in one set the most important works discussed in the text. Whichever records are used, the text should serve only as an introduction to the music itself.

I am heavily indebted to David Hamilton and Claire Brook for their devoted reading of the manuscript, and to Hinda Keller Farber for her care in preparing it for publication. I am especially grateful to Martin Williams for adding to his illuminating discussion of jazz. And I very much want to thank the many colleagues who were sufficiently interested in the project of revision to send me their suggestions for making this a better book.

The text, naturally, covers a much wider field than the course, but like the course it strives never to lose sight of my main goal—to create music lovers. In this connection it is well to recall Stravinsky's wonderful remark, "The trouble with music appreciation in general is that people are taught to have too much respect for music; they should be taught to love it instead."

JOSEPH MACHLIS

ONE
The Materials of Music

"There are only twelve tones. You must treat them carefully." — PAUL HINDEMITH

1 By Way of Introduction

"You use a glass mirror to see your face; you use works of art to see your soul."
— GEORGE BERNARD SHAW

Why a Book on Music?

The need for art lies deep in human nature. Children spontaneously make up stories and poems, create songs, and paint. We find art in the most primitive societies, where everybody takes part in the dancing, singing, and ceremonies of the tribe.

But as society develops, life becomes more complex. The creation of art becomes a specialty, the personal domain of the artist; and what he creates becomes ever more sophisticated. Eventually the simpler art of the folk is separated from the cultivated art of a leisure class. Poets, painters, and musicians begin to create their works for an audience that is socially high above the peasants from whom art originally sprang. In this aristocratic setting art takes on a wealth of subtleties that can be fully appreciated only by people who have the time and the tradition.

Our age is the first when, because of technological advances—radio and television, long-playing records, paperbacks and cheap reproductions —art has become accessible to all members of society. Given this process, we confront an ever more decisive gap between the great tradition of art and the new mass audience. It is in order to close this gap that our schools and universities offer courses in the appreciation of painting, literature, and music, and our publishers turn out books that instruct novices how to get more out of the poems, symphonies, and paintings to which they are exposed.

There can be only one justification for such books—to heighten the reader's enjoyment. His understanding can be deepened, he can be made more aware of what he hears, sees, or reads, if he is properly introduced to the vocabulary of a particular art, its basic concepts, and techniques. At the same time he must not be overwhelmed with too many technical details, or he will end by being more bewildered and baffled than when he began.

A book about music must be doubly careful to avoid this danger, for it can too easily bog down in material that concerns the professional rather

Responding to music has always been the most natural thing in the world. **Bauerntanz,** an anonymous Swiss engraving (c. 1520).

than the layman. As a matter of fact, millions of people enjoy music who never read a book about it. Many feel that the less said the better, since it would only spoil their enjoyment if they knew too much. They happen to be wrong. Much can be told listeners that will enable them to listen more intelligently, hear more clearly, and respond on a deeper level to the patterns of sound as they float through the air: much that will heighten their perceptions, enrich their awareness, and increase their enjoyment. It is to this body of knowledge that our book addresses itself.

The Art of Listening

Responding to music is the most natural thing in the world, judging from the multitudes who sing, dance, hum, whistle, nod, and tap. But to listen perceptively to a great musical work—that is, really to *hear* it—is an art in itself: an art that may come more easily to some than to others, but one that can be acquired through practice and application.

Our time, unfortunately, does not encourage this art. What with radio, television, recordings, jukeboxes, and cassettes, music surrounds us everywhere. Anything that is so easy to come by is, in the end, taken for granted. People have only to flick a knob to have music flood their living room. They converse, eat, telephone, read the comics, do crossword puzzles, and all the while that ceaseless tinkle-tinkle is floating past their ears, half-heeded, quarter-heeded, or unheeded. By a supreme irony, the very invention that brought music into every home in the land has all but ended the art of listening to it. People think they've been listening just because their ears happened to be in the path of the sounds. They do not realize that there is only one way to listen to music, and that is—to listen!

As a matter of fact, we vary greatly in our way of responding to music.

During the playing, shall we say, of the *Triumphal March* from *Aïda,* one listener will summon up a vision of ancient tombs and Pharoahs. Another floats off in a daydream equally far removed from the music and the world. A third is filled with a strange sense of power at the ringing tone of the trumpets. His neighbor for no apparent reason recalls the half hour he spent in the dentist's chair. This one is pleased with himself for having noticed the reappearance of a theme. That one has decided that the conductor is a shoemaker and wonders how he ever managed to get an orchestra. The musicologist reflects upon the contribution of Verdi to grand-opera style. The critic polishes a phrase for his next review. The budding composer is oppressed by a suspicion that he was born too late.

Listening to music combines intellectual, emotional, and sensuous elements in an altogether special way. Our minds can be aware of the way a piece is put together even while our hearts respond to its emotional appeal and our senses are ravished by the physical beauty of the sound. The goal of all training in listening is to combine all three levels. If we succeed in doing this, listening becomes a total experience in which mind, heart, and senses are nourished together.

Listening to music combines intellectual, emotional, and sensuous elements. A free concert in the Grand Foyer at the Kennedy Center. *(Photo by Richard Braaten.)*

"To understand," said Raphael, "is to equal." When we completely understand a great work of music we grasp the "moment of truth" that gave it birth. For the nonce we become, if not the equal of the master who created it, at least worthy to sit in his company. We receive his message, we fathom his intention. In effect, we listen perceptively. And that is the one sure road to the enjoyment of music.

2 Art as Experience

"Art postulates communion, and the artist has an imperative need to make others share the joy which he experiences himself." — IGOR STRAVINSKY

What Art Offers

Art, like love, is easier to experience than to define. That is because, like love, it is experienced on different levels. There is art that serves as entertainment and offers a pleasant escape from the cares of life. There is art that propagates the artist's point of view, whether religious, political, or philosophical. There is art that fulfills Aristotle's precept by purging our emotions "through pity and terror." There is art that leads us to a broader understanding and compassion.

The important thing is that, wherever men have lived together, art has sprung up among them as a language surcharged with feeling and significance. The desire to create such a language—whether through poetry, drama and the novel, painting, sculpture and architecture, music and dance—appears to be universal. It is part of man's need to impose his will on the universe, to bring order out of chaos, to endow his moments of highest awareness with enduring form and substance.

Because of its diversity, art has been defined in many ways. Santayana considered art to be "the response to the demand for entertainment, for the stimulation of our senses and imagination." In similar vein Alfred North Whitehead wrote, "Art is the imposing of a pattern on experience, and our esthetic enjoyment in recognition of the pattern." On the other hand, a long line of philosophers considered art important because its moral effect on our nature extended far beyond affording us relaxation and pleasure. "The introduction of a new kind of music," Plato stated, "must be shunned as imperiling the whole state, since styles of music are never disturbed without affecting the most important political institutions." More than two thousand years later Tolstoy set forth an equally idealistic definition: "Art is a human activity having for its purpose the transmission to others of the highest and best feelings to which man has risen." How close this is to Shelley's famous definition of poetry as "the record of the best and happiest moments of the happiest and best minds." Or to André Malraux's profound remark: "The function of literature is to reveal to man his hidden greatness."

Clearly no two philosophers would agree on a definition. We may say that art concerns itself with the communication of certain ideas and feelings by means of a sensuous medium—color, sound, bronze, marble, words. This medium is fashioned into works marked by beauty of design and coherence of form, works that appeal to our minds, arouse our emotions, kindle our imagination, and enchant our senses.

Music and Life: The Sources of Musical Imagery

How did music come into being? A number of theories have been advanced to explain its origins. One derives music from the inflections of speech, another from mating calls and bird calls, a third from the cries of battle and signals of the hunt, a fourth from the rhythms of collective labor. Some attribute the rise of music to the imitation of nature's sounds, others connect it with the play impulse, with magic and religious rites, or with the need for emotional expression. All these explanations relate music to the deepest experiences of the individual and the group. Underlying all is the fact that man possesses in his vocal cords a means of producing music, in his body an instrument for rhythmic movement, and in his mind the capacity to imagine and to recognize musical sounds.

The art of music has come a long way from its primitive stage. But it has retained its connection with the springs of human feeling, with the accents of joy and sorrow, tension and release. In this sense we may speak of

Singing is the most widespread way of making music. An etching by Francesco Bartolozzi (1727–1815) of a lute player and a singer.

Dance is the physical response to the power of rhythm. A lithograph of Jane Avril by Henri de Toulouse-Lautrec (1864–1901). *Collection, The Museum of Modern Art, New York; Gift of Abby Aldrich Rockefeller.)*

music as a universal language, one that transcends the barriers which men put up against each other. Its procedures have been shaped by thousands of years of human experience; its expressive content mirrors man's existence, his place in nature and in society.

Song is the most natural form of music. Issuing from within the body, it is projected by means of the most personal of all instruments, the human voice. From time immemorial singing has been the most widespread way of making music. In folk music we have a treasury of song that reflects all phases of life—work songs, love songs, drinking songs, cradle songs,

Music plays an important role in the religious experience. A photo of a fragment of the altarpiece by Adriaen van Wesel (1420–80?) depicting three angel musicians and St. Joseph.

Throughout history, music has been an integral part of processions and ceremonies. An engraving by Hieronymus Hess (1799–1850) of a *Carnival Reveille* in Basel.

patriotic songs, dance songs, play songs, marching songs, songs of mourning, narrative songs. Some are centuries old, others are of recent origin; but all come out of human experience and affirm the indissoluble bond between music and life.

An equally fertile source of music is the dance. The love of dancing springs from man's joy in his body, his release of tension through movement and gesture, his capacity for living in the moment. In a larger sense dance mirrors the structure of society. The dance of the countryside is different from the city dance; and both, throughout the ages, were set off from the court dance. Folk, popular, and court dances nourished centuries of European art music. Certain dance pieces exude a peasant gusto, others idealize the spirit of the dance. But all testify to the power of rhythm and mirror the patterns of man's physical presence in the world.

The march (a kind of dance) descends from the ceremonial processions of tribal life. Its music is associated with trumpets and drums and the pageantry of great civic occasions. So too the religious impulse has motivated a considerable amount of the world's great music. Most works in this category were composed for use in the church service; others are concert pieces on sacred themes. In either case they have that spiritual quality which music is particularly able to achieve. Opera too forms a potent link between life and music. Its theme is man, his passions, his conflicts, his actions. Through opera, composers learned to transform into musical images the most varied sentiments and situations drawn from the human condition.

Then there is the great body of abstract instrumental music that is nourished by all the images we have mentioned but presents them in an abstract way, lifted from the particular to the general, from the specific to the universal. Here the music is filled with an emotion to which it is neither possible nor desirable to attach a label. Perhaps we would do best to call it simply the emotion of music. When Beethoven was once asked what a composition of his meant, he sat down at the piano and played it again; which was his way of saying that it meant—itself! This power of music to communicate feelings in the abstract (which painting and sculpture have achieved only in our time) impelled Walter Pater to his celebrated statement that "All art constantly aspires towards the condition of music."

The first step toward understanding music is to become aware of the elements of which it is composed. We will discuss each of these separately in the following chapters. Then you will be able to understand how they combine to form the whole.

3 Melody: Musical Line

"It is the melody which is the charm of music, and it is that which is most difficult to produce. The invention of a fine melody is a work of genius." — JOSEPH HAYDN

Melody is that element of music which makes the widest and most direct appeal. It has been called the soul of music. It is generally what we remember and whistle and hum. We know a good melody when we hear it and we recognize its unique power to move us, although we might be hard put to explain wherein its power lies. The melody is the musical line—or curve, if you prefer—that guides our ear through a composition. The melody is the plot, the theme of a musical work, the thread upon which hangs the tale. As Aaron Copland aptly put it, "The melody is generally what the piece is about."

A *melody* is a succession of single tones perceived by the mind as a unity. In order to perceive a melody as a unity, we must find a significant relationship among its constituent tones. We must derive from them an impression of a conscious arrangement: the sense of a beginning, a middle, and an end. We hear the words of a sentence not singly but in relation to the thought as a whole. So too we perceive tones not separately but in relation to each other within a pattern. A melody seems to move up and down, its individual tones being higher or lower than each other. It also moves forward in time, one tone claiming our attention for a longer or shorter duration than another. From the interaction of the two dimensions emerges the total unit which is melody.

Melodic range   In addition, a melody may move stepwise along the scale or it may leap to a tone several degrees away. The leap may be narrow or wide, as may be the *range* of the melody (the distance from its lowest to highest tone). Compare the narrow range and stepwise movement of *America* with the bold leaps and far-flung activity of *The Star-Spangled Banner*. Clearly *The Star-Spangled Banner* is the more vigorous melody. A melody may be fast or slow, loud or soft. A loud and fast tune such as *Dixie* creates the atmosphere of jaunty activity proper to a marching song as surely as a soft, slow melody like *Silent Night* suggests a hymnlike serenity and peace. In short, the character of a melody is determined by its overall pattern of movement.

The Structure of Melody

Let us examine the pattern of a well-known tune.

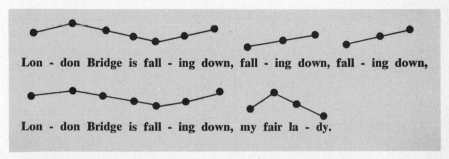

Lon - don Bridge is fall - ing down, fall - ing down, fall - ing down,

Lon - don Bridge is fall - ing down, my fair la - dy.

The phrase   You will notice that this melody divides itself into two halves. Such symmetry is found frequently in melodies dating from the eighteenth and nineteenth centuries. Each of these halves is called a *phrase*. In music, as in language, a phrase denotes a unit of meaning within a larger structure. Two phrases together form a musical *period*.

Each phrase ends in a kind of resting place that punctuates the flow of the music. Such a resting place is known as a *cadence*. The first phrase of *London Bridge* ends in an upward inflection, like a question. This is an inconclusive type of cadence, indicating, like a comma in punctuation, that more is to come. The second phrase ends in a full cadence that creates a sense of conclusion. The vigorous downward inflection on the word "la-dy" contributes to this decisive ending. (It should be pointed out, however, that not all final cadences move downward.) Both phrases of *London Bridge* combine in a question-and-answer formation: the second phrase grows out of the first and completes its meaning. We find here the quality of organic unity that is of prime importance in art.

The composer unifies his structure by repeating some of his musical ideas. Thus both phrases of *London Bridge* begin in identical fashion. The necessary contrast is supplied by fresh material, which in our example comes on the words "my fair lady." Through repetition and contrast the composer achieves both unity and variety. This combination of traits is basic to musical architecture, for without unity there is chaos, without variety—boredom.

The melodic line does not leave off haphazardly, as if it suddenly found something better to do. On the contrary, it gives the impression of having reached its goal. If you will hum the last phrase of several well-known tunes such as *The Star-Spangled Banner, America,* and *Auld Lang Syne,* you will notice they all end on a tone that produces this effect of finality. We encounter here what for centuries has been a basic principle in our music: one tone is singled out as the center of the group and serves as a landmark for the others. This central tone is the one to which, in most cases, the melody ultimately returns.

The phrase as a whole may trace an upward or downward curve. Not infrequently, the one is balanced by the other. *The Farmer in the Dell* presents an ascending first phrase which is answered by a descending second phrase:

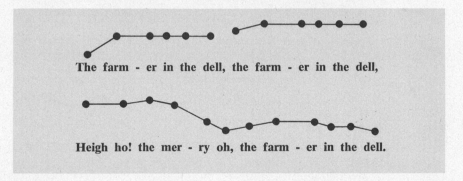

The farm - er in the dell, the farm - er in the dell,

Heigh ho! the mer - ry oh, the farm - er in the dell.

The melody moves forward in time, now faster, now slower, in a rhythmic pattern that holds our attention even as does its up and down movement. Without the rhythm the melody loses its aliveness. Try singing *London Bridge* or *The Farmer in the Dell* in tones of equal duration, and see how much is lost of the quality of the pattern. Without rhythm, the melody could not be organized into clear-cut phrases and cadences.

Our gestures when we speak are purely physical movements, yet they carry emotional meaning. In the same way, the physical facts that make up a melody take on psychological implications. The melodic line may be described as angular or smooth, tense or relaxed, energetic or languid. Above all, the melody must be interesting. We say of a painter that he has a sense of line, meaning that he is able to sustain movement over the whole of his canvas. The same holds for the unfolding melodic line with its rising and falling, its peaks and valleys. A melody has to have what musicians call the "long line." It must build tension as it rises from one level to the next, and must retain its drive until the final note.

What makes a striking effect on the listener is the climax, the high point

The undulating line in a painting or a melody sustains movement. A drawing by Pablo Picasso (1881–1975), **Four Ballet Dancers.** *(Collection, The Museum of Modern Art, New York; Gift of Abby Aldrich Rockefeller.)*

Melodic shape

in the melodic line that usually represents the peak of intensity. The climax gives purpose and direction to the melodic line. It creates the impression of crisis met and overcome. Our national anthem contains a fine climax in the last phrase, on the words "O'er the land of the free." There can be no doubt in anybody's mind that this song is about freedom. Clearly, too, freedom must be striven for, to judge from the effort we have to make to get up to the crucial tone.

The principles we have touched upon are to be found in the melodies of the masters. Let us take some familiar examples. Brahms's popular *Hungarian Dance No. 5* opens with vigorous upward leaps. The impression of energy is reinforced by the lively rhythm. As is often the case with dance tunes, the phrases are symmetrical, with a clearly marked cadence at the end of each. The activity of this melodic line contrasts with the gentle flow of the Air from Bach's *Suite No. 3* for orchestra, which moves at a much slower pace. Chopin's lively *Mazurka in B flat,* Opus 7, No. 1, exemplifies a type of melody that, because of its wide range and leaps, is more suitable for an instrument than for voice. (*Opus,* abbreviated Op., the Latin for "work," is used together with a number to indicate the chronological position of a piece—or a group of pieces—in a composer's output. The opus number may refer to either the order of composition or the order of publication.) Notice the contrast between this melody and the restricted activity of Chopin's *Prelude in E minor,* which moves mostly stepwise and within a narrow range. A fine example of how rhythm can make a melody memorable is offered by the *Hallelujah Chorus* from Handel's *Messiah.* The sharply defined rhythm on the word "Hallelujah," repeated again and again in the course of the piece, stamps itself unforgettably on the mind.

"Melody," writes the composer Paul Hindemith, "is the element in which the personal characteristics of the composer are most clearly and most obviously revealed." For melody is the essential unit of communication in music: the direct bearer of meaning from composer to listener.

4 Harmony: Musical Space

"Music, to create harmony, must investigate discord." — PLUTARCH

We are accustomed to hearing melodies against a background of harmony. To the movement of the melody, harmony adds another dimension —depth. Harmony is to music what perspective is to painting. It introduces the impression of musical space. The supporting role of harmony is apparent when a singer accompanies his melody with chords on the guitar or banjo, or when a pianist plays the melody with his right hand while the left strikes the chords. We are jolted if the wrong chord is sounded, for at that point we become aware that the necessary unity of melody and harmony has been broken.

Interval and chord

Harmony pertains to the movement and relationship of intervals and chords. An *interval* may be defined as the distance—and relationship— between two tones. In the familiar *do-re-mi-fa-sol-la-ti-do* scale, the interval *do-re* is a second, *do-mi* is a third, *do-fa* a fourth, *do-sol* a fifth, *do-la* a sixth, *do-ti* a seventh, and from one *do* to the next is an octave. The tones of the interval may be sounded in succession or simultaneously.

A *chord* may be defined as a combination of three or more tones that constitutes a single unit of harmony. Just as the vaulting arch rests upon columns, so melody unfolds above the supporting chords, the harmony. The melodic line constitutes the horizontal aspect of music; the harmony, consisting of blocks of tones (chords), constitutes the vertical:

The Function of Harmony

Chords have meaning only in relation to other chords: that is, only as each leads into the next. Harmony therefore implies movement and progression. In the larger sense, harmony denotes the overall organization of tones in a musical work in such a way as to achieve order and unity.

The triad

The most common chord in our music is a certain combination of three tones known as a *triad.* Such a chord may be built by combining the first, third, and fifth degrees of the *do-re-mi-fa-sol-la-ti-do* scale: *do-mi-sol.* A triad may be built on the second degree (steps 2–4–6 or *re-fa-la*); on the third degree (steps 3–5–7 or *mi-sol-ti*); and similarly on each of the other degrees of the scale. The triad is a basic formation in our music. "In the world of tones," observes one authority, "the triad corresponds to the force of gravity. It serves as our constant guiding point, our unit of measure, and our goal."

Although the triad is a vertical block of sound, its three tones often appear horizontally as a melody. The first three tones of the *Blue Danube Waltz* form a triad, as do the first three of our national anthem (on the words "O-oh-say"). When the lowest tone (or root) of the chord is duplicated an octave above, we have a four-tone version of the triad. This happens at the beginning of *The Star-Spangled Banner,* on the words "say can you see." It is apparent that melody and harmony do not function independently of one another. On the contrary, the melody implies the harmony that goes with it, and each constantly influences the other.

Active and Rest Chords

Music is an art of movement. Movement to be purposeful must have a goal. In the course of centuries musicians have tried to make the progression of chords meaningful by providing such a goal.

Tonic and Dominant

We noticed, in the previous chapter, that a number of melodies ended—that is, came to rest—on a central tone. This is the *do* which comes both first and last in the *do-re-mi-fa-sol-la-ti-do* scale. The triad on *do* (*do-mi-sol*) is the I chord or *Tonic,* which serves as the chord of rest. But rest has meaning only in relation to activity. The chord of rest is counterposed to other chords which are active. The active chords seek to be completed, or *resolved,* in the rest chord. This striving for resolution is the dynamic force in our music. It shapes the forward movement, imparting direction and goal.

The fifth step of the *do-re-mi-fa-sol-la-ti-do* scale is the chief representative of the active principle. We therefore obtain two focal points: the active triad on *sol* (*sol-ti-re*), the V chord or *Dominant,* which seeks to be resolved to the restful triad on *do.* Dominant moving to Tonic constitutes a compact formula of activity completed, of movement come to rest.

The cadence   We saw that the cadence is a point of rest in the melody. This point of rest is underlined by the harmony. For example, Dominant resolving to Tonic is the most common final cadence in our music. We hear it asserted over and over again at the end of many compositions dating from the eighteenth and nineteenth centuries. After generations of conditioning we feel a decided expectation that an active chord will resolve to the chord of rest.

Following is the harmonic structure of *London Bridge*, involving a simple progression from Tonic to Dominant and back.

London Bridge is	falling down,	falling down,	falling down:
I———	I———	V———	I———
London Bridge is	**falling down,**	**my fair**	**lady.**
I———	I———	V———	I———

The   The triad built on the fourth scale step *fa* (*fa-la-do*) is known as the
Subdominant   IV chord or *Subdominant*. This too is an active chord, but less so than the Dominant. The progression IV—I creates a less decisive cadence than the other. It is familiar to us from the two chords associated with the Amen often sung at the end of hymns.

These three triads, the basic ones of our system, suffice to harmonize many a famous tune.

Silent night!	Holy night!	All is calm,	all is bright,
I———	I———	V———	I———
Round yon Virgin	**Mother and Child!**	**Holy Infant, so**	**tender and mild,**
IV———	I———	IV———	I———
Sleep in heavenly	**peace,**	**sleep in heavenly**	**peace.**
V———	I———	I——V——	I———

Consonance and Dissonance

Harmonic movement, we saw, is generated by the tendency of active chords to be resolved to chords of rest. This movement receives its maximum impetus from the dissonance. *Dissonance* is restlessness and activity, *consonance* is relaxation and fulfillment. The dissonant chord creates tension. The consonant chord resolves it.

Dissonance introduces the necessary tension into music. Without it, a work would be intolerably dull and insipid. What suspense and conflict are to the drama, dissonance is to music. It creates the areas of tension without which the areas of relaxation would have no meaning. Each complements the other; both are a necessary part of the artistic whole.

In general, music has grown more dissonant through the ages. It is easy

Harmony lends a sense of depth to music, as perspective does to painting. A painting by Meindert Hobbema (1638–1709), **The Avenue, Middleharnis.** *(Courtesy of the Trustees, The National Gallery, London.)*

to understand why. A combination of tones that sounded extremely harsh when first introduced began to seem less so as the sound became increasingly familiar. As a result, a later generation of composers had to find ever more dissonant tone-combinations in order to produce the same amount of tension as their predecessors. This process has extended across the centuries, as is apparent if we listen in succession to music of different epochs. For example, the Sanctus from the *Missa Ascendo ad Patrem* by Palestrina (late seventeenth century) has all the seraphic calm we associate with the sacred music of that composer; yet it must have sounded considerably less consonant to Palestrina's contemporaries than it does to us. Next, listen to the second movement of Mozart's *Eine kleine Nachtmusik* or the duet *Là ci darem la mano* from his opera *Don Giovanni:* both works date from 1787. The harmony will strike you as predominantly consonant, although less so than the Palestrina piece. In the Prelude to his most romantic music drama, Wagner tried to express the unfulfilled yearning of Tristan for Isolde (1859). There is a markedly higher level of dissonance tension here than in the music of Mozart. Finally, for an example of twentieth-century dissonance, listen to the *Dance of the Adolescents* from Igor Stravinsky's *Rite of Spring* (1913). This piece will suggest to you the distance that separates the music of our century, in regard to dissonance tension, from the music of earlier times.

Harmony is a much more sophisticated phenomenon than melody. Historically it appeared much later, about a thousand years ago. Its real development took place only in the West. The music of the Orient to this day is largely melodic. Indeed, we may consider the great achievement of Western music to be harmony (hearing in depth), even as in painting it is perspective (seeing in depth). Our harmonic system has advanced steadily over the past ten centuries. Today it is adjusting to new needs. These constitute the latest chapter in man's age-old attempt to impose law and order upon the raw material of sound; to organize tones in such a way that they will manifest a unifying idea, a selective imagination, a reasoning will.

5 Rhythm: Musical Time

"In the beginning was rhythm." — HANS VON BÜLOW

Rhythm—the word means "flow" in Greek—is the term we use to refer to the controlled movement of music in time. The duration of the tones, their frequency, and the regularity or irregularity with which they are sounded determine the rhythm of a musical passage. Rhythm is the element of music most closely allied to body movement, to physical action. Its simpler patterns when repeated over and over can have a hypnotic effect on us. For this reason rhythm has been called the heartbeat of music, the pulse that betokens life. It is this aspect of rhythm that people have in mind when they say of a musician that "he's got rhythm," meaning an electrifying quality, an aliveness almost independent of the notes. Yet, since music is an art that exists solely in time, rhythm in the larger sense controls all the relationships within a composition, down to the minutest detail. Hence Roger Sessions's remark that "an adequate definition of rhythm comes close to defining music itself."

The Nature of Rhythm

It is rhythm that causes people to fall in step when the band plays, to nod or tap with the beat. Rhythm releases our motor reflexes even if we do not respond with actual physical movement. We feel it in ourselves as a kind of ideal motion; we seem to dance without leaving our chairs.

Rhythm springs from the need for order inherent in the human mind. Upon the tick-tock of the clock or the clacking of train wheels we automatically impose a pattern. We hear the sounds as a regular pulsation

In architecture, symmetry and repetition of elements are expressions of rhythm. A photo of the Guggenheim Museum, New York City.

of strong and weak beats. In brief, we organize our perception of time by means of rhythm.

The ancients discerned in rhythm the creative principle of the universe manifested alike in the regular movement of planets, the cycle of seasons and tides, of night and day, desire and appeasement, life and death. Yet these rhythms framed an existence that all too often lacked design and meaning. Rivers overflowed for no good reason, lightning struck, enemies pillaged. Exposed to the caprice of a merciless destiny, man fashioned for himself an ideal universe where the unforeseen was excluded and divine order reigned. This universe was art; and its controlling principle was rhythm. The symmetrical proportions of architecture, the balanced groupings of painting and sculpture, the patterns of the dance, the regular meters of poetry—each in its own sphere represents man's deep-seated need for rhythmical arrangement. But it is in music, the art of ideal movement, that rhythm finds its richest expression.

Meter

If we are to grasp the flow of music through time, time must be organized. Musical time is usually organized in terms of a basic unit of length, known as a *beat*—the regular pulsation to which we may tap our feet. Some beats are stronger than others—these are known as *accented* or *strong* beats. In much of the music we hear, these strong beats occur at regular

intervals—every other beat, every third beat, every fourth, and so on—
and thus we perceive the beats in groups of two, three, four, or more.
These groups are known as *measures,* each containing a fixed number of
beats. The first beat of the measure generally receives the strongest accent.

Meter, therefore, denotes the fixed time patterns within which musical
events take place. Within the underlying metrical framework, the rhythm
flows freely. In a dance band, the drummer will beat a regular pattern,
with an accent on the first beat of every measure, while the trumpeter or
another soloist will play a melody, containing many notes of different
lengths, flowing freely over the regular pattern. Together, both of them
articulate the rhythm or overall flow of the music. We may say that all
waltzes have the same meter: ONE-two-three ONE-two-three. Within
that meter, however, each waltz follows its own rhythmic pattern.

Although meter is one element of rhythm, it is possible to draw a subtle
distinction between them. This may be noted in the domain of poetry.
A metrical reading of a poem—such as these lines by Robert Frost—will
bring out the regular pattern of accented and unaccented syllables:

> The wóods are lóve-ly, dárk and déep.
> But Í have próm-is-és to kéep,

When we read rhythmically, on the other hand, we bring out the natural
flow of the language within the basic meter and, more important, the
expressive meaning of the words. It is this distinction that the English
critic Fox-Strangways has in mind when he observes: "A melody—an
Irish reel perhaps—is in strict time, or people could not dance to it correctly; but if it had not also rhythm, they would not dance to it passionately."

Metrical Patterns

The simpler metrical patterns, in music as in poetry, depend on the regular recurrence of accent. Simplest of all is a succession of beats in which
a strong alternates with a weak: ONE-two ONE-two—or in marching,
LEFT-right LEFT-right. This is known as duple meter and is often encountered as two-four time ($\frac{2}{4}$). The pattern occurs in many nursery
rhymes and marching songs.

Twín - kle	twín - kle	lít - tle	stár———,
ONE - two	ONE - two	ONE - two	ONE - two

Hów I	wón - der	what you	áre———.
ONE two	ONE - two	ONE - two	ONE two

The best way to perceive rhythm is through physical response. The above tune can be accompanied, while singing, with a downward movement of the hand on ONE and an upward movement on *two*.

Duple meter   *Duple meter,* then, contains two beats to the measure, with the accent generally falling on the first beat. Within this meter a tune such as *Yankee Doodle* presents a somewhat more active rhythmic pattern than the above example. That is, in *Twinkle, twinkle, little star* there is mostly one melody note to a beat. *Yankee Doodle* contains, for the most part, two melody notes to a beat. Here the meter is the steady ONE-two ONE-two that constitutes the underlying beat, above which flows the rhythmic pattern of the melody.

Yánkee Doodle	wént to town	Ríding on a	pó - ny
ONE - two	ONE - two	ONE - two	ONE - two

Triple meter   Another basic metrical pattern is that of three beats to the measure, or *triple meter,* with the accent normally falling on the first beat. This is the pattern of three-four time (¾) traditionally associated with the waltz and minuet.

Two celebrated examples of triple meter are *America* and *The Star-Spangled Banner.*

Mý	coun - try	'tís——of thee,
ONE - two - three		ONE - two - three

Swéet	land of	lí——ber - ty
ONE - two - three		ONE - two - three

Óf	thee I	síng——————
ONE - two - three		ONE - two - three

Oh	sáy can you	sée———
three	ONE - two - three	ONE - two -

by the	dáwn's ear - ly	líght———
three	ONE - two - three	ONE - two

Quadruple meter   *Quadruple meter,* also known as *common time,* contains four beats to the measure. The primary accent falls on the first beat of the measure, with a secondary accent on the third: ONE-two-THREE-four. Quadruple meter, generally encountered as four-four time (⁴⁄₄), is found in some of our most widely sung melodies: *Good Night Ladies; Annie Laurie;* the *Battle Hymn of the Republic; Long, Long Ago; Auld Lang Syne,* and a host of others.

Góod night, lá-dies!——   Góod night, lá-dies!——
ONE - two - Three - four   ONE - two - Three - four

Góod night, lá-dies!——We're   goíng to leave you nów————.
ONE - two - Three - four   ONE - two -   Three - four

Should   aúld——ac-quain - tance   bé——for - got,
four   ONE - two - Three - four   ONE - two - Three

and   né————ver brought to   mínd——————,
four   ONE - two - Three - four   ONE - two - Three

Compound meters   Duple, triple, and quadruple meter are regarded as the *simple meters.* The *compound meters* contain five, six, seven, or more beats to the measure, with primary and secondary accents marking the metrical pattern. Most frequently encountered among the compound meters is *sextuple meter:* six-four or six-eight time. This is often marked by a gently flowing effect. Popular examples are *My Bonnie Lies over the Ocean, Sweet and Low, Silent Night, Believe Me if All Those Endearing Young Charms, Drink to Me Only with Thine Eyes.*

Dríňk to   me   ón————ly   wíth—— thine eyes——— and
ONE - two - three - Four - five - six   ONE - two - three - Four - five - six

Í————will   pledge—— with   míne————————
ONE - two - three - Four - five - six   ONE - two - three - Four - five - six

You may hear examples of duple meter in Schubert's *Marche militaire,* Brahms's *Hungarian Dance No. 5,* and the Gavotte from Bach's *Suite No. 3.* Three-four time is exemplified by the Minuet from Mozart's *Eine kleine Nachtmusik,* Chopin's *Mazurka in B flat,* Opus 7, No. 1, and the *Emperor Waltz* of Johann Strauss. The *Triumphal March* from Verdi's *Aïda* is a good example of ¼ time, as is the March from Prokofiev's *The Love for Three Oranges.* For examples of ⁶⁄₈ time listen to *Morning* from *Peer Gynt Suite No. 1* by Grieg or Mendelssohn's *Venetian Boat Song.* When ⁶⁄₈ time is taken at a rapid pace the ear hears the six beats in two groups of three, so that the effect is akin to that of duple meter. An example is the Gigue from Bach's *Suite No. 3.*

The four meters just mentioned are the ones most frequently encountered in folk music and in the art music of the eighteenth and nineteenth centuries.

Syncopation

In music based on dance rhythm the meter has to be very clearly defined. This accounts for the decisive accents in a piece such as Brahms's *Hungarian Dance No. 5* or Chopin's *Mazurka in B flat.* Lyric pieces, on the other hand, achieve a more flowing effect by not emphasizing the accent so strongly, as in *Morning* or the *Venetian Boat Song.* In Debussy's popular piece *Clair de lune* (Moonlight) there is hardly any accent at all, so that the meter flows dreamily from one measure to the next.

Composers devised a number of ways to keep the recurrent accent from becoming monotonous. They used ever more complex rhythmic patterns within the measure, and learned how to vary the underlying beat in many subtle ways. The most common of these procedures is *syncopation.* This term denotes a deliberate upsetting of the normal accent. The accent, instead of falling on a strong beat of the measure is shifted to a weak beat, or to an *offbeat* (between the beats), as in *Good Night, Ladies,* on the second syllables of *ladies.* Through this irregularity the accent is made to conflict with the pattern that has been set up in the listener's mind. The pleasure of satisfying his expectations is abandoned for the equally important pleasure of surprise. Syncopation has figured in European art music for centuries, and was used by the masters with great subtlety. It is associated in the popular mind with the Afro-American dance rhythms out of which modern jazz developed.

To sum up: music is an art of movement in time. Rhythm, the artistic organization of musical movement, permeates every aspect of the musical process. It shapes the melody and harmony, and binds together the parts within the whole: the notes within the measure, the measures within the phrase, the phrases within the period. Through the power of rhythm the composer achieves a dimension in time comparable to what painter, sculptor, and architect achieve in space.

Time is the crucial dimension in music. And its first law is rhythm.

6 Tempo: Musical Pace

"The whole duty of a conductor is comprised in his ability to indicate the right tempo."
— RICHARD WAGNER

Meter tells us how many beats there are in the measure, but it does not tell us whether these beats occur slowly or rapidly. The *tempo,* by which we mean the rate of speed, the pace of the music, provides the answer to this vital matter. Consequently the flow of the music in time involves both the meter and the tempo.

Tempo carries emotional implications. We hurry our speech in moments of agitation. Our bodies press forward in eagerness, hold back in lassitude. Vigor and gaiety are associated with a brisk gait as surely as despair demands a slow one. In an art of movement such as music, the rate of movement is of prime importance. We respond to musical tempo physically and psychologically. Our pulse, our breathing, our entire being adjusts to the rate of movement and to the feeling engendered thereby on the conscious and subconscious levels.

Because of the close connection between tempo and mood, tempo markings indicate the character of the music as well as the pace. The tempo terms are generally given in Italian, a survival from the time when the opera of that nation dominated the European scene. In the following table, *andante* (literally, "going," from the Italian *andare,* to go) indicates the speed of a normal walking pace. With this term as a midpoint, the table gives the most common Italian markings for the various tempos:

solemn (very, very slow):	*grave*
broad (very slow):	*largo*
quite slow:	*adagio*
slow:	*lento*
a walking pace:	*andante*
somewhat faster than andante:	*andantino*
moderate:	*moderato*
moderately fast:	*allegretto*
fast (cheerful):	*allegro*
lively:	*vivace*
very fast:	*presto*
very, very fast:	*prestissimo*

(For the pronunciation of these and other terms see the Index.) Frequently encountered too are modifying adverbs such as *molto* (very), *meno* (less), *poco* (a little), and *non troppo* (not too much). It should be noted that andante, which in the eighteenth century indicated a "going" pace, in the nineteenth came to mean "fairly slow."

Of great importance are the terms indicating a change of tempo. The principal ones are *accelerando* (getting faster) and *ritardando* (holding back, getting slower); *a tempo* (in time) indicates a return to the original pace.

For examples of the various tempos, listen to the opening section of the following works:

largo   Dvořák, *New World Symphony,* second movement
         Chopin, *Prelude in E minor*

adagio	Beethoven, *Sonata pathétique,* second movement
lento	Chopin, *Etude in E major,* Opus 10, No. 3
andante	Beethoven, *Symphony No. 5,* second movement
	Mozart, *Là ci darem la mano* from *Don Giovanni*
andantino	Schubert, *Trout Quintet,* theme of the fourth movement
allegretto	Mozart, *Symphony in G minor,* Minuet (third movement)
	Tchaikovsky, *Arabian Dance* from *Nutcracker Suite*
allegro	Mozart, *Eine kleine Nachtmusik,* fourth movement
	Beethoven, *Sonata pathétique,* third movement
vivace	Chopin, *Mazurka in B flat,* Opus 7, No. 1
presto	Beethoven, *Symphony No. 5,* final section
accelerando	Grieg, *In the Hall of the Mountain King* from *Peer Gynt*
ritardando	Tchaikovsky, *1812 Overture,* transition into the final section

Wagner's statement about tempo, quoted at the head of this chapter, is of course an exaggeration; the conductor has many other duties besides setting the tempo. It does make clear, however, that when a conductor hits on "the right tempo" he has correctly gauged the meaning and intent of the music.

7 Dynamics: Musical Volume

"The player must be guided by the passion. Sometimes a note requires a rather vigorous attack, at other times a moderate one, at still other times one that is barely audible."

— LEOPOLD MOZART (1756)

Dynamics denotes the degree of loudness or softness at which the music is played. In this area, as in that of tempo, certain responses seem to be rooted in the nature of our emotions. Mystery and fear call for a whisper, even as jubilation and vigorous activity go with full resonance. A lullaby or love song moves in another dynamic range than a triumphal march. Modern instruments place a wide gamut of dynamic effects at the composer's disposal.

The principal dynamic indications are:

very soft:	*pianissimo (pp)*
soft:	*piano (p)*
moderately soft:	*mezzo piano (mp)*
moderately loud:	*mezzo forte (mf)*
loud:	*forte (f)*
very loud:	*fortissimo (ff)*

A page from the score of Bach's *Brandenburg Concerto No. 2.* (Note the lack of expression marks.)

A page from the score of Tchaikovsky's *Pathétique Symphony.* (Observe the profusion of expression marks.)

Of special importance are the directions to change the dynamics. Such changes are indicated by words or signs. Among the commonest are:

growing louder: *crescendo* (━━◁)
growing softer: *decrescendo* or *diminuendo* (▷━━)
sudden stress: *sforzando* (*sf,* forced)—accent on a single note
  or chord

As the orchestra increased in size and precision, composers extended the range of dynamic markings in both directions, so that we find *ppp* and *fff.* Ultimately four and even five *p*'s or *f*'s were used.

The markings for tempo and dynamics are so many clues to the expressive content of a piece of music. These so-called "expression marks" steadily increased in number during the late eighteenth century and during the nineteenth, as composers tried to indicate their intentions ever more precisely. In this regard it is instructive to compare a page of Bach (early eighteenth century) with one of Tchaikovsky (late nineteenth century; see pp. 26-27).

Tempo and Dynamics as Elements of Musical Expression

Crescendo and diminuendo are among the important expressive effects available to the composer. Through the gradual swelling and diminishing of the tone volume, the illusion of distance enters music. It is as if the source of sound were approaching us and then receding. As orchestral style developed, composers quickly learned to take advantage of this

Dynamic contrasts in music are analogous to light and shade in painting. **The Calling of Saint Matthew,** a painting by Caravaggio (1573–1610).

procedure. Rossini, for example, was so addicted to employing a long-drawn-out swell of tone for the sake of dramatic effect that he was caricatured in Paris as "Monsieur Crescendo." The impact of such a crescendo can be little short of electrifying, as is apparent from the closing section of his Overture to *The Barber of Seville.* A similar effect is to be observed in Ravel's *Bolero,* in which an extended melody is repeated over and over while the music grows steadily louder. The crescendo is achieved, first, by piling on instruments one after the other; second, by causing the various instruments to play progressively louder.

Wagner's Prelude to *Lohengrin* is intended to depict the descent from heaven of the Holy Grail. The image of a band of angels approaching from the distance and then receding is translated into what has become a basic pattern in music, the crescendo-and-decrescendo (◁══════▷). Other striking examples of this dynamic scheme are to be found in the second half of Debussy's nocturne for orchestra, *Fêtes* (Festivals), and in the first movement of Bartók's *Music for Strings, Percussion, and Celesta.*

Crescendo in conjunction with accelerando (louder and faster) creates excitement as surely as decrescendo together with ritardando (softer and slower) slackens it. The effect of an intensification of volume and pace is exemplified in Honegger's *Pacific 231,* in which the composer tries to suggest the sense of power conjured up by a locomotive as it gradually builds up momentum and tears through the night. Here crescendo and accelerando are translated into the imagery of motion, as is the case in the finale of Tchaikovsky's *Waltz of the Flowers,* which is designed to build up to a rousing curtain for the *Nutcracker Ballet.* In the Tchaikovsky piece the music climbs steadily from the middle register to the bright and nervous high, so that the three elements—acceleration of pace, increase in volume, and rise in pitch—reinforce one another to create the climax.

Devices of this kind never fail in their effect upon audiences, which would seem to indicate that they are not the arbitrary procedures of a single imagination but are rooted in certain basic responses inherent in our nature.

8 Instruments of the Orchestra (I)

"With these artificial voices we sing in a manner such as our natural voices would never permit." — JOHN REDFIELD: *Music—A Science and an Art*

Properties of Musical Sound

A note played on a trumpet will sound altogether different from the same note played on a violin or a flute. The difference lies in the tone-color

Timbre
characteristic of each instrument, its *timbre*. (The word retains its French pronunciation, *tám'br*.)

The composer has at his disposal two basic media—human voices and musical instruments. He may write for either or both, according to his purpose. If he is writing for a group of instruments, he tries to make each instrument do the things for which it is best suited, taking into account its capacities and limitations. There are, to begin with, the limits of each instrument's range—the distance from its lowest to its highest tone, beyond which it cannot go. There are also the limits of dynamics—the degree of softness or loudness beyond which it cannot be played. There are technical peculiarities native to its low, middle, and high register, as a result of which a certain formation of notes will be executed more easily on one instrument than another. (By *register* we mean a specific area in the range of an instrument or voice, such as low, middle, or high.) These and a host of similar considerations determine the composer's choice as he clothes his ideas in their instrumental garb.

An *instrument* is a mechanism that is able to generate musical vibrations and launch them into the air. Each instrument, according to its capacities, enables us to control the four properties of musical sound: pitch, duration, volume, and color.

Pitch
By *pitch* we mean the location of a tone in the musical scale in relation to high or low. The pitch is determined by the rate of vibration, which to a large extent depends on the length of the vibrating body. Other conditions being equal, the shorter a string or column of air, the more rapidly it vibrates and the higher the pitch. The longer a string or column of air, the fewer the vibrations per second and the lower the pitch. The width, thickness, density, and tension of the vibrating body also affect the outcome.

Duration
Duration depends on the length of time over which vibration is maintained. We hear tones as being not only high or low but also short or long.

Volume
Volume (dynamics) depends on the degree of force of the vibrations, as a result of which the tone strikes us as being loud or soft. As for the *timbre* or tone color, that is influenced by a number of factors, such as the size, shape, and proportions of the instrument, the material of which it is made, and the manner in which vibration is set up.

Instruments figure in our music singly; in small groups (chamber music); and as part of that most spectacular of ensembles, the orchestra. In the orchestra they are divided into four sections (or choirs): string, woodwind, brass, and percussion.

The String Section

The string section of the orchestra includes four instruments—violin, viola, violoncello, and double bass. These have four strings, which are set vibrating by either drawing a bow across them or plucking them.

The hair of the bow is rubbed with rosin so that it will "grip" the strings. The player holds the bow in his right hand. He *stops* the string by pressing down a finger of his left hand at a particular point on the fingerboard, thereby leaving a certain portion of the string free to vibrate. By stopping the string at another point he changes the length of the vibrating portion, and with it the rate of vibration and the pitch.

Violin   The *violin* was brought to its present form by the brilliant instrument makers who flourished in Italy from around 1600 to 1750. Most famous among them were the Amati and Guarneri families—in these dynasties the secrets of the craft were transmitted from father to son—and the master builder of them all, Antonio Stradivari (c. 1644–1737).

The violin, the highest-pitched of the string choir, is universally admired for its singing tone, which brings it of all instruments closest to the human voice. Pre-eminent in lyric melody, the violin is also capable of brilliance and dramatic effect, of subtle nuances from soft to loud, of the utmost rhythmic precision and great agility in rapid passages. It has an extremely wide range. (For the comparative range of the instruments and the tuning of the strings, see Appendix II.)

Viola   The *viola* is somewhat larger than the violin, and is lower in range. Its strings are longer, thicker, heavier. The tone is husky in the low register, somber and penetrating in the high. The viola is an effective melody instrument, and often serves as a foil for the more brilliant violin by playing a secondary melody. It usually fills in the harmony, or may *double* another part; that is, reinforce it by playing the same notes an octave higher or lower.

Violoncello   The *violoncello,* popularly known as *cello,* is lower in range than the viola and is notable for its lyric quality, which takes on a dark resonance in the low register. Composers value highly its expressive tone. In the orchestra the cellos perform functions similar to those of the violins and violas. They often carry the melody. They enrich the sonority with their full-throated songfulness. They accentuate the rhythm. And together with the basses they supply the foundation for the harmony of the string choir.

Double bass   The *double bass,* known also as *contrabass* or *bass viol,* is the lowest in range of the string section. Accordingly, it plays the bass part—that is, the foundation of the harmony. Its deep indistinct tones come into focus when they are duplicated (doubled) an octave higher, usually by the cello. When this is done, the double bass assumes great carrying power and furnishes basic support for the entire orchestra. In more recent music, the dark timbre of the instrument has also been much used to achieve special color effects.

The string instruments are pre-eminent in playing *legato* (smooth and connected), though they are capable too of the opposite quality of tone, *staccato* (short and detached). A special effect, *pizzicato* (plucked), is executed by the performer's plucking the string with his finger instead of using the bow. *Vibrato* denotes a throbbing effect achieved by a rapid

Violinist Itzhak Perlman.

Walter Trampler playing the viola.

Mstislav Rostropovich, cellist.

Gary Karr playing the double bass.

wrist-and-finger movement that slightly alters the pitch. In *glissando* the player moves a finger of his left hand rapidly along the string while the right hand draws the bow, thereby sounding all the pitches of the scale. *Tremolo,* the rapid repetition of a tone through a quick up-and-down movement of the bow, is associated in the popular mind with suspense and excitement. No less important is the *trill,* a rapid alternation between a tone and its neighbor. *Double-stopping* involves playing two strings simultaneously; when three or four strings are played simultaneously, it is called *triple-* or *quadruple-stopping.* Thereby the members of the violin family, essentially melodic instruments, became capable of harmony. The *mute* is a small attachment that fits over the bridge, muffling (and changing) the sound. *Harmonics* are crystalline tones in the very high register. They are produced by lightly touching the string at certain points while the bow is drawn across the string. (For an explanation of harmonics, see Appendix V.)

The string section has come to be known as "the heart of the orchestra." This term indicates the versatility and general usefulness of this choir. The strings also figure prominently as solo instruments and in chamber music: in duets, trios, quartets, quintets, and the like.

The Woodwind Section

In the woodwind instruments the tone is produced by a column of air vibrating within a pipe that has little holes in its side. When one or another of these holes is opened or closed, the length of the vibrating air column within the pipe is changed. The woodwind instruments are capable of remarkable agility by means of an intricate mechanism of keys arranged so as to suit the natural position of the fingers.

The woodwinds are a less homogeneous group than the strings. Nowadays they are not necessarily made of wood, and they represent several methods of setting up vibration: by blowing across a mouth hole (flute family); by blowing into a mouthpiece that has a single reed (clarinet and saxophone families); by blowing into a mouthpiece fitted with a double reed (oboe and bassoon families). They do, however, have one important feature in common: the holes in the side of the pipes. In addition, their timbres are such that composers think of them and write for them as a group.

Flute   The *flute* is the soprano voice of the woodwind choir. Its timbre ranges from the poetic to the brilliant. Its tone is cool and velvety in the expressive low register, and smooth in the middle. In the upper part of the range the timbre is bright, birdlike, and stands out against the orchestral mass. The present-day flute, made of a silver alloy rather than wood, is a cylindrical tube that is held horizontally. It is closed at one end. The player positions his lips (*embouchure*), blowing across a mouth hole cut in the side of the pipe at the other end. The flute is much prized as a melody instrument and offers the player complete freedom in playing rapid repeated notes, scales, and trills.

Piccolo

The *piccolo* (from the Italian *flauto piccolo,* "little flute") has a piercing tone that produces the highest notes in the orchestra. In its upper register it takes on a shrillness that is easily heard even when the orchestra is playing fortissimo. For this reason the instrument contributes to many an orchestral climax. On the other hand, composers are coming more and more to make use of the limpid singing quality of its lower register.

Oboe

The *oboe* is made of wood. Its mouthpiece is a double reed consisting of two slips of cane bound together so as to leave between them an extremely small passage for air. Because of this compression, the tone is focused and intense in all registers. Oboe timbre is generally described as plaintive, nasal, reedy. The instrument is associated with pastoral effects and with nostalgic moods. The pitch of the oboe is not readily subject to change, for which reason it is chosen to sound the A for the other instruments when the orchestra is tuning up.

English horn

The *English horn* is an alto oboe. Its wooden tube is wider and longer than that of the oboe and ends in a pear-shaped bell, which largely accounts for its soft, somewhat mournful timbre. The instrument would be well named were it not for the fact that it is neither English nor a horn. Its expressive, gently poignant tone has made it a favorite with composers.

Clarinet

The *clarinet* has a single reed, a small flexible piece of cane fastened against its chisel-shaped mouthpiece. The instrument possesses a beautiful liquid tone, clear and powerful in the high register, relaxed in the middle, cool and almost spectral in the low. It has a remarkably wide range from low to high and from soft to loud. The clarinet is a favorite instrument when it comes to playing melody. Almost as agile as the flute, it has an easy command of rapid scales, trills, and repeated notes.

Bass clarinet

The *bass clarinet* is one octave lower in range than the clarinet. Its rich singing tone, flexibility, and wide dynamic range make it an invaluable member of the orchestral community.

Bassoon

The *bassoon* belongs to the double-reed family. Its tone is weighty and thick in the low register, dry and sonorous in the middle, reedy and intense in the upper. Capable of a hollow-sounding staccato and wide leaps that create a humorous effect, it is at the same time a highly expressive instrument.

Contra-bassoon

The *contrabassoon,* known also as double bassoon, produces the lowest tone in the orchestra. Its tube, over sixteen feet in length, is folded four times around to make it less unwieldly. Its function in the woodwind section may be compared to that of the double bass among the strings, in that it supplies a foundation for the harmony.

Saxophone

The *saxophone* is of more recent origin, having been invented by Adolphe Sax of Brussels in 1840. It was created by combining the features of several other instruments—the single reed of the clarinet, the conical tube of the oboe, and the metal body of the brass instruments.

Paula Robison, flute virtuoso.

Lady Evelyn Barbirolli playing the oboe.

Mary Ellis studies the piccolo at the Mannes School in New York.

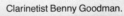
Clarinetist Benny Goodman.

Bernard Garfield, principal bassoon, the Philadelphia Orchestra.

The saxophone blends well with either woodwinds or brass. In the 1920s it became the characteristic instrument of the jazz band. Although it figures prominently in a number of important modern scores, it has not yet established itself as a permanent member of the orchestra.

9 Instruments of the Orchestra (II)

"Lucidity is the first purpose of color in music." — ARNOLD SCHOENBERG

The Brass Section

The brass section consists of the French horn, trumpet, trombone, and tuba. These instruments have cup-shaped mouthpieces (except for the horn, whose mouthpiece is shaped like a funnel). The tube flares at the end into an opening known as a *bell*. The column of air within the tube is set vibrating by the tightly stretched lips of the player, which act as a kind of double reed. To go from one pitch to another involves not only mechanical means, such as a slide or valves, but also variation in the pressure of the lips and breath. This demands great muscular control.

Horns and trumpets were widely used in the ancient world. The primitive instruments were fashioned from the horns and tusks of animals, which at a more advanced stage of civilization were reproduced in metal. They were used chiefly in religious ceremonies and for military signals. Their tone was on the terrifying side, as is evidenced by what happened to the walls of Jericho.

French horn The *French horn*—generally referred to simply as horn—is descended from the ancient hunting horn. Its golden resonance lends itself to a variety of uses: it can be mysteriously remote in soft passages, and nobly sonorous in loud. The timbre of the horn blends equally well with woodwinds, brass, and strings, for which reason it serves as the connecting link among them. Although capable of considerable agility, the horn is at its best in sustained utterance; for sheer majesty, nothing rivals the sound of several horns intoning a broadly flowing theme in unison. The muted horn has a poetic faraway sound; if the muted tone is forced, however, the result is an ominous rasping quality.

Trumpet The *trumpet,* highest in pitch of the brass choir, possesses a firm, brilliant timbre that lends radiance to the orchestral mass. It is associated with martial pomp and vigor. Played softly, the instrument commands a lovely round tone. The muted trumpet is much used; the mute, a pear-shaped device of metal or cardboard, is inserted in the bell. When the muted tone is forced, a harsh snarling sound results that is not soon forgotten. Jazz

Barry Tuckwell and the French Horn
with an interested audience.

Tuba player Steven Johns.

J. J. Johnson plays the trombone.

Gerard Schwartz, trumpet.

trumpet players have experimented with various kinds of mutes, and these are gradually finding their way into the symphony orchestra.

Trombone   The *trombone*—the Italian word means "large trumpet"—has a grand sonorousness that combines the brilliance of the trumpet with the majesty of the horn. In place of valves it has a movable U-shaped slide that alters the length of the vibrating air column in the tube. (There is a valve trombone that is used occasionally, but it lacks the rich tone of the slide trombone.) Composers consistently avail themselves of the trombone to achieve effects of nobility and grandeur.

Tuba   The *tuba* is the bass of the brass choir. Like the string bass and contrabassoon, it furnishes the foundation for the harmonic fabric. It is surprisingly responsive for so unwieldly an instrument. To play it requires— among other things—good teeth and plenty of wind. The tuba adds body to the orchestral tone, and a dark resonance ranging from velvety softness to a growl.

Mention should be made, too, of the brass instruments used in military and outdoor bands. Most important of these is the *cornet,* which was developed early in the nineteenth century from the posthorn. The cornet has a shorter body than the trumpet and possesses greater agility. (It is basically an instrument of conical shape, whereas the body of the trumpet is cylindrical for the greater part of its length.) The tone of the cornet is rounder but less brilliant than that of the trumpet. Because of the comparative ease with which it is played, the cornet has become the mainstay of school and municipal bands. Among the brass-band instruments are the *flügelhorn,* which is similar in shape to the cornet but wider; the *baritone* and *euphonium,* which are tenor tubas; and the *helicon,* which is a double-bass tuba, circular in form so that the player is able to carry the instrument over his shoulder. (An American type of helicon is the *sousaphone,* named after John Philip Sousa, who suggested its specially designed bell.) The *bugle,* originally a hunter's horn, has a powerful tone that carries in the open air. Since it is not equipped with valves, it is able to sound only certain tones of the scale, which accounts for the familiar pattern of duty calls in the army.

The Percussion Instruments

The percussion section comprises a variety of instruments that are made to sound by striking or shaking. Certain ones are made of metal or wood. In others, such as the drums, vibration is set up by striking a stretched skin.

The percussion section of the orchestra is sometimes referred to as "the battery." Its members accentuate the rhythm, generate excitement at the climaxes, and inject splashes of color into the orchestral sound. Like seasoning in food, they are most effective when used sparingly.

Tuned percussion

The percussion instruments fall into two categories: those which are capable of being tuned to definite pitches, and those which produce a single sound in the borderland between music and noise (instruments of indefinite pitch). In the former class are the *kettledrums,* or *timpani,* which are generally used in sets of two or three. The kettledrum is a hemispheric copper shell across which is stretched a "head" of calfskin held in place by a metal ring. Adjustable screws or a pedal mechanism enable the player to change the tension of the calfskin head, and with it the pitch. The instrument is played with two padded sticks, which may be either soft or hard. Its dynamic range extends from a mysterious rumble to a thunderous roll. The muffled drum frequently figures in passages that seek to evoke an atmosphere of mystery or mourning. The *glockenspiel* (German for "set of bells") consists of a series of horizontal tuned plates of various sizes, made of steel. The player strikes these with mallets, producing a bright metallic sound. The *celesta,* which in appearance resembles a miniature upright piano, is a kind of glockenspiel that is operated by a keyboard: the steel plates are struck by small hammers and produce an ethereal sound. The *xylophone* consists of tuned blocks of wood laid out in the shape of a keyboard. Struck with mallets with hard heads, the instrument produces a dry, crisp timbre. If mallets with soft heads are used, the tone is warmer and mellower. Expert xylophone players attain dazzling speed and accuracy. The *marimba* is a more mellow xylophone of African and South American origin, pitched an octave lower. The *vibraphone* combines the principle of the glockenspiel with resonators, each containing revolving disks operated by electric motors. Its highly unusual tone is marked by an exaggerated vibrato, which can be controlled by changing the speed of the motor. Also known as a *vibraharp,* this instrument plays a prominent part in jazz, and has been used by a number of contemporary composers. *Chimes* consist of a set of tuned metal tubes of various lengths suspended from a frame and struck with a hammer. They have a broad dynamic range, from a metallic tinkle to a sonorous clang, and are frequently called upon to simulate church bells.

Unpitched percussion

In the other group are the percussion instruments that do not produce a definite pitch. The *side drum* or *snare drum* (also known as *military drum*) is a small cylindrical drum with two heads stretched over a shell of metal. It is played with two drumsticks, and owes its brilliant tone to the vibrations of the lower head against taut snares (strings). The *tenor drum* is larger in size, with a wooden shell, and has no snares. The *bass drum,* played with a large soft-headed stick, produces a low heavy sound. It is much used in dance bands. The *tom-tom* is a name given to American Indian or Oriental drums of indefinite pitch, imitations of which are often used in dance bands. The *tambourine* is a small round drum with "jingles"—little metal plates—inserted in its rim. It is played by striking the drum with the fingers or elbow, by shaking, or by passing the hand over the jingles. The tambourine is much used in the folk dances of Italy. *Castanets* are widely

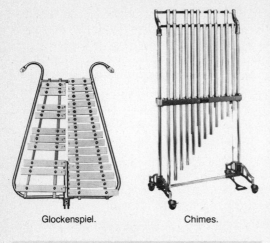
Glockenspiel.

Chimes.

Bobby Christian playing the timpani.

Al Payson with the snare drum.

Celesta.

Gong.

The bass drum is played by Jacqueline Meyer of Indiana State Universit

used in Spain. They consist of little wooden clappers moved by the thumb and forefinger of the player. The *triangle* is a small round bar of steel bent in the shape of a triangle. It is open at the upper end and, when struck with a steel beater, gives off a bright tinkling sound. *Cymbals* are two large circular brass plates of equal size. When struck sidewise against each other, they produce a shattering sound. A suspended cymbal, when struck lightly with a drumstick, produces a mysterious sound. The *gong,* or *tam-tam,* is a broad circular disk of metal, suspended in a frame so as to hang freely. When struck with a heavy drumstick, it produces a deep roar. If a soft stick is used the effect can be ghostly, even terrifying.

Other Instruments

Besides the instruments just discussed, several are occasionally used in the orchestra without being an integral part of it. Among these are the harp, piano, and organ.

Harp

The *harp* is one of the oldest of musical instruments. It appears in its earliest form on Babylonian inscriptions of over four thousand years ago. It was the traditional instrument of the bards of ancient Britain and Ireland, and became the national emblem of the latter country. Its strings are played by plucking and produce a crystalline tone that sounds lovely, both alone and in combination with other instruments. The pedals are used to tighten the strings, hence to raise the pitch. Chords on the harp are frequently played in broken form; that is, the tones are sounded one after another instead of simultaneously. From this circumstance comes the term *arpeggio,* which means a broken chord (*arpa* is the Italian for "harp"). Arpeggios occur in a variety of forms on many instruments.

Piano

The *piano* was originally known as the *pianoforte,* the Italian for "soft-loud," which indicates its wide dynamic range and its capacity for nuance. Its strings are struck with little hammers controlled by a keyboard mechanism. The piano cannot sustain tone as well as the string and wind instruments, but in the hands of a fine performer it is capable nonetheless of singing melody. Each string (except in the highest register) is covered by a damper that stops the sound when the finger releases the key. There are three pedals. If the one on the right is pressed down, all the dampers are raised, so that the strings continue to vibrate, producing that luminous haze of sound which the great piano composers used to such advantage. The pedal on the left shifts the hammers to reduce the area of impact on the strings, thereby inhibiting the volume of sound; hence it is known as the "soft pedal." The middle pedal (lacking on upright pianos) is the sustaining pedal, which sustains only the tones held down at the moment the pedal is depressed. The piano is pre-eminent for brilliant scales, arpeggios and trills, rapid passages and octaves. It has a wide range from lowest to highest tone and commands great rhythmic vitality.

Organ

The *organ,* once regarded as "the king of instruments," is a wind instru-

Van Cliburn at the piano.

Harp.

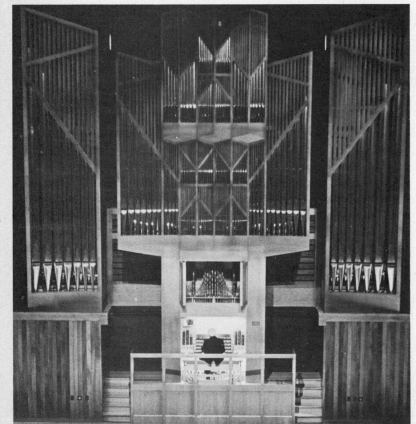

André Marchal playing the great tracker organ in Alice Tully Hall, New York.

ment; air is fed to its pipes by mechanical means. The pipes are controlled by two or more keyboards and a set of pedals. Gradations in the volume of tone are made possible on the modern organ by means of swell boxes. The organ possesses a multicolored sonority and majestic harmonies that fill a huge space. Nowadays the electronic organ is coming into use. Here the sound is produced not by wind but by electrical oscillators.

The instruments described in this chapter form a vivid and diversified group. To composer, performer, and listener alike they offer an endless variety of colors and shades of expression.

10 The Orchestra

"Orchestration is part of the very soul of the work. A work is thought out in terms of the orchestra, certain tone-colors being inseparable from it in the mind of its creator and native to it from the hour of its birth." — NICHOLAS RIMSKY-KORSAKOV

From the group of approximately twenty instruments that Bach had at his disposal or the forty-odd that Mozart knew, the modern orchestra has grown into an ensemble that may call for more than a hundred players. These musicians, many of artist stature, give their full time to rehearsal and performance, achieving a precision unknown in former times.

The orchestra is constituted with a view to securing the best balance of tone. The performers are divided into the four sections we have described. In large orchestras approximately two thirds are string players, one fourth are wind players. From three to five men take care of the percussion. The following distribution is typical of the orchestras of our largest cities:

strings:	18 first violins
	15 second violins
	12 violas
	12 violoncellos
	9 double basses
woodwinds:	3 flutes, 1 piccolo
	3 oboes, 1 English horn
	3 clarinets, 1 bass clarinet
	3 bassoons, 1 double bassoon
brass:	4–6 horns
	4 trumpets
	3 trombones
	1 tuba

percussion:
1 kettledrum player
2–4 performers for bass and side drum, glockenspiel, celesta, xylophone, triangle, cymbals, tambourine, etc.

It will be noticed that the violins are divided into two groups, first and second. Each group functions as a unit and plays a separate part. In gen-

The Chicago Symphony Orchestra with its conductor, Sir George Solti.

The seating plan of the Chicago Symphony Orchestra.

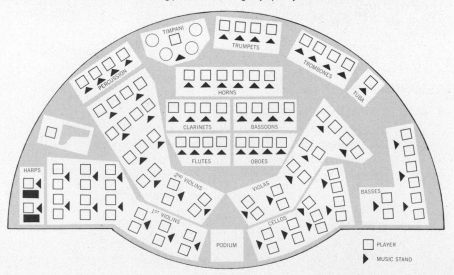

eral, the size of the orchestra varies according to the demands of the music. Included in the largest ensembles are two harps and, for certain works, a piano or organ.

The instruments are arranged so as to secure the best balance of tone. Most of the strings are up front. Brass and percussion are at the back. A characteristic seating plan is shown on p. 44; this arrangement varies somewhat from one orchestra to the next.

The conductor   The ensemble is directed by the conductor, who beats time and indicates the entrances of the various instruments, the shadings in the volume of tone, the principal and subordinate lines, and a host of related details that serve to make clear the structure of the work. Beyond that, like any performing artist, he presents his personal interpretation of what the composer has written. He has before him the *score* of the work. This consists of from a few to as many as twenty-five or more staves (staffs), each representing one or more instrumental parts. All the staffs together comprise a single composite line. What is going on at any moment in the orchestra is indicated at any given point straight down the page. It will be observed from the illustration on p. 46 that the instruments are grouped in families, woodwinds on top, then brass, percussion, and strings.

The Art of Orchestration

The composer bent over a page of score paper envisions the colors in his imagination as he blends and contrasts the timbres. He judges accurately the kind of sound he desires, be it powerful, caressing, or delicate; and he uses color to highlight the rhythmic patterns and the architectural design, to set off the principal ideas from the subordinate, and to weld the innumerable details into a whole.

The foregoing should dispel the widespread misconception that one man writes the music while another orchestrates it. This is true of most popular music, the score of a musical comedy, and the movie industry. But in art music, as the quotation from Rimsky-Korsakov makes clear, the two functions cannot be separated. What the composer says and how he says it are part and parcel of his individual manner of conceiving sound.

Erroneous too is the notion that the composer first writes his orchestral piece for the piano and then arranges it for instruments. An orchestral work, from its inception, is conceived in terms of the orchestra. If many composers like to have a piano in the room while writing, it is primarily because this gives them contact with the living sound. But the piano is no more able to render a symphonic piece than a black-and-white reproduction can reveal the colors of a Raphael or a Titian.

Listening to the orchestra is a favorite pastime of the musical public today. Most of this listening is done via recordings, radio, and television, so that many listeners never come in contact with the living orchestral sound. A pity, for the best way to become familiar with the orchestral instruments

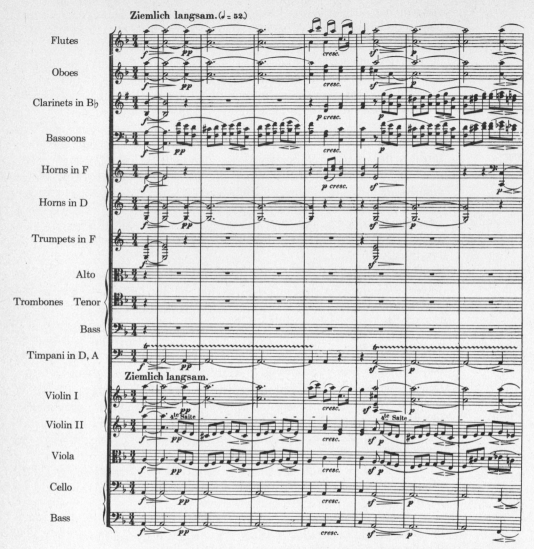

A page from Schumann's *Fourth Symphony,* showing the arrangement of instrumental parts.

is to be in the concert hall, where one can see as well as hear them. Recorded music plays a vital role in our musical life, but it should be regarded as a preparation for the live performance, not as a substitute.

The Orchestra in Action: Tchaikovsky's Nutcracker Suite

We shall in the course of this book have ample occasion to comment on how various composers wrote for the orchestra. At this point, however, the reader may find a helpful introduction to the orchestra in a work such as Tchaikovsky's *Nutcracker Suite,* which is a particularly fine example of vivid orchestral sonorities. The word *suite* indicates an instrumental work consisting of a number of short pieces (*movements*) related to a central idea. The suite may be either an independent work or a set of pieces drawn from a larger work. The *Nutcracker Suite* was drawn from a Christmas Eve ballet concerning a little girl who dreams that the nutcracker she received as a gift has turned into a handsome prince. Russian nutcrackers are often shaped like a human head, hence the transformation. The fairy-tale atmosphere impelled Tchaikovsky to some enchanting music.

March
Side 1/1
(S and E II) *

Three excerpts from the ballet will serve to illustrate Tchaikovsky's masterful handling of the orchestra. The *March,* which accompanies the entrance of the guests to the Christmas Eve party, is in a lively ⁴⁄₄ time. The characteristic march rhythm is set forth by clarinets, horns, and trumpets. Winds are answered by strings—a widely used orchestral device. Worthy of note is the filigree work in the accompaniment, in this case presented by the cellos and double basses pizzicato, an effect dear to Tchaikovsky's heart. In the middle section a staccato theme in high register is presented by three flutes and clarinet, mezzo forte, and vividly conveys a suggestion of ballet movement. The first part is repeated and the piece ends fortissimo.

Arab Dance
Side 1/2
(S and E II)

The little girl and her prince are entertained by various sweetmeats in the castle of the Sugar-Plum Fairy. The character representing Coffee dances the *Arab Dance,* a subdued number marked Allegretto. It is in ³⁄₈ time. Muted violas and cellos set up a *rhythmic ostinato*—that is, an "obstinate" rhythm repeated over and over with an almost hypnotic insistence. Against this dark curtain of sound, after introductory chords in the woodwinds, the muted violins unfold an Oriental-sounding melody. Striking is the long-drawn-out Oriental wail of the oboe, in the upper register, over the quiet movement of the melody and harmony in the strings below. The music dies away at the end.

Dance of the Toy Flutes
Side 1/3
(S and E II)

The *Dance of the Toy Flutes,* marked Moderato assai (very moderate) and in ²⁄₄ time, has always been a favorite with devotees of Tchaikovsky. Against a pizzicato accompaniment of violas, cellos, and double basses, three flutes outline a suave and beguiling melody. A short solo on the English horn arrests the ear, after which the opening theme returns. The middle section of the piece is devoted to a telling idea presented by the trumpets against a background of brass and percussion sounds, with a slight crescendo as the melodie line ascends and a decrescendo as it moves downward. After this the gracious melody of the flutes is heard again.

The modern orchestra, with its amplitude of tonal resources, its range of dynamics and infinite variety of color, offers a memorable experience both to the musician and the music lover. There is good reason for the widespread conviction that it is one of the wonders of our musical culture.

* For all selections included in the Recordings that accompany this text, references have been provided to the specific sides and bands. Thus, the *March* from *The Nutcracker* may be found on Side 1, Band 1 of both the Standard (*S*) version of the Recordings and the Expanded (*E*) version, volume II.

11 Form: Musical Structure and Design

"The principal function of form is to advance our understanding. It is the organization of a piece which helps the listener to keep the idea in mind, to follow its development, its growth, its elaboration, its fate." — ARNOLD SCHOENBERG

Form is that quality in a work of art which presents to the mind of the beholder an impression of conscious choice and judicious arrangement. It represents clarity and order in art. It shows itself in the selection of certain details and the rejection of others. Form is manifest too in the relationship of the parts to the whole. It helps us to grasp the work of art as a unity. It can be as potent a source of beauty as the content itself.

Whether in the domestic arts—the setting of a table, the weaving of a basket—or in the loftier ones, a balance is required between unity and variety, between symmetry and asymmetry, activity and repose. Nor is this balance confined to art. Nature has embodied it in the forms of plant and animal life and in what man likes to think of as her supreme handiwork— his own form.

Form in Music

Repetition and contrast

Our lives are composed of sameness and differentness: certain details are repeated again and again, others are new. Music mirrors this dualism. Its basic law of structure is *repetition* and *contrast*—unity and variety. Repetition fixes the material in our minds and ministers to our need for the familiar. Contrast sustains our interest and feeds our love of change. From the interaction of the familiar and the new, the repeated elements and the contrasting ones, result the lineaments of musical form. These are to be found in every type of musical organism, from the nursery rhyme to the symphony.

The principle of form is embodied in a variety of musical forms. These utilize procedures worked out by generations of composers. No matter how diverse, they are based in one way or another on repetition and contrast. The forms, however, are not fixed molds into which the composer pours his material. What gives a piece of music its aliveness is the fact that it adapts a general plan to its own requirements. All faces have two eyes, a nose, and a mouth. In each face, though, these features are to be found in a wholly individual combination. The forms that students in composition follow are ready-made formulas set up for their guidance. The forms of the masters are living organisms in which external organization is delicately adjusted to inner content. No two symphonies of Haydn or Mozart, no two sonatas of Beethoven are exactly alike. Each is a fresh and unique solution to the problem of fashioning musical material into a logical and coherent form.

Three-Part or Ternary Form (A-B-A)

A basic pattern in music is *three-part* or *ternary form*. Here the composer presents a musical idea, next presents a contrasting idea, and then repeats the first. Hence this type of structure embodies the principle of "statement-departure-return" (a-b-a). The repetition safeguards the unity, while variety is supplied by the middle section.

This principle is manifest in its simplest form in a nursery song such as *Twinkle, Twinkle, Little Star:*

a—Twinkle, twinkle, little star, how I wonder what you are.
b—Up above the world so high, like a diamond in the sky!
a—Twinkle, twinkle, little star, how I wonder what you are.

Often the first phrase is immediately repeated, so as to engrave it on the mind. This a-(a)-b-a structure is to be found in many melodies such as *Believe Me If All Those Endearing Young Charms; Maryland, My Maryland*; and *Old Man River*. It is the standard formula for the tunes of Tin Pan Alley. Our need for security is so great that, in a song consisting of four phrases, we are quite content to hear the opening phrase three times.

The four phrases in the a-a-b-a structure make up a unit that corresponds roughly to a paragraph in prose. Such a unit may be built up into a larger formation. For instance, a contrasting unit may be fashioned from new material (melodies c and d), after which the composer repeats the first unit, either as before or with some variation. There results a large A-B-A structure, each section of which is itself a three-part form or some variant thereof. (Notice that we use capital letters for the overall sections and small letters for the components within the section.) Tchaikovsky's *Waltz of the Flowers* (after the introduction) is a good example of this kind of formation:

A	B	A	
a-b-a-b	**c-d-c**	**a-b-a-b**	**Coda**

Coda, the Italian word for "tail," indicates the concluding section of a composition, which is added to the form proper to round it off.

Three-part form became the standard pattern for innumerable short pieces of a simple song or dance type. This pattern is clear in several of the compositions mentioned in the preceding chapters. You will have no difficulty in recognizing the basic pattern of statement-departure-return in such pieces as the minuets from Mozart's *Eine kleine Nachtmusik* and *Symphony in G minor,* or Chopin's *Etude in E major* and the *Dance of the Toy Flutes* from Tchaikovsky's *Nutcracker Suite.*

Three-part (a-b-a) form is as effective to the eye as it is to the ear. An etching by Giovanni Battista Piranesi (1720-78) of the Piazza of St. Peter's, Rome. *(New York Public Library.)*

With its attractive symmetry and its balancing of the outer sections against the contrasting middle one, the three-part or ternary form constitutes a simple, clear-cut formation that is a favorite in painting and architecture no less than in music.

The statement-departure-return principle is presented most effectively when there is a real departure; that is to say, when the middle section offers a decided contrast to the first and third parts. This contrast may show itself in a number of ways. An agitated first section may be opposed to a lyric middle part. The first part may lie in the dark lower register, the second in the middle or upper range. The contrast may be further underlined by opposing loud to soft, fast to slow, staccato to legato, strings to woodwinds and/or brass. These and similar ways serve to emphasize the contrast between the first and second sections as well as between the second section and the return of the first. Thus, in Chopin's celebrated *Fantasie-Impromptu* for piano, the first section is based on an impetuous running melody that extends across the keyboard, while the middle part presents a serenely songlike idea in the treble register.

Two-Part or Binary Form (A-B)

Two-part or *binary form* is based on a statement and a departure, without a return to the opening section. This type of structure can be observed in the question-and-answer formation of a tune like *America*. A similar structure is to be observed in the Italian folksong *Santa Lucia* and in Brahms's *Lullaby*. Binary form is much in evidence in the short pieces that made up the suite of the seventeenth and eighteenth centuries, a period of lively experimentation in the realm of musical structure. Since each section generally is repeated, two-part form is not quite as apparent to the ear as is the three-part pattern. You will hear examples of A-B form in the Allemande from Corelli's *Sonata,* Opus 4, No. 1 and the Gigue from Bach's *Suite No. 3.*

We will examine in subsequent chapters the great forms of Western music. No matter how imposing their dimensions, they all show the principle of repetition and contrast, of unity and variety, that we have traced here. In all its manifestations our music displays the striving for organic form that binds together the individual tones within the phrase, the phrases within the musical period, the periods within the section, the sections within the movement, and the movements within the work as a whole; even as, in a novel, the individual words are bound together in phrases, sentences, paragraphs, sections, chapters, and parts.

It has been said that architecture is frozen music. By the same token, music is floating architecture. Form is the structural principle in music. It distributes the areas of activity and repose, tension and relaxation, light and shade, and integrates the multitudinous details, large and small, into the spacious structures that are the glory of Western music.

12 Musical Style

"A good style should show no sign of effort. What is written should seem a happy accident."
— SOMERSET MAUGHAM

Style may be defined as the characteristic manner of presentation in any art. The word may refer to the element of fitness that shapes each type of art work to its function. We distinguish between the style of the novel and that of the essay, between the style of the cathedral and that of the palace. The word may also indicate an artist's personal manner of expression, i.e., the distinctive flavor that sets him apart from all others. Thus we speak of the style of Dickens or Thackeray, or Raphael or Michelangelo, of Wagner or Brahms. In a larger sense we often identify style with national culture, as when we speak of French, Italian, or German style; or with an entire civilization, as when we contrast the musical style of the West with that of the Orient.

Style periods

Since all the arts change from one age to the next, one very important use of the word is in connection with the various historical periods. Here the concept of style enables us to draw the proper connection between the artist and his time, so that the art work is placed in its socio-historical frame. No matter how greatly the artists of a particular era may vary in personality and outlook, when seen in the perspective of time they turn out to have certain qualities in common. The age has put its stamp upon all. Because of this we can tell at once that a work of art—whether music, poetry, painting, or architecture—dates from the Middle Ages or the Renaissance, from the eighteenth century or the nineteenth. The style of a period, then, is the total art-language of all its artists as they react to the forces—artistic, political, economic, religious, philosophic—that shape their environment.

Scholars will always disagree as to precisely where one style period ends and the next begins. Each period leads by imperceptible degrees into the following one, dates and labels being merely convenient signposts. The following outline shows the main style periods in the history of Western music. Each represents a conception of form and technique, an ideal of beauty, a manner of expression and performance attuned to the cultural climate of the period; in a word—a style! (The dates, naturally, are approximate.)

350–600 A.D.	Period of the Church Fathers
600–850	Early Middle Ages. Gregorian Chant
850–1150	Romanesque. Development of the staff in musical notation, about 1000
1150–1450	Gothic
1450–1600	Renaissance
1600–1750	Baroque
1725–1775	Rococo
1775–1825	Classical
1820–1900	Romantic
1890–1915	Post-Romantic, including Impressionism
1910–	Twentieth century

13 Musical Notation

"Musical notation is so familiar to us that few are aware of the difficulty of the problems which had to be solved, and the innumerable experiments undertaken for the invention and perfection of a satisfactory method of recording musical sounds."

— SYLVIA TOWNSEND WARNER

Our musical notation is the result of an evolution that reaches back to antiquity. It has adapted itself to successive systems of musical thought, and continues to do so. It is by no means a perfect tool, but it has proved adequate to the constantly new demands made upon it.

The Notation of Pitch

Staff

Musical notation presents a kind of graph of the sounds with regard to their duration and pitch. These are indicated by symbols called *notes,* which are written on the *staff,* a series of five parallel lines with four spaces between:

The position of the notes on the staff indicates the pitches, each line and space representing a different degree of pitch.

Clefs

A symbol known as a *clef* is placed at the left end of the staff, and determines the group of pitches to which that staff refers. The *treble clef* (𝄞) is used for pitches within the range of the female singing voices, and the *bass clef* (𝄢) for a lower group of pitches, within the range of the male singing voices.

Pitch names

Pitches are named after the first seven letters of the alphabet, from A to G; the lines and spaces are named accordingly. (From one note named A to the next is the interval of an octave, which—as we have seen—is the distance from one *do* to the next in the *do-re-mi-fa-sol-la-ti-do* scale). The pitches on the treble staff are named as follows:

E   F   G   A   B   C   D   E   F

And those on the bass staff:

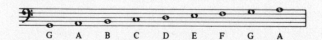

G   A   B   C   D   E   F   G   A

For pitches above and below these, short extra lines called *ledger lines* can be added:

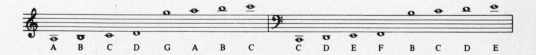

A B   C   D   G   A   B   C   C   D   E   F   B   C   D   E

Middle C—the C that, on the piano, is situated approximately in the center of the keyboard—comes between the treble and bass staffs. It is represented by either the first ledger line above the bass staff or the first ledger line below the treble staff, as the following example, makes clear. This combination of the two staffs is called the *great staff* or *grand staff:*

C D E F G A B C D E F G A B C

Accidentals   There are also signs known as *accidentals,* which are used to alter the pitch of a written note. A *sharp* (♯) before the note indicates the pitch a semitone above; a *flat* (♭) indicates the pitch a semitone below. A *natural* (♮) cancels a sharp or flat. Also used are the *double sharp* (𝄪) and *double flat* (♭♭), which respectively raise and lower the pitch by two half-tones—that is, a whole tone.

Semitones   The piano keyboard exemplifies this arrangement of whole and half tones. The distance from one piano key to its nearest neighbor is a *semitone* (also called a *half tone,* or *half step.*) This is true whether the adjacent keys are both white, or one white and the other black: thus, from E to F is a semitone, also from C to C♯.

Each of the black keys has two names, depending on whether it is considered in relation to its upper or lower neighbor. For example, the black key between C and D can be called either C♯ or D♭. Similarly, D♯ is the same as E♭, F♯ as G♭, G♯ as A♭, and A♯ as B♭.

In many pieces of music, where certain sharped or flatted notes are used consistently throughout the piece, the necessary sharps or flats are written at the beginning of each line of music, in order to save repetition. This may be seen in the following example of piano music. Notice that piano music is written on the great staff, with the right hand usually playing the notes written on the upper staff and the left hand usually playing the notes written on the lower:

The Notation of Rhythm

The duration of tones is indicated by the appearance of the notes placed on the staff. These use a system of relative values. For example, in the following table each note represents a duration half as long as the preceding one:

Note values

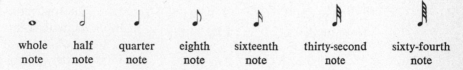

| whole note | half note | quarter note | eighth note | sixteenth note | thirty-second note | sixty-fourth note |

In any particular piece of music, these note values are related to the beat of the music. If the quarter note represents one beat, then a half note lasts for two beats, a whole note for four, with two eighth notes on one beat, or four sixteenths. The following chart makes this clear:

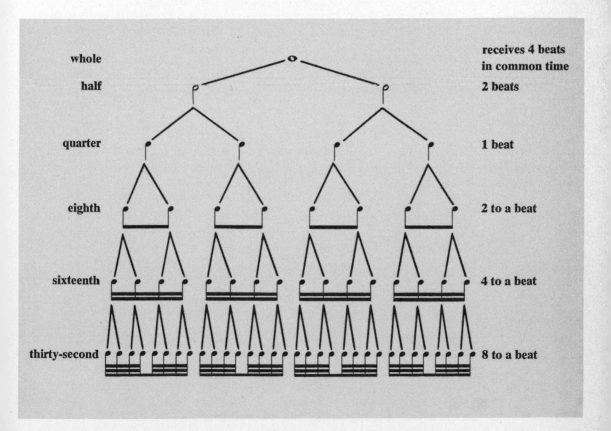

Triplet

When a group of three notes is to be played in the time normally taken up by only two of the same kind, we have a *triplet:*

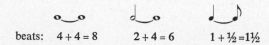

Tie

It is possible to combine successive notes of the same pitch, using a curved line known as a *tie:*

beats: 4 + 4 = 8   2 + 4 = 6   1 + ½ = 1½

Augmenta-tion dot

A *dot* after a note extends its value by half:

beats: 4 + 2 = 6   2 + 1 = 3   1 + ½ = 1½   ½ + ¼ = ¾

Rests

Time never stops in music, even when there is no sound. Silence is indicated by symbols known as *rests,* which correspond in time value to the notes:

whole rest	half rest	quarter rest	eighth rest	sixteenth rest	thirty-second rest	sixty-fourth rest

Time signature

The metrical organization of a piece of music is indicated by the *time signature,* which specifies the meter. This consists of two numbers, written one above the other. The upper numeral indicates the number of beats within the measure; the lower one shows which unit of value equals one beat. Thus, the time signature ¾ means that there are three beats to a measure, with the quarter note equal to one beat. In 6/8 time there are six beats in the measure, each eighth note receiving one beat. Following are the most frequently encountered time signatures:

duple meter	2/2	2/4	2/8	
triple meter	3/2	3/4	3/8	3/16
quadruple meter		4/4	4/8	
sextuple meter		6/4	6/8	

Also in use are 9/8 (3 groups of 3) and 12/8 (4 groups of 3). Contemporary music shows a wide use of nonsymmetrical patterns such as 5/4 or 5/8 (3 + 2 or 2 + 3) and 7/4 or 7/8 (4 + 3, 3 + 4, 2 + 3 + 2, etc.).

Four-four (4/4) is known as *common time* and is often indicated by the sign **C** . A vertical line drawn through this sign (**¢**) indicates *alla breve* or *cut time,* generally quick, with the half note receiving one beat instead of the quarter; in other words, two-two (2/2).

The following examples show how the system works. It will be noticed that the measures are separated by a vertical line known as a *barline;* hence a measure is often referred to as a *bar*. As a rule, the barline is followed by the most strongly accented beat, the ONE.

Lon - don Bridge is   fall - ing   down,   Fall - ing   down,   fall - ing   down,

Lon - don Bridge is   fall - ing   down,   My   fair   la - dy.

The   farm - er   in   the   dell,____   The   farm - er   in   the   dell,____

Heigh   ho!   the   mer - ry   oh,   The   farm - er   in   the   dell.____

My coun - try   'tis   of thee,   Sweet land of   lib - er - ty,   Of thee   I   sing.

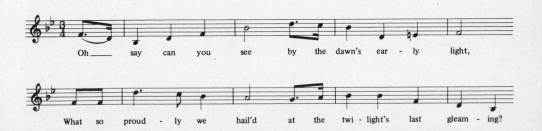

Oh ____   say   can   you   see   by   the dawn's   ear - ly   light,

What   so   proud - ly   we   hail'd   at   the   twi - light's   last   gleam - ing?

TWO

Nineteenth-Century Romanticism

"Music is the most romantic of all the arts—one might almost say, the only genuinely romantic one—for its sole subject is the infinite. Music discloses to man an unknown realm, a world in which he leaves behind him all definite feelings to surrender himself to an inexpressible longing." — E. T. A. HOFFMANN (1776–1822)

14 The Romantic Movement

"Romanticism is beauty without bounds—the beautiful infinite."
— JEAN PAUL RICHTER (1763–1825)

Historians observe that style in art moves between two poles, the classic and the romantic. Both the classic artist and the romantic strive to express significant emotions, and to achieve that expression within beautiful forms. Where they differ is in their point of view. The classical spirit seeks order, poise, and serenity as surely as the romantic longs for strangeness, wonder, and ecstasy. The classic artist is apt to be more objective in his approach to art and to life. He tries to view life sanely and "to see it whole." The romantic, on the other hand, is apt to be intensely subjective, and views the world in terms of his personal feelings. The German philosopher Friedrich Nietzsche, in his writings on art, dramatized the contrast between the two through the symbol of Apollo, god of light and measure, as opposed to Dionysus, god of intoxication and passion. Classic and romantic have alternated and even existed side by side from the beginning of time, for they correspond to two basic impulses in man's nature: on the one hand his need for moderation, his desire to have emotion purged and controlled; on the other, his desire for uninhibited emotional expression, his longing for the unknown and the unattainable.

Specifically, the classic and romantic labels are attached to two important periods in European art. The one held the stage in the last quarter of the eighteenth century and the early decades of the nineteenth. The other, stemming out of the social and political upheavals that followed in the wake of the French Revolution, came to the fore in the second quarter of the nineteenth century.

Romanticism in the Nineteenth Century

The French Revolution was the outcome of momentous social forces. It signalized the transfer of power from a hereditary feudal-agricultural aristocracy to the middle class, whose position depended on commerce and industry. As in the case of the American Revolution, this upheaval heralded a social order shaped by the technological advances of the Industrial Revolution. The new society, based on free enterprise, emphasized

Revolutionary ardor was one of the mainsprings of the Romantic period. A painting by Eugène Delacroix (1798–1863), **Liberty Leading the People.**

the individual as never before. Freedom—political, economic, religious, personal—was its watchword. On the artistic front this urge for individualism found expression in the Romantic movement.

The slogan of "Liberty, Equality, Fraternity" inspired hopes and visions to which few artists failed to respond. Sympathy for the oppressed, interest in simple folk and in children, faith in man and his destiny—all these, so intimately associated with the time, point to the democratic character of the Romantic movement. Whereas the eighteenth century had found inspiration in the art of ancient Greece, the Romantics discovered the so-called Dark Ages. King Arthur and Siegfried, fairy tale and medieval saga usurped the place formerly held by the gods and heroes of antiquity. Romantic architecture fell under the spell of the Gothic revival. So too, the formal gardens of the eighteenth century, with their spacious symmetries, were supplanted in public favor by picturesque grottoes and mysterious bowers. The Romantics became intensely aware of nature, but nature as a backdrop for the inner conflicts of man. When the heroine of a Romantic novel felt sad, it rained.

The Romantic poets rebelled against the conventional form and matter of their Classical predecessors; they leaned toward the fanciful, the picturesque, and the passionate. In Germany a group of young writers, following in the footsteps of Goethe and Schiller, created a new kind of lyric poetry that culminated in the art of Heinrich Heine; he became one of the favorite poets of the Romantic composers. A similar movement in France was led by Victor Hugo, its greatest prose writer, and Alphonse Lamartine, its greatest poet. In England the revolt against the formalism of the Classical age numbered among its adherents a line of lyric poets such as Gray, Cowper and Burns, Wordsworth and Coleridge, Byron, Shelley, and Keats. The new spirit of individualism expressed itself in the Romantic artist's sense of his uniqueness, his heightened awareness of himself as an individual apart from all others. "I am different from all the men I have seen," proclaimed Jean Jacques Rousseau. "If I am not better, at least I am different."

Thus, one of the prime traits of Romantic art was its emphasis on an intensely emotional type of expression. It has been well said that with Romanticism the pronoun "I" made its appearance in poetry. Gone were the elegantly abstract couplets of the eighteenth-century Classicists. The new age found expression in the passionate lyricism of such lines as Shelley's—

> Oh! lift me as a wave, a leaf, a cloud!
> I fall upon the thorns of life! I bleed!

or Keats's—

> When I have fears that I may cease to be
> Before my pen has gleaned my teeming brain . . .

The newly won freedom of the artist proved a not unmixed blessing. He confronted a philistine world from which he felt himself more and more cut off. A new type emerged—the artist as bohemian, the rejected dreamer who starved in an attic and through peculiarities of dress and behavior "shocked the bourgeois." This was the sensitive individual who was both too good for the moneyed world about him and not good enough. Increasingly the Romantic artist found himself arrayed against the established order. He was free from the social restraints imposed by court life; but he paid dearly for his freedom in loneliness, in knowing himself apart from his fellows. Withdrawal from the world brought a preoccupation with inner problems. Eternal longing, regret for the lost happiness of childhood, an indefinable discontent that gnawed at the soul—these were the ingredients of the Romantic mood. Yet the artist's pessimism was not without its basis in external reality. It became apparent that the high hopes fostered by the Revolution were not to be realized overnight. Despite the brave slogans, men were not yet equal or free. Inevitably optimism gave way to doubt and disenchantment—"the illness of the century."

This malaise was reflected in the art of the time. Thus, Balzac's *Human Comedy* depicted the warping of human relationships in the new society. Hugo dedicated *Les Misérables* "to the unhappy ones of the earth." The nineteenth-century novel found its great theme in the conflict between the individual and society. Jean Valjean and Heathcliff, Madame Bovary and Anna Karenina, Oliver Twist, Tess of the d'Urbervilles, and the Karamazovs—a varied company rises from those impassioned pages to point up the frustrations and guilts of the nineteenth-century world.

Hardly less persuasive was the art of those who sought escape. Some glamorized the past, as did Walter Scott and Alexandre Dumas. Longing for far-off lands inspired the exotic scenes that glow on the canvases of Turner and Delacroix. The Romantic poets and painters showed a remarkable fondness for the picturesque, the fantastic, and the macabre. Theirs was a world of "strangeness and wonder": the eerie landscape we encounter in the writings of a Coleridge, a Hawthorne, or a Poe.

Romanticism, in fine, dominated the art output of the nineteenth century. It gave its name to a movement and an era, and created a multitude of colorful works that still hold millions in thrall.

15 Romanticism in Music

"Music is the melody whose text is the world." — SCHOPENHAUER

Great changes in the moral, political, and social climate of an epoch seek to be expressed also in the art of that epoch. But they cannot be unless the new age places in the artist's hand the means of giving expression to new ideas. This was precisely the achievement of the Romantic movement in music—that it gave composers the means of expressing what the age demanded of them.

Improvements in instruments

In the first place, the Industrial Revolution brought with it not only the production of cheaper and more responsive instruments, but also introduced important improvements in the wind instruments that strongly influenced the sound of Romantic music. For example, the addition of valves to the brass instruments made them much more maneuverable, so that composers like Wagner and Tchaikovsky could assign melodies to the horn that would have been unplayable in the time of Haydn and Mozart. So too, as a result of improved manufacturing techniques, the piano acquired a cast-iron frame and thicker strings that gave it a deeper and more brilliant tone. If the impassioned *Sonata* of Liszt sounds different from a sonata of Mozart it is not only because Liszt's time demanded of him a different kind of expression, but also because it put at his disposal a piano capable of effects that were neither available nor necessary in the earlier period.

The nineteenth-century orchestra offered the composer increased range and variety. Contemporary wood-cut of an orchestral concert at the Covent Garden Theater, London, 1846.

Secondly, the gradual democratization of society brought with it a broadening of educational opportunities. Conservatories that trained more and better musicians than formerly were established in the chief cities of Europe. As a result, nineteenth-century composers could count on instrumental performers whose skill was considerably in advance of what it had been in former times. As music moved from palace and church to the public concert hall, orchestras increased in size and efficiency, and gave the composer a means of expression more varied and colorful than he had ever had before. This naturally had a direct influence upon the sound. For example, where most eighteenth-century music ranged in dynamic level from piano to forte, the dynamic range of the orchestra in the nineteenth century was far greater. Now came into fashion the heaven-storming crescendos, the violent contrasts of loud and soft that lend such drama to the music of the Romantics. As orchestral music became more and more important, the technique of writing for orchestra—that is, orchestration

The public concert hall

—became almost an art in itself. At last the musician had a palette comparable to the painter's, and used it as the painter did—to conjure up sensuous beauty and enchantment, to create mood and atmosphere, to suggest nature scenes and calm or stormy seascapes.

Increased expressiveness

The desire for direct communication led composers to use a large number of expressive terms intended to serve as clues to the mood of the music, with the result that a highly characteristic vocabulary sprang up. Among the directions frequently encountered in nineteenth-century scores are *dolce* (sweetly), *cantabile* (songful), *dolente* (weeping), *mesto* (sad), *maestoso* (majestic), *gioioso* (joyous), *con amore* (with love, tenderly), *con fuoco* (with fire), *con passione, espressivo, pastorale, agitato, misterioso, lamentoso, trionfale*. These suggest not only the character of the music but the frame of mind behind it.

Use of folklore

The interest in folklore and the rising tide of nationalism impelled the Romantic musicians to make use of the folk songs and dances of their native lands. As a result, a number of national idioms—Hungarian, Polish, Russian, Bohemian, Scandinavian—came to the fore and opened up new areas to European music, greatly enriching its melody, harmony, and rhythm.

Romantic melody

Even when written for instruments, Romantic melody was easy to sing and hum. The nineteenth century above all was the period when musicians tried to make their instruments "sing." It is no accident that the themes from Romantic symphonies, concertos, and other instrumental works have been transformed into popular songs; for Romantic melody was marked by a lyricism that gave it an immediate emotional appeal, as is evidenced by the enduring popularity of the tunes of Schubert, Chopin, Verdi, and their fellows. Through innumerable songs and operas as well as instrumental pieces, Romantic melody appealed to a wider audience than had ever existed before.

Romantic man desired to taste all experience at its maximum intensity. He was enchanted in turn by literature, music, painting. How much more intoxicating, he reasoned, would be a "union of the arts" that combined all three. Music in the nineteenth century drew steadily closer to literature and painting—that is, to elements that lay outside the realm of sound. The connection with Romantic poetry and drama is most obvious, of course, in the case of music with words. However, even in their purely orchestral music the Romantic composers responded to the mood of the time and captured with remarkable vividness the emotional atmosphere that surrounded nineteenth-century poetry and painting.

The result of all these tendencies was to make Romanticism as potent a force in music as it was in the other arts. Nineteenth-century music was linked to dreams and passions, to profound meditations on life and death, man's destiny, God and nature, pride in one's country, desire for freedom, the political struggles of the age, and the ultimate triumph of good over evil. These intellectual and emotional associations, nurtured by the Romantic movement, enabled music to achieve a commanding position in the nineteenth century as a moral force, a vision of man's greatness, and a direct link between his inner life and the world around him.

16 The Short Lyric Forms as an Expression of Romanticism

"Out of my great sorrows I make my little songs." — HEINRICH HEINE

Through the short lyric forms the Romantic movement satisfied its need for intimate personal expression. Coming into prominence in the early decades of the century, the song and piano piece emerged as particularly attractive examples of the new lyricism.

The Song

The repertory of song—folk, popular, and art—is more extensive than that of all other types of music. For song combines two musical elements of universal appeal—melody and the human voice. A *song* is a short lyric composition for solo voice based on a poetic text. The vocal melody is presented as a rule with an instrumental accompaniment that gives it harmonic background and support.

A great poem is complete in itself and needs nothing more to enhance it. A melody, too, is a thing complete in itself. To blend the two into an artistic whole requires imagination of the highest order. The creators of the Romantic art song were so successful in combining words and music that many of the lyric poems they used have survived mainly in their musical settings.

Types of Song Structure

We distinguish between two main types of song structure. In *strophic form* the same melody is repeated with every stanza, or strophe, of the poem. This formation, which occurs very frequently in folk and popular song, permits of no great closeness between words and music. Instead it sets up a general atmosphere that accommodates itself equally well to all the stanzas. The first may tell of the lover's expectancy, the second of his joy at seeing his beloved, the third of her father's harshness in separating them, and the fourth of her sad death, all these being sung to the same tune. The prevalence of strophic song throughout the ages points to one

Strophic song

conclusion: the folk learned early that a lovely tune is a joy in itself, and that it heightens emotion no matter what the content of a particular stanza.

Through-composed song

The other type is what the Germans call *durchkomponiert,* literally "through-composed"—that is, composed from beginning to end, without repetitions of whole sections. Here the music follows the story line, changing with each stanza according to the text. This makes it possible for the composer to mirror every shade of meaning in the words.

There is also an intermediate type that combines the repetition of the strophic song with the freedom of the song that is through-composed. The same melody may be repeated for two or three stanzas, with new material introduced when the poem seems to require it, generally at the climax. Schubert's celebrated *Ständchen* (Serenade) is a fine example of this structure.

The Art Song in the Romantic Period

Despite the prominence of song throughout the ages, the art song as we know it today was a product of the Romantic era. It was created by the

The immense popularity of the Romantic art song was due in part to the emergence of the piano as the universal household instrument. A lithograph by Achille Devéria (1800–57), **In the Salon.**

Lied

union of poetry and music in the early nineteenth century. This union was consummated with such artistry by Franz Schubert and his successors, notably Robert Schumann and Johannes Brahms, that the new genre came to be known all over Europe by the German word for song—*Lied* (plural, *Lieder*).

The lied depended for its flowering on the upsurge of lyric poetry that marked the rise of German Romanticism. Goethe (1749–1832) and Heine (1799–1856) are the two leading figures among a group of poets who, like Wordsworth and Byron, Shelley and Keats in English literature, cultivated a subjective mode of expression through the short lyric poem. The lied brought to flower the desire of the Romantic era for the union of music and poetry, ranging from tender sentiment to dramatic balladry. Its favorite themes were love and longing, the beauty of nature, the transience of human happiness.

The triumph of the Romantic art song was made possible by the emergence of the piano as the universal household instrument of the nineteenth century. The piano accompaniment translated the poetic images into musical ones. Voice and piano together created a short lyric form charged with feeling, suited alike for amateurs and artists, for the home as for the concert room. Within a short time the lied achieved immense popularity and made a durable contribution to world art.

The Piano Piece

The short lyric piano piece was the instrumental equivalent of the song in its projection of lyric and dramatic moods within a compact frame. Among the titles most frequently used for it are *bagatelle* (literally, "a trifle"), *impromptu* ("on the spur of the moment"), *intermezzo* (interlude), *nocturne* (night song), *novelette* (short story), *moment musical, song without words, album leaf, prelude, romance, capriccio* (caprice); and, of larger dimensions, the *rhapsody* and *ballade*. In the dance category are the *waltz, mazurka, polka, écossaise* (Scottish dance), *polonaise* (Polish dance), *march,* and *country dance.* Composers also used titles of a fanciful and descriptive nature. Typical are Schumann's *In the Night, Soaring,* and *Whims;* Liszt's *Forest Murmurs* and *Fireflies.* The nineteenth-century masters of the short piano piece—Schubert, Chopin and Liszt, Mendelssohn, Schumann and Brahms, and their fellows—showed inexhaustible ingenuity in exploiting the technical resources of the instrument and its capacities for lyric-dramatic expression.

The short lyric forms sprang out of the composer's realization that size is no criterion in art, and that an exquisitely wrought miniature may contain as much beauty as a symphony. In the song and piano piece, nineteenth-century Romanticism found one of its most characteristic means of expression.

17 Franz Schubert

"When I wished to sing of love it turned to sorrow. And when I wished to sing of sorrow it was transformed for me into love."

In the popular mind Franz Schubert's life has become a romantic symbol of the artist's fate. He suffered poverty and was neglected during his lifetime. He died young. And after his death he was enshrined among the immortals.

His Life

He was born in 1797 in a suburb of Vienna, the son of a schoolmaster. The boy learned the violin from his father, piano from an elder brother; his beautiful soprano voice gained him admittance to the imperial chapel and school where the court singers were trained. His teachers were duly astonished at the musicality of the shy, dreamy lad. One of them remarked that Franz seemed to learn "straight from Heaven."

His schooldays over, young Schubert tried to follow in his father's footsteps, but he was not cut out for the routine of the classroom. He found escape in the solitude of his attic, immersing himself in the lyric poets who were the first voices of German Romanticism. As one of his friends said, "Everything he touched turned to song." With a spontaneity comparable to Mozart's, the melodies took shape that gave to the new Romantic lyricism its ideal expression. *Gretchen at the Spinning Wheel,* to Goethe's verses, was written in a single afternoon—when he was seventeen. A year later came his setting of the same poet's *Erlking.* One of his greatest songs, it was the work of a few hours.

Schubert's talent for friendship attracted to him a little band of followers. Their appreciation of his genius comforted him for the neglect and incomprehension of the world. With their encouragement Schubert, not yet twenty, broke with the drudgery of his father's school. In the eleven years that were left him he occupied no official position (although he occasionally made half-hearted attempts to obtain one). He lived with one or another of his friends in a mixture of poverty and camaraderie, hope and despair. And steadily, with an almost self-devouring intensity, the music poured from the bespectacled young man. "How do you compose?" he was asked. "I finish one piece," was the answer, "and begin the next."

Schubert was singularly unable to stand up to the world. Songs that in time sold in the hundreds of thousands he surrendered literally for the price of a meal. As the years passed, the buoyancy of youth gave way to

Franz Schubert.

a sense of loneliness, the tragic loneliness of the Romantic artist. "No one feels another's grief," he wrote, "no one understands another's joy. People imagine that they can reach one another. In reality they only pass each other by." Yet he comprehended—and in this he was the Romantic—that his very suffering must open to his art new layers of awareness. "My music is the product of my talent and my misery. And that which I have written in my greatest distress is what the world seems to like best."

He still yielded to flurries of optimism when success appeared to lie within his grasp, but eventually there came to him an intimation that the struggle had been decided against him. "It seems to me at times that I no longer belong to this world." This was the emotional climate of the magnificent song cycle *Die Winterreise* (The Winter Journey), in which he struck a note of somber lyricism new to music. Depressed by illness and poverty, he abandoned himself to the mournful images of Wilhelm Müller's poems. The long, dark journey—was it not the symbol of his own life? Overcoming his discouragement, he embarked on his last effort. To the earlier masterpieces was added, in that final year, an amazing list that includes the *Symphony No. 9 in C major,* the *Mass in E flat,* the *String Quintet in C,* the three posthumous piano sonatas, and thirteen of his finest songs, among them the ever-popular *Serenade.*

With the great *C-major Symphony* behind him, he made arrangements to study counterpoint. "I see now how much I still have to learn." Ill with typhus, he managed to correct the proofs of the last part of *Die Winterreise.* The sense of defeat accompanied him through the final delirium; he fancied that he was being buried alive. "Do I not deserve a place above the ground?" His last wish was to be buried near the master he worshiped above all others—Beethoven.

He was thirty-one years old when he died in 1828. His possessions consisted of his clothing, his bedding, and "a pile of old music valued at ten florins": his unpublished manuscripts. In the memorable words of Sir George Grove, "There never has been one like him, and there never will be another."

His Music

Schubert stood at the confluence of the Classic and Romantic eras. His symphonic style bespeaks the heir of the Classical tradition; but in his songs and piano pieces he was wholly the Romantic, an artist whose magical lyricism impelled Liszt to call him "the most poetic musician that ever was."

In the *Impromptus* and *Moments musicaux* (Musical Moments) the piano sings the new lyricism. Caprice, spontaneity, and the charm of the unexpected take their place as elements of Romantic art. Of comparable freshness is the popular tone of the dance pieces, waltzes, *ländlers* (Austrian peasant dances), and écossaises. His piano sonatas were neglected for years, but have now found their rightful place in the repertory.

Finally there are the songs, more than six hundred of them. Many were written down at white heat, sometimes five, six, seven in a single morning. Certain of his melodies achieve the universality of folk song, others display the highest sophistication. In either case they issue directly from the heart of the poem. Their eloquence and freshness of feeling have never been surpassed. Of special moment are the accompaniments: a measure or two, and the rustling brook is conjured up, the dilapidated hurdy-gurdy, or the lark "at heaven's gate." Of Schubert's songs may be said what Schumann remarked about the *Symphony in C major:* "This music transports us to a region where we cannot remember ever to have been before."

Erlkönig

Side 1/4
(S and E II)

This masterpiece of Schubert's youth (1815) captures the Romantic "strangeness and wonder" of Goethe's celebrated ballad. *Erlkönig* (the Erlking) is based on the legend that whoever is touched by the King of the Elves must die. The poem has four characters: the narrator, the father, the child, and the seductive Elf.

Narrator

Wer reitet so spät durch Nacht und Wind?	Who rides so late through night and wind?
Es ist der Vater mit seinem Kind;	It is the father with his child.
er hat den Knaben wohl in dem Arm,	He holds the boy firmly in his arm,
er fasst ihn sicher, er hält ihn warm.	He clasps him tight, he keeps him warm.

Father

"Mein Sohn, was birgst du so bang dein Gesicht?"	"My son, why hide your face in fear?"

Son

"Siehst, Vater, du den Erlkönig nicht?
den Erlenkönig mit Kron' und Schweif?"

"Father, do you not see the Erlking?
The Erlking with crown and tail?"

Father

"Mein Sohn, es ist ein Nebelstreif."

"My son, it is only a streak of mist."

Erlking

"Du liebes Kind, komm, geh mit mir!
gar schöne Spiele spiel' ich mit dir;
manch bunte Blumen sind an dem Strand;
meine Mutter hat manch' gülden Gewand."

"You sweet child, come, go with me!
Such pleasant games I'll play with you.
Many bright flowers bloom along the shore,
My mother has many a robe of gold."

Son

"Mein Vater, mein Vater, und hörest du
    nicht,
was Erlenkönig mir leise verspricht?"

"Oh father, father, do you not hear

What the Erlking gently promises me?"

Father

"Sei ruhig, bleibe ruhig, mein Kind;
in dürren Blättern säuselt der Wind."

"Be calm, my child, stay calm;
It is only the wind among the dead leaves."

Erlking

"Willst, feiner Knabe, du mit mir gehn?
meine Töchter sollen dich warten schön;
meine Töchter führen den nächtlichen
    Reihn
und wiegen und tanzen und singen dich ein,

sie wiegen und tanzen und singen dich ein."

"Lovely boy, will you come with me?
My daughters will serve you well.
My daughters keep nightly revels.

They'll sing and dance and rock you to
    sleep.
They'll sing and dance and rock you to
    sleep."

Son

"Mein Vater, mein Vater, und siehst du
    nicht dort
Erlkönigs Töchter am düstern Ort?"

"Oh father, father, do you not see

The Erlking's daughters in the darkness?"

Father

"Mein Sohn, mein Sohn, ich seh' es genau,
es scheinen die alten Weiden so grau."

"My son, my son, I see quite clearly
The old willow trees gleaming gray."

Erlking

"Ich liebe dich, mich reizt deine schöne
    Gestalt,
und bist du nicht willig, so brauch' ich
    Gewalt."

"I love you, your beauty charms me,

And if you're not willing, I'll use force!"

Son

"Mein Vater, mein Vater, jetzt fasst er
    mich an!
Erlkönig hat mir ein Leids gethan!"

"Oh father, father, he seizes me!

The Erlking has done me harm!"

Narrator

Dem Vater grauset's, er reitet geschwind,	The father shudders, he rides swiftly,
er hält in Armen das ächzende Kind,	Holding fast the moaning child.
erreicht den Hof mit Müh' und Noth:	He reaches home with pain and dread:
in seinen Armen das Kind war todt.	In his arms the child lay dead!

The eerie atmosphere of the poem is established by the piano part. Galloping triplets are heard against a rumbling figure in the bass. This motive, so Romantic in tone, pervades the canvas and imparts to it an astonishing unity.

Schnell (Fast)

The characters are vividly differentiated through changes in the melody, harmony, rhythm, and type of accompaniment. The child's terror is suggested by clashing dissonance. The father, allaying his son's fears, is represented by a more rounded vocal line. As for the Erlking, his cajoling is given in suavely melodious phrases.

The song is through-composed; the music follows the unfolding of the narrative with a steady rise in tension—and pitch—that builds to the climax. Abruptly the obsessive triplet rhythm lets up, giving way to a ritard as horse and rider reach home. "In his arms the child"—a dramatic pause precedes the two final words—"lay dead."

The thing seems strangely simple, inevitable. The doing of it by a marvelous boy of eighteen was a milestone in the history of Romanticism.

An Sylvia

Side I/5
(S and E II)

This song, composed in 1826, contrasts with *Erlkönig* in tempo, dynamics, form, and mood. It is lyrical where the other is dramatic, serene where the other is stormy. The tempo marking is Moderato, the accompaniment mostly pianissimo. The form is strophic; the same melody is repeated for the three stanzas drawn from Shakespeare's *The Two Gentlemen of Verona*.

An Sylvia	*To Sylvia*
Was ist Sylvia, saget an,	Who is Sylvia? what is she,
dass sie die weite Flur preist?	That all our swains commend her?
Schön und zart seh' ich sie nah'n,	Holy, fair and wise is she;
auf Himmels Gunst und Spur weis't,	The heaven such grace did lend her,
dass ihr Alles unterthan,	That she might admired be,
dass ihr Alles unterthan.	That she might admired be.

Ist sie schön und gut dazu?	Is she kind as she is fair?
Reiz labt wie milde Kindheit;	For beauty lives with kindness:
ihrem Aug' eilt Amor zu,	Love doth to her eyes repair,
dort heilt er seine Blindheit,	To help him of his blindness;
und verweilt in süsser Ruh',	And, being help'd, inhabits there,
und verweilt in süsser Ruh'.	And, being help'd, inhabits there.
Darum Sylvia tön', o Sang,	Then to Sylvia let us sing,
der holden Sylvia Ehren!	That Sylvia is excelling;
Jeden Reiz besiegt sie lang,	She excels each mortal thing
den Erde kann gewähren:	Upon the dull earth dwelling;
Kränze ihr und Saitenklang,	To her let us garlands bring,
Kränze ihr und Saitenklang.	To her let us garlands bring.

The piano introduction presents repeated chords in the right hand, in regular eighth notes, over a dotted-note rhythm in the left. This pattern persists throughout, a background for one of Schubert's most beautiful melodies. Each phrase of six bars is followed by a single-measure comment on the piano, like an echo of the voice. There results a seven-bar unit, which is most unusual.

The melody flows gently, by step or narrow leap:

However, on the last line of each stanza it broadens out with two octave leaps in succession. This imparts tension to the melodic line and brings the stanza to a fine climax. Yet it is a climax that does not disturb the lyric mood, The little piano introduction serves also as an interlude between the stanzas and as postlude at the end.

In this enchanting song are manifest the qualities that set Schubert apart: his charm of melody, his tenderness, and an ineffably romantic longing that can only be described as Schubertian.

18 Robert Schumann

"Music is to me the perfect expression of the soul."

The turbulence of German Romanticism, its fantasy and subjective emotion, found their voice in Robert Schumann. His music is German to the core, yet he is no local figure. A true lyric poet, he rose above the national to make his contribution to world culture.

Robert Schumann.

His Life and Music

Robert Schumann (1810–56) was born in Zwickau, a town in Saxony, son of a bookseller whose love of literature was reflected in the boy. He studied law first at the University of Leipzig, then at Heidelberg. The inevitable decision to abandon law for music filled him with happiness. "I am so fresh in soul and spirit," he exulted, "that life gushes and bubbles around me in a thousand springs."

In a burst of creative energy he produced, while still in his twenties, his most important works for the piano. The spontaneity of his production astonished him. "Everything comes to me of itself," he wrote, "and indeed it sometimes seems as if I could play on eternally and never come to an end." Such intensity—the prime quality of the lyricist—carried with it a premonition of early doom. "Oh I cannot help it, I should like to sing myself to death like a nightingale . . ."

He found ideal happiness in his marriage to Clara Wieck, one of the great pianists of his day. She became the first interpreter of his piano works and contributed substantially to the spreading of his fame. Yet neither her love nor that of their children could ward off his increasing withdrawal from the world. Moodiness and nervous exhaustion culminated in periods of severe depression; some years later he began to complain of "unnatural noises" in his head. His last letter to the violinist Joachim, two weeks before the final breakdown, is a farewell to his art. "The music is silent now . . . I will close. Already it grows dark." In a fit of melancholia he threw himself into the Rhine, was rescued by fishermen, and placed in a private asylum near Bonn. Despite occasional flashes of lucidity the darkness did not lift. He died two years later at the age of forty-six.

As a piano composer Schumann was one of the most original figures of the century. Whimsy and ardent expressiveness pervade his miniatures, which brim over with impassioned melody and vigorous rhythms. Typical titles are *Fantasy Pieces, Romances, Scenes from Childhood*. His songs are second only to Schubert's. His favorite theme is love, particularly from the woman's point of view. His favored poet was Heine, for whom he had an affinity like that of Schubert for Goethe.

The four symphonies are marked by lyric freshness. What could be closer to the essence of German Romanticism than the "nature sound" of the horns and trumpets at the opening of the *Spring Symphony,* his first? "Could you infuse into the orchestra," he wrote the conductor, "a kind of longing for spring? At the first entrance of the trumpets I should like them to sound as from on high, like a call to awakening."

Mondnacht

Side 1/6
(S and E II)

Mondnacht (Moonlit Night) exemplifies the intimate quality of Schumann's lyricism at its best. The poem by Joseph von Eichendorff inspired the composer to an intensely personal song.

Es war, als hätt' der Himmel
   die Erde still geküsst,
dass sie im Blüthenschimmer
   von ihm nur träumen müsst'.
	It seemed as if heaven
	   Quietly kissed the earth,
	So that mid the shimmering blossoms
	   She must dream only of him.

Die Luft ging durch die Felder,
   die Aehren wogten sacht,
es rauschten leis' die Wälder,
   so sternklar war die Nacht.
	A breeze floated through the fields,
	   The stalks of corn waved lightly;
	The forest leaves murmured gently,
	   And starlit was the night.

Und meine Seele spannte
   weit ihre Flügel aus,
flog durch die stillen Lande,
   als flöge sie nach Haus.
	And my soul boldly
	   Outspread her wings,
	Floated over the quiet earth,
	   As if homeward bound.

Schumann's direction, Zart, heimlich (tender, mysterious), sets the Romantic mood. The brief introduction on the piano evokes a serene landscape. Over gently dissonant harmonies the vocal line unfolds in a broad curve, the upward glide of the first phrase balanced by downward movement in the second.

This is a strophic song with much repetition. The music for the first two lines is repeated in the next two, and the second stanza repeats the first. In other words, the opening phrase is heard four times in a row, with subtle changes in the accompaniment.

The emotional climax of the song comes with the third stanza, at which point the poet becomes subjective, rapturous ("And my soul boldly outspread her wings"). Here there is a broadening in both harmony and dynamics. A slight retard in the piano part brings on the final appearance of the main phrase, on the last two lines of the poem. As in *To Sylvia* the introduction serves also as interlude between the stanzas and as a postlude at the end, fading away in pianissimo harmonies.

We see here the perfect mating of Romantic poetry and Romantic music. The result is magic.

19 Frédéric François Chopin

"My life . . . an episode without a beginning and with a sad end."

In the annals of his century Chopin (1810–49) is known as the "Poet of the Piano." The title is a valid one. His art, issuing from the heart of Romanticism, constitutes the golden age of that instrument.

His Life

The national composer of Poland was half French. His father emigrated to Warsaw, where he married a lady-in-waiting to a countess and taught French to the sons of the nobility. Frédéric, who displayed his musical gift in childhood, was educated at the newly-founded Conservatory of Warsaw. His student years were climaxed by a mild infatuation with a young singer, Constantia Gladkowska, who inspired him with sighs and tears in the best nineteenth-century manner. "It was with thoughts of this beautiful creature that I composed the Adagio of my new concerto." The concerto was the one in F minor. Frédéric was nineteen.

When the young artist set forth to make a name in the world, his comrades sang a farewell cantata in his honor. Frédéric wept, convinced he would never see his homeland again. In Vienna the news reached him that Warsaw had risen in revolt against the Tsar. Gloomy visions tormented him; he saw his family and friends massacred. He left Vienna in the summer. On reaching Stuttgart he learned that the Polish capital had been captured by the Russians. The tidings precipitated a torrent of grief, and the flaming defiance that found expression in the *Revolutionary Etude.*

In September, 1831, the young man reached Paris. He thought of continuing to London, even to America. But he was introduced by his countryman, Prince Radziwill, into the aristocratic salons and there created a

Frédéric Chopin. A painting by Eugène Delacroix.

sensation. His decision was made, and the rest of his career was linked to the artistic life of his adopted city. Paris in the 1830s was the center of the new Romanticism. The circle in which Chopin moved included as brilliant a galaxy of artists as ever gathered anywhere. Among the musicians were Liszt and Berlioz, Rossini and Meyerbeer. The literary figures included Victor Hugo, Balzac, Lamartine, George Sand, de Musset, and Alexandre Dumas. Heinrich Heine was his friend, as was the painter Delacroix. Although Chopin was a man of emotions rather than ideas, he could not but be stimulated by his contact with the leading intellectuals of France.

Through Liszt he met Mme. Aurore Dudevant, "the lady with the somber eye," known to the world as the novelist George Sand. She was thirty-four, Chopin twenty-eight when the famous friendship began. Mme. Sand was brilliant and domineering; her need to dominate found its counterpart in Chopin's need to be ruled. She left a memorable account of this fastidious artist at work: "His creative power was spontaneous, miraculous. It came to him without effort or warning . . . But then began the most heartrending labor I have ever witnessed. It was a series of attempts, of fits of irresolution and impatience to recover certain details. He would shut himself in his room for days, pacing up and down, breaking his pens, repeating and modifying one bar a hundred times . . . He would spend six weeks over a page, only to end by writing it out finally just as he had sketched it in the original draft."

For the next eight years Chopin spent his summers at Mme. Sand's chateau at Nohant, where she entertained the cream of France's intelligentsia. These were productive years for him, although his health grew progressively worse and his relationship with Mme. Sand ran its course from love to conflict, from jealousy to hostility. They parted in bitterness.

According to his friend Liszt, "Chopin felt and often repeated that in breaking this long affection, this powerful bond, he had broken his life." Chopin's creative energy, which had lost its momentum in his middle thirties, came to an end. The "illness of the century," the lonely despair of the Romantic artist pervades his last letters. "What has become of my art?" he writes during a visit to Scotland. "And my heart, where have I wasted it? I scarce remember any more how they sing at home. That world slips away from me somehow. I forget. I have no strength. If I rise a little I fall again, lower than ever."

He returned to Paris suffering from tuberculosis and died some months later, at the age of thirty-nine. His funeral was his greatest triumph. Princesses and artists joined to pay him homage. Meyerbeer, Berlioz, and Delacroix were among the mourners. George Sand stayed away. His heart was returned to Poland, the rest of him remained in Paris. And on his grave a friendly hand scattered a gobletful of Polish earth.

His Music

Chopin was one of the most original artists of the Romantic era. His idiom is so entirely his own there is no mistaking it for any other. He was the only master of first rank whose creative life centered about the piano. From the first, his imagination was wedded to the keyboard, to create a universe within that narrow frame. His genius transformed even the limitations of the instrument into sources of beauty. (The prime limitation, of course, is the piano's inability to sustain tone for any length of time.) Chopin overcame these with such ingenuity that to him as much as to any individual is due the modern piano style. The widely spaced chords in the bass, sustained by pedal, set up masses of tone that wreathe the melody in enchantment. "Everything must be made to sing," he told his pupils. The delicate ornaments in his music—trills, grace notes, runs of gossamer lightness—seem magically to prolong the single tones. And all this generally lies so well for the hand that the music seems almost to play itself.

It is remarkable that so many of his works have remained in the pianist's repertory. His Nocturnes—night songs, as the name implies—are tinged with varying shades of melancholy. They are usually in three-part form. The Preludes are visionary fragments; some are only a page in length, several consist of two or three lines. The Etudes crown the literature of the study piece. Here piano technique is transformed into poetry. The Impromptus are fanciful, capricious, yet they have a curious rightness about them. The Waltzes capture the brilliance and coquetry

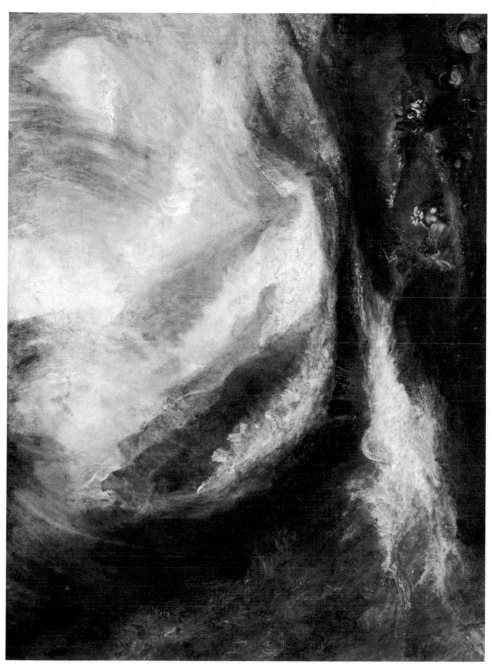

Romantics such as J. M. W. Turner (1775–1851) used nature as a backdrop for the inner conflicts of man. **Valley of Aosta—Snowstorm, Avalanche and Thunderstorm.** *(The Art Institute of Chicago.)*

Romanticism seized on themes of passionate intensity. This is clearly demonstrated in the famous painting **The Raft of the "Medusa,"** by Theodore Gericault (1791–1824). *(The Louvre, Paris.)*

of the salon. They are veritable dances of the spirit. The Mazurkas, derived from a Polish peasant dance, evoke the idealized landscape of his youth.

Among the larger forms are the four Ballades. These are epic poems of spacious structure, like sagas related by a bard. The Polonaises revive the stately processional dance in which Poland's nobles were wont to hail their kings. Heroic in tone, they resound with the clangor of battle and brave deeds. In reminding his countrymen of their ancient glory the national poet strengthens their will to freedom. The *Berceuse* (Cradle Song), the *Barcarolle* (Boat Song), the *Fantasy in F minor,* and the dramatic Scherzos reveal the composer at the summit of his art. The *Sonatas in B minor* and *B-flat minor* are thoroughly Romantic in spirit as are the *Piano Concertos in E minor* and *F minor.*

Chopin's style emerged fully formed when he was twenty. It was not the result of an extended intellectual development, as was the case with masters like Beethoven or Wagner. In this he was the true lyricist, along with his contemporaries Schumann and Mendelssohn. All three died young, and all three reached their peak through the spontaneous lyricism of youth. In them the first period of Romanticism found its finest expression.

Mazurka in C-sharp minor

Side 1/7
(S and E II)

The *Mazurka in C-sharp minor,* Opus 6, No. 2, belongs to Chopin's youthful works. It was published in 1832, when he was twenty-two. The piece, which takes about two minutes to play, reveals Chopin's imaginative handling of the lively dance rhythms of his native land. It shows too his affinity for the short lyric form. The piece follows the basic principle of three-part (A-B-A) structure, modified according to the composer's fancy and presenting a flow of endearing melody.

A brief introduction marked Sotto voce ("below the voice"—that is, whispered), with the melody in an inner voice, prepares the way for the main idea. It has been said of Chopin's mazurkas that some dance with the heart, others with the heel. This one dances with the heart:

Characteristic are the dotted rhythms and the occasional shifting of the accent from the first to the second or third beat. Notice the simple dynamic scheme: a statement begins softly and works up to a forte at the close. The first section (A) has a poignance about it, a kind of bitter-sweet quality that informs certain dances of Eastern Europe. For contrast, the middle section (B) is in a happier mood. It is marked Gajo—gay. The music dies down. We hear again the Sotto voce of the opening, and the first section is repeated in abbreviated form.

Etude in A minor

Side 1/8
(S and E II)

An *etude* is a study piece that deals with a specific technical problem, such as rapid scales, arpeggios, octaves, and the like. Every instrumentalist has to spend hours practicing such study pieces which, apart from their use as exercises, have either very little or no musical value.

It was Chopin's achievement to lift the study piece from its purely utilitarian level into the high realm of art. His Etudes are little tone poems suffused with all the glow of his creative imagination. At the same time they approach the technical problems of a new style of Romantic piano playing with an inventiveness that had never been envisaged before.

Typical is the *Etude in A minor,* Opus 25, No. 11. The technical problem here is one that the pianist encounters fairly frequently: a melody in the left hand articulated against rapid passages in the right. To meet these requirements Chopin created one of his most tumultuous tone paintings. The right hand alone, then both together announce the brief theme on which the piece is based—a solemn melody, like a summons, marked Lento:

This motto gives rise to a theme that shapes the piece, projected at first in tumultuous, quasi heroic accents. The tension abates for an instant when the melody is switched to the right hand while the left takes over the passage work. Eventually both hands play the rapid passages simultaneously, building a tremendous climax. Throughout, the piece demands from the pianist the utmost accuracy, speed and endurance. Finally the motto thunders from the bass, then in massive chords. A sweeping scale in both hands concludes this tonal epic.

One is swept along by the tremendous drive, the almost explosive force of the music. This Etude is popularly known as the *Winter Wind,* one of a series of fanciful titles that affixed themselves to various works of Chopin long after he had written them.

Prelude in E minor

Side 2/1
(S and E II)
The *Prelude in E minor,* Opus 28, No. 4 (1839) reveals Chopin's uncanny power to achieve the utmost expressiveness with the simplest means. The melody hardly moves, unfolding in sustained tones over a succession of chords that change very subtly, usually one note at a time:

The music strikes a gently mournful mood that is of the essence of Romanticism. Tension gathers slowly; there is something inevitable about the rise to the climax, where the melody, advancing in bold leaps, takes on the character of a passionate outcry that subsides to a sorrowful pianissimo ending. Rarely has so much been said in a single page. Schumann did not exaggerate when he said of the Preludes, "In each piece we find in his own hand, 'Frédéric Chopin wrote it!' He is the boldest, the proudest poet of his time."

His countrymen have enshrined Chopin as the national composer of Poland. Withal he is a spokesman of European culture. It is not without significance that despite his homesickness he spent the whole of his adult life in Paris. Thus Poland was idealized in his imagination as the symbol of that unappeasable longing which every Romantic artist carries in his heart: the longing for the lost land of happiness that may never be found again. Heine, himself an expatriate, divined this when he wrote that Chopin is "neither a Pole, a Frenchman, nor a German. He reveals a higher origin. He comes from the land of Mozart, Raphael, Goethe. His true country is the land of poetry."

20 The Nature of Program Music

"... The renewal of music through its inner connection with poetry." — FRANZ LISZT

Program music is instrumental music endowed with literary or pictorial associations; the nature of these associations is indicated by the title of the piece or by an explanatory note—the "program"—supplied by the composer. Program music is distinguished from *absolute* or *pure music,* which consists of musical patterns devoid of literary or pictorial connotations.

Program music was of special importance in a period like the nineteenth century when musicians became sharply conscious of the connection between their art and the world about them. It helped them to bring music closer to poetry and painting, and to relate their work to the moral and political issues of their time. It also helped them to approach the forms of absolute music in a new way. All the same, the distinction between absolute and program music is not as rigid as many suppose. A work entitled *Symphony No. 1* or *Third String Quartet* falls into the former category. Yet the composer in the course of writing it may very well have had in mind specific images and associations that he has not seen fit to divulge. Beethoven, whom we think of as the master of absolute music, confessed to a friend, "I have always a picture in my thoughts when I am composing, and work to it." Conversely, a piece called *Romeo and Juliet Overture* comes under the heading of program music. Yet if we were not told the title we would listen to it as a piece of absolute music. This is what we are apt to do in any case once we get to know the work. What concerns us ultimately is the destiny not of the lovers but of the themes.

Varieties of Program Music

The concert overture   A primary impulse toward program music derived from the opera house, where the overture was a rousing orchestral piece in one movement designed to serve as an introduction to an opera (or a play). Many operatic overtures achieved independent popularity as concert pieces. This pointed the way to a new type of overture not associated with an opera: a single-movement concert piece for orchestra, based on a striking literary idea, such as Tchaikovsky's *Romeo and Juliet*. This type of composition, the *concert overture,* might be descriptive, like Mendelssohn's seascape *Hebrides (Fingal's Cave)*; or it could embody a patriotic idea, as does Tchaikovsky's *1812 Overture.*

The concert overture, despite its literary program, retained the design traditionally associated with the first movement of a symphony (what will be discussed in a later chapter as *sonata-allegro form*). This consists of three sections—the *Exposition* (or *Statement*), in which the themes are presented; the *Development;* and the *Recapitulation* (or *Restatement*). In other words, the concert overture retained a form associated with absolute music, but combined it with the poetic or pictorial ideas associated with program music. Thus, it offered composers a single-movement form of orchestral music which they were able to invest with the imagery of a romantic story or scene.

Incidental music   An engaging species of program music is that written for plays, generally consisting of an overture and a series of pieces to be performed between the acts and during the important scenes, known as *incidental music.* Nineteenth-century composers produced a number of works of this type that were notable for tone painting, characterization, and theater atmosphere.

The most successful pieces were generally arranged into suites, a number of which became vastly popular. Mendelssohn's music for *A Midsummer Night's Dream* is one of the most successful works in this category. Hardly less appealing are the two suites from Bizet's music for Alphonse Daudet's play *L'Arlésienne* (The Woman of Arles) and the two from Grieg's music for Henrik Ibsen's poetic drama *Peer Gynt.*

The program symphony

The impulse toward program music was so strong that it invaded even the hallowed form of absolute music—the symphony. Composers tried to retain the grand form of Beethoven and at the same time to associate it with a literary theme. Thus came into being the *program symphony.* The best known examples are three program symphonies of Berlioz—*Symphonie fantastique, Harold in Italy, Romeo and Juliet*—and two of Liszt, the *Faust* and *Dante* symphonies.

The symphonic poem

As the nineteenth century wore on, the need was felt more and more for a large form of orchestral music that would serve the Romantic era as well as the symphony had served the Classical. Toward the middle of the century the long-awaited step was taken with the creation of the symphonic poem. This was the nineteenth century's one original contribution to the large forms. It was the achievement of Franz Liszt, who first used the term in 1848. His *Les Préludes* is among the best known examples of this type of music.

A *symphonic poem* is a piece of program music for orchestra, in one movement, which in the course of contrasting sections develops a poetic idea, suggests a scene, or creates a mood. It differs from the concert overture in one important respect: whereas the concert overture generally retains one of the traditional Classical designs, the symphonic poem is much freer in form. The name is used interchangeably with *tone poem.* The symphonic poem as cultivated by Liszt and his disciples was an immensely flexible form that permitted its course to be shaped by the literary idea. The programs were drawn from poets and painters dear to the Romantic temperament: Shakespeare, Dante, Petrarch; Goethe and Schiller; Michelangelo and Raphael; Byron and Victor Hugo. A strong influence was the "return to nature" that had been advocated by Rousseau. The symphonic poem gave composers the canvas they needed for a big single-movement form. It became the most widely cultivated type of orchestral program music throughout the second half of the century.

The varieties of program music just described—concert overture, incidental music, program symphony, and symphonic poem—comprise one of the striking manifestations of nineteenth-century Romanticism. This type of music emphasized the descriptive element; it impelled composers to try to express specific feelings; and it proclaimed the direct relationship of music to life.

21 Berlioz: *Symphonie fantastique*

"The prevailing characteristics of my music are passionate expression, intense ardor, rhythmic animation, and unexpected turns. To render my works properly requires a combination of extreme precision and irresistible verve, a regulated vehemence, a dreamy tenderness, and an almost morbid melancholy."

His Life

Hector Berlioz (1803–69) was born in France in a small town near Grenoble. His father, a well-to-do physician, expected him to follow in his footsteps, and at eighteen Hector was dispatched to the medical school in Paris. The Conservatory and the Opéra, however, exercised an infinitely greater attraction than the dissecting room. The following year the fiery youth made a decision that horrified his upper-middle-class family: he gave up medicine for music.

The Romantic revolution was brewing in Paris. Berlioz, along with Victor Hugo and the painter Delacroix, found himself in the camp of "young France." Having been cut off by his parents, he gave lessons, sang in a theater chorus, and turned to various musical chores. He fell under the spell of Beethoven; hardly less powerful was the impact of Shakespeare, to whose art he was introduced by a visiting English troupe. For the actress whose Ophelia and Juliet excited the admiration of the Parisians, young Berlioz conceived an overwhelming passion. In his *Memoirs,* which read like a Romantic novel, he describes his infatuation for Harriet

Hector Berlioz. A painting by Gustave Courbet (1819–77).

Smithson: "I became obsessed by an intense, overpowering sense of sadness. I could not sleep, I could not work, and I spent my time wandering aimlessly about Paris and its environs."

In 1830 came the first official recognition of Berlioz's gifts. He was awarded the coveted Prix de Rome, which gave him a stipend and an opportunity to live and work in the Eternal City. That year also saw the composition of what has remained his most celebrated work, the *Symphonie fantastique*. Upon his return from Rome a hectic courtship of Miss Smithson ensued. There were strenuous objections on the part of both their families and violent scenes, during one of which the excitable Hector attempted suicide. He was revived. They were married.

Now that the unattainable ideal had become his wife, his ardor cooled. It was Shakespeare he had loved rather than Harriet, and in time he sought the ideal elsewhere. All the same, the first years of his marriage were the most fruitful of his life. By the time he was forty he had produced most of the works on which his fame rests.

To earn money he turned to music criticism, producing a stream of reviews and articles. His literary labors were a necessary part of his musical activity; he had to propagandize for his works and create an audience capable of understanding them. In the latter part of his life he conducted his music in all the capitals of Europe. But Paris never wholly accepted him. Year after year he dissipated his energies in reviewing the works of nonentities while his own were neglected. Disgust and misanthropy settled upon him; for the last seven years of his life the embittered master wrote no more. He died at sixty-six, tormented to the end. "Some day," wrote Richard Wagner, "a grateful France will raise a proud monument on his tomb." The prophecy has been fulfilled.

His Music

Berlioz was one of the boldest innovators of the nineteenth century. His approach to music was wholly original, his sense of sound unique. From the start he had an affinity—where orchestral music was concerned—for the vividly dramatic or pictorial program.

Berlioz's most important opera, *Les Troyens* (The Trojans), on his own libretto based on Vergil, has been successfully revived in recent years. The *Requiem* (Mass for the Dead; 1837) and the *Te Deum* (Hymn of Praise; 1849) are conceived on a grandiose scale. This love of huge orchestral and choral forces represents only one aspect of Berlioz's personality. No less characteristic is the tenderness that finds expression in the oratorio *L'Enfance du Christ* (Childhood of Christ; 1854); the fine-spun lyricism that wells up in his songs; the sensibility that fills his orchestra with Gallic clarity and grace.

It was in the domain of orchestration that Berlioz's genius asserted itself most fully. His daring originality in handling the instruments opened up a new world of Romantic sonority. Until his time, as Aaron Copland pointed out, "composers used instruments in order to make them sound like themselves; the mixing of colors so as to produce a new result was his achievement." His scores abound in novel effects and discoveries that served as models to all who came after him. Indeed, the conductor Felix Weingartner called Berlioz "the creator of the modern orchestra."

Symphonie fantastique: *Fourth Movement*

Berlioz's best-known symphony was written at the height of his infatuation with Harriet Smithson, when he was twenty-seven years old. It is hardly to be believed that this remarkable "novel in tones" was conceived by a young man only three years after the death of Beethoven. Extraordinary is the fact that he not only attached a program to a symphony, but that he drew the program from his personal life. In this autobiographical approach to his art Berlioz is a true Romantic. "A young musician of morbid sensibility and ardent imagination in a paroxysm of lovesick despair has poisoned himself with opium. The drug, too weak to kill, plunges him into a heavy sleep accompanied by strange visions. His sensations, feelings, and memories are translated in his sick brain into musical images and ideas. The beloved one herself becomes for him a melody, a recurrent theme [*idée fixe*] that haunts him everywhere."

The "fixed idea" that symbolizes the beloved—the basic theme of the symphony—is subjected to variation in harmony, rhythm, meter, and tempo; dynamics, register, and instrumental color. These transformations take on literary as well as musical significance. Thus the basic motive, re-

curring by virtue of the literary program, becomes a musical thread unifying five movements that are diverse in mood and character.

Fourth movement
Side 2/2 (S)
Side 3/2
(E II)

The fourth movement is the famous *March to the Scaffold*. "He dreams that he has killed his beloved, that he has been condemned to die and is being led to the scaffold. The procession moves to the sounds of a march now somber and wild, now brilliant and solemn. . . . At the very end the 'fixed idea' reappears for an instant, like a last thought of love interrupted by the fall of the axe."

Marked Allegretto non troppo in 4/4, the march movement exemplifies the nineteenth-century love of the fantastic. Not easily forgotten is the sound of the opening: muted horns, timpani, pizzicato chords on cellos and double basses. The lower strings play an energetic theme that strides down the scale:

After this idea is given to the violins, the diabolical march emerges in the woodwinds and brass:

The theme of the beloved appears at the very end, on the clarinet, and is cut off by a grim fortissimo chord. The effect ("a last thought of love interrupted by the fall of the axe") has been much criticized as being too realistic. One must remember, however, that when Berlioz wrote it he was opening up new fields of expression for his art.

There is a bigness of line and gesture about the music of Berlioz, an overflow of vitality and inventiveness. He is one of the major prophets in the Romantic era.

22 Tchaikovsky: *Romeo and Juliet*

"Truly there would be reason to go mad were it not for music."

Few composers typify the end-of-the-century mood as does Peter Ilyich Tchaikovsky (1840–93). He belonged to a generation that saw its truths crumbling and found none to replace them. He expressed as did none other the pessimism that attended the final phase of the Romantic movement.

His Life

Tchaikovsky was born at Votinsk in a distant province of Russia, son of a government official. His family intended him for a career in the government. He graduated at nineteen from the aristocratic School of Jurisprudence at St. Petersburg and obtained a minor post in the Ministry of Justice. Not till he was twenty-three did he reach the decision to resign his

Peter Ilyich Tchaikovsky, in a painting by N. D. Kuznetsov.

post and enter the newly founded Conservatory of St. Petersburg. "To be a good musician and earn my daily bread"—his was a modest goal.

He completed the course in three years and was immediately recommended by Anton Rubinstein, director of the school, for a teaching post at the new Conservatory of Moscow. Despite the long hours and large classes, the young professor of harmony applied himself assiduously to composition. His twelve years at Moscow saw the production of some of his most successful works.

Extremely sensitive by nature, Tchaikovsky was subject to attacks of depression aggravated by his irregular personal life. In the hope of achieving some degree of stability, he entered into an ill-starred marriage with a student of the Conservatory, Antonina Miliukov, who was hopelessly in love with him. His sympathy for Antonina soon turned into uncontrollable aversion, and in a fit of despair he wandered into the icy waters of the Moscow River. Some days later he fled, on the verge of a serious breakdown, to his brothers in St. Petersburg.

In this desperate hour, as in one of the fairy tales he liked to turn into ballets, there appeared the kind benefactress who enabled him to go abroad until he had recovered his health, freed him from the demands of a teaching post, and launched him on the most productive period of his career. Nadezhda von Meck, widow of an industrialist, was an imperious and emotional woman. She lived the life of a recluse in her mansion in Moscow, from which she ran her railroads, her estates, and the lives of her eleven children. Her passion was music, especially Tchaikovsky's. Bound by the rigid conventions of her time and her class, she had to be certain that her enthusiasm was for the artist, not the man; hence she stipulated that she was never to meet the recipient of her bounty.

Thus began the famous friendship by letter which soon assumed a tone of passionate attachment. For the next thirteen years Mme. von Meck made Tchaikovsky's career the focal point of her life, providing for his needs with exquisite devotion and tact. Save for an accidental glimpse of one another at the opera or during a drive, they never met.

The correspondence gives us an insight into Tchaikovsky's method of work. "You ask me how I manage the instrumentation. I never compose in the abstract. I invent the musical idea and its instrumentation simultaneously." Mme. von Meck inquires if the *Fourth Symphony* (which he dedicated to her) has a definite meaning. Tchaikovsky replies, "How can one express the indefinable sensations that one experiences while writing an instrumental composition that has no definite subject? It is a purely lyrical process. It is a musical confession of the soul, which unburdens itself through sounds just as a lyric poet expresses himself through poetry. The difference lies in the fact that music has far richer resources of expression and is a more subtle medium. . . . As Heine said, "Where words leave off music begins.' "

The years covered by the correspondence saw the spread of Tchaikovsky's fame. He was the first Russian whose music appealed to Western tastes, and in 1891 he was invited to come to America to participate in the ceremonies that marked the opening of Carnegie Hall. From New York he wrote, "These Americans strike me as very remarkable. In this country the honesty, sincerity, generosity, cordiality, and readiness to help you without a second thought are extremely pleasant. . . . The houses downtown are simply colossal. I cannot understand how anyone can live on the thirteenth floor. I went out on the roof of one such house. The view was splendid, but I felt quite giddy when I looked down on Broadway. . . . I am convinced that I am ten times more famous in America than in Europe."

The letters of his final years breathe disenchantment and the suspicion that he had nothing more to say. "Is it possible that I have completely written myself out? I have neither ideas nor inclinations!" But ahead of him lay his two finest symphonies.

Immediately after finishing his *Sixth Symphony,* the *Pathétique,* he went to St. Petersburg to conduct it. The work met with a lukewarm reception, due in part to the fact that Tchaikovsky, painfully shy in public, conducted his music without any semblance of conviction. Some days later, although he had been warned of the prevalence of cholera in the capital, he carelessly drank a glass of unboiled water and contracted the disease. He died within the week, at the age of fifty-three. The suddenness of his death and the tragic tone of his last work led to rumors that he had committed suicide. Almost immediately there accrued to the *Symphonie pathétique* the sensational popularity it has enjoyed ever since.

His Music

"He was the most Russian of us all!" said Stravinsky. In the eyes of his countrymen Tchaikovsky is a national artist. He himself laid great weight on the Russian element in his music. "Why is it that the simple Russian landscape, a walk in summer through Russian fields and forest or on the steppes at evening can affect me so that I have lain on the ground numb, overcome by a wave of love for nature."

Tchaikovsky cultivated all branches of music. Of prime importance are his last symphonies, the *Fourth* (1877), the *Fifth* (1888), and the *Sixth* (1893). They abound in spectacular climaxes that endear them to the virtuoso conductor. In the domain of program music two arresting works continue to be played: the overture-fantasy *Romeo and Juliet* and the symphonic fantasy *Francesca da Rimini* (1876). Hardly less popular is the colorful *Capriccio italien* (1880). Of his eight operas, two hold the international stage: *Eugene Onegin* (1877–78) and *Pique Dame* (Queen of Spades, 1890). Based on librettos derived from the national poet Pushkin, both are essentially lyric in character. Tchaikovsky's ballets enjoy immense popularity. *Swan Lake* (1876), *The Sleeping Beauty* (1889), and *The Nutcracker* (1892) are appreciated both in the ballet theater and in the concert hall.

Overture-Fantasy: Romeo and Juliet

Side 3/2 (S)
Side 4/2
(E II)

Romeo and Juliet, the first work that fully revealed Tchaikovsky's gifts, was written in 1869, when the composer was twenty-nine. In 1881 he thoroughly revised the piece. The term *overture-fantasy* suggests his imaginative approach to the material. It also makes clear that this is not an overture to an opera but an independent concert piece. The form is similar to that which may be found in Mendelssohn's Overture to *A Midsummer Night's Dream:* a large three-section structure called sonata-allegro form, that allows for the presentation, development, and restatement of musical ideas (Exposition-Development-Recapitulation). In this case the form is enlarged by means of a spacious introduction and epilogue. It was in no sense the composer's intent to give a detailed musical depiction of the Shakespearean drama. Rather, he selected three salient images that lent themselves to musical treatment—the gentle Friar Laurence, the feud between the two noble families of Verona, and the love of Romeo and Juliet.

Friar Laurence is evoked by a chorale which is presented in four-part harmony by two clarinets and two bassoons, Andante non tanto quasi moderato (not too slow, almost moderate; a *chorale* is a hymn or a hymn-like tune). This chorale, with its organ-like chords, creates a medieval atmosphere. It expands into a lengthy introduction, and returns at the end of the piece in a prelude-postlude formation.

The Allegro giusto (fast, in strict time) begins the Exposition with the "Feud" theme.

The brusque rhythm with its strong syncopation suggests violent action, as do the full orchestral tone and explosive accompaniment. Characteristic of Tchaikovsky are the sweeping runs, ascending and descending, on the violins.

The love theme is a melody long of line and tenderly lyrical, sung by English horn and muted violas. The youthful composer created here a broadly spun song whose ardor is not unworthy of Shakespeare's lovers. The

mood is rounded off by a subsidiary idea of great expressiveness, played by the muted strings. With this the Exposition section comes to an end.

The agitated development section is based mainly on the Feud theme, interspersed with references to the Friar Laurence music in the horns and, ultimately, the trumpets. In the working out of his musical ideas Tchaikovsky achieves that building up of tension and momentum which is the essence of symphonic development. The Recapitulation brings back the feud theme substantially as before. The love music is now expanded and rises, wave upon wave of sumptuous orchestral sound, to one of those torrential climaxes that only an uninhibited romantic could achieve.

The epilogue is fashioned out of the love theme. Muffled drums beat a dirge for the dead lovers, and the chorale of the opening is heard again, balancing the architecture.

This is young man's music, fervid, communicative, and fashioned along broad simple lines. It captures a characteristic moment in the thought and feeling of the late Romantic era. Beyond that it remains one of the more beguiling—and solidly wrought—examples of nineteenth-century program music.

23 Nationalism and the Romantic Movement

"I grew up in a quiet spot and was saturated from earliest childhood with the wonderful beauty of Russian popular song. I am therefore passionately devoted to every expression of the Russian spirit. In short, I am a Russian through and through!" — TCHAIKOVSKY

The Rise of Musical Nationalism

In giving voice to his personal view of life the artist also expresses the hopes and dreams of the group with which he is identified. It is this identification, seeping through from the most profound layers of the unconscious, that makes Shakespeare and Dickens so English, Dostoevsky so Russian, Proust so French. Yet this national quality does not cut the artist off from other peoples. Shakespeare, Dostoevsky, and Proust belong not only to their own nations but to all mankind. In depicting the life they knew they expressed what all men feel.

Alongside the national artist stands the nationalist, who affirms his national heritage in a more conscious way. Needless to say, the two categories overlap. This was especially true in nineteenth-century Europe, where political conditions encouraged the growth of nationalism to such a degree that it became a decisive force within the Romantic movement. National tensions on the Continent—the pride of the conquering nations and the struggle for freedom of the subjugated ones—gave rise to emotions that found an ideal expression in music. The Romantic composers expressed their nationalism in a number of ways. Several based their music on the songs and dances of their people: Chopin in his Mazurkas, Liszt in his *Hungarian Rhapsodies,* Dvořák in the *Slavonic Dances,* Grieg in the *Norwegian Dances*. A number wrote dramatic works based on folklore or the life of the peasantry. Examples are the German folk opera *Der Freischütz* by Carl Maria von Weber, the Czech national opera *The Bartered Bride* by Bedřich Smetana, as well as the Russian fairy-tale operas and ballets of Tchaikovsky and Rimsky-Korsakov. Some wrote symphonic poems and operas celebrating the exploits of a national hero, a historic event, or the scenic beauty of their country. Tchaikovsky's *1812 Overture* and Smetana's *The Moldau* exemplify this trend, as does the glorification of the gods and heroes of German myth and legend in Richard Wagner's music dramas, especially *The Ring of the Nibelung,* a vast epic centering about the life and death of Siegfried. The nationalist composer might unite his music with the verses of a national poet or dramatist. Schubert's settings of Goethe fall into this category; also Grieg's music for Ibsen's *Peer Gynt* and Tchaikovsky's operas based on the dramas of Alexander Pushkin, the Russian national poet who also inspired Rimsky-Korsakov and Musorgsky. Of special significance was the role of music in periods of political turmoil, when the nationalist composer was able to give emotional expression to the aspirations of his people, as Verdi did when Italy was striving for unification, or Sibelius did when Finland struggled against its Russian rulers at the end of the century.

The political implications of musical nationalism were not lost upon the authorities. Verdi's operas had to be altered again and again to suit the Austrian censor. Sibelius's tone poem *Finlandia* with its rousing trumpet calls was forbidden by the tsarist police when Finland was demanding her independence at the turn of the century. During World War II the Nazis forbade the playing of *The Moldau* in Prague and of Chopin's Polonaises in Warsaw because of the powerful symbolism residing in these works.

Nationalism added to the language of European music a variety of national idioms of great charm and vivacity. By associating music with the love of homeland, nationalism enabled composers to give expression to the cherished aspirations of millions of people. In short, national consciousness

The Romantic imagination was captured by exotic locales and picturesque effects. A painting by Eugène Delacroix, **Women of Algiers in Their Apartment.** *(Louvre, Paris.)*

pervaded every aspect of the European spirit in the nineteenth century. The Romantic movement is unthinkable without it.

Exoticism

Exoticism in music, painting, and literature evokes the picturesque atmosphere and color of far-off lands. The trend, needless to say, was strongly encouraged by the Romantic movement. Nineteenth-century exoticism manifested itself, in the first place, as a longing of the northern nations for the warmth and color of the south; in the second, as a longing of the West for the fairy-tale splendors of the Orient. The former impulse found expression in the works of German, French, and Russian composers who turned for inspiration to Italy and Spain. The long list includes several well-known works by Russian composers: Glinka's two *Spanish Overtures,* Tchaikovsky's *Capriccio italien,* and Rimsky-Korsakov's *Capriccio on Spanish Themes.* The German contribution includes Mendelssohn's *Italian Symphony,* Hugo Wolf's *Italian Serenade,* and Richard Strauss's *Aus Italien.* Among the French works are Chabrier's *España* and Lalo's *Symphonie espagnole.* The masterpiece in this category is, of course, Bizet's *Carmen.*

Russian national school

The glamor of the East was brought to international prominence by the Russian national school. In an empire that stretched to the borders of Persia, exoticism was really a form of nationalism. The fairy-tale background of Asia pervades Russian music. Rimsky-Korsakov's orchestrally resplendent *Scheherazade* and his opera *Sadko,* Alexander Borodin's opera *Prince Igor* and symphonic poem *In the Steppes of Central Asia,* and Ippolitov-Ivanov's *Caucasian Sketches* are among the many orientally inspired works that for a time found favor throughout the world. A number of French and Italian composers also utilized exotic themes: Saint-Saëns in *Samson and Delilah,* Delibes in *Lakmé,* Massenet in *Thaïs,* Verdi in *Aïda,* and Puccini in his operas *Madame Butterfly* and *Turandot.*

24   Nationalism in the Symphonic Poem

"I am no enemy of the old forms in the old music. But I do not hold that we now have to follow them. I have come to the conclusion that the forms of the past are finished. Absolute music is quite impossible for me." — BEDŘICH SMETANA

Smetana: The Moldau

Side 3/1 (S)
Side 4/1 (E II)

The Czech national school was founded by Bedřich Smetana (1824–84). As in the case of several nationalist composers, Smetana's career unfolded

The Moldau flows in majestic peace through Prague.

against a background of political agitation. Bohemia stirred restlessly under Austrian rule, caught up in a surge of nationalist fervor that culminated in the uprisings of 1848. Young Smetana aligned himself with the
patriotic cause. After the revolution was crushed, the atmosphere in Prague
was oppressive for those suspected of sympathy with the nationalists. In
1856 Smetana accepted a post as conductor in Sweden. A disciple of
Berlioz and Liszt, he turned to the writing of symphonic poems during his
stay abroad. On his return to Bohemia in 1861 he resumed his career as a
national artist and worked for the establishment of a theater in Prague
where the performances would be given in the native tongue.

Of his eight operas on patriotic themes, several still hold the boards in
the theaters of his native land. One—*The Bartered Bride*—attained world-
wide fame. Hardly less important in the establishing of Smetana's reputation was the cycle of six symphonic poems entitled *My Country,* which occupied him from 1874 to 1879. These works are steeped in the beauty of
Bohemia's countryside, the rhythm of her folk songs and dances, the
pomp and pageantry of her legends. Best known of the series is the second,
Vltava (The Moldau), Smetana's finest achievement in the field of orchestral music.

In this tone poem the famous river becomes a poetic symbol that suffuses
the musical imagery with patriotic associations. The program appended to
the score explains the composer's intention. "Two springs pour forth in the

shade of the Bohemian forest, one warm and gushing, the other cold and peaceful." These join in a brook that becomes the river Moldau. "Coursing through Bohemia's valleys, it grows into a mighty stream. Through thick woods its flows as the gay sounds of the hunt and the notes of the hunter's horn are heard ever closer. It flows through grass-grown pastures and lowlands where a wedding feast is being celebrated with song and dance. At night, wood and water nymphs revel in its sparkling waves. Reflected on its surface are fortresses and castles—witnesses of bygone days of knightly splendor and the vanished glory of martial times." The stream races ahead through the Rapids of St. John, "finally flowing on in majestic peace toward Prague and welcomed by historic Vysehrad"—the legendary site of the castle of the ancient Bohemian kings. "Then it vanishes far beyond the poet's gaze."

The opening is marked Allegro commodo non agitato (moderately fast, not agitated). A rippling figure is heard as a dialogue between two flutes against a pizzicato accompaniment by violins and harp. From this emerges a broadly flowing melody played by oboe and violins—the theme of the river—that describes a broad arc in its stepwise movement along the scale. Smetana adapted his melody from a Czech folk song.

This theme subsequently is heard with the G raised to G sharp, which subtly alters the effect:

After a repetition of this idea, horns, woodwinds, and trumpets evoke a hunting scene. A fanfare such as the following not only creates an outdoor atmosphere but also underlines the descent of the modern French horn from the old hunting horn:

The section labeled *Peasant Wedding* is in the spirit of a rustic dance. Presented by clarinets and first violins against a staccato accompaniment, the melody has the stepwise movement, narrow skips within a narrow range, and repeated-note figures that we associate with folk song and dance:

Where the score is marked *Moonlight—Nymphs' Revels,* the mood changes to one of mystery. An atmosphere of woodland enchantment is evoked by the muted strings against a background of flute, clarinet, horn, and harp.

A gradual crescendo leads to the return of the principal melody. The pace quickens as the music graphically depicts the Rapids of St. John, with full use of the brass choir against the rippling of the strings. As the river approaches the ancient site of the royal castle, the principal melody returns in an exultant mood with certain tones (G and C) raised a half step to G sharp and C sharp. The result, as we shall learn in a later chapter, is to shift the tune from minor to major. This is taken care of by the change in key signature, which becomes four sharps:

Now the brass and woodwinds intone a triumphal chorale, as though the composer were promising his countrymen that their former glory will return.

There is a diminuendo to the end as the river "vanishes far beyond the poet's gaze."

The Czechs regard this symphonic landscape as a national tone poem that mirrors the very soul of their land. The rest of the world sees in it one of the more attractive examples of late Romantic tone painting.

25 The Symphony

"A great symphony is a man-made Mississippi down which we irresistibly flow from the instant of our leave-taking to a long foreseen destination." — AARON COPLAND

Absolute music is music for which the composer has not indicated to us any nonmusical associations, whether of story, scene, or mood. Here the musical ideas are organized in such a way that, without any aid from external images, they give the listener a satisfying sense of order and continuity.

The Nature of the Symphony

A *symphony* is a large-scale work for orchestra, in several parts or movements. These generally are three or four in number, in the sequence fast-slow-fast or fast-slow-moderately fast-fast. (There are many exceptions to this pattern.) The movements contrast in character and mood. Taken together they form an architectural entity and establish the symphony as the most exalted type of absolute music. (By a *movement* we mean a complete and comparatively independent part of a larger musical work.)

First movement   We will postpone a detailed discussion of symphonic structure to a later part of this book. It will suffice for the present to establish the character of the first movement of the cycle as a large form based on three sections—Exposition (Statement), Development, and Recapitulation (or Restatement). Sometimes a slow introduction leads into the movement proper. The Exposition usually presents two contrasting themes—one strongly rhythmic, the other lyric—which expand into contrasting sections. There is a bridge or transitional passage that leads from the first theme group to the second. A *codetta* (little coda) completes the Exposition. The Development is marked by a tremendous increase in tension. Here the composer may break the themes into fragments, recombining them in fresh patterns and revealing them in a new light. As he does so he explores the possibilities of the material for dynamic growth and development. Conflict and drama are of the essence in the Development. In the Recapitulation we hear again the themes of the Exposition more or less in their original guise, but with the wealth of new meaning that these have taken on in the course of the movement. There follows the coda, whose function is to round off the action and to bring the movement to its appointed conclusion.

The first movement is generally the most dramatic of the cycle. It is written in what is known as *sonata form, sonata-allegro form* (because the tempo of this movement is almost always allegro), or *first-movement form*. This form may also be used for an independent piece such as the overture. We encountered sonata-allegro form in the *Romeo and Juliet Overture*.

Second movement   In contrast to the first movement, the second—in the nineteenth-century symphony—is generally a slow movement of tenderly lyric nature. It may, however, vary in mood from the whimsical, even playful, to the tragic and passionate. The tempo marking in most cases is andante, adagio, or largo. This movement may be in three-part (A-B-A) form; sometimes it is a theme and variations. (Other possibilities are indicated in later chapters.)

Third movement   Third in the cycle, in the symphonies of the Romantic period, is the strongly rhythmic and impetuous scherzo, with overtones of humor, surprise, whimsy, or folk dance. As you may already know, *scherzo* is the Italian word for "jest"; but the mood may range from elfin lightness to demonic energy. The tempo marking indicates a lively pace—allegro, allegro molto, vivace, or the like. The form is usually a large A-B-A; the middle section, known as the *trio,* is of a somewhat quieter nature. In some symphonies the scherzo comes second.

Fourth movement   The fourth and last member of the cycle is of a dimension and character to balance the first. It may bring the symphony to a close on a note of triumph. The movement is generally a spirited allegro. In most of the Romantic symphonies to be discussed in the next chapters the final movement, like the first, is based on sonata-allegro form.

We have here given the barest outline of symphonic form, not attempting a complete picture until after we shall have heard several representative symphonies. What is important at this point is to understand that the symphony is a drama whose several movements are concerned with the presentation of abstract musical ideas. These ideas unfold in such a way as to give each movement a quality of logical continuity. The essence of symphonic style is dramatic contrast and development. It arouses emotion in the listener, but emotion not directed to any specific image.

Themes   The word *theme* figures prominently in any serious discussion of musical form. By a theme we mean a distinctive musical idea that serves as a building block, a germinating element in a large musical work. The theme may be a fully rounded melody or it may be a compact melodic-harmonic-rhythmic kernel that is capable of further growth and flowering. The theme may be broken down into its constituent fragments, which are known as

Motives   *motives.* For example, the melody of *London Bridge* might serve as a theme in a large work. The first four notes (on the words "London Bridge is") could constitute one motive, the next three notes (on the words "falling down"), another. In the unfolding of a work this theme and its motives might undergo continual development, in the course of which their capacity for growth would be explored. We shall have more to say on theme and motive when we discuss the Classical form in detail.

The nineteenth-century symphony holds a place of honor in the output of the Romantic era. It retains its hold on the public, and remains one of the striking manifestations of the spirit of musical Romanticism.

26 Dvořák: *New World Symphony*

"In the Negro melodies of America I discover all that is needed for a great and noble school of music. These beautiful and varied themes are the product of the soil. They are American. They are the folk songs of America, and your composers must turn to them."

Antonín Dvořák (1841–1904) is one of several late Romantic composers who based their personal style on the songs and dances of their native lands. He stands alongside Bedřich Smetana as a founder of the Czech national school.

His Life

Dvořák was born in a village near Prague where his father kept an inn and butcher shop. Poverty for a time threatened to rule out a musical career. However, the boy managed to get to Prague when he was sixteen. There he mastered his craft and became a viola player in the orchestra of the Czech National Theater. Success as a composer came slowly, but in time he was able to resign his orchestra post and devote himself to composing, teaching, and conducting. By the time he was forty Dvořák had left behind the material cares that plagued the first years of his career. As professor of composition at the Conservatory of Prague he was able to exert an important influence on the musical life of his time.

The spontaneity and melodious character of his music assured its popularity. When the last decade of the century arrived, Dvořák was known throughout Europe. In 1892 he was invited to become director of the National Conservatory of Music in New York City. He received fifteen

Antonín Dvořák.

thousand dollars a year at the Conservatory—a fabulous sum in those days —as compared with the six hundred dollars that made up his annual salary as a professor in Prague. His stay in the United States was fruitful. He produced what has remained his most successful symphony, *From the New World;* a number of chamber works, including the *American Quartet;* and the *Concerto for Cello and Orchestra.* Dvořák spent a summer at the Czech colony in Spillville, Iowa, in an atmosphere congenial to his simple tastes. Although every effort was made to induce him to continue at the Conservatory, his homesickness overrode all other considerations. After three years he returned to his beloved Bohemia.

Dvořák spent his remaining years in Prague in the happy circle of his wife and children, students and friends. He died in his sixty-third year, revered as a national artist throughout his native land.

His Music

Dvořák was a natural musician, a type that has always been abundant in Bohemia. Songfulness was native to a temperament in which intuition predominated over the intellectual process. Having sprung from the village, he never lost touch with the soil that was the source of his strength. At the same time, he achieved a solid craftsmanship in his art that enabled him to shape his musical impulses into large forms notable for their clarity and rightness.

Coming to the United States as one of the leading nationalists of Europe, Dvořák tried to influence his American pupils toward a national art. One of his pupils was Henry T. Burleigh, the Black baritone and arranger of spirituals. The melodies he heard from Burleigh stirred the folk poet in Dvořák, and strengthened him in his conviction that American composers would find themselves only when they had thrown off the European past and sought inspiration in the songs—Indian, Negro, cowboy—of their own country.

The time was not ripe for his advice to be heeded. But his instinct did not mislead him concerning the future of American music. One has but to consider the rich harvest of modern American works based on folklore to realize how fruitful, in the main, was his view.

The New World Symphony

The subtitle *From the New World* defines the scope and intent of the *Symphony No. 9 in E minor,* Opus 95 (1893). Dvořák was too much the Czech to presume to write an American work. His aim was to express his emotional response to a young and growing land, even while he longingly evoked the landscape of his own Bohemia. The work consequently is a mixture of Czech and American elements.

The symphony opens with a slow introduction. Cellos introduce a serene melody:

First movement
Side 4/1 (S)
Side 5/1 (E II)

This atmospheric introduction leads into a vigorous Allegro molto. The first theme is an energetic idea that opens with an upthrusting arpeggio figure, wide of span and syncopated in rhythm. The first phrase is presented by the horns against a curtain of string tone. The second phrase, marked by staccato, strong accents (indicated in the example by arrow-shaped signs), and dotted rhythm, is played by the woodwinds. Notice the syncopation in the second measure, where the accent falls on the offbeat (an eighth note followed by a dotted quarter), and in the fourth measure, where an eighth note is followed by a quarter:

The dotted rhythm persists throughout the bridge passage that leads into the next theme. This transition is based on a motive from the second phrase which is restated several times at lower pitches. Such a duplication of a pattern at a higher or lower pitch is known as a *sequence.*

The second theme is a plaintive tune of Bohemian folk character that is introduced by a flute and oboe. It has the narrow range and repetition of tones associated with folk song.

This theme is soon repeated on higher pitches (ascending sequence) and sounds different because of a basic change—what we shall come to recognize in a later chapter as a shift from minor to major:

Third is a songful theme announced by flute solo and taken over, in the answering phrase, by the violins. Its outlines were suggested by Dvořák's favorite Negro spiritual, *Swing Low, Sweet Chariot.* Notice again the syncopation in the second and sixth measures: an eighth note followed by a dotted quarter. Notice, too, how the upward inflection in measure 3 is subtly balanced by the downward inflection at the end of the second phrase.

A codetta, fortissimo, rounds off the Exposition.

The development explores the possibilities of the thematic material. The following examples show how Dvořák goes about reworking his themes and motives.

1. A motive from Theme 3 answered by a motive from Theme 1:

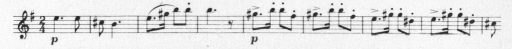

2. The opening motive of Theme 3, with slight changes of melody and rhythm in measures 3 and 4, combined with a motive from Theme 1, slightly changed:

3. The first phrase of Theme 1 combined with new material:

4. A motive from the second phrase of Theme 1 spun out through sequence and rhythmic transformation:

5. A motive from Theme 1, with slight melodic and rhythmic changes, serving as a transition to the Recapitulation:

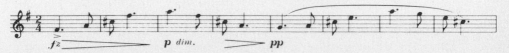

It is upon procedures such as these that the Development section of sonata-allegro form depends.

The Recapitulation restates the thematic material. There is a grandiose coda to which descending chromatic scales lend excitement, culminating in a fortissimo statement of the basic arpeggio figure.

Second movement
Side 4/2 (S)
Side 5/2 (E II)

The slow movement is a Largo, in ¼ time consisting of three sections (A-B-A), each of which contains subdivisions and repetitions of material. Out of the introductory chords, marked *ppp*, issues the famous melody assigned to the English horn. It shows several characteristics we associate with folk song: a narrow range, much repetition, and small skips alternating with stepwise movement:

The middle section (B) opens with a melody in the flutes and oboes, pianissimo, against a sustained tremolo in the second violins and violas. Marked "a little faster," it consists of two four-measure phrases that move by step and small skip within a narrow range:

A contrasting melody is then sung by the clarinets, *pp,* taking on a dark coloring from the pizzicato accompaniment of the double basses:

Both melodies are repeated. This section is followed by an interlude in which a staccato melody on the flute creates an outdoor atmosphere. The transition back to the first section combines simultaneously motives from theme 1 of the first movement (trombone), the main Largo theme (trumpets), and Theme 3 of the first movement (horns and violins):

When a composition is in several movements and themes from the earlier movements recur in the later ones, the piece is said to be in *cyclical form.* Such reminiscence, it goes without saying, offers a most effective way of tying the movements together. The reappearance of the first-movement themes at this point creates a dramatic moment. The first section (A) is repeated in shortened form, and the Largo ends with mysterious chords, *ppp,* which recall those at the beginning of the movement.

Third movement
Side 4/3 (S)
Side 5/3 (E II)

The Scherzo, marked Molto vivace (very lively) is a dance movement in ¾ time. Its first theme (a) is of an impetuously rhythmic character. Indeed, this theme is as much a rhythm as a melody:

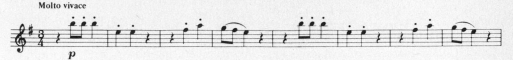

This is contasted with a suave subject (b), rich in folkloric charm, introduced by flute and oboe. Its lyric character makes it a perfect foil for the opening tune:

The opening theme returns, so that this A section of the Scherzo is really an a-b-a.

A transition leads into the Trio or middle section (B) which also alternates two themes. The first (c) is a kind of rustic waltz played by flutes and oboes:

The second (d), played by the violins, is a dancelike tune to which wide leaps and trills in descending sequence impart a lilting gayety.

These two melodies are repeated in the pattern c-c-d-c-d-c. A brief transition leads back to the repetition of the first section, the Scherzo proper. The coda again underlines the cyclical form of the symphony by bringing back motives from earlier movements. This Scherzo demonstrates how a large-scale symphonic movement can be built up through the repetition of fairly short units:

A	bridge	B	bridge	A	Coda
a-a-b-a		c-c-d-c-d-c		a-b-a	themes from earlier movements

Fourth movement
Side 5/1 (S)
Side 6/1 (E II)

The finale, Allegro con fuoco (fast, with fire) is an ample sonata-allegro form in $\frac{4}{4}$ time. The stormy introduction leads into a vigorous melody in the character of a march, played by trumpets and horns.

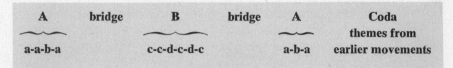

The second theme is a flowing, lyrical idea, a reverie sung by the clarinet.

The third theme is in the nature of a popular song. Its symmetrical phrases end in three descending notes that appear to be derived from the familiar round, *Three Blind Mice.*

This little figure takes on prominence as it is bandied about by the various instrumental groups. Here, for example, is how it is spun out as a codetta to the Exposition:

The following examples from the Development well illustrate the thematic-motivic process as Dvořák and his contemporaries practiced it.

1. Opening motive of the march theme in a new rhythm:

2. A motive derived from the march theme becomes an accompaniment for a motive from the Largo:

3. The Largo theme in two different rhythms:

4. The opening arpeggio of the first movement combined with the march theme in changed rhythm:

The Recapitulation presents the three themes of the Exposition in somewhat shortened form. And the coda further affirms the cyclical form of the symphony by touching upon the opening chords of the Largo, now played fortissimo by woodwinds and brass, by combining the Largo and Scherzo themes, and by bringing the symphony to an end with the triumphal proclamation of the up-and-down arpeggio with which the first Allegro began. Notice the chromatic scales that supply excitement, and the diminuendo at the very end.

The *New World Symphony* has always been a favorite in the United States. Its continuity of thought, clarity of outline, and vivacity of detail command the respect of musicians, while its appealing melodies and accessible ideas are such as make the popular classic.

27   Brahms: *Symphony No. 3*

"It is not hard to compose, but it is wonderfully hard to let the superfluous notes fall under the table."

Against the colorful program art of Berlioz, Liszt, and Wagner there arose an austere, high-minded musician dedicated to the purity of the

Classical style. His veneration for the past and his mastery of the architecture of absolute music brought him closer to the spirit of Beethoven than were any of his contemporaries.

His Life

Johannes Brahms (1833–97) was born in Hamburg, son of a double-bass player whose love of music was greater than his attainments. As a youngster of ten Johannes helped increase the family income by playing the piano in the dance halls of the slum district where he grew up. By the time he was twenty he had acquired sufficient reputation as a pianist to accompany the Hungarian violinist Eduard Reményi on a concert tour.

His first compositions made an impression on Joseph Joachim, leading violinist of the day, who made possible a visit to Robert Schumann at Düsseldorf. Schumann recognized in the shy young composer a future leader of the camp dedicated to absolute music. He published in his journal the famous essay entitled "New Paths," in which he named the twenty-year-old "young eagle" as the one who "was called forth to give us the highest ideal expression of our time." Brahms awoke to find himself famous.

Robert and Clara took the fair-haired youth into their home. Their friendship opened up new horizons for him. Five months later came the tragedy of Schumann's mental collapse. With a tenderness and strength he had not suspected in himself, Brahms tided Clara over the ordeal of Robert's illness.

The older man lingered for two years while the younger was shaken by the great love of his life. Fourteen years his senior and the mother of seven children, Clara Schumann appeared to young Brahms as the ideal of womanly and artistic perfection. What had begun as filial devotion ripened into romantic passion. She for her part found a necessary source of strength in the loyalty of the "young eagle." For Johannes this was the period of storm and stress, as his letters to her reveal. "You have taught me and every day teach me more and more to marvel at the nature of love, affection, and self-denial. I can do nothing but think of you." At the same time he was rent by feelings of guilt, for he loved and revered Schumann, his friend and benefactor, above all others. He thought of suicide and spoke of himself, as one may at twenty-two, as "a man for whom nothing is left."

This conflict was resolved the following year by Schumann's death; but another conflict took its place. Now that Clara was no longer the unattainable ideal, Brahms was faced with the choice between love and freedom. Time and again in the course of his life he was torn between the two, with the decision going always to freedom. His ardor subsided into a lifelong friendship. Two decades later he could still write her, "I love you more than myself and more than anybody and anything on earth."

Johannes Brahms. A portrait by
J. B. Laurens when the composer
was twenty years old.

His appointment as musician to the Prince of Detmold inaugurated his professional career. After four years at this post he returned to Hamburg to devote himself to composition. But he failed to obtain an official appointment in his native city—the directors of the Philharmonic never forgot that Johannes came from the slums—and settled in Vienna, which remained the center of his activities for thirty-five years. In the stronghold of the Classical masters he found a favorable soil for his art, his northern seriousness refined by the grace and congeniality of the South. The time was ripe for him. His fame filled the world and he became the acknowledged heir of the Viennese masters.

Just as in early manhood his mother's death had impelled him to complete *A German Requiem,* so the final illness of Clara Schumann in 1896 gave rise to the *Four Serious Songs.* Her death profoundly affected the composer, already ill with cancer. He died ten months later, at the age of sixty-four, and was buried not far from Beethoven and Schubert.

His Music

Brahms was a traditionalist. His aim was to show that new and important things could still be said in the tradition of the Classical masters. In this he differed from avowed innovators such as Berlioz, Liszt, and Wagner.

Brahms's four symphonies (1876, 1877, 1883, 1885) are unsurpassed in

Symphonies　the late Romantic period for breadth of conception and design. In the two concertos for piano and orchestra (1858, 1881) and the one for violin (1878), the solo instrument is integrated into a fullscale symphonic structure.

Chamber music　The duo sonatas, trios, quartets, quintets, and sextets for string and wind instruments, with and without piano, comprise a body of works marked by lyricism and a quality of introspection peculiarly his own. He is an important figure too in piano music.

Songs　As a song writer Brahms stands in the direct line of succession to Schubert and Schumann. His output includes about two hundred solo songs and an almost equal number for two, three, and four voices.

In his waltzes he paid tribute to the popular dance of his beloved Vienna, but he knew he was too much the north German to capture the real Viennese flavor. When he gave his autograph to Johann Strauss's daughter—composers customarily inscribed a few bars of their music—he wrote the opening measures of the *Blue Danube Waltz* and noted beneath it, "Not, alas, by Johannes Brahms."

The Third Symphony: *Third Movement*

The *Symphony No. 3 in F major,* Opus 90, was completed in 1883 when Brahms was fifty years old. The rugged melodies and vigorous rhythm of this work are characteristic of his music, as is the subdued orchestral color. Woodwinds and brass are used in their lower register, blending with the strings in a silver-gray sonority that has a warmth all its own.

Third movement
Side 2/3 (S)
Side 3/3 (E II)
The third movement of a symphony was usually an impetuous Allegro. For this Brahms substituted a lyrical movement in moderate tempo. Characteristic of this change is the third movement of this symphony, marked Poco allegretto. It is in impassioned, darkly colored orchestral song wholly Brahmsian in tone and feeling. The opening theme is a melody of powerful appeal played by the cellos:

After suitable expansion this tune is contrasted with a lighter idea in the middle part. When the opening section is repeated, the melody originally played by the cellos is assigned first to the French horn, then to the oboe. The movement is a superb example of Brahms's introspective lyricism.

His art marks the end not only of a century but of a cultural epoch. This profound rhapsodist remains an impressive figure, one of the last representatives of nineteenth-century German idealism.

Francisco Goya (1746–1828), long considered the greatest painter of the late eighteenth century, stood outside the Classical stream. In this famous canvas, **Majas on a Balcony,** his passionate realism anticipates a later age. *(The Metropolitan Museum of Art, Bequest of Mrs. H. O. Havemeyer, 1929. The H. O. Havemeyer Collection.)*

The rise of nationalism is reflected in this heroic painting by Jacques Louis David (1748–1825), entitled **Bonaparte Crossing the Alps.** *(Chateau, Malmaison.)*

28   The Concerto

"We are so made that we can derive intense enjoyment only from a contrast."
— SIGMUND FREUD

The Nature of the Concerto

A *concerto* is a large-scale work in several movements for solo instrument and orchestra. (Occasionally, more than one soloist is involved.) Here the attention is focused upon the solo performer. This circumstance helps determine the style. The dramatic tension between soloist and orchestra is analogous to that between protagonist and chorus in Greek tragedy. The massive sonorities of the piano, the sweetness of the violin, or the dark resonance of the cello may be pitted against the orchestra. This opposition of forces constitutes the essential nature of the concerto.

Form   In its dimensions the concerto is comparable to a symphony. Most concertos are in three movements: a dramatic allegro, usually in sonata form, is followed by a songful slow movement and a brilliant finale. In the opening movement, as in the first movement of a symphony, contrasting themes are stated ("exposed"), developed, and restated. In this case, however, the tension is twofold: not only between the contrasting ideas but also between the opposing forces—that is, the solo instrument against the group. Each of the basic themes may be announced by the *tutti* (literally, "all"; i.e., the orchestra as a whole) and then taken up by the solo part. Or the latter may introduce the ideas and the orchestra expatiate upon them.

Cadenza   A characteristic feature of the concerto is the *cadenza,* which is a fanciful solo passage in the manner of an improvisation that is interpolated into the movement. The cadenza came out of a time when improvisation was an important element in art music, as it still is today in jazz. Taken over into the solo concerto, the cadenza made a dramatic effect: the orchestra fell silent and the soloist launched into a free play of fantasy on one or more themes of the movement. Before the nineteenth century the performer was usually the composer; consequently the improvisation was apt to be of the highest caliber. With the rise of a class of professional players who interpreted the music of others but did not invent their own, the art of improvisation declined. Thus the cadenza came to be composed before hand, either by the composer or the performer.

The concerto has to be a "grateful" vehicle that will enable the performing artist to exhibit his gifts as well as the capacities of the instrument. This element of technical display, combined with appealing melodies, has helped to make the concerto one of the most widely appreciated types of concert music.

29 Mendelssohn: *Violin Concerto*

"I should like to write a violin concerto for you next winter. One in E minor is running through my head, and the beginning does not leave me in peace." (Letter to Ferdinand David)

Felix Mendelssohn stands out in the roster of musicians for the fortunate circumstances that attended his career: he was born to wealth; he found personal happiness; and he was the idol of a vast public, not only in his German homeland, but also in England.

His Life

Felix Mendelssohn (1809–47) was the grandson of Moses Mendelssohn, the Jewish philosopher who expounded Plato to the eighteenth century. His father was an art-loving banker; his mother read Homer in the original. They joined the Protestant faith when Felix was still a child. The Mendelssohn home was a meeting place for the wit and intellect of Berlin. The garden house, seating several hundred guests, was the scene of memorable musicales where an orchestra under the boy's direction performed his numerous compositions. Here, when he was seventeen, his Overture to *A Midsummer Night's Dream* was presented to an enraptured audience.

Felix Mendelssohn.

Mendelssohn's misfortune was that he excelled in a number of roles—as pianist, conductor, organizer of musical events, and educator. For the last fifteen years of his life his composing was carried on amid the distractions of a taxing public career. At twenty-six he was conductor of the Gewandhaus Orchestra at Leipzig, which he transformed into the finest in Europe. He was summoned to Berlin by Frederick William IV to carry out that monarch's plans for an Academy of Music. Later he founded the Conservatory of Leipzig, which raised the standards for the training of musicians. He made ten visits to England, where his appearances elicited a fenzy of enthusiasm. All this in addition to directing one or another of the provincial festivals that formed the backbone of musical life in Germany. This continual pouring out of his energies finally took its toll: at the age of thirty-eight, he succumbed to a stroke. Huge throngs followed his bier. Condolences came from all over Europe. A world figure had died.

His Music

Mendelssohn was dedicated to a mission: to preserve the tradition of the Classical forms in an age that was turning from them. But it should not be supposed that he was untouched by Romanticism. In his early works he is the ardent poet of nature, a landscape painter of gossamer brush. Tenderness and manly fervor breathe from his music and a gentle melancholy that is very much of the age.

Of his symphonies the best known are the third, the *Scotch,* and the fourth, the *Italian*—mementos of his youthful travels. The *Concerto for Violin and Orchestra* (1844) retains its position as one of the most popular ever written. The *Octet for Strings,* which he wrote when he was sixteen, is much admired, as are the *Songs without Words* (1829–42), a collection of short piano pieces. Mendelssohn was also a prolific writer for the voice.

In England Mendelssohn was admired as no composer had been since Handel and Haydn. The first edition of Grove's Dictionary, which appeared in 1880, devoted its longest article to him—sixty-eight pages. Bach received eight.

Violin Concerto

First movement
Side 2/4 (S)
Side 6/2 (E II)

The *Violin Concerto in E minor* (1844), a staple of the repertory, dates from the latter part of Mendelssohn's career. The work reveals his special gifts: clarity of form and grace of utterance, a subtle orchestral palette, and a vein of sentiment that is tender but reserved. The first movement, Allegro molto appassionato (very fast and impassioned), is a shapely example of sonata-allegro form. The customary orchestral introduction is omitted; the violin announces the main theme of the movement almost immediately. This is a resilient and active melody in the upper register, marked by decisive rhythm and a broad arch that unfolds in symmetrical phrases.

Allegro molto appassionato

The expansion of this theme gives the violinist opportunity for brilliant passage work, much of it in triplets. These serve as a unifying element throughout the movement. The theme is then proclaimed by full orchestra (tutti).

The main function of the bridge is to lead from the first theme to the second. Sometimes, however, this transition is made so attractive that it takes on the character of a new idea. Such is the case with this energetic melody of wide range:

The contrasting second theme is narrow of range and characterized by stepwise movement and narrow leaps. It is introduced by clarinets and flutes, tranquillo and pianissimo over a sustained tone on the open G string

A violin concerto performed in the Hall of the Paris Conservatory, 1843. From a contemporary woodcut after a sketch by P.-S. Germain.

of the solo instrument. Such a sustained tone in one part while the harmonies change in the other parts is known as a *pedal point* (or *organ point*, from the fact that it occurs frequently in organ music as a note sustained by one of the pedal keys). The lyric theme provides an area of relaxation in the precipitous forward drive of the movement.

The development section explores motives of the principal theme and the transitional idea. It is marked by genuine symphonic momentum, culminating in the cadenza which, instead of coming at the end of the movement as is customary, serves as a link between the Development and a shortened Recapitulation. Under a curtain of widely spaced arpeggios on the violin the opening theme emerges in the orchestra. From here to the coda the movement gains steadily in power.

Felicitous in melody and graceful in form, the Concerto displays the tender sentiment and Classic moderation that are so typical of Mendelssohn's style.

30   The Nature of Opera

"It is better to invent reality than to copy it." — GIUSEPPE VERDI

For well over three hundred years the opera has been one of the most alluring forms of musical entertainment. A special glamor is attached to everything connected with it—its arias, singers, and roles, not to mention its opening nights. Carmen, Mimi, Violetta, Tristan—what character in fact or fiction can claim, generation after generation, so constant a public?

An *opera* is a drama that is sung. It combines the resources of vocal and instrumental music—soloists, ensembles, chorus, orchestra and ballet—with poetry and drama, acting and pantomime, scenery and costumes. To weld the diverse elements into a unity is a problem that has exercised some of the best minds in the history of music.

At first glance opera would seem to make impossible demands on the credulity of the spectator. It presents us with human beings caught up in dramatic situations, who sing to each other instead of speaking. The reasonable question is (and it was asked most pointedly throughout the history of opera by literary men): how can an art form based on so unnatural a procedure be convincing? The question ignores what must al-

The interior of the Comédie d'Amsterdam seen from the stage during an opera performance, 1768. From a contemporary engraving.

ways remain the fundamental aspiration of art: not to copy nature but to heighten our awareness of it. True enough, people in real life do not sing to each other. Neither do they converse in blank verse, as Shakespeare's characters do; nor live in rooms of which one wall is conveniently missing so that the audience may look in. All the arts employ conventions that are accepted both by the artist and his audience. The conventions of opera are more in evidence than those of poetry, painting, drama, or film, but they are not different in kind. Once we have accepted the fact that the carpet can fly, how simple to believe that it is also capable of carrying the prince's luggage.

Opera functions in the domain of poetic drama. It uses the human voice to impinge upon the spectator the basic emotions—love, hate, jealousy, joy, grief—with an elemental force possible only to itself. The logic of reality gives way on the operatic stage to the transcendent logic of art, and to the power of music over the life of the heart.

The Components of Opera

Recitative In the classic type of opera the explanations necessary to plot and action are presented in a kind of musical declamation known as *recitative*. This vocal style imitates the natural inflections of speech; its rhythm is curved to the rhythm of the language. Instead of a purely musical line, recitative is often characterized by a rapid patter and "talky" repetition of the same note; also by rapid question-and-answer dialogue that builds dramatic tension in the theater.

Aria

Recitative gives way at the lyric moments to the *aria,* which releases the emotional tension accumulated in the course of the action. The aria is a song, generally of a highly emotional kind. It is what audiences wait for, what they cheer, and what they remember. An aria, because of its beauty, may be effective even when removed from its context. Many arias are familiar to multitudes who never heard the operas from which they are excerpts.

Opera types

Grand opera is sung throughout. In opera of the more popular variety the recitative is generally replaced by spoken dialogue. This is the type known among us as *operetta* or *musical comedy,* which has its counterpart in the French *opéra-comique* and German *Singspiel.* Interestingly enough, in Italy—the home of opera—even the comic variety, the *opera buffa,* is sung throughout.

Voice classifications

The emotional conflicts in opera are linked to universal types and projected through the contrasting voices. Soprano, mezzo-soprano, and contralto are counterposed to tenor, baritone, and bass. The coloratura soprano has the highest range and greatest agility in the execution of trills and rapid passages. The dramatic soprano is preferred for dynamic range and striking characterization, the lyric for gentler types. If the heroine is a soprano, her rival for the hero's love will often be a contralto. The tenor may be lyric or dramatic. German opera has popularized the *Heldentenor* (heroic tenor) who, whether as Siegfried or Tristan, is required to display endurance, brilliance, and expressive power.

Ensembles

An opera may contain ensemble numbers—trios, quartets, quintets, sextets, septets—in which the characters pour out their respective feelings. The unique quality of an ensemble number lies in its ability to project several contrasting emotions at the same time, the music binding these together into an artistic whole.

Chorus

The chorus is used in conjunction with the solo voices or it may function independently in the mass scenes. It may comment and reflect upon the action, in the manner of the chorus in Greek tragedy. Or it may be integrated into the action. In either case choral song offers the composer rich opportunities for varied musical-dramatic effects.

Orchestra and ballet

The orchestra provides the accompaniment. It sets the mood and creates the atmosphere for the different scenes. It also functions independently, in the overture, preludes to the acts, interludes, and postludes. Sometimes the ballet provides an eye-filling diversion in the scenes of pageantry that are an essential feature of grand opera. In the folk operas of the nineteenth century the ballet was used to present peasant and national dances.

Libretto

The *libretto,* or text, of an opera must be devised so as to give the composer his opportunity for the set numbers—the arias, duets, ensembles, choruses, marches, ballets, and finales—that are the traditional features of this art form. The librettist must not only create characters and plot with some semblance of dramatic insight, but he also has to fashion situations that justify the use of music and could not be fully realized without it.

Opera appeals primarily to those composers and music lovers· who are given to the magic of the theater. It exerts its fascination upon those who love to hear singing. Thousands who do not feel at home with the abstract instrumental forms warm to opera, finding there a graphic kind of music linked to action and dialogue, whose meaning it is impossible to mistake. Countless others are attracted for the very good reason that opera contains some of the grandest music ever written.

31 Verdi: *La traviata*

"Success is impossible for me if I cannot write as my heart dictates!"

In the case of Giuseppe Verdi (1813–1901), the most widely loved of operatic composers, it happened that the time, the place, and the personality were happily met. He inherited a rich tradition, his capacity for growth was matched by masterful energy and will, and he was granted a long span of life in which his gifts attained their full flower.

His Life

Born in a hamlet in northern Italy where his father kept a little inn, the shy, taciturn lad grew up amid the poverty of village life. His talent attracted the attention of a prosperous merchant in the neighboring town of Busseto, a music lover who made it possible for the youth to pursue his studies. After two years in Milan he returned to Busseto to fill a post as organist. When he fell in love with his benefactor's daughter, the merchant in wholly untraditional fashion accepted the penniless young musician as his son-in-law. Verdi was twenty-three, Margherita sixteen.

Three years later he returned to the conquest of Milan with the manuscript of an opera. *Oberto, Count of San Bonifacio* was produced at La Scala in 1839 with fair success. The work brought him a commission to write three others. Shortly after, Verdi faced the first crisis of his career. He had lost his first child, a daughter, before coming to Milan. The second, a baby boy, was carried off by fever, a catastrophe followed several weeks later by the death of his young wife. "My family had been destroyed, and in the midst of these trials I had to fulfill my engagement and write a comic opera!" *Un giorno di regno* (King for a Day) failed miserably. "In a sudden moment of despondency I despaired of finding any comfort in my art and resolved to give up composing."

The months passed; the distraught young composer adhered to his decision. One night he happened to meet the impresario of La Scala, who forced him to take home the libretto of *Nabucco* (Nebuchadnezzar, King of Babylon). "I came into my room and, throwing the manuscript angrily on the writing table, I stood for a moment motionless before it. The book opened as I threw it down. My eyes fell on the page and I read the line *Va pensiero sull' ali dorate* (Go, my thought, on golden wings—first line of the chorus of captive Jews who by the waters of Babylon mourn their ravished land). Resolved as I was never to write again, I stifled my emotion, shut the book, went to bed, and put out the candle. I tried to sleep, but *Nabucco* was running a mad course through my brain." In this fashion the musician was restored to his art. *Nabucco*, presented at La Scala in 1842, was a triumph for the twenty-nine-year-old composer and launched him on a spectacular career.

Italy at this time was in the process of birth as a nation. The patriotic party aimed at liberation from the Hapsburg yoke and the establishment of a united kingdom under the House of Savoy. Verdi from the beginning identified himself with the national cause. "I am first of all an Italian!" In this charged atmosphere his works took on special meaning for his countrymen. No matter in what time or place the opera was laid, they interpreted it as an allegory of their plight. The chorus of exiled Jews from *Nabucco* became a patriotic song. As the revolutionary year 1848 approached, Verdi's works—despite the precautions of the Austrian censor—continued to nourish the zeal of the nationalists. In *Attila* the line of the Roman envoy to the leader of the Huns, "Take thou the universe—but leave me Italy!" provoked frenzied demonstrations. When, in *The Battle of Legnano,* a chorus of medieval Italian knights vowed to drive the German invaders beyond the Alps, audiences were aroused to indescribable enthusiasm. Rarely has a musician more ideally filled the role of a people's artist.

His death at eighty-eight was mourned throughout the world. Italy accorded him the rites reserved for a national hero. From the thousands who followed his bier there sprang up a melody—*Va pensiero sull' ali dorate*. It was the chorus from *Nabucco* that he had given his countrymen as a song of solace sixty years before.

His Music

Verdi's music struck his contemporaries as the epitome of dramatic energy and passion. Endowed with an imagination that saw all emotion in terms of action and conflict—that is, in terms of the theater—he was able to imbue a dramatic situation with shattering expressiveness. Again and

Giuseppe Verdi. *(Museo Teatrale della Scala.)*

again he demanded of his librettists "a short drama, swift-moving and full of passion . . . Passions above all!" True Italian that he was, he based his art on melody, which to him was the most immediate expression of human feeling. "Art without spontaneity, naturalness, and simplicity," he maintained, "is no art."

Early period Of his first fifteen operas the most important is *Macbeth* (1847), in which for the first time he derived his story material from Shakespeare, whom he called "the great searcher of the human heart." There followed in close succession the three operas that established his international fame: *Rigoletto* in 1851, based on Victor Hugo's drama *Le Roi s'amuse* (The King is Amused); *Il trovatore* (The Troubadour) in 1853, derived from a fanciful Spanish play; and *La traviata* (The Lost One), also produced in 1853, which he adapted from the younger Dumas's play *La Dame aux camélias* (The Lady of the Camellias). In these works of sustained pathos the musical dramatist stands before us in full stature.

Middle period The operas of the middle period are on a more ambitious scale, showing Verdi's attempt to assimilate elements of the French grand opera. The three most important are *Un ballo in maschera* (A Masked Ball; 1859), *La forza del destino* (The Force of Destiny; 1862), and *Don Carlos* (1867). In these the master fought his way to a higher conception of dramatic unity.

Final period These aims came to fruition in *Aïda,* the work that ushers in his final period (1870–93). Verdi found his ideal librettist in Arrigo Boito (1842–

1918). For their first collaboration they turned to Shakespeare. The result was *Otello* (1887), the apex of three hundred years of Italian lyric tragedy. After its opening night the seventy-four-year-old composer declared, "I feel as if I had fired my last cartridge. Music needs youthfulness of the senses, impetuous blood, fullness of life." He disproved his words when six years later, working once more with Boito, Verdi—approaching eighty—astonished the world with *Falstaff* (1893). Fitting crown to the labors of a lifetime, this luminous comic opera ranks with Mozart's *Figaro,* Rossini's *Barber of Seville,* and Wagner's *Meistersinger.*

La traviata

Based on a libretto by Francesco Piave, *La traviata* is a work suffused with intimate lyricism and emotion. The heroine is Violetta Valéry, one of the reigning beauties of Paris, who already is suffering from the first ravages of tuberculosis (the nineteenth-century word was consumption) when the drama begins. She lives for the pleasure of the moment until Alfredo Germont, a young man of good Provençal family, falls in love with her and offers to take her away from the fast life that is killing her.

La traviata, Act II, Scene 1. Violetta (Maria Callas) with Germont (Ettore Bastianini) in the famous Visconti production at La Scala. *(Photo by Erio Piccagliani.)*

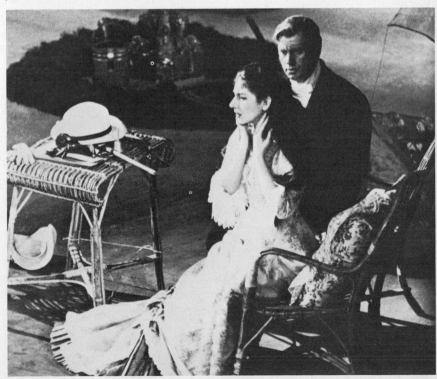

The first act takes place at a party in Violetta's house, to which Alfredo has been brought by a friend. When the guests go in to supper, Alfredo tells Violetta that he has loved her ever since he first saw her. She shrugs off his declaration; friendship, she tells him, is all she has to offer. He persists in his words of devotion. She unpins the white flower that she always wears (hence the title of Dumas's novel and play, which in English became *Camille*), hands it to him and tells him to come back when it has faded. "Tomorrow?" he asks. He takes the flower and leaves, full of hope.

Side 6/1 (S)
Side 7/1 (E II)
After her guests have departed Violetta, alone, is torn between her need for love and her fear of a serious involvement. The two moods alternate in the long soliloquy that becomes the final scene of Act I. The first mood is evoked in a tender Andantino in which she expresses her yearning for someone to give meaning to her life.

This section reaches its climax when Verdi brings back the phrase in which Alfredo declared his love, a phrase that becomes the love theme of the opera:

The contrasting mood is an Allegro brillante in which the disillusioned woman of the world rejects the idea of love. Freedom is what she desires above all, freedom from any attachment or responsibility. This is a light-hearted melody whose nimble leaps and runs show off the coloratura voice at its most beguiling:

At the height of it we hear Alfredo's voice, offstage, repeating the love theme. We may assume that he is singing the melody as he leaves her house or, symbolically, that she remembers his declaration and hears it in her mind. The scene mounts in tension to a brilliant close.

The opera, like the novel and play on which it was based, centers about the tragic conflict between the individual and society that was one of the main preoccupations of Romantic literature. The lovers are separated when

Alfredo's father—the epitome of bourgeois morality—appeals to Violetta not to ruin the young man's life. Society, he tells her, will never accept Alfredo's marriage with a demi-mondaine; sooner or later he will tire of her and leave her. Violetta yields and returns to her former lover, Baron Douphol. The third act is a gambling party in the home of Violetta's friend Flora. Alfredo wins huge sums from the Baron and, convinced that Violetta left him because he had no money, insults her publicly by flinging his winnings at her. The Baron challenges him to a duel. The fourth act unfolds in Violetta's bedroom; she is alone and in the final stage of her illness. Alfredo returns to seek her forgiveness. He is followed by the elder Germont, who is so moved by her nobility of character that he is ready to accept her as his daughter. It is too late; she dies in Alfredo's arms.

This is Romantic opera at its best. Dumas's heroine lives on in the opera house—a perennially appealing figure whose all-too-human frailties have been endowed with nobility and pathos by the lovely strains with which Verdi invested her love, her suffering, and her death.

32 Wagner: *Tristan und Isolde*

"The error in the art genre of opera consists in the fact that a means of expression—music—has been made the object, while the object of expression—the drama—has been made the means."

Richard Wagner (1813–83) looms as probably the single most important phenomenon in the artistic life of the latter half of the nineteenth century. Historians, not without justice, divide the period into "Before" and "After" Wagner. The course of post-Romantic music is unthinkable without the impact of this complex and fascinating figure.

His Life

He was born in Leipzig, son of a minor police official who died when Richard was still an infant. The future composer was almost entirely self-taught; he had in all about six months of instruction in music theory. At twenty he abandoned his academic studies at the University of Leipzig and obtained a post as chorus master in a small opera house. In the next six years he gained practical experience conducting in provincial theaters. He married the actress Minna Planer when he was twenty-three, and produced his first operas—*Die Feen* (The Fairies; 1834) and *Das Liebesverbot* (The Ban on Love, after Shakespeare's *Measure for Measure;* 1836). As with all his later works, he wrote the librettos himself. He was in this way able to achieve a unity of the musical-dramatic conception beyond anything that had been known before.

Success came to him when, after his opera *Rienzi* was acclaimed at Dresden, the thirty-year-old composer was appointed conductor to the King of Saxony. But he was already moving away from grand opera based on history and political intrigue to a simpler, more universal type of drama based on folk legends. *The Flying Dutchman* (1841) was followed by the two dramas of the Dresden period—*Tannhäuser* (1843–45) and *Lohengrin* (1846–48)—which bring to its peak the German Romantic opera of the first half of the nineteenth century. These works use subjects derived from Medieval German epics, display a profound feeling for nature, employ the supernatural as an element of the drama, and glorify the German land and people. But the Dresden public was not prepared for *Tannhäuser*. They had come to see another *Rienzi* and were disappointed.

Wagner the revolutionary   A dedicated artist who made no concessions to popular taste, Wagner dreamed of achieving for opera something of the grandeur that had characterized the ancient Greek tragedy. To this task he addressed himself with the fanaticism of the born reformer. He was increasingly alienated from a frivolous court that regarded opera as an amusement; from the bureaucrats in control of the royal theaters, who thwarted his plans; and from Minna, his wife, who was delighted with their social position in Dresden and had no patience with what she considered his utopian schemes. He was persuaded that the theater was corrupt because the society around it was corrupt. His beliefs as an artist led him into the camp of those who, as the fateful year 1848 approached, dreamed of a

Richard Wagner.

revolution in Europe that would end the power of the reactionary rulers. With reckless disregard of the consequences, Wagner appeared as speaker at a club of radical workingmen, and published two articles in an anarchist journal: "Man and Existing Society" and "The Revolution." "The present order," he wrote, "is inimical to the destiny and the rights of man. The old world is crumbling to ruin. A new world will be born from it!"

The revolution broke out in Dresden in May 1849. King and court fled. Troops dispatched by the King of Prussia crushed the insurrection. Wagner escaped to his friend Franz Liszt at Weimar, where he learned that a warrant had been issued for his arrest. With the aid of Liszt he was spirited across the border and found refuge in Switzerland.

The Zurich years

In the eyes of the world—and of Minna—he was a ruined man; but Wagner did not in the least share this opinion. "It is impossible to describe my delight when I felt free at last—free from the world of torturing and ever unsatisfied desires, free from the distressing surroundings that had called forth such desires." He settled in Zurich and entered on the most productive period of his career. He had first to clarify his ideas to himself, and to prepare the public for the novel conceptions toward which he was finding his way. For four years he wrote no music, producing instead his most important literary works, *Art and Revolution, The Art Work of the Future,* and the two-volume *Opera and Drama* which sets forth his theories of the *music drama,* as he named his type of opera. He next proceeded to put theory into practice in the cycle of music dramas called *The Ring of the Nibelung.* He began with the poem on Siegfried's death that came to be known as *Götterdämmerung* (Dusk of the Gods). Realizing that the circumstances prior to this action required explaining, he added the drama on the hero's youth, *Siegfried.* The need

The Ring

for still further background led to a poetic drama concerning the hero's parents, *Die Walküre* (The Valkyrie). Finally, the trilogy was prefaced with *Das Rheingold* (The Rhinegold), a drama revolving about the curse of gold out of which the action stems.

Although he wrote the four librettos in reverse order, he composed the operas in sequence. When he reached the second act of *Siegfried* he grew tired, as he said, "of heaping one silent score upon the other," and laid aside the gigantic task. There followed his two finest works—*Tristan und Isolde* (1857–59) and *Die Meistersinger von Nürnberg* (The Mastersingers of Nuremberg; 1862–67). The years following the completion of *Tristan* were the darkest of his life. The mighty scores accumulated in his drawer without hope of performance: Europe contained neither theater nor singers capable of presenting them. Wagner succumbed to Schopenhauer's philosophy of pessimism and renunciation—he who could never renounce anything. He was estranged from Minna, who failed utterly to understand his artistic aims. His involvement with a series of women who did understand him—but whose husbands objected—brought the *Tristan* triangle into his own life and catapulted him into lonely despair. As he

The Festival Playhouse, Bayreuth, 1876. From a contemporary print. *(Bildarchiv Bayreuther Festspiele.)*

passed his fiftieth year, his indomitable will was broken at last. He contemplated in turn suicide, emigration to America, escape to the East.

At this juncture intervened a miraculous turn of events. An eighteen-year-old boy who was a passionate admirer of his music ascended the throne of Bavaria as Ludwig II. One of the young monarch's first acts was to summon the composer to Munich. The King commissioned him to complete the *Ring,* and Wagner took up the second act of *Siegfried* where he had left off a number of years before. A theater was planned especially for the presentation of his music dramas, which ultimately resulted *Bayreuth* in the festival playhouse at Bayreuth. And to crown his happiness he found, to share his empire, a woman equal to him in will and courage—Cosima, the daughter of his old friend Liszt. For the last time the *Tristan* pattern thrust itself upon him. Cosima was the wife of his fervent disciple, the conductor Hans von Bülow. She left her husband and children in order to join her life with Wagner's. They were married some years later, after Minna's death.

The Wagnerian gospel spread across Europe, a new art-religion. Wagner societies throughout the world gathered funds to raise the temple at Bayreuth. The radical of 1848 found himself, after the Franco-Prussian War, the national artist of Bismarck's German Empire. The *Ring* cycle was completed in 1874, twenty-six years after Wagner had begun it, and the four dramas were presented to worshipful audiences at the first Bayreuth festival in 1876.

One task remained. To make good the financial deficit of the festival the master undertook his last work, *Parsifal* (1877–82), a "consecrational festival drama" based on the legend of the Holy Grail. He finished it as he approached seventy. He died shortly after, in every sense a conqueror, and was buried at Bayreuth.

His Music

Wagner gave shape to the desire of the Romantic era for the closest possible connection between music and dramatic expression; and beyond that, for the closest connection between music and life. "Every bar of dramatic music," he maintained, "is justified only by the fact that it explains something in the action or in the character of the actor."

He did away with the old "number" opera with its arias, duets, ensembles, choruses, and ballets. His aim was a continuous tissue of melody that would never allow the emotions to cool. The focal point of Wagnerian music drama, however, is the orchestra. Here is the nub of his operatic reform. He developed a type of symphonic opera as native to the German genius as vocal opera is to the Italian. The orchestra is the unifying principle of his music drama. It is both participant and ideal spectator; it remembers, prophesies, reveals, comments. The orchestra floods the action, the characters, and the audience in a torrent of sound that incarnates the sensuous ideal of the Romantic era.

Leitmotifs The orchestral tissue is fashioned out of concise themes, the *leitmotifs,* or "leading motives"—Wagner called them basic themes—that recur throughout the work, undergoing variation and development even as the themes and motives of a symphony. The leitmotifs carry specific meanings, like the "fixed idea" of Berlioz's symphony or the main theme of a symphonic poem. They have an uncanny power of suggesting in a few strokes a person, an emotion, or an idea; an object—the gold, the ring, the sword; or a landscape—the Rhine, Valhalla, the lonely shore of Tristan's home. Through a process of continual transformation the leitmotifs trace the course of the drama, the changes in the characters, their experiences and memories, their thoughts and hidden desires. As the leitmotifs accumulate layer upon layer of meaning, they themselves become characters in the drama, symbols of the relentless process of growth and decay that rules the destinies of gods and heroes.

Harmonic innovations Wagner's musical language was based on chromatic harmony, which he pushed to its then farthermost limits. Chromatic dissonance imparts to Wagner's music its restless, intensely emotional quality. Never before had the unstable tone combinations been used so eloquently to portray states of soul. The active chord (Dominant) seeking resolution in the chord of rest (Tonic) became in Wagner's hands the most romantic of symbols: the lonely man—Flying Dutchman, Lohengrin, Siegmund, Tristan—seeking redemption through love, the love of the ideal woman, whether Senta or Elsa, Sieglinde or Isolde.

Tristan und Isolde

For unity of mood, sustained inspiration, and intensity of feeling *Tristan und Isolde* is the most perfectly realized of Wagner's lyric tragedies. Certainly no more eloquent tribute has ever been offered to consuming passion.

Isolde, proud princess of Ireland, has been promised in marriage to the elderly King Mark of Cornwall. Tristan, the King's nephew and first knight of his court, is sent to bring her to her new home. They had met before when Tristan fought against her country. What had begun as hate, wounded pride, and desire for revenge turns to overpowering love—a love that can have only a tragic solution because, in yielding to it, the lovers betray her husband, the King.

Prelude
Side 5/2 (S)
Side 8/1 (E II)

The Prelude to the drama depicts the passion that enmeshes them. This extraordinary tone poem evolves from a leitmotif that recurs throughout the opera. Used always to suggest the yearning, tenderness, and rapture of the lovers, the famous progression is the epitome of chromatic—that is, Romantic—harmony. Notice how the voices move by half step along the chromatic scale:

Prelude, in Wagner's use of the term, indicates a freer and more flexible form than overture. It is more in the character of a fantasy, lyric rather than dramatic, contemplative rather than narrative. This Prelude comes as close as any piece ever did to those twin goals of musical romanticism: intoxication and ecstasy.

Wagner satisfied the need of an era for sensuous beauty, for the heroic, the mystical, the grandiose. He takes his place in history as the most commanding figure of the Romantic period: a master whose achievements have become part and parcel of our musical heritage.

33 Puccini: *La bohème*

"Almighty God touched me with his little finger and said, 'Write for the theater—mind you, only for the theater!' And I have obeyed the supreme command."

The Italian operatic tradition was carried on, in the post-Romantic era, by a group of composers led by Giacomo Puccini (1858–1924). His generation included Ruggiero Leoncavallo, remembered for *I pagliacci* (The Clowns; 1892), and Pietro Mascagni, whose reputation likewise rests on a single success, *Cavalleria rusticana* (Rustic Chivalry; 1890). These Italians were associated with the movement known as *verismo* (realism), which tried to bring into the lyric theater the naturalism of Zola, Ibsen, and their contemporaries. Instead of choosing historical or mythological themes, they picked subjects from everyday life and treated them in down-to-earth fashion. Puccini was strongly influenced by this trend towards operatic realism.

His Life

He was born in 1858 in Lucca, son of a church organist in whose foot-steps he expected to follow. It was at Milan, where he went to complete his studies, that his true bent came to the fore. He studied at the Conservatory with Amilcare Ponchielli, composer of *La gioconda*. The ambitious young musician did not have to wait long for success. His first opera,

Giacomo Puccini.

Le villi (The Spirits; 1884), produced when he was twenty-six, was received with enthusiasm. *Manon Lescaut* (1893), based on the novel of Abbé Prévost, established him as the most promising among the rising generation of Italian composers. In Luigi Illica and Giuseppe Giacosa he found an ideal pair of librettists, and with this writing team he produced the three most successful operas of the early twentieth century: *La bohème* in 1896; *Tosca* in 1900; and *Madame Butterfly,* after a play by David Belasco, in 1904. The dates should dispel the popular notion of Puccini as a facile melodist who tossed off one score after another. Each of his operas represented years of detailed work involving ceaseless changes until he was satisfied.

The Girl of the Golden West (1910) was based, like its predecessor, on a play by Belasco. The world premiere at the Metropolitan Opera House was a major event. A more substantial achievement was the trio of one-act operas: *Il tabarro* (The Cloak), *Suor Angelica* (Sister Angelica), and the comic opera *Gianni Schicchi* (1918). The first two are not heard frequently. The third is a masterpiece.

Handsome and magnetic, Puccini was idolized and feted wherever he went. His wife was jealous not without reason. "I am always falling in love," he confessed. "When I no longer am, make my funeral." As he entered middle age this singer of youth and love began to feel that his time was running out. "I am growing old and that disgusts me. I am burning to start work but have no libretto and am in a state of torment. I need work just as I need food." After much seeking he found a story that released the music in him and embarked on his final task—*Turandot.* He labored for four years on this fairy-tale opera about the beautiful and cruel princess of China. A work of consummate artistry, it is his most polished score. Puccini, ill with cancer, pushed ahead with increasing urgency. "If I do not succeed in finishing the opera someone will come to the front of the stage and say, 'Puccini composed as far as this, then he died.'"

He was sent to Brussels for treatment, accompanied by his son and the rough draft of the final scene. He died in 1924, following an operation, at the age of sixty-six. *Turandot* was completed from his sketches by his friend Franco Alfano. However, at the first performance at La Scala on April 25, 1926, the composer's wish was fulfilled. Arturo Toscanini, his greatest interpreter, laid down the baton during the lament over the body of Liù. Turning to the audience he said in a choking voice, "Here ends the master's work."

La bohème

Puccini's best-loved work is based on Henri Murger's *La Vie de bohème* (Bohemian Life). The novel depicts the joys and sorrows of the young artists who flock to Paris in search of fame and fortune, congregating

La bohème, Act I: Mimi (Katia Ricciarelli) asks Rodolfo (José Carreras) to light her candle, and their romance is begun. Metropolitan Opera production. *(Photo copyright by Beth Bergman.)*

in the Latin Quarter on the Left Bank of the Seine. "A gay life yet a terrible one," Murger called their precarious existence woven of bold dreams and bitter realities. Puccini's music was peculiarly suited to this atmosphere of "laughter through tears." Remembering his own life as a struggling young musician in Milan, he recaptured its wistfulness and charm.

The first act discloses to us the attic where live four impecunious young Bohemians—Rodolfo the poet, Marcello the painter, Schaunard the musician, and Colline, who is a philosopher by nature but has no other trade. Rodolfo and Marcello are trying to work but can think of nothing but the cold; the stove has run out of fuel. They are presently joined, first by Colline, then by Schaunard, who by a stroke of luck has come on some money. The landlord arrives with a nasty word—rent!—and is gotten rid of. The young men go off to the Café Momus to celebrate Christmas Eve, Rodolfo remaining behind to finish an article he is writing.

Side 6/2 (S)
Side 7/2 (E II)

There is a knock on the door. Enter Mimi and romance. Her arrival is heralded in this act as in later ones by a poignant phrase in the orchestra. Her candle has gone out. Will Rodolfo light it? Their dialogue, bathed by the orchestra in a current of emotion, exemplifies the spell that Puccini casts over the homeliest sentiments. "A little wine? . . . Thank you . . . Here it is . . . Not so much . . . Like this? . . . Thank you."

Mimi returns, having lost her key. Their candles are extinguished by a gust of wind; they search for the key on the floor, in the dark. Rodolfo, finding it, has the presence of mind to slip it into his pocket. Their hands touch and Rodolfo sings his aria *Che gelida manina* (How cold your little hand, let me warm it here in mine). Here is the Italian cantabile, the melody gliding along the scale and rising in a broad golden curve to its crest. Three centuries of operatic tradition stand behind an aria such as this.

Rodolfo asks who she is. Mimi replies with the aria *Mi chiamano Mimi:*

There follows a duet, based on a phrase from Rodolfo's aria, which now becomes the love theme of the opera.

Rodolfo, smitten, invites her to the café, to phrases that have become part of the Italian folklore of flirtation. "Give me your arm, my little one. . . . I obey you, signor." The act ends, as it should, with a high C on the word "amor."

The subsequent acts trace the stormy love of Rodolfo and Mimi, together with the no less tempestuous relationship of Marcello and Musetta. Mimi leaves Rodolfo, unable to put up with his jealousy. In the final act she returns to the attic, her beauty ravaged by poverty and illness. The lovers remember the night they met, and Puccini underlines their blasted hopes by quoting the music of that first encounter. Mimi's death is presented with enormous pathos. Puccini wrote the scene with tears in his eyes. It has been listened to in like fashion.

La bohème has retained its freshness for more than half a century. Within its genre it is a masterpiece.

34   The Nature of Choral Music

"In a sense no one is ignorant of the material from which choral music springs. For this material is, in large measure, the epitomized thought, feeling, aspiration of a community rather than an individual." — PERCY M. YOUNG: *The Choral Tradition*

By *choral music* we mean music performed by many voices—a chorus, a choir, or a glee club. A *chorus* is a fairly large body of singers, generally consisting of both men and women. (The term also refers to the pieces that such a group sings.) A *choir* is a smaller group, usually connected with a church. A *glee club* functions as a rule in a college and performs popular music and college songs along with more serious works.

The chorus consists of four groups, corresponding to the principal vocal ranges: sopranos, altos, tenors, and basses. Choral music therefore is usually arranged in four parts. The groups may be subdivided into first and second sopranos, first and second altos, and so on, so that the music may unfold in from five to eight or more parts. But four parts is the standard arrangement. Choral music consequently differs in one important respect from most of the instrumental and vocal music we have discussed thus far. There the ear followed a single melody line that was supported by a background of harmony. In choral music, on the other hand, the ear is aware of several voice parts. These unfold like so many threads that interweave in an ever changing pattern. Often an idea is presented in one voice and imitated in turn by each of the other voices. The result is a different kind of musical texture.

In earlier times choral music was often performed without accompaniment. By the eighteenth century the orchestra had firmly established itself as a partner of the chorus. This trend continued throughout the nineteenth century. Choral music consequently offered the composer exciting opportunities for contrast: between voices and orchestra, between men's and women's voices, between high and low voices, between solo voices and chorus, as well as all possible combinations of these. Small wonder that works for soloists, chorus, and orchestra challenged the imagination of composers and brought forth some of their finest efforts.

Choral Music in the Nineteenth Century

The nineteenth century, we found, witnessed a broadening of the democratic ideal and an enormous expansion of the musical public. This climate was uniquely favorable to choral music, which flowered as an enjoyable group activity involving increasing numbers of music lovers.

As a result, choral music came to play an important part in the musical life of the Romantic era.

Amateur choral groups

Singing in a chorus required less skill than playing in an orchestra. It attracted many music lovers who had never learned to play an instrument, or who could not afford to buy one. With a modest amount of rehearsal (and a modest amount of voice), they could learn to take part in the performance of great choral works. The music they sang, being allied to words, was somewhat easier to understand than absolute music, both for the performers and the listeners. The members of the chorus not only enjoyed a pleasant social evening once or twice a week but also, if their group was good enough, became a source of pride to their community.

The repertory centered about the great choral heritage of the past. Nevertheless, if choral music was to remain a vital force, its literature had to be enriched by new works that would reflect the spirit of the time. Accordingly, we find some of the most important composers active in this field.

We will discuss a movement from Verdi's *Requiem Mass*. A *Mass* is a setting of the most solemn service of the Roman Catholic Church, and a *Requiem* is a setting of the Mass for the Dead. It takes its name from the opening line of the text: "Requiem aeternam dona eis Domine" (Give them eternal rest, O Lord). The Mass was originally intended to be performed in church, but by the nineteenth century it has found a wider audience in the concert hall.

In the nineteenth century, enormous choral and orchestral forces were the order of the day. A contemporary woodcut depicting the opening concert at St. Martin's Hall, London, 1850.

Verdi: Messa da Requiem

"I am not a learned composer, but I am a very experienced one."

Verdi's *Requiem* (1874) was written in memory of Alessandro Manzoni, the poet-novelist who was the leading Italian writer during the mid-nineteenth century. In a larger sense the *Requiem* was a tribute to the Italian genius. As Verdi put it, "It was a crying need of my heart to do all in my power to honor this great spirit, whom I valued so highly as a writer and revered as a man—the true pattern of patriotic virtue."

Like many liberals of his time, Verdi was a free-thinker; his wife called him "a man of little faith." Nonetheless the Catholic tradition of his childhood retained its hold upon him, as is evident from the many religious episodes in his operas. He approached the supreme liturgy of the Church with utter assurance. The old masters did not draw an artificial distinction between sacred and secular music. When they wished to honor God they spoke the living musical language of their time. Verdi did likewise. His natural language was Italian opera, and this became the language of his *Requiem Mass.* (More than a century earlier, even Bach had been accused of being too "operatic" in the *St. Matthew Passion.*) Verdi saw the text of the *Requiem* as a great spiritual drama, a conflict between man's fear of death and his hope for salvation in the hereafter. He treated this conflict with the dramatic power that was uniquely his. There resulted a work of shattering force and sensuous lyricism.

Second movement
Side 15/1 (S)
Side 9/1 (E II)
His vision of the Last Judgment, the *Dies irae,* is the central fresco of the *Requiem*. It has been compared—not inappropriately—to Michelangelo's. Marked Allegro agitato, the movement opens with crashing chords in the orchestra and headlong descending scales that suggest the terror of Judgment Day. The chorus hurls out the text like an imprecation:

Dies irae, dies illa,	That day of wrath, that day of anger
solvet saeclum in favilla,	Will dissolve the world in ashes,
teste David cum Sibylla.	As David prophesied, and the Sibyl.

The next verse describes the trembling when the Judge will appear to weigh men's deeds. Tremolos in the string instruments vividly suggest the shuddering of the sinners. Trumpets "from afar and invisible"—that is, backstage—are echoed by trumpets in the main orchestra. There is a tremendous upsurge of sound as the brass and drums take over, ushering in

A recent performance of Verdi's *Messa da Requiem* conducted by Claudio Abbado with the chorus and orchestra of La Scala in the Concert Hall of the John F. Kennedy Center for the Performing Arts, on September 10, 1976. (Photo by Richard Braaten.)

the next section, *Tuba mirum*. This is marked Allegro sostenuto and is in ¼. The music is a powerful evocation of the text:

Tuba mirum spargens sonum   The trumpet, hurling its wondrous sound
per sepulcra regionum,   Over the graves of the world,
coget omnes ante thronum.   Will summon all before the throne.

Trumpet calls and mighty strokes on the kettledrum convey the terror of that awesome moment. The next verse, for solo bass, describes how Death and Nature alike will be astounded when all creation rises again to answer the Judge. The key word, "mors" (death), is repeated with chilling impact. The section ends *pppp*.

This music suggests the rich tradition out of which came the choral works of the nineteenth century. They represented an important current in the art of the Romantic era, and continue to give pleasure to a worldwide audience.

THREE
More Materials of Music

"In any narrative—epic, dramatic or musical—every word or tone should be like a soldier marching towards the one, common, final goal: conquest of the material. The way the artist makes every phrase of his story such a soldier, serving to unfold it, to support its structure and development, to build plot and counterplot, to distribute light and shade, to point incessantly and lead up gradually to the climax—in short, the way every fragment is impregnated with its mission towards the whole, makes up this delicate and so essential objective which we call FORM." — ERNST TOCH

35 The Organization of Musical Sounds: Key and Scale

"All music is nothing more than a succession of impulses that converge towards a definite point of repose." — IGOR STRAVINSKY

At the beginning of this book we discussed various elements of music. Now that we have had occasion to hear how these are interwoven in a number of works, we are ready to consider the materials of music on a more advanced level, particularly as they relate to the organization of the large Classical forms.

Tonality

A system of music must have set procedures for organizing tones into intelligible relationships. One of the first steps in this direction is to select certain tones and arrange them in a family or group. In such a group one tone assumes greater importance than the rest. This is the *do,* the Tonic or keynote around which the others revolve and to which they ultimately gravitate.

Key
  By a *key* we mean a group of related tones with a common center or Tonic. The tones of the key serve as basic material for a given composition. When we listen to a composition in the key of A we hear a piece based in large part upon the family of tones that revolve around and gravitate to the common center A.

This "loyalty to the Tonic" is inculcated in us by most of the music we hear. It is the unifying force in the *do-re-mi-fa-sol-la-ti-do* scale that was taught us in our childhood. You can test for yourself how strong is the pull to the Tonic by singing the first seven tones of this pattern, stopping on *ti.* You will experience an almost physical compulsion to resolve the *ti* up to *do.*

The sense of relatedness to a central tone is known as *tonality.* This sense, needless to say, resides in our minds rather than in the tones themselves. Tonality underlies the whole system of relationships among tones as embodied in keys, scales, and the harmonies based on those, such relationships converging upon the "definite point of repose." Specifically, tonality refers to those relationships as they were manifest in Western music from around 1600 to 1900.

The "Miracle of the Octave"

A string of a certain length, when set in motion, vibrates at a certain rate per second and produces a certain pitch. Given the same conditions, a string half as long will vibrate twice as fast and sound an octave above. A string twice as long will vibrate half as fast and sound an octave below. When we sound together on the piano two tones other than an octave, such as C–D or C–F, the ear distinctly hears two different tones. But when we strike an octave such as C–C or D–D, the ear recognizes a very strong similarity between the two tones. Indeed, if one were not listening carefully one would almost believe that he was hearing a single tone. This "miracle of the octave" was observed at an early stage in all musical cultures, with the result that the octave became the basic interval in music. (An interval, we saw, is the distance and relationship between two tones.)

Division of the octave

The method of dividing the octave determines the scales and the character of a musical system. It is precisely in this particular that one system differs from another. In Western music the octave is divided into twelve equal intervals. The fact is apparent from the look of the piano keyboard, where counting from any tone to its octave we find twelve keys—seven white and five black. These twelve tones are a half tone (semitone) apart. That is, from C to C sharp is a half step, as is from C sharp to D. The half step is the smallest unit of distance in our musical system. From C to D is a distance of two semitones, or a whole tone.

Oriental music is based on other units. In India, for example, quarter-tone scales are used. The Javanese divide the octave into five nearly equal parts. Arabic music contains a scale that divides the octave into seventeen parts. We are not able to play Oriental music on the piano, which is tuned in semitones. Nor could we readily sing it, since we have been trained to think in terms of the whole- and half-tone intervals of our system.

The twelve semitones into which Western music divides the octave con-

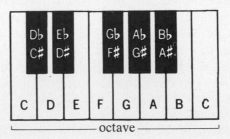

Note: The black keys are named in relation to their white neighbors. When the black key between C and D is thought of as a semitone higher than C, it is known as C sharp. When it is regarded as a semitone lower than D, the same key is called D flat. Thus D sharp is the same tone as E flat, F sharp is the same tone as G flat, and G sharp is the same tone as A flat. Which of these names is used depends upon the scale and key in which a particular sharp or flat appears.

stitute what is known as the *chromatic scale*. They are duplicated in higher and lower octaves. No matter how vast and intricate a musical work, it is made up of the twelve basic tones and their higher and lower duplications.

The Major Scale

The scale   A *scale* is a series of tones arranged in consecutive order, ascending or descending. Specifically, a scale presents the tones of a key. The word is derived from the Italian *scala,* "ladder." In the widest sense a scale is a musical alphabet revealing at a glance the principle whereby tones are selected and related to one another in a given system.

The music of the Classic-Romantic period is based on two contrasting scales, the *major* and the *minor*. These consist of seven different tones, with the octave *do* added at the end of the series. The major scale has the familiar *do-re-mi-fa-sol-la-ti-do* pattern. Its seven tones are picked out of the possible twelve in order to form a centralized family or key out of which musical compositions may be fashioned. It becomes clear that compositions based on the major scale represent a "seven out of twelve" way of hearing music.

The major scale   If you play the white keys on the piano from C to C you will hear the familiar *do-re-mi-fa-sol-la-ti-do* series; in other words, the major scale. Let us examine this series a little more closely.

We notice that there is no black key on the piano between E–F (*mi-fa*) and B–C (*ti-do*). These tones, therefore, are a semitone apart, while the others are a whole tone apart. Consequently, when we sing the *do-re-mi-fa-sol-la-ti-do* sequence we are measuring off a pattern of eight tones that are a whole tone apart except steps 3–4 (*mi-fa*) and 7–8 (*ti-do*). In other words, we are singing the pattern *do,* whole step, whole step, half step, whole step, whole step, whole step, half step. You will find it instructive to sing this scale trying to distinguish between the half- and whole-tone distances as you sing.

This scale implies certain relationships based upon tension and resolution. We have already indicated one of the most important of these—the thrust of the seventh step to the eighth (*ti* seeking to be resolved to *do*). There are others: if we sing *do-re* we are left with a sense of incompleteness that is resolved when *re* moves back to *do; fa* gravitates to *mi; la* descends to *sol*. These tendencies, we saw, reside not in the tones but in our minds. They are the meanings attached by our musical culture to the raw material of nature.

Most important of all, the major scale defines the two poles of Classical harmony: the *do* or Tonic, the point of ultimate rest; and the *sol* or Dominant, representative of the active harmony. Upon the trackless sea of sound this relationship imposes direction and goal. Tonic going to Dominant and returning to tonic becomes a basic progression of Classical harmony. It will also serve, we shall find, as a basic principle of Classical form.

The Key as an Area in Musical Space

The major scale, we said, is a "ladder" of whole and half tones.

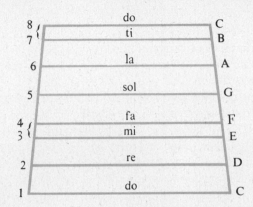

A ladder may be placed on high ground or low, but the distance between its steps remains the same. So too the major scale may be measured off from one starting point or another without affecting the sequence of whole and half steps within the pattern.

The Tonic
Any one of the twelve tones of our octave may serve as starting point for the scale. Whichever it is, that tone at once assumes the function of the Tonic or key center. The other tones are chosen according to the pattern of the ladder. They immediately assume the functions of activity and rest implicit in the major scale. Most important, they all take on the impulse of gravitating more or less directly to the Tonic.

With each different Tonic we get another group of seven tones out of the possible twelve. In other words, every major scale has a different number of sharps or flats. The scale of C major is the only one that has no sharps or flats. If we build the major scale from G we must include an F sharp in order to conform to the pattern of whole and half steps. (Try building the pattern whole step, whole step, half step, whole step, whole step, whole step, half step, from G. You will find that F natural does not fit this pattern.) If we build the major-scale pattern from D, we get a group of seven that includes two sharps. If F is our starting point the scale includes B flat. (The twelve major scales are listed in Appendix III.) When we play a tune like *America* on the piano with C as keynote—that is, in the key of C major—we use only the white keys. Should we play it with G as a keynote —that is, in the key of G major—we should in the course of it have to sound F sharp, not F natural. Were we to play F natural we would be off key.

Tonal position and function
It becomes clear that the meaning of a tone, its direction and drive, are determined not by its intrinsic nature but by its position in the scale. The tone C may be the Tonic or point of rest in one scale. In another it may be the seventh step seeking to be resolved by ascending to the eighth. In still

another it may be the second step thrusting down to the first. In any case its impulse of activity or rest depends not on its character as the tone C but on its function as the *do,* the *ti,* or the *re*—the 1, 7, or 2—of that particular key and scale. The Classical system is based on the eminently social doctrine that the significance of a tone depends not upon itself but upon its relationship to other tones.

The key serves as a means of identification. The title *Symphony in A major* refers to a work based in large measure upon the tones of the A-major scale and the harmonies fashioned from those, with the keynote A serving as the central tone to which the others gravitate. This group is the one that includes three sharps.

The Minor Scale

Whether the major scale begins on C, D, E, or any other tone, it follows the same pattern in the arrangement of the whole and half steps. Such a pattern is known as a *mode.* Thus, all the major scales exemplify the major mode of arranging whole and half steps.

The natural minor

There is also a *minor mode,* which complements and serves as a foil to the major. It differs primarily from the major in that its third degree is lowered a half step; that is, the scale of C minor has E flat instead of E. In the pure or *natural minor scale* the sixth and seventh steps are also lowered: C–D–E♭ F–G A♭ B♭ C. (For two other versions of the minor scale—*harmonic* and *melodic*—see Appendix III.) The minor is pronouncedly different from the major in mood and coloring. *Minor,* the Latin word for "smaller," refers to the fact that the distinguishing interval C–E♭ is smaller than the corresponding interval C–E in the major ("larger") scale.

Music in the minor modes

Like the major, the pattern of the minor scale may begin on each of the twelve tones of the octave. In each case there will be a different group of seven tones out of twelve; that is, each scale will include a different number of sharps or flats. It becomes clear that every tone in the octave may serve as starting point or keynote for a major and a minor scale. This gives us twelve keys according to the major mode and twelve keys according to the minor mode. If the mode of a work is not specified, the major is implied, as when we speak of the *Melody in F, Minuet in G,* or *Symphony in A.* The minor is always specified, as in the case of Schubert's *Symphony in B minor* or Mendelssohn's *Violin Concerto in E minor.*

Is the minor "sadder" than the major? Such connotations exist only in reference to the music of a particular time and place. The nineteenth century seems to have regarded the minor as more somber than the major. The funeral music of Beethoven, Mendelssohn, Chopin, Wagner, and Grieg is conspicuously in the minor, while the triumphal finales of a number of symphonies and overturnes of the same period are as conspicuously in the major.

The minor mode has a certain exotic ring to Western ears and is associated in the popular view with Oriental and east European music. This aspect of the minor is prominent in such works as the *Turkish Rondo* of Mozart; in a number of pieces in Hungarian style by Schubert, Liszt, and Brahms; in the main theme of Rimsky-Korsakov's *Scheherazade,* César Cui's *Orientale,* and similar exotica. The folk songs of certain regions appear to incline to the major while others lean toward the minor. There are, however, so many exceptions that such a generalization must be viewed with caution.

The contrast between minor and major became an element of musical structure during the Classic-Romantic period. For example, in A-B-A form, the outer sections might be in one mode and the contrasting middle section in the other. Or a symphony might start out in the minor and shift to the major in an access of triumph, as in Beethoven's *Fifth,* Franck's *D minor,* and Tchaikovsky's *Fifth.* Thus the distinction between major and minor lent itself to contrasts of color, mood, and emotional intensity.

Key signatures

The key signature at the head of a piece announces the number of sharps or flats that prevail in that particular composition. Notice that beneath each major key in the example is listed the minor key with the same number of sharps or flats. This is known as its *relative minor.*

| G major | D major | A major | E major | F major | Bb major | Eb major | Ab major |
| E minor | B minor | F# minor | C# minor | D minor | G minor | C minor | F minor |

The twelve major and twelve minor keys make up the harmonic system of the Classical period. There had to come into existence an art form that would mobilize the resources of this system, that would bring into focus its capacities for dramatic conflict and architectural expanse. It was the great achievement of the eighteenth century to evolve and perfect this form.

36 The Major-Minor System

"Form follows function." — LOUIS SULLIVAN

Transposition

Suppose a certain melody begins on G. If one felt that the song lay a little too high for his voice, he might begin on F instead of G and shift all the tones of the melody one step lower. Someone else might find that the song lay too low for his voice. He would begin on A and sing each tone of the melody one step higher than it was written. The act of shifting all the tones of a musical composition a uniform distance to a higher or lower level of pitch is called *transposition*.

When we transpose a piece we shift it to another key. We change the level of pitch, the keynote, and the number of sharps or flats. But the melody line remains the same because the pattern of its whole and half steps has been retained in the new key as in the old. That is why the same song can be published in various keys for soprano, alto, tenor, and bass.

We have all transposed melodies without being aware of it. For example, a group of children will begin a song from a certain note. If the melody moves too high or too low for comfort, their teacher will stop them and have them begin again from another tone. On an instrument, transposing is a more complicated matter. The player must adjust his fingers to another arrangement of sharps or flats. If he is a pianist or organist he must shift not only the melody but the harmonies as well. The ability to transpose a piece at sight is a skill that musicians regard with respect. It is a necessity for professional accompanists, who are constantly required to transpose songs to higher or lower keys to suit the range of singers.

Choice of key

Why does a composer choose one key rather than another for his piece? In former times external factors strongly influenced this choice. Up to the time of Beethoven, for example, the brass instruments were not able to change keys as readily as they are now. In writing for the string instruments composers considered the fact that certain effects, such as playing on the open strings, could be achieved in one key rather than another. Several composers of the Romantic period seemed to associate a certain emotional atmosphere or color with various keys. Characteristic was Mendelssohn's fondness for E minor, Chopin's for C-sharp minor.

Modulation

If a piece of music can be played in one key as in another, why not put all music in the key of C and be done with it? Because the contrast between keys and the movement from one key to another is an essential element of musical structure. We have seen that the tones of the key form a group of "seven out of twelve," which imparts coherence and focus to the music. But this closed group may be opened up, in which case we are shifted—either gently or abruptly—to another area centering about another keynote. Such a change gives us a heightened sense of activity. It is an expressive gesture of prime importance.

The process of passing from one key to another is known as *modulation*. There is no way to describe in words something that can be experienced only in the domain of sound. Suffice it to say that the composer has at his disposal a number of ways of modulating; therewith he "lifts" the listener from one tonal area to another. As Arnold Schoenberg put it, "Modulation is like a change of scenery."

The twelve major and twelve minor keys may be compared to so many rooms in a house, with the modulations equivalent to corridors leading from one to the other. The eighteenth-century composer as a rule established the home key, shaped the passage of modulation—the "corridor"—in a clear-cut manner, and usually passed to a key area that was not too far away from his starting point. There resulted a spaciousness of structure that was the musical counterpart of the rolling sentences of the eighteenth-century novel and the balanced façades of eighteenth-century architecture.

Nineteenth-century Romanticism, on the other hand, demanded a whipping-up of emotions, an intensifying of all musical processes. In the Romantic era modulations were ever more frequent and abrupt. There came into being a hyperemotional music that wandered restlessly from key to key in accord with the need for excitement of the mid- and late-Romatic era. By the same token, the balanced structure of the Classical system, with its key areas neatly marked off one from the other, began to disintegrate.

Chromaticism

When seven tones out of twelve are selected to form a major or minor key, the other five become extraneous in relation to that particular Tonic. They enter the composition as transients, mainly to embellish the melody or harmony. If the piece is to sound firmly rooted in the key, the seven tones that belong to the key must prevail. Should the composer allow the five foreign tones to become too prominent in his melody and harmony, the relationship to the key center would be weakened and the key feeling become ambiguous. The distinction between the tones that do not belong within the key area and those that do is made explicit in the contrasting terms *chromatic* and *diatonic*. Chromatic, as we saw, refers to the twelve-tone scale including all the semitones of the octave. Chromatic melody or harmony moves by half steps, taking in the tones extraneous to the key. The word comes from the Greek *chroma,* which means "color." Diatonic, on the other hand, refers to musical progression based on the seven tones of a major or minor scale, and to harmonies that are firmly rooted in the key.

Diatonic vs. chromatic harmony

Diatonic harmony went hand in hand with the clear-cut key feeling that marked the late-eighteenth-century style. We may say that the music of Haydn, Mozart, and Beethoven tends to be diatonic. (There are of course many passages in their music, especially in their late works, that belie this generalization.) Chromatic harmony, on the other hand, characterized the ceaseless modulation and surcharged emotional atmosphere of nineteenth-century music. The Romantic composers, from Schubert to Wagner and his followers, indefatigably explored the possibilities of chromaticism. In an earlier section of this book we described the Romantic movement in music.

We may now establish, as one of its important characteristics, a tendency toward chromatic harmony.

The Key as a Form-Building Element

By marking off an area in musical space with a fixed center, the key provides the framework within which musical growth and development take place. The three main harmonies of the key—Tonic (I), Dominant (V), and Subdominant (IV)—become the focal points over which melodies and chord progressions unfold. In brief, the key is the neighborhood inhabited by a tune and its harmonies. Thus the key becomes a prime factor for musical unity.

At the same time the contrast between keys may further the cause of variety. The Classical composer pitted one key against another, thereby achieving a dramatic opposition between them. He began by establishing the home key. Presently he modulated to a related key, generally that of the Dominant (for example, from C major with no sharps or flats to G major, one sharp; or from G major to D major, two sharps). In so doing he established a tension, since the Dominant key was unstable compared to the tonic. This tension required resolution, which was provided by the return to the home key.

The progression from home key to contrasting key and back outlined the basic musical pattern of statement-departure-return. The home key was the anchorage, the safe harbor; the foreign key represented adventure. The home key was the symbol of unity; the foreign key ensured variety and contrast.

The tension between two keys and their ultimate reconciliation became the motive power of the music of the Classical era. This conflict-and resolution found its frame in the grand form of the latter half of the eighteenth century—the ideal tone-drama known as the sonata.

37 The Development of Themes: Musical Logic

"I alter some things, eliminate and try again until I am satisfied. Then begins the mental working out of this material in its breadth, its narrowness, its height and depth."

— LUDWIG VAN BEETHOVEN

Thinking, whether in words or tones, demands continuity and sequence. Every thought must flow out of the one before and lead logically into the next. In this way is created a sense of steady progression toward a goal. If we were to join the beginning of one sentence to the end of another, it would not make any more sense than if we united the first phrase of one melody and the second of another. In our discussion of melody (pages 10-14) we compared the two phrases of *London Bridge* to a question-and-answer formation. A similar impression of cause and effect, of natural flow and continuity, must pervade the whole musical fabric.

Theme   When a melodic idea, we noted, is used as a building block in the construction of a musical work it is known as a theme or subject. The theme is the first in a chain of musical situations, all of which must grow out of the basic idea as naturally as does the plant from the seed. The process of spinning out a theme, of weaving and reweaving the threads of which it is composed, is the essence of musical thinking. This process of expansion has its parallel in prose writing, where an idea stated at the beginning of a paragraph is embroidered and enlarged upon until all its aspects appear in view. Each sentence leads smoothly into the one that follows. In similar fashion, every measure takes up where the one before left off and brings us inexorably to the next.

Thematic   The most tightly knit kind of expansion in our music is known as
development *thematic development*. To develop a theme means to unfold its latent energies, to search out its capacities for growth and bring them to fruition. Thematic development represents the constructional element in music. It is one of the most important techniques in musical composition, demanding of the composer imagination, master craftsmanship, and intellectual power.

In the process of development, certain procedures have proved to be particularly effective. The simplest is repetition, which may be either exact or varied; or the idea may be restated at another pitch. For example, in *America,* the melodic idea on the words "Land where my fathers died" is restated immediately, but a tone lower, on the words "Land of the pilgrims' pride." Such a restatement at a higher or lower pitch level is
Sequence   known, we saw, as a sequence. The original idea may also be varied in regard to melody, harmony, rhythm, timbre, dynamics, and register. It may be attended by expansion or contraction of the note values as well as by bold and frequent changes of key.

A basic technique in thematic development is the breaking up of the
Motive   theme into its constituent motives. A motive, we found, is the smallest fragment of a theme that forms a melodic-rhythmic unit. The motives are the cells of musical growth. Through fragmentation of themes, through repeating and varying the motives and combining them in ever fresh patterns the composer imparts to the musical organism the quality of dynamic evolution and growth.

Thematic development is too complex a technique to appear to advantage in short lyric pieces, songs, or dances. In such compositions a simple contrast between sections and a modest expansion within each section supplies the necessary continuity. By the same token, thematic development finds its proper frame in the large forms of music. To those forms it imparts an epic-dramatic quality, along with the clarity, coherence, and logic that are the indispensable attributes of this most advanced type of musical thinking.

38   The Sonata: The First Movement

"The history of the sonata is the history of an attempt to cope with one of the most singular problems ever presented to the mind of man, and its solution is one of the most successful achievements of his artistic instincts." — HUBERT PARRY

The name sonata comes from the Italian *suonare,* "to sound," indicating a piece to be sounded on instruments, as distinct from cantata, a piece to be sung. A *sonata* (as Haydn, Mozart, and their successors understood the term) is an instrumental work consisting of a series of contrasting movements, generally three or four in number. The name sonata is used when the piece is intended for one or two instruments. If more than two are involved the work is called, as the case may be, a trio, quartet, quintet, sextet, septet, octet, or nonet. A sonata for solo instrument and orchestra is called a concerto; a sonata for the whole orchestra, a symphony. The sonata, clearly, accounts for a large part of the instrumental music we hear.

Sonata-Allegro Form

The most highly organized and characteristic member of the several movements that make up the sonata cycle is the opening movement. This is what is variously known as *first-movement form, sonata-allegro form,* or *sonata form.* Each of these names is useful but somewhat misleading. "First-movement form" is good provided we remember that this form may also be used for the other movements, and also for single-movement works. "Sonata-allegro form" is appropriate, since this type of movement is at its most characteristic in a lively or allegro movement. Unfortunately, the name fails to take into account that slow movements were sometimes cast in this form, especially in the eighteenth century. "Sonata form" is correct, and is much used by modern writers; but it is too easily confused with the term "sonata," which includes all the movements.

A movement in sonata-allegro form is based on two assumptions. The first is that a musical movement takes on direction and goal if, after establishing itself in the home key, it modulates to other areas and ultimately returns to the home key. We may therefore regard sonata form as a drama between two contrasting key areas. The "plot," the action, and the tension derive from this contrast. Sonata-allegro form, in brief, is an artistic embodiment of the principles underlying the major-minor system—the establishment, that is, of different key areas which serve as points of reference for a statement, a departure, and a return.

Second is the assumption that a theme may have its latent energies released through the development of its constituent motives. Most useful for this purpose is a brief, incisive theme, one that has momentum and tension, and that promises more than at first sight it reveals. The themes will be stated or "exposed" in the first section; developed in the second; and restated or "recapitulated" in the third.

The Exposition (Statement)

The opening section, the Exposition or Statement, sets forth the two opposing keys and their respective themes. (A theme may consist of several related ideas, in which case we speak of it as a theme group.) The first theme and its expansion establish the home key. A transition or bridge leads into a contrasting key; in other words, the function of the bridge is to modulate. The second theme and its expansion establish the contrasting key. A closing section or codetta rounds off the Exposition in the contrasting key. In the Classical sonata form the Exposition is repeated. The adventurous quality of the Exposition derives in no small measure from the fact that it brings us from the home key to the contrasting key.

The Development

The Development wanders further through a series of foreign keys, building up tension against the inevitable return home. Temperature is kept at fever pitch through frequent modulation, resulting in a sense of breathless activity and excitement.

At the same time the composer proceeds to reveal the potentialities of his themes. He breaks them into their component motives; recombines them into fresh patterns; and releases their latent energies, their explosive force. Conflict and action are the essence of drama. In the development section the conflict erupts, the action reaches maximum intensity. The protagonists of the drama are hurled one against another; their worlds collide. Emotion is transformed into motion. The theme may be modified or varied, turned upside down (*inversion*), expanded to longer note values (*augmentation*), contracted into shorter note values (*diminution*), combined with other motives or even with new material. If the sonata is for orchestra—that is, a symphony—a fragment of the theme may be presented by one group of instruments and imitated by another. Now it appears in the upper register, now deep in the bass. Each measure seems to grow out of the preceding by an inescapable law of cause and effect. Each adds to the drive and the momentum. Unity and diversity, logic and passion fuse at white heat to create much out of little.

The Recapitulation (Restatement)

When the developmental surge has run its course, the tension abates. A transition passage leads back to the home key. The beginning of the third section, the Recapitulation or Restatement, is in a sense the psychological climax of sonata form, just as the peak of many a journey is the return home. The first theme appears as we first heard it, in the home key, proclaiming the victory of unity over diversity, of continuity over change.

The Recapitulation follows the general path of the Exposition, restating the first and second themes more or less in their original form, but with the wealth of additional meaning that these have taken on in the course of their wanderings. Most important of all, in the Recapitulation the opposing elements are reconciled, the home key emerges triumphant. For this reason, the third section differs in one important detail from the Exposition: the composer now remains in the home key. He generally shifts the second theme, which was originally in a contrasting key, to the home area. In other words, although the second theme and its expansion unfold in substantially the same way as before, we now hear this material transposed into the home key. There follows the final pronouncement, the coda, in the home key. This is fashioned from material previously heard in the codetta, to which new matter is sometimes added. The coda rounds off the movement and asserts the victory of the home key with a vigorous final cadence.

Coda

The procedure just described is summed up in the following outline:

Sonata-Allegro Form (Sonata Form)

Exposition * (or Statement)	Development	Recapitulation (or Restatement)
First theme (or theme group) and its expansion in home key	Builds up tension against the return to home key by	First theme (or theme group) and its expansion in home key
Bridge—modulates	1. Frequent modulation to foreign keys	Bridge
Second theme (or theme group) and its expansion in contrasting key	2. Fragmentation and manipulation of themes and motives	Second theme (or theme group) and its expansion transposed to home area
Codetta. Cadence in contrasting key	Transition back to home key	Coda. Cadence in home key

* Note: The Exposition may be preceded by a slow introduction. Also, certain Classical masters, especially Haydn, occasionally based the sonata-allegro movement on a single theme, which appeared first in the home key, then in the contrasting key. However, as time went on composers preferred a movement based on contrasting themes.

The main features of the outline above are present in one shape or another in innumerable sonata-allegro movements, yet no two are exactly alike in their disposition of the material. Each constitutes a unique solution of the problem in terms of character, mood, and relation of forces, for the true artist—and it is his work alone that endures—shapes the form according to what he desires to express; so that what looks on paper like a fixed plan becomes, when transformed into living sound, a supple framework for infinite variety.

Thematic opposition

Even as the dramatist creates opposing personalities as the chief characters of his work, so the composer achieves a vivid contrast between the musical ideas that form the basis of the movement. The opposition between two themes may be underlined in a number of ways. Through a contrast in dynamics—loud against soft; in register—low against high; in timbre—strings against winds, one instrumental combination against another; in rhythm and tempo—an animated pattern against one that is sustained; in tone production—legato against staccato; in type of melody—an active melody line with wide range and leaps against one that moves quietly along the scale; in type of harmony—consonance against dissonance, diatonic harmony against chromatic; in type of accompaniment—quietly moving chords against extended arpeggios. Not all of these may appear in a given work. One contrast, however, is required, being the basis of the form: the contrast of key. And the opposition may be further intensified by putting one theme in the major and the other in minor.

The reader should be cautioned, in conclusion, against a widespread misconception. The conventional description of sonata-allegro form, by its emphasis upon the few themes that serve as building blocks for an instrumental movement, seems to imply that everything between these themes is in the nature of filling-in or transitional material. Unfortunately many people listen in precisely this way to a symphonic movement, waiting for the themes—that is, the melodies they recognize—just as, in another context, they wait for the arias in an opera. But from everything we have said it is clear that the sonata-allegro movement is an organic unity in which the growth, the development, the destiny of a theme is no less important than the theme itself (just as, in assessing a human action, we consider its consequences no less than the deed proper). The music examples in the past chapters and in those to come represent what is generally regarded as "Theme 1," "Theme 2," or "Theme 3" of a sonata movement. They are actually only the kernels, the beginnings of themes. The theme, in the profoundly musical sense, must be considered to include not only the few notes in the example but also the "etc."—that is, the passage or section that constitutes the flowering of the idea. It is only when we take this larger view of the theme (or theme group) that we come to understand the symphonic movement for what it is: a continuous expansion and growth of musical ideas from first note to last, from which not a measure may be omitted without disturbing the equilibrium and the organic oneness of the whole. Only by listening to the movement in this way do we apprehend the essential qualities of sonata style, its concentration, its continuity, its unflagging dynamism. It should be added that sonata-allegro form is the representative form of the Classical period.

39   The Sonata, Continued: The Other Movements

"To write a symphony means, to me, to construct a world." — GUSTAV MAHLER

We now consider the other types of musical structure that came to be included in the sonata cycle.

Theme and Variations

We found that repetition is a basic element of musical structure. This being so, composers devised ways of varying an idea when they restated it. Variation is an important procedure that is to be found in every species of music. But there is one type of piece in which it constitutes the ruling principle—the *theme and variations*. The theme is stated at the outset, so that the audience will know the basic idea that serves as the point of departure. The melody may be of the composer's invention, as in the second movement of Haydn's *Surprise Symphony;* or one that he has borrowed from another, as in the case of Brahms's *Variations on a Theme by Paganini*. The theme is apt to be a small two- or three-part form, simple in character so as to allow room for elaboration. There follows a series of variations in which certain features of the original idea are retained while others are altered. Each variation sets forth the idea with some new modification—one might say in a new disguise—through which the listener glimpses something of the original theme.

Melodic variations   To the process of variation the composer brings all the techniques of musical embellishment. He may, to begin with, vary the melody. To indicate the simplest way that this is done, suppose a melodic line moves C–D–E. One may ornament it by including intermediate notes, transforming the melodic progression into C–D–D♯–E or C–C♯–D–E, or C–C♯–D–D♯–E. In this way a more florid line results, although the melody is not fundamentally changed. Conversely, one may omit certain notes and thereby reduce the melody to its skeletal outline: C–E. Or one may shift the melody to another key, thereby throwing new light upon it. Melodic variation is a favorite procedure in the jazz band and rock group, where the solo player embellishes a popular tune with a series of arabesques.

Harmonic variation   In harmonic variation the chords that accompany a melody are replaced by others. Diatonic harmonies may give way to chromatic, simple triads to complex dissonances. Or the melody may be entirely omitted, the variation being based on the harmonic skeleton. The type of accompaniment may be changed; for example, from chords in block formation to decorative broken chords (arpeggios). Or the melody may be shifted to a lower register with new harmonies sounding above it.

Rhythmic
variation

So too the rhythm, meter, and tempo may be varied, with interesting changes in the nature of the tune. This may take on the guise of a waltz, a polka, a minuet, a march. The texture may be enriched by interweaving the melody with new themes. Or the original theme may itself become an accompaniment for a new melody. By combining these methods with changes in dynamics and tone color, the expressive content of the theme may be changed, so that it is presented now as a funeral march, now as a serenade, folk dance, caprice, or boat song. This type of character variation was much in favor in the Romantic era.

The theme with variations challenges the composer's inventiveness and enables him to achieve a high degree of unity in diversity. One therefore understands why variation form has attracted composers for more than three hundred years, both as an independent piece and as one of the movements of the sonata.

Minuet and Trio

The *minuet* originated in the French court in the mid-seventeenth century; its stately ¾ time embodied the ideal of grace of an aristocratic age. In the eighteenth century the minuet was taken over into the sonata, where it served as the third movement, occasionally the second.

Since dance music lends itself to symmetrical construction, we often find in the minuet a clear-cut structure based on phrases of four and eight measures. (All the same, the minuets of Haydn and Mozart reveal an abundance of nonsymmetrical phrases.) In tempo the minuet ranges from stateliness to a lively pace and whimsical character. As a matter of fact, certain of Haydn's minuets are closer in spirit to the village green than to the palace ballroom.

The custom prevailed of presenting two dances as a group, the first being repeated at the end of the second (A–B–A). The one in the middle was frequently arranged for only three instruments; hence the name *trio,* which persisted even after the customary setting for three was abandoned. The trio as a rule is lighter in texture and quieter of gait. Frequently woodwind tone figures prominently in this section, creating an out-of-doors atmosphere that lends it a special charm. At the end of the trio we find *da capo* or D.C. ("from the beginning"), signifying that the first section is to be played over again. Minuet-trio-minuet is a symmetrical three-part structure in which each part in turn is a small two-part or three-part form:

Minuet (A)	Trio (B)	Minuet (A)
a-b-a	c-d-c	a-b-a
or	or	or
a-b	c-d	a-b

This structure is elaborated through repetition of the subsections, a procedure that the composer indicates with a *repeat sign* (:||:). However, when the minuet returns after the trio the repeat signs are customarily ignored. A codetta may round off each section.

Minuet (A)	Trio (B)	Minuet (A)
||: a :|||: b-a(codetta) :||	||:c :|||: d-c :||	a-b-a (codetta)
or	or	or
||: a :|||: b(codetta) :||	||: c :|||: d :||	a-b (codetta)

Scherzo   In the nineteenth-century symphony the minuet was displaced by the scherzo. This is generally the third movement, occasionally the second. It is usually in ¾ time. Like the minuet, it is a three-part form (scherzo-trio-scherzo), the first section being repeated after the middle part. But it differs from the minuet in its faster pace and vigorous rhythm. The scherzo—the name, as you will recall, is the Italian word for "jest"—is marked by abrupt changes of mood ranging from the humorous or the whimsical to the mysterious and even demonic. In the hands of Beethoven the scherzo became a movement of great rhythmic drive.

The Rondo

The *rondo* is a lively movement suffused with the spirit of the dance. Its distinguishing characteristic is the recurrence of a central idea—the rondo theme—in alternation with contrasting elements. Its symmetrical sections create a balanced architecture that is satisfying esthetically and easy to grasp. In its simplest form, A-B-A-B-A, the rondo is an extension of three-part form. If there are two contrasting themes the sections may follow an A-B-A-C-A or similar pattern.

The true rondo as developed by the Classical masters was more ambitious in scope. Characteristic was the formation A-B-A-C-A-B-A. The first A-B-A was in the nature of an Exposition and the corresponding A-B-A at the end was a Recapitulation. Between them was the C section, which served as a kind of Development. What with contrasts of key and elaborate transitional passages, this type of rondo took on the spaciousness of sonata from and came to be known as a *rondo-sonata*.

Actually one may speak of rondo style as well as rondo form, for the essence of the rondo—at any rate as Haydn and Mozart cultivated it—is its vivacity and good humor. Because the theme is to be heard over and over again it must be catchy and relaxing. One should point out, however, that not every movement that follows the rondo form has the spirit of the gay Classical rondo. The rondo figured in eighteenth- and nineteenth-century music both as an independent piece and as a member of the sonata cycle. In the sonata it often served as the final movement.

The Sonata Cycle as a Whole

The four-movement cycle of the Classical masters, as found in their symphonies, concertos, sonatas, string quartets, and other types of chamber music, became the vehicle for their most important instrumental music. The following outline sums up the common practice of the Classic-Romantic era. It will be helpful to the reader, provided he remembers that it is no more than a general scheme and does not necessarily apply to all works of this kind. In Beethoven's *Ninth Symphony,* for example, the scherzo is the second movement while the Adagio comes third.

Movement	Character	Form	Tempo
First	Epic-dramatic	Sonata-allegro	Allegro
Second	Slow and lyrical	Theme and variations Sonata form A-B-A	Andante, Adagio, Largo
Third	Dancelike: Minuet (18th century) Scherzo (19th century)	Minuet and trio Scherzo and trio	Allegretto Allegro
Fourth	Lively, "happy ending" (18th century) Epic-dramatic, with triumphal ending (19th century)	Sonata-allegro Rondo Rondo-sonata Theme and variations	Allegro, Vivace, Presto

The Classical masters of the sonata thought of the four movements of the cycle as self-contained entities connected by identity of key. First, third, and fourth movements were in the home key, with the second movement in a contrasting key. The nineteenth century sought a more obvious connection between movements—a thematic connection. This need was met by cyclical structure, in which a theme from the earlier movements appeared in the later ones as a kind of motto or unifying thread.

The sonata cycle satisfied the need of composers for an extended instrumental work of an abstract nature. It mobilized the contrasts of key and mode inherent in the major-minor system. With its fusion of sensuous, emotional, and intellectual elements, its intermingling of lyric contemplation and action, the sonata cycle may justly claim to be one of the most ingenious art forms ever devised by man.

FOUR

Eighteenth–Century Classicism

"When a nation brings its innermost nature to consummate expression in arts and letters we speak of its classic period. Classicism stands for experience, for spiritual and human maturity which has deep roots in the cultural soil for the nation, for the mastery of the means of expression in technique and form, and for a definite conception of the world and of life; the final compression of the artistic values of a people."

— PAUL HENRY LANG: *Music in Western Civilization*

40 The Classical Spirit

" 'Tis more to guide, than spur the Muse's steed;
Restrain his fury, than provoke his speed;
The winged courser, like a gen'rous horse,
Shows most true mettle when you check his course."
— ALEXANDER POPE: *Essay on Criticism*

The dictionary defines Classicism in two ways: in general terms, as pertaining to the highest order of excellence in literature and art; specifically, pertaining to the culture of the ancient Greeks and Romans. Implicit in the Classical attitude is the notion that supreme excellence has been reached in the past and may be attained again through adherence to tradition.

Being part of a tradition implies a relationship to things outside oneself. The Classical artist neither glories in nor emphasizes his apartness from other men. He regards neither his individuality nor his personal experience as the primary material of his art. For him, therefore, the work of art exists in its own right rather than as an extension of his ego. Where the Romantic is inclined to regard art primarily as a means of self-expression, the Classicist stresses its powers as a means of communication. His atten-

The Parthenon, Athens.

tion is directed to clarity of thought and beauty of form. In effect, he is considerably more objective in his approach than is the Romantic. For the extremely personal utterance of the Romantic, he substitutes symbols of universal validity. Classicism upholds the control and the discipline of art, its potentialities for rational expression and exquisite workmanship, its vision of an ideal beauty. This wholeness of view encourages the qualities of order, stability, and harmonious proportion that we associate with the Classical style.

As we pointed out in our discussion of Romanticism, neither the Classical nor the Romantic spirit is limited to any one time. Both have alternated throughout the history of culture. However, just as conditions in the nineteenth century gave rise to an extended period of Romanticism, so the social climate of the eighteenth century favored the emergence of the Classical spirit.

Eighteenth-Century Classicism

Aristocratic patronage
The culture of the eighteenth century was under the patronage of an aristocracy for whom the arts were a necessary adornment of life. Art was part of the elaborate ritual that surrounded the existence of princes. In such a society, where the ruling caste enjoys its power through hereditary right, tradition is apt to be prized and the past revered. The center of art life is the palace and the privileged minority residing therein. In these high places the emphasis is on elegance of manner and beauty of style.

The art of the eighteenth century bears the imprint of the spacious palaces and formal gardens, with their balanced proportions and finely wrought detail, that formed the setting for enlightened despotism. In the middle of the century, Louis XV presided over the extravagant fetes in Versailles (although he foresaw the deluge). Frederick the Great ruled in Prussia, Maria Theresa in Austria, Catherine the Great in Russia. Yet disruptive forces were swiftly gathering beneath the glittering surface. The American Revolution dealt a shattering blow to the doctrine of the divine right of kings. And before the century had ended, Europe was convulsed by the French Revolution.

Bourgeois revolution
The second half of the eighteenth century, consequently, witnessed both the twilight of the *ancien régime* and the dawn of a new political-economic alignment in Europe; specifically, the transfer of power from the aristocracy to the middle class, whose wealth was based on a rapidly expanding capitalism, on mines and factories, steam power and railroads. This shift was made possible by the Industrial Revolution, which gathered momentum in the mid-eighteenth century with a series of important inventions, from Watt's steam engine and Hargreaves's spinning jenny in the 1760s to Cartwright's power loom in 1785 and Eli Whitney's cotton gin in 1793.

These decades saw significant advances in science. Benjamin Franklin discovered electricity in 1752, Priestley discovered oxygen in 1774, Jenner

Eighteenth-century Classicism drew its inspiration from the art and culture of ancient Greece. A painting by Jacques-Louis David (1748–1825), **Oath of Horatii.**

perfected vaccination in 1796, Laplace advanced his mechanistic view of the universe and Volta invented the voltaic pile in 1800. There were important events in intellectual life, such as the publication of Winckelmann's *History of Ancient Art* (1764), of the French *Encyclopédie* (1751–72), and the first edition of the *Encyclopaedia Britannica* (1771). The final quarter of the century produced such landmarks as Adam Smith's *The Wealth of Nations,* Kant's *Critique of Pure Reason,* Rousseau's *Confessions,* Gibbon's *Decline and Fall of the Roman Empire,* Boswell's *Life of Johnson,* and Malthus's *Essay on Population.*

Intellectual dualism   The intellectual climate of the Classical era, consequently, was nourished by two opposing streams. On the one hand Classical art captured the exquisite refinement of a way of life that was drawing to a close. On the other it caught the intimations of a new way of life that was struggling to be born. This dualism is of the essence in the Classical era and pervades all its attitudes. For example, the eighteenth century has been called the Age of Reason; but the two opposing camps invoked reason in diametrically opposite ways. The apologists of the status quo appealed to reason in order to justify the existing order. Early in the century Leibnitz taught that this was "the best of all possible worlds," and Pope proclaimed that "Whatever is, is right." As the century wore on, however, this spurious optimism became ever more difficult to maintain. The opponents of the established order, the *philosophes* who created the *Grande Encyclopédie* as an instrument of the Enlightenment—Voltaire, Diderot, Rousseau, Condorcet, d'Alembert and their comrades—also invoked reason, but for the purpose of attacking the existing order. Therewith these spokesmen for the rising middle class became the prophets of the approaching upheaval.

The Romantics, we saw, idealized the Middle Ages. But to eighteenth-century thinkers the Medieval period represented a thousand years of barbarism—the Dark Ages. The term *Gothic* represented everything that was opposed to what they regarded as rational and cultivated. Their ideal was the civilization of ancient Greece and Rome. To the Gothic cathedral, with its stained-glass windows, its bizarre gargoyles, its ribbed columns soaring heavenward in passionate mysticism, they opposed the Greek temple, a thing of beauty, unity and proportion, lightness and grace.

Classical ideals

Yet here too the revival of interest in Classical Antiquity meant different things to the opposing camps. The aristocrats and their spokesmen exalted Hellenism as the symbol of a rational, objective attitude that guarded one against becoming too deeply involved with the issues of life. They saw the ancient gods, kings, and heroes as a reflection of themselves—themselves ennobled, transfigured. But to the protagonists of the middle class, Greece and Rome represented city-states that had rebelled against tyrants and thrown off despotism. It was in this spirit that the foremost painter of revolutionary France, Jacques-Louis David, decked his canvases with the symbols of Athenian and Roman democracy. In this spirit, too, Thomas Jefferson praised David for having "ennobled the contemporary countenance with the classical quality of ancient republican virtue." Jefferson patterned both the Capitol and the University of Virginia after Greek and Roman temples, thereby giving strength to the Classic revival in this country, which made Ionic, Doric, and Corinthian columns an indispensable feature of our public buildings well into the twentieth century.

The Augustan Age

The Classical point of view held sway in English letters to such an extent that the mid-eighteenth century is known as the Augustan Age (after the Roman emperor Augustus, patron of the poet Vergil). Its arbiter was Samuel Johnson, whose position of leadership in literature was as undisputed as was that of his friend Sir Joshua Reynolds in painting. Both men upheld a highly formal, aristocratic type of art. Yet within the formal stream of Augustan Classicism we become aware of a current of tender sentiment that is an early sign of the Romantic spirit. The novels of Samuel Richardson, Henry Fielding, Laurence Sterne, and Tobias Smollett were suffused with homely bourgeois sentiment, as were the poems of Thomas Gray, Oliver Goldsmith, and William Cowper. For the Age of Reason was

The Age of Sensibility

also, curiously, the Age of Sensibility, and the sensibility steadily broadens into a trend toward the Romantic.

Thus it is that the Age of Reason begins to give way to the Age of

Romance considerably earlier than is commonly supposed. In the 1760s there already appeared a number of works—such as Percy's *Reliques of Ancient English Poetry*—that clearly indicate the new interest in a romantic medievalism. In the same decade Rousseau, the "father of Romanticism," produced some of his most significant writings. His celebrated

The library at the University of Virginia, designed by Thomas Jefferson, is a Roman Pantheon in red brick and white woodwork.

Sturm und Drang

dictum, "Man is born free and everywhere he is in chains," epitomizes the temper of the time. So too the first outcropping of the Romantic spirit in Germany, the movement known as *Sturm und Drang* (Storm and Stress), took shape in the 1770s, when it produced two characteristic works by its most significant young writers—the *Sorrows of Werther* by Goethe and *The Robbers* by Schiller. (Goethe, it will be remembered, became a favorite lyric poet of the Romantic composers.) By the end of the century the atmosphere had completely changed. The two most important English poets of the late eighteenth century—Robert Burns and William Blake— stand entirely outside the Classical stream, as does the greatest end-of-the-century painter, Goya, whose passionate realism anticipates a later age.

Late eighteenth-century culture, therefore, is neither as exclusively aristocratic nor as exclusively Classical as we have been taught to believe. It assimilated and was nourished by both democratic and Romantic elements. Precisely its dual nature lends it its subtle charm.

The Artist under Patronage

The eighteenth-century artist generally functioned under the system of aristocratic patronage. He created for a public high above him in social rank; his patrons were interested in his product rather than in his personality. Inevitably he was directed toward a Classical objectivity and reserve.

The artist under patronage was a master craftsman, an artisan working on direct commission from his patron. He produced works for immediate use, sustained by daily contact with his public. It is true that in point of social status the artist in livery was little better than a servant. This was not quite as depressing as it sounds, for in that society virtually everybody was a servant of the prince save other princes. The patronage system gave the artist economic security and a social framework within which he could function. It offered important advantages to the great artists who successfully adjusted to its requirements, as the career of Haydn richly shows. On the other hand, Mozart's tragic end illustrates how heavy was the penalty exacted from those unable to make that adjustment.

Eighteenth-century Classicism, then, mirrored the unique moment in history when the old world was dying and the new was in process of being born. From the meeting of two historic forces emerged an art of noble simplicity whose achievement in music constitutes one of the pinnacles of Western culture.

41 Classicism in Music

"Ought not the musician, quite as much as the poet and painter, to study nature? In nature he can study man, its noblest creature." — JOHANN FRIEDRICH REICHARDT (1774)

The Classical period in music (c. 1775–1825) centers about the achievements of the four masters of the Viennese school—Haydn, Mozart, Beethoven, and Schubert—and their contemporaries. Their art reached its flowering in a time of great musical experimentation and discovery, when musicians were confronted by three challenging problems: first, to explore to the full the possibilities offered by the major-minor system; second, to perfect a large form of absolute instrumental music that would mobilize those possibilities to the fullest degree; and third, having found this ideal form in the sonata cycle, to differentiate between its various types—the solo and duo sonata, trio, quartet, and other kinds of chamber music, the concerto, and the symphony.

If by Classicism we mean adherence to traditional forms we certainly cannot apply the term to the composers of the Viennese school. They ex-

The Vien-
nese school

perimented boldly and ceaselessly with the materials at their disposal. An enormous distance separates Haydn's early symphonies and string quartets from his later ones; the same is true of Mozart, Beethoven, and Schubert. Nor can we call these masters Classical if we mean that they—like the poets and painters of the mid-eighteenth century—subordinated emotional expression to accepted "rules" of form. The slow movements of Haydn and Mozart are filled with emotion of the profoundest kind. What could be more impassioned than Beethoven's music, or more suffused with lyric tenderness than Schubert's?

Even in point of time the Classical label does not fit music very well. The Classical era in literature and painting spread across the middle of the eighteenth century, whereas in music it appeared several decades later, in the last quarter of the eighteenth and the first quarter of the nineteenth centuries, when the forces of Romanticism already were coming to the fore. It should not surprise us that Romantic elements abound in the music of Haydn, Mozart, and Beethoven, especially in their late works. As for Schubert, although his symphonies and chamber music fall within the Classical orbit, his songs and piano pieces—as we saw in an earlier section of this book—stamp him a Romantic.

In consequence, the term Classicism applies to the art of the four Viennese masters in only one—but that one perhaps the most important —of its meanings: "as pertaining to the highest order of excellence." They and their contemporaries solved the problems presented to them so brilliantly that their symphonies and concertos, piano sonatas, duo sonatas, trios, string quartets, and similar works remained as unsurpassable models for all who came after. They evolved a dynamic instrumental language that was the perfect vehicle for the processes of thematic growth and development. They perfected spacious designs born of reason and logic, whose overall structure was flexible enough to allow for free expression of the most varied sentiments. And in doing so they created a new world of musical thought and sound.

Vocal Music in the Classical Period

Classical
opera

The opera house was a center of experimentation in the Classical era. Opera was the most important branch of musical entertainment and the one that reached the widest public. Classical opera was based on principles directly opposite to those that prevailed in the Romantic music drama. The music was the point of departure and imposed its forms on the drama. Each scene was a closed musical unit. The separate numbers were conceived as parts of the whole and held together in a carefully planned framework. There was the greatest possible distinction between the rapid patter of recitative and the lyric curve of aria. The voice reigned supreme, yet the orchestra displayed all the vivacity of the Classical instrumental style.

A significant development was the importance of Italian comic opera

Opera buffa   (opera buffa), which adopted certain features of the serious opera and in turn influenced the latter. Far from being an escapist form of entertainment, comic opera was directly related to the life of the time. Its emphasis was on the affairs of "little people," on swift action, pointed situations, spontaneous emotion, and sharpness of characterization. This popular lyric theater showed an abundance of racy melody, brilliant orchestration, and lively rhythms. Characteristic were the ensemble numbers at the end of the act, of a verve and drive that influenced all branches of music. From its cradle in Italy, Classical opera buffa spread all over Europe, steadily expanding its scope until it culminated in the works of the greatest musical dramatist of the eighteenth century—Mozart.

Liturgical music   As a center of music making, the Church retained its importance alongside opera house and aristocratic salon. Whereas the first half of the century had seen the high point of Protestant music in the art of Bach and his contemporaries, the Catholic countries now assumed first place, especially the Hapsburg domains. The masters of the Viennese Classical school produced a great deal of Catholic church music: Masses, vespers, litanies, and the like. They did as composers have always done: they used the living idiom of their day (an idiom based on opera and symphony) to express their faith in God and man.

Instrumental Music of the Classical Period

The Classical masters established the orchestra as we know it today. They based the ensemble on the blending of the four instrumental groups. The heart of this orchestra was the string choir. Woodwinds, used with great imagination, ably seconded the strings. The brass sustained the harmonies and contributed body to the tone mass, while the kettledrums supplied

The 18th-century orchestra   rhythmic life and vitality. The eighteenth-century orchestra numbered from thirty to forty players. The volume of sound was still considered in relation to the salon rather than the concert hall. (It was toward the end of the Classical period that musical life began to move from the one to the other.) Foreign to Classical art were the swollen sonorities of the late nineteenth century. The orchestra of Haydn and Mozart lent itself to delicate nuances in which each timbre stood out radiantly.

It follows that the Classical masters conceived their works on a smaller scale than did their nineteenth-century successors. They created a dynamic style of orchestral writing in which all the instruments participated actively. The interchange and imitation of themes among the various instrumental groups assumed the excitement of a witty conversation. The Classical orchestra brought to absolute music a number of effects long familiar in the opera house. The gradual crescendo and decrescendo established themselves as staples of the new symphonic style. Hardly less conspicuous were the abrupt alternations of soft and loud, sudden accents, dramatic pauses, the use of tremolo and pizzicato. These and similar

The eighteenth-century orchestra was relatively small, scaled to perform in the salons of the wealthy. In this painting by Francesco Guardi (1712–93), **The Gala Concert,** the orchestra perches in the balcony at the left. *(Alte Pinakothek, Munich.)*

devices of operatic music added drama and tension to the Classical orchestral style.

The symphony   The central place in Classical instrumental music was taken by the "sonata for orchestra"—the symphony. This grew rapidly in dimension and significance until, with the final works of Mozart and Haydn, it became the most important type of absolute music (which it remained throughout the Romantic period). Important, too, was the "sonata for solo instrument *The concerto* and orchestra"—the concerto, which combined a virtuoso part for the featured player with the resources of the orchestra. The piano concerto was the chief type, although other solo instruments were not neglected.

Chamber music   Chamber music enjoyed a great flowering in the Classical era, as did a type of composition that stood midway between chamber music and symphony, known as *divertimento*. The title fixes the character of this category of music as sociable diversion or entertainment. Closely related were the serenade, the *notturno* (night piece), and the *cassation* (a term of obscure origin probably referring to something in the streets or out-of-doors). Contemporary acounts tell of groups of street musicians who performed these works—for strings, winds, or both—outside the homes of the wealthy or in a quiet square before an appreciative audience of their fellow townsmen. At this time too the piano came into favor, supplanting harpsichord and clavichord as an instrument for the home. The piano sonata became the most ambitious form of solo music, in which composers worked out new conceptions of keyboard style and sonata structure, creating a rich literature for both the amateur and the virtuoso.

Sonata form   Classical sonata form was based upon a clear-cut opposition of keys. This demanded a harmony well rooted in the key. What gives certain works of Haydn and Mozart their pure, even chaste quality is the fact that their harmony is firmly diatonic, as distinct from the tendency toward chromaticism that gained strength throughout the nineteenth century.

Other Aspects of Musical Classicism

The Classical era created a universal style disseminated through two international art forms—Italian opera and Viennese symphony. These represented an all-European culture that transcended national boundaries. In *International* this regard Classicism reflected the international character of the two most *style* powerful institutions in eighteenth-century society, the aristocracy and the Church. Indeed, the eighteenth century was the last stronghold of internationalism in art (until the twentieth began). German, French, and Italian influences intermingle in the art of Haydn and Mozart. These masters were not German in the way that Wagner was, or Schumann, or Brahms. Romantic nationalism, we saw, opened up new dialects to composers. By the same token something was lost of the breadth of view that made artists like Beethoven and Goethe citizens of the world in the highest sense.

The Classical composers were far less concerned with exotic atmosphere than the Romantics (in spite of the *Turkish Rondo* of Mozart and the *Turkish March* of Beethoven). They already were strongly influenced by the "return to nature," especially Haydn in *The Creation* and *The Seasons* and Beethoven in the *Pastoral Symphony;* these works foreshadowed the numerous landscapes and sea scenes that were to play such an important part in nineteenth-century music. Also, significantly, despite the aristocratic spirit of the late eighteenth century, folklore elements entered increasingly into the Classical style. Popular song and dance are manifest not only in the German dances, contradances, ländler, and waltzes of the Viennese masters but also in the allegros and rondos of their larger works.

Classicism, to sum up, achieved the final synthesis of the intellectual currents of eighteenth-century life. The great theme of this pure and serene art was man, the measure of all things: a rational creature working out his destiny in an ordered universe whose outer garment was the beauty of nature and whose inner law was the clarity of reason. The Classical masters struck a perfect balance between emotion and intellect, heart and mind. So delicate an equilibrium is as rare in art as in life.

We have made reference to Nietzsche's distinction between the Dionysian and the Apollonian. The Classical spirit finds a fit symbol in the god of light, whose harmonious proportions so eloquently proclaim the cult of ideal beauty.

42 Joseph Haydn

"I have only just learned in my old age how to use the wind instruments, and now that I do understand them I must leave the world."

The long career of Joseph Haydn (1732–1809) spanned the decades when the Classical style was being formed. He imprinted upon it the stamp of his personality, and made a contribution to music that in scope and significance was second to none.

His Life

He was born in Rohrau, a village in Lower Austria, son of a wheelwright. Folk song and dance were his natural heritage. Displaying uncommon musical aptitude as a child, he was taught the rudiments by a distant relative, a schoolmaster. The beauty of his voice secured him a place as chorister in St. Stephen's Cathedral in Vienna, where he remained till he was sixteen. With the breaking of his voice his day at the choir school came to an end. He established himself in an attic in Vienna, managed to obtain a dilapidated clavier, and set himself to master his craft. He eked out a living through teaching and accompanying, and often joined the roving bands of musicians who performed in the streets. In this way the popular Viennese idiom entered his style along with the folk idiom he had absorbed in childhood.

Joseph Haydn.

The performance of *The Creation* in Haydn's honor at the University of Vienna one year before his death.

Esterházy patronage

Haydn before long attracted the notice of the music-loving aristocracy of Vienna, and was invited to the country house of a nobleman who maintained a small group of musicians. His next patron kept a small orchestra, so that he was able to experiment with more ample resources. In 1761, when he was twenty-nine, he entered the service of the Esterházys, a family of enormously wealthy Hungarian princes famous for their patronage of the arts. He remained in their service for almost thirty years— that is, for the greater part of his creative career. The palace of the Esterházys was one of the most splendid in Europe, and music played a central part in the constant round of festivities there. The musical establishment under Haydn's direction included an orchestra, an opera company, a marionette theater, and the chapel. The agreement between prince and composer sheds light on the social status of the eighteenth-century artist. Haydn is required to abstain "from undue familiarity and from vulgarity in eating, drinking, and conversation." He is enjoined to act uprightly and to influence his subordinates "to preserve such harmony as is becoming in them, remembering how displeasing any discord or dispute would be to His Serene Highness. . . . It is especially to be observed that when the orchestra shall be summoned to perform before company the said Joseph Heyden shall take care that he and all the members of his orchestra do follow the instructions given and appear in white stockings, white linen, powdered, and with a pigtail or tie-wig."

Haydn's life is the classic example of the patronage system operating at its best. Though he chafed occasionally at the restrictions imposed on him by court life, he inhabited a world that questioned neither the supremacy of princes nor the spectacle of a great artist in livery. His final estimate of his position in the Esterházy household was that the advantages outweighed the disadvantages. "My Prince was always satisfied with my works. I not only had the encouragement of constant approval but as conductor of an orchestra I could make experiments, observe what produced an effect and what weakened it, and was thus in a position to improve, alter, make additions or omissions, and be as bold as I pleased. I was cut off from the world, there was no one to confuse or torment me, and I was forced to become *original*."

Later years   Haydn had married when still a young man, but did not get on with his wife. They ultimately separated, and he found consolation elsewhere. By the time he reached middle age his music had brought him fame throughout Europe. He was asked to appear at various capitals but accepted none of these invitations as long as his patron was alive. After the Prince's death he made two visits to England (1791–92, 1794–95), where he conducted his works with phenomenal success. He returned to his native Austria laden with honors and financially well off.

His Music

Instrumental music   It was Haydn's historic role to help perfect the new instrumental language of the late eighteenth century, a language based on the dynamic development of themes and motives. The string quartet occupied a central position in Haydn's art. The eighty-three quartets he left are an indispensable part of the repertory. One understands Mozart's remark, "It was from Haydn that I first learned the true way to compose quartets." Like the quartets, the symphonies—over a hundred in number—extend across the whole of Haydn's career. Of these works it may be said, as it has been of his quartets, that they are the spiritual birthplace of Beethoven. Haydn also enriched the literature of the divertimento and concerto. His piano sonatas, of late years unjustly neglected, are returning to favor.

Vocal music   Haydn was a prolific composer of vocal music, religious and secular. Among the works for soloists, chorus, and orchestra are fourteen Masses and *The Creation* (1797–98), on verses drawn from the Bible and Milton's *Paradise Lost*. His numerous operas and marionette plays were designed specifically for the entertainment needs of the Esterházy court. "My operas are calculated exclusively for our own company and would not produce their effect elsewhere." But several, revived in recent years, have given delight.

The Surprise Symphony

The best known of Haydn's symphonies, the *Surprise,* in G major, is one
of the set of six written for his first visit to London in 1791. The orchestra
that presented these compositions to the world consisted of about forty
players: a full string section, two each of flutes, oboes, bassoons, horns,
and trumpets, with harpsichord and timpani.

*First
movement*
Side 7/1 (S)
Side 8/1 (E I)

The first movement opens with a brief introduction marked Adagio
cantabile. This passage in Haydn's most reflective mood is notable for its
limpid scoring for winds and strings. The movement proper is a forceful
Vivace assai (very lively) in sonata-allegro form, imbued with all the
symphonic drive and forthrightness of the Classical style.

The first theme, assigned to the first violins, is in the home key of G
major.

Notice that the first five notes are immediately restated a step lower, that is,
in sequence. They constitute a motive that will figure prominently in the
Development. This idea flowers into a vigorous section, at the close of
which a bridge passage leads into the contrasting key of D major. In the
course of this transition the basic motive, momentarily in D minor, takes on
a new shape:

The second theme, in D, is played by the first violins.

As often happens in Haydn, the two basic ideas do not present a marked
contrast to one another. The movement is built rather on the opposition
between home and contrasting key. A graceful closing theme rounds off the
Exposition:

The transparent orchestration and economy of means are characteristic
traits of Haydn's style, as are the breadth of design and prevailing good
humor.

He begins the Development by changing the first interval of his basic motive.

A segment of the basic motive leads to a new idea:

Out of these and similar threads Haydn weaves a closely-knit fabric. Frequent modulations give that sense of excitement, of releasing hidden energies, which marks the Development. The abrupt changes from *p* to *f* impart a dynamic quality to the music. They are characteristic of Haydn's orchestral writing, and look ahead to Beethoven's dramatic style.

The Recapitulation presents the material in shortened form. The second theme is transposed from the contrasting key of D to the home key of G—that is, from the Dominant key to the Tonic. The coda brings the movement to an affirmative cadence in G.

Second movement
Side 7/2 (S)
Side 8/2 (E I)

The second movement is the Andante, a theme and variations in C major. The theme is of a folksong simplicity. It is announced by the violins, staccato.

The eight-bar phrase is repeated pianissimo and ends in an abrupt fortissimo crash—the "surprise" that gives the symphony its name. "There," Haydn told a friend, "all the ladies will scream." But despite the famous anecdote, in an artist of Haydn's stature one must seek a deeper motivation for the effect. The contrast between soft and loud was one of the dynamic elements of the new orchestral language and was bound to fascinate an innovative artist like Haydn, quite apart from the ladies.

Haydn's variations are notable for their ease, taste, humor, and workmanship.

Variation 1. The theme is combined with arabesques in the first violins.

Variation 2. The theme is shifted into the minor and is played fortissimo by all the woodwinds and strings.

Variation 3 returns to the major. The theme is heard piano in a new rhythm.

In the second half of this variation the theme is heard underneath counter-melodies traced by solo flute and oboe.

Variation 4 brings changes in dynamics (fortissimo), register (high and middle), orchestration (melody in the woodwinds and brass), and a new triplet rhythm in the first violins against fortissimo chords on the offbeat in the other strings. The melody, too, is subtly changed.

The second half of this variation introduces a new version of the melody based on dotted rhythm.

This striking variation ends on a sustained chord which leads into the coda. The theme is wreathed in new harmonies. The final measures, which are in the nature of a gentle summing up, have a wonderful sound.

Third
movement
Side 7/3 (S)
Side 8/3 (E I)

The third movement, a Minuet in G major, is a rollicking Allegro molto that leaves far behind it the manner of the courtly dance. Peasant humor and the high spirits of folk dance permeate this movement.

The first section (A) shows a structure typical of the Classical minuet: ||:a:||:b-a-codetta:||. At the very outset we encounter one of Haydn's delightful irregularities in structure: two four-bar phrases are answered by one of four and another of six bars. The b section ends with an inimitably droll effect when flute and oboe are answered in low register by bassoon and cello. The Trio (section B) is quieter in movement, combining bassoon and violins in octaves. The form of this section is ||:c:||:d-c:||.

The Minuet proper is repeated da capo, giving the movement a clear-cut A-B-A form.

Fourth
movement
Side 7/4 (S)
Side 8/4 (E I)

The fourth movement is a vigorous Allegro molto (very lively) in sonata-allegro form. Like the first and third movements, it is in G major. Imbued with the spirit of popular dance, this Allegro has all the verve of the Haydn finale. The principal theme establishes the home key of G.

An energetic bridge passage leads to the second theme in the contrasting key, D major. This is a roguish little tune that is followed by a codetta in the same key. The first theme undergoes a forceful development, in the course of which the music touches upon various major and minor keys. In the Restatement, both first and second themes are in the home key of G. The coda sustains the jovial mood; and an energetic cadence in G major ends a work which captured, for Haydn's aristocratic listeners, all the charm and humor of the folk.

43 Wolfgang Amadeus Mozart

"People make a mistake who think that my art has come easily to me. Nobody has devoted so much time and thought to composition as I. There is not a famous master whose music I have not studied over and over."

Something of the miraculous hovers about the music of Mozart (1756–91). One sees how it is put together, whither it is bound, and how it gets there; but its beauty of sound and perfection of style, its poignancy and grace defy analysis and beggar description. For one moment in the history of music all opposites were reconciled, all tensions resolved. That luminous moment was Mozart.

His Life

He was born in Salzburg, son of Leopold Mozart, an esteemed composer-violinist attached to the court of the Archbishop. He began his career as the most extraordinarily gifted child in the history of art. He first started to compose before he was five, and performed at the court of the Empress Maria Theresa at the age of six. The following year his ambitious father organized a grand tour that included Paris, London, and Munich. By the time he was thirteen the boy had written sonatas, concertos, *Early works* symphonies, religious works, an opera buffa, and the operetta *Bastien and Bastienne.*

He reached manhood having attained a mastery of all forms of his art. The speed and sureness of his creative power, unrivaled by any other composer, is best described by himself: "Though it be long, the work is complete and finished in my mind. I take out of the bag of my memory what has previously been collected into it. For this reason the committing to paper is done quickly enough. For everything is already finished, and it rarely differs on paper from what it was in my imagination. At this work I can therefore allow myself to be disturbed. Whatever may be going on about me, I write and even talk."

From patronage to free artist His relations with his patron, Hieronymus von Colloredo, Prince-Archbishop of Salzburg, were most unhappy. The high-spirited young artist rebelled against the social restrictions imposed by the patronage system. At length he could endure his position no longer. He quarreled with the Archbishop, was dismissed, and at twenty-five established himself in Vienna to pursue the career of a free artist, the while he sought an official appointment. Ten years remained to him. These were spent in a tragic struggle to achieve financial security and to find again the lost serenity of his childhood. Worldly success depended on the protection

Wolfgang Amadeus Mozart.

of the court. But the Emperor Joseph II—who referred to him as "a decided talent"—either passed him by in favor of lesser men or, when he finally took Mozart into his service, assigned him to tasks unworthy of his genius such as composing dances for the court balls. Of his remuneration for this work Mozart remarked with bitterness, "Too much for what I do, too little for what I could do."

Marriage to Constanze

In 1782 he married Constanze Weber, against his father's wishes. The step signalized Mozart's liberation from the close ties that had bound him to the well-meaning but domineering parent who strove so futilely to ensure the happiness of the son. Constanze brought her husband neither the strength of character nor the wealth that might have protected him from a struggle with the world for which he was singularly unequipped. She was an undistinguished woman to whom Mozart, despite occasional lapses, was strongly attached. It was not till many years after his death that she appears to have realized, from the adulation of the world, the stature of her husband.

Late years

His final years were spent in growing want. The frequent appeals to his friends for aid mirror his despair and helplessness. He describes himself as "always hovering between hope and anxiety." He speaks of the black thoughts that he must "repel by a tremendous effort." The love of life that had sustained him through earlier disappointments began to desert him. Again and again he embarked on a journey that seemed to promise a solution to all his difficulties, only to return empty-handed.

In the last year of his life, after a falling off in his production, he nerved himself to the final effort. For the popular Viennese theater he wrote *The Magic Flute,* on a libretto by the actor-impresario-poetaster Emanuel Schikaneder. Then a flurry of hope sent him off to Prague for the coronation of the new Emperor, Leopold II, as King of Bohemia. The festival opera he composed for this event, *The Clemency of Titus,* failed to impress a court exhausted by the protracted ceremonies of the coronation. Mozart returned to Vienna broken in body and spirit. With a kind of fevered desperation he turned to his last task, the *Requiem.* It had been commissioned by a music-loving count who fancied himself a composer and intended to pass off the work as his own. Mozart in his overwrought state became obsessed with the notion that this *Mass for the Dead* was intended for himself and that he would not live to finish it. A tragic race with time began as he whipped his faculties to this masterwork steeped in visions of death.

He was cheered in his last days by the growing popularity of *The Magic Flute.* The gravely ill composer, watch in hand, would follow the performance in his mind. "Now the first act is over . . . Now comes the aria of the Queen of Night . . ." His premonition concerning the *Requiem* came true. He failed rapidly while in the midst of the work. His favorite pupil, Süssmayr, completed the Mass from the master's sketches, with some additions of his own.

Mozart died in 1791, shortly before his thirty-sixth birthday. In view of his debts he was given "the poorest class of funeral." His friends followed to the city gates; but the weather being inclement, they turned back, leaving the hearse to proceed alone. "Thus, without a note of music, forsaken by all he held dear, the remains of this prince of harmony were committed to the earth—not even in a grave of his own but in the common paupers' grave."

His Music

Many view Mozart as one in whom the elegance of court art reached its peak. To others he represents the spirit of artless youth untouched by life. Both views are equally far from the truth. Neither the simplicity of his forms nor the crystalline clarity of his texture can dispel the intensity of feeling that pervades the works of his maturity. Because of the mastery with which everything is carried out, the most complex operations of the musical mind are made to appear effortless. This deceptive simplicity is truly the art that conceals art.

It has been said that Mozart taught the instruments to sing. Into his exquisitely wrought instrumental forms he poured the lyricism of the great vocal art of the past. The peasant touch is missing from Mozart's music, which draws its inspiration neither from folk song nor nature. It is an indoor art, sophisticated, rooted in the culture of two musical cities—Salzburg and Vienna.

Instrumental music   The Salzburg years saw the composition of a quantity of social music, divertimentos and serenades of great variety. In chamber music he favored the string quartet. His works in this form range in expression from the bouyantly songful to the austerely tragic. One of the outstanding pianists of his time, Mozart wrote copiously for his favorite instrument. He led the way in developing the concerto for piano and orchestra, and wrote more than twenty works for this medium. They established the piano concerto as one of the important types of the Classical era.

Symphonies
The more than forty symphonies—their exact number has not been determined—that extend across his career tend toward ever greater richness of orchestration, freedom of part writing, and depth of emotion. The most important are the six written in the final decade of his life—the *Haffner,* in D (1782), the *Linz,* in C (1783), the *Prague,* in D (1786), and the three composed in 1788. With these works the symphony achieves its position as the most weighty form of abstract music. In an age when composers produced their works almost exclusively on commission, it is significant that Mozart's last three symphonies were never performed during his lifetime: he wrote them for no specific occasion but from inner necessity. They came into being because the composer had something in him that had to be said, no matter who heard.

Operas
But the central current in Mozart's art that nourished all the others was opera. Here were embodied his joy in life, his melancholy, all the impulses of his many-faceted personality. None has ever surpassed his power to delineate character in music and to make his puppets come alive. His lyric gift, molded to the curve of the human voice, created a wealth of melody whose sensuous loveliness sets it apart in music. His orchestra, although it never obtrudes upon the voice, becomes the magical framework within which the action unfolds.

In Lorenzo da Ponte, an Italian-Jewish adventurer and poet who was one of the picturesque figures of the age, Mozart found a librettist whose dramatic vitality was akin to his own. (Da Ponte ultimately emigrated to America, operated a grocery store and sold illicit liquor on the side, taught Italian at Columbia College, was one of the first impresarios to bring Italian opera to New York, wrote a fascinating book of memoirs, and died in 1838.) The collaboration produced three works: *The Marriage of Figaro* (1786), which da Ponte adapted from the comedy of Beaumarchais satirizing the old regime; *Don Giovanni* (1787), "the opera of all operas"; and *Così fan tutte* (1790), which has been translated in a variety of ways from "So do all women" to "Girls will be girls!" These crown the history of Classical opera buffa, just as *The Abduction from the Seraglio* (1782) and *The Magic Flute* (1791), a gigantic fantasy steeped in the symbolism of Freemasonry, bring to its apex the German *Singspiel* (song-play). Abounding in irony and satire, these masterpieces reach beyond the world of satin and lace whence they issued. They achieve what da Ponte set forth as his and Mozart's intention: "To paint faithfully and in full color the divers passions."

Don Giovanni

Conceived in the tradition of the opera buffa, *Don Giovanni* oversteps that tradition into the realm covered by our term tragicomedy. Da Ponte called it a "jocose" or cheerful drama. The opera is unique for its range of emotions.

Da Ponte's Don heralds a new type in literature as in society: the supreme individualist who brooks no restraints and brushes aside every obstacle in the way of his self-realization. Don Juan is the eternal type of libertine for whom the pursuit of pleasure has become the final assertion of will. Mozart's music humanizes him, transforms him into one of the boldest conceptions in the entire range of the lyric theater.

In the opening scene Don Giovanni, having broken into Anna's chamber, rushes out of the house struggling with her and concealing his face. Donna Anna, determined to discover the identity of her assailant, calls for help. Her father—the Commandant—appears, drawing his sword. Donna Anna withdraws into the house. The Don does not wish to fight the old man but is goaded into a duel in the course of which he mortally wounds the Commandant. The conversation between Don Giovanni and Leporello establishes the moral climate they inhabit. "Who is dead, you or the old man?" "Silly question. The old man." "Bravo. Nice work—attacking the daughter and murdering the father." "He asked for it." "And Donna Anna, what did she ask for?" "Shut up and come away. Unless you too are asking for something." "Oh no, master. I shan't say another word." They escape. Donna Anna comes out of the house with Don Ottavio, her betrothed. She discovers her father's body and is overcome by grief. In the ensuing duet she

Don Giovanni, Act I, Scene 3: The Don (Sherrill Milnes) woos Zerlina (Teresa Stratas) in the duet *Là ci darem la mano.* Metropolitan Opera production. *(Photo copyright by Beth Bergman.)*

Catalogue Aria

Side 8/5 (S)
Side 10/4 (E I)

and Don Ottavio swear to track down the murderer and make him pay for his crime.

Leporello's *Catalogue Aria* is sung to Donna Elvira, who still loves the Don even though he has abandoned her.

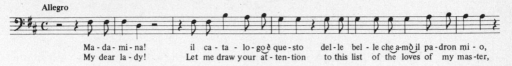

Ma - da - mi - na! il ca - ta - lo - go è que - sto del - le bel - le che a-mò il pa - dron mi - o,
My dear la - dy! Let me draw your at - ten - tion to this list of the loves of my mas - ter,

To persuade her of the futility of her passion Leporello reads her the list of his master's amours. "In Italy six hundred and forty. In Germany two hundred and thirty-one. A hundred in France, in Turkey ninety-one. But in Spain it's already one thousand and three (*'mille e tre'*). Country girls, servant girls, city girls, countesses, baronesses, princesses. All ranks, all shapes, all ages . . ." What is left unsaid in the vocal line is filled in by the saucy accompaniment. This comic aria, in which the singer with a knowing wink takes the audience into his confidence, is in the great tradition of the theater of buffoons.

Duet

Side 8/6 (S)
Side 10/5 (E I)

In the next scene, *Là ci darem la mano*—a little duet, as Mozart called it—is sung by Don Giovanni and Zerlina, the artless peasant maid who has momentarily caught his fancy. He succeeds in detaching her from

Là ci da - rem la ma - no, là mi di - rai di sì,
Give me your hand, sweet maid - en, Whis - per a gen - tle "yes,"

her fiancé, the country bumpkin Masetto, assures her that he intends to marry her, and invites her to come with him to his villa. The voices alternate, the phrases becoming ever shorter as he grows more ardent and she more amenable. "I should feel happy. What if he's only making sport of me . . . Come, my delight . . . I'm sorry for Masetto . . . I'll change your life . . . How quickly I yield . . ." The tempo changes from andante to allegro; 2/4 time gives way to 6/8 as she throws herself into his arms. Together they sing, "Let us go, my dearest, and ease the pangs of innocent love." There is much repetition of the key word "andiam" (let us go) to allow for musical expansion. The melody is Mozart at his suavest.

The opera traces the course of Don Giovanni's escapades until the final scene, when the sinner receives the punishment he deserves.

Eine kleine Nachtmusik

Mozartian elegance and delicacy of touch are embodied in this serenade for strings (K. 525, 1787), whose title means "A Little Night Music." Probably the work was intended for a double string quartet supported by a bass. The version we know has four movements, compact, intimate, and beautifully proportioned; originally there were five.

First movement
Side 8/1 (S)
Side 7/3 (E I)

The opening Allegro is a sonata form in $\frac{4}{4}$ time in G major. As was customary in music of this type, the first movement has a marchlike character—as if the musicians were arriving for their cheerful task.

Second and third movements
Side 8/2-3 (S)
Side 7/4-5 (E I)

Fourth movement
Side 8/4 (S)
Side 7/6 (E 1)

Second is the Romanza, an eighteenth-century Andante that maintains the balance between lyricism and a pleasant reserve. The key is C, the meter ₵; symmetrical sections are arranged in an A-B-A-C-A structure. The Minuet, marked Allegretto, is in G major and regular four-bar structure. The Trio, which is marked sotto voce (in an undertone, subdued), traces a soaring curve of Mozartian melody; after which the Minuet is repeated.

The rondo finale, Allegro, is in cut time in the home key of G. It is based on a vivacious principal theme:

This alternates with a subordinate idea. (The sign over the last note in measure 2 of the example indicates a *turn,* a type of ornament or embellishment.)

The movement displays certain features of sonata form—opposition between home and contrasting key, development of the rondo theme, and modulation far afield. We have said that there is a rondo style as well as a rondo form. This is the perfect example, bright, jovial, and—a trait inseparable from this master—stamped with an aristocratic refinement.

In the music of Mozart subjective emotion is elevated to the plane of the universal. The restlessness and the longing are exorcised by the ideal loveliness of Apollonian art. Mozart is one of the supreme artists of all time; the voice of pure beauty in music, and probably the most sheerly musical composer that ever lived.

Symphony No. 40 in G minor

It was in the summer of 1788, during the darkest period of his life, that Mozart in the space of a little over six weeks composed his last three symphonies: in E flat (K. 543); in G minor (K. 550); and in C, the *Jupiter* (K. 551). They are popularly known as Nos. 39, 40, and 41.

The *G-minor Symphony* represents that mingling of Classic and Romantic elements which marked the final decades of the eighteenth century. Along with several important works that preceded it, the Symphony strikes an impassioned note, especially in its first and fourth movements.

First
movement
Side 11/1 (S)
Side 10/1 (E 1)

The first movement, in sonata-allegro form, plunges immediately into the Allegro molto. The Exposition opens with an intense theme for the violins that establishes the home key of G minor. Pointing to a new expressiveness

in music, it flowers out of a three-note germ motive (A) that is genuinely symphonic in its capacity for growth and contains two other motives (B and C) that play their part in the development of the material. Notice that the second phrase is a sequence, one step lower, of the first. Great rhythmic activity gives the melody a feeling of restlessness that is heightened by the animated accompaniment of the lower strings. Stepwise movement in the first measure is balanced by the dramatic upward leap in the second and the gradual descent of the melody in the third. A vigorous bridge passage that sustains tension through a steady crescendo leads into the contrasting key, the relative major—B flat. The second theme, shared by woodwinds and strings, provides an area of comparative relaxation in the headlong drive of the movement. This melody is in direct contrast to the restlessness of the first subject. It moves in a flowing rhythm, mostly stepwise and within a narrow range. Notice that each phrase begins by gliding downward along the chromatic scale:

The codetta, in which we hear echoings of the basic motive (A), establishes the cadence in the contrasting key. In most recordings of this work the Exposition is repeated, which is in accordance with Classical usage. (The short exposition of the Classical symphony demands to be repeated, otherwise the whole design is upset. As the Exposition grew ever longer in nineteenth-century music, the practice was abandoned.)

The Development is brief and packed with action. It searches out the possibilities of the opening theme, concentrating on the three-note motive. The music wanders far afield, modulating rapidly from one foreign key to the next. Here are some examples of Mozart's developmental technique:

1. Theme 1 with change at the end:

2. Theme 1 in the bass with a new melody above it:

3. Expansion through a pattern combining motives C and B, which is repeated in a descending sequence:

4. Expansion through repetition of motive A, forming a pattern that is repeated in a descending sequence:

5. Inversion of motive A (upside-down), used together with the motive in its original position as part of the transition back to the home key:

Never slackening its course, the Development is crowned by the transition back to the home key, one of those miraculous passages that only Mozart could have written. We hear the initial theme as it sounded in the beginning.

The Recapitulation follows the course of the first section. The bridge is expanded and circles about the home key. The second theme is given in G minor rather than major, taking on a strangely tender tone. The coda energetically confirms the home key.

Fourth movement
Side 11/2 (S)
Side 10/2 (E I)

The finale, Allegro assai (very fast), is a compact sonata-allegro form, abrupt and imperious. A tragic restlessness lurks beneath its polished surface. The first subject, in G minor, is presented by the first violins. Based on an upward-bounding arpeggio, it represents a pattern dear to the Classical era and known as a *rocket theme*.

The contrasting theme, sung by the first violins in the related key of ·B-flat major, provides the necessary foil in point of serenity and grace. It has longer—that is, fewer—notes, moves within a narrow range, mostly step-wise or with narrow leaps, and is rhythmically quieter.

It is repeated, with subtle embellishments, by the clarinet.

The Development is highly dramatic. The rocket motive is bandied about by various instruments that crowd upon one another in hurried imitation as they spin out a complex orchestral fabric. Tension is maintained at maximum pitch by the rapid modulations through foreign keys. The Recapitulation presents the material again with certain changes, most important of which is the shifting of the second theme into the home key of G minor. From that moment of enchantment until the final cadence we witness the exciting spectacle of a great artist functioning at the summit of his powers.

44 Ludwig van Beethoven

"Freedom above all!"

Beethoven (1770–1827) belonged to the generation that received the full impact of the French Revolution. He was nourished by its vision of the freedom and dignity of the individual. The time, the place, and the personality combined to produce an artist sensitive in the highest degree to the impulses of the new century. He created the music of a heroic age and in accents never to be forgotten proclaimed its faith in the power of man to shape his destiny.

His Life

He was born in Germany, in the city of Bonn in the Rhineland, where his father and grandfather were singers at the court of the local prince,

Ludwig van Beethoven.

the Elector Max Friedrich. The family situation was unhappy, the father being addicted to drink, and Ludwig at an early age was forced to take over the support of his mother and two younger brothers. At eleven and a half he was assistant organist in the court chapel. A year later he became harpsichordist in the court orchestra. A visit to Vienna in his seventeenth year enabled him to play for Mozart. The youth improvised so brilliantly on a theme given him by the master that the latter remarked to his friends, "Keep an eye on him—he will make a noise in the world some day."

Arrangements were made some years later for him to study with Haydn in Vienna at the Elector's expense. He left his native town when he was twenty-two, never to return. Unfortunately, the relationship between pupil and teacher left much to be desired. The aging Haydn was ruffled by the young man's volcanic temperament and independence of spirit. Beethoven worked with other masters, the most academic of whom declared that "he has learned nothing and will never do anything in decent style."

Meanwhile his powers as a pianist took the music-loving aristocracy by storm. He was welcomed in the great houses of Vienna by the powerful patrons whose names appear in the dedications of his works—Prince Lichnowsky, Prince Lobkowitz, Count Razumovsky, and the rest. Archduke Rudolph, brother of the Emperor, became his pupil and devoted friend. These connoisseurs, no less than the public, were transported by his highly personal style of improvisation, by the wealth of his ideas, the novelty of their treatment, and the surging emotion behind them.

The rebel

To this "princely rabble," as he called them, the young genius came—in an era of revolution—as a passionate rebel, forcing them to receive him as an equal and friend. "It is good to move among the aristocracy," he observed, "but it is first necessary to make them respect you." Beethoven, sensitive and irascible, stood up for his rights as an artist. When Prince Lichnowsky, during the Napoleonic invasion, insisted that he play for some French officers, Beethoven stormed out of the palace in a rage, demolished a bust of Lichnowsky that was in his possession, and wrote to his exalted friend: "Prince! what you are, you are through the accident of birth. What I am, I am through my own efforts. There have been many princes and there will be thousands more. But there is only one Beethoven!" Such was the force of his personality that he was able to make the aristocrats about him accept this novel idea. Beneath the rough exterior they recognized an elemental power akin to a force of nature.

Beethoven functioned under a modified form of the patronage system. He was not attached to the court of a prince. Instead, the music-loving aristocrats of Vienna helped him in various ways—by paying him handsomely for lessons, or through gifts. He was also aided by the emergence of a middle-class public and the growth of concert life and music publishing. At the age of thirty-one he was able to write, "I have six or seven publishers for each of my works and could have more if I chose. No more bargaining. I name my terms and they pay." A youthful exuberance pervades the first decade of his career, an almost arrogant consciousness of his strength. "Power is the morality of men who stand out from the mass, and it is also mine!" Thus spoke the individualist in the new era of individualism.

Deafness

Then, as the young eagle was spreading his wings, fate struck in a vulnerable spot: he began to lose his hearing. His helplessness in the face of this affliction dealt a shattering blow to his pride. "Ah, how could I possibly admit an infirmity in the one sense that should have been more perfect in me than in others. A sense I once possessed in highest perfection. Oh I cannot do it!" As his deafness closed in on him—the first symptoms appeared when he was in his late twenties—it became the symbol of his terrible sense of apartness from other men, of all the defiance and insecurity and hunger for love that had rent him for as long as he could remember. Upon the mistaken advice of his doctors he retired in 1802 to a summer resort outside Vienna called Heiligenstadt. A titanic struggle shook him, between the destructive forces in his soul and his desire to live and create. It was one of those searing experiences that either break a man or leave him stronger. "But little more and I would have put an end to my life. Only art it was that withheld me. Ah, it seemed impossible to leave the world until I had produced all that I felt called upon to produce, and so I endured this wretched existence."

It was slowly borne in on him that art must henceforth give him the happiness life withheld. Only through creation could he attain the victory of which fate had threatened to rob him. The will to struggle asserted itself; he fought his way back to health. "I am resolved to rise superior to every obstacle. With whom need I be afraid of measuring my strength? If possible I will bid defiance to my fate, although there will be moments in life when I will be the unhappiest of God's creatures . . . I will take Fate by the throat. It shall not overcome me. Oh how beautiful it is to be alive—would that I could live a thousand times!" He had stumbled on an idea that was to play a decisive part in nineteenth-century thought: the concept of art as refuge, as compensation for the shortcomings of reality; art as sublimation, atonement, faith—the idealized experience, the ultimate victory over life.

Having conquered the chaos within himself he came to believe that man could conquer chaos. This became the epic theme of his music: the progression from despair to conflict, from conflict to serenity, from serenity to triumph and joy. The revelation that had come to him through suffering was a welcome message to the world that was struggling to be born. The concept of man the master of his fate hit off the temper of the new middle-class society in its most dynamic phase. In giving expression to his personal faith Beethoven said what his generation needed to hear. He became the major prophet of the nineteenth century, the architect of its heroic vision of life. "I am the Bacchus who presses out the glorious wine for mankind. Whoever truly understands my music is freed thereby from the miseries that others carry about in them."

The final years

The remainder of his career was spent in an unremitting effort to subjugate the elements of his art to the expressive ideal he had set himself. Fellow musicians and critics might carp at the daring of his thoughts, but his victory was assured. A growing public, especially among the younger generation, responded to the powerful thrust of his music. His life was outwardly uneventful. There were the interminable quarrels with associates and friends—he grew increasingly suspicious and irritable, especially in his last years, when he became totally deaf. There were the complicated dealings with his publishers, in which he displayed an impressive shrewdness; his turbulent love affairs (he never married); his high-handed interference in the affairs of his brothers; his tortured relationship with his nephew Carl, an ordinary young man upon whom he fastened a tyrannical affection. All these framed an inner life of extraordinary intensity, an unceasing spiritual development that reached down to ever profounder levels of insight and opened up new domains to tonal art.

Biographers and painters have made familiar the squat, sturdy figure—he was five foot four, the same as that other conqueror of the age, Napoleon—walking hatless through the environs of Vienna, the bulging brow

The Theater an der Wien, shown here in a contemporary engraving, was the site of the first public performances of *Fidelio* (1805), the *Eroica Symphony* (1805), the *Violin Concerto* (1806), and the *Pastoral Symphony* (1808).

furrowed in thought, stopping now and again to jot down an idea in his sketchbook; an idea that, because he was forever deprived of its sonorous beauty, he envisioned all the more vividly in his mind. A ride in an open carriage in inclement weather brought on an attack of dropsy that proved fatal. He died in his fifty-seventh year, famous and revered.

His Music

Beethoven is the supreme architect in music. His genius found expression in the structural type of thinking embodied in the sonata-symphony. The sketchbooks in which he worked out his ideas show how gradually they reached their final shape and how painstakingly he molded the material into its one inevitable form. "I carry my thoughts within me long, often very long before I write them down. In doing this my memory stands me in such good stead that even years afterward I am sure not to forget a theme I have once grasped . . . As I know what I want, the fundamental idea never deserts me. It mounts, it grows in stature. I hear, I see the picture in its whole extent standing all of a piece before my spirit, and there remains for me only the task of writing it down."

Inheriting the sonata form from Haydn and Mozart, he transformed it

Treatment of Classical forms

into a spacious frame for his ideas. He expanded the dimensions of the first movement, especially the coda. Like Haydn and Mozart, he treated the Development section as the dynamic center of sonata-form. His short incisive themes offer limitless opportunity for expansion and development; they unfold with volcanic energy and momentum. The slow movement acquired in his hands a hymnic character, the embodiment of Beethovenian pathos. He transformed minuet into scherzo, making it a movement of rhythmic energy ranging from "cosmic laughter" to mystery and wonder. He enlarged the finale into a movement comparable in size and scope to the first, ending the symphony on a note of triumph.

Sonatas and symphonies

The piano occupied a central position in Beethoven's art. His thirty-two sonatas are an indispensable part of its literature, whether for the amateu. pianist or concert artist. They are well called the pianist's New Testament (the Old being the *Well-Tempered Clavier* of Bach). In the symphony Beethoven found the ideal medium wherein to address mankind. His nine symphonies are spiritual dramas of universal appeal. Their sweep and tumultuous affirmation of life mark them a pinnacle of the rising democratic art. They are conceived on a scale too grand for the aristocratic salon; they demand the amplitude of the concert hall.

The concerto offered Beethoven a congenial public form in which he combined virtuosity with symphonic architecture. Most popular of his works in the medium are the *Third Piano Concerto;* the *Fourth,* in G (1806); the *Fifth,* in E flat (the *Emperor,* 1809); and the noble *Concerto for Violin,* in D (1806). He wrote much chamber music, the string quartet being closest to his heart. His supreme achievements in this area are the last five quartets, which occupied the final years of his life. In these, as in the last five piano sonatas, the master's gaze is focused within, encompassing depths that music never before had plumbed.

Vocal music

Although his most important victories were won in the instrumental field, Beethoven enriched the main types of vocal music. Of his songs the best known is the cycle of six, *An die ferne Geliebte* (To the Distant Beloved). His sole opera *Fidelio* (originally called *Leonora,* completed in 1805) centers about wifely devotion, human freedom, and the defeat of those who would destroy it. The *Missa solemnis* (Solemn Mass in D; 1818–23) ranks in importance with the *Ninth Symphony* and the final quartets. The work transcends the limits of any specific creed or dogma. Above the Kyrie of the Mass he wrote a sentence that applies to the whole of his music: "From the heart . . . may it find its way to the heart."

His creative activity, extending over a span of thirty-five years, bears witness to a ceaseless striving after perfection. "I feel as if I had written scarcely more than a few notes," he remarked at the end of his career. And a year before his death: "I hope still to bring a few great works into the world." Despite his faith in his destiny he knew the humility of the truly great. "The real artist has no pride. Unfortunately he sees that his art has no limits, he feels obscurely how far he is from the goal. And while he is perhaps being admired by others, he mourns the fact that he has not yet reached the point to which his better genius, like a distant sun, ever beckons him."

The Fifth Symphony

The most popular of all symphonies, Beethoven's *Fifth,* in C minor, Opus 67, is also the most concentrated expression of the frame of mind and spirit that we have come to call Beethovenian. It embodies in supreme degree the basic principle of symphonic thinking—the flowering of an extended composition from a kernel by a process of organic growth. The popular story that Beethoven, when asked for the meaning of the opening theme, replied, "Thus Fate knocks at the door," is probably not authentic. Such literalness seems unlikely in one who was so completely the tone poet. If the work continues to be associated with Fate it is rather because of the inevitable, the relentless logic of its unfolding.

*First
movement
Side 10/1 (S)
Side 12/1 (E I)*

The first movement, marked Allegro con brio (lively, with vigor), springs out of the rhythmic idea of "three shorts and a long" that dominates the symphony. Announced in unison by strings and clarinets (Beethoven holds his full forces in reserve), the motive establishes the home key of C minor. It is the most compact and commanding gesture in the whole symphonic literature.

Out of this motive flowers the first theme, which is a repetition, at different levels of the scale and with altered intervals, of the germinating rhythm.

a) The motive. b) Sequence, with smaller interval. c) Sequence. d) The motive with larger interval. e) Same as b. f) Sequence of motive. g) Motive with the interval filled in. h) Inversion (upside-down) of g.

The power of the movement springs from the almost terrifying single-mindedness with which the underlying idea is pursued. It is rhythm, torrential yet superbly controlled, that is the generating force behind this "storm and stress." Beethoven here achieved a vehemence that was new in music. The bridge to the related key of E-flat major is fashioned out of the basic motive. Notice how much more compact is this bridge than the leisurely transition in the first movement of Mozart's *G-minor Symphony:*

We reach an area of relaxation with the lyric second theme. Yet even here the headlong course of the movement does not slacken. As the violins, clarinet, and flute sound the gentle melody in turn, the basic rhythm of "three shorts and a long" persists in the cellos and double basses.

Basic rhythm

The Exposition is rounded off with a short section (codetta) reaffirming the basic rhythm.

The Development is dramatic, peremptory, compact. The following examples show how Beethoven weaves a tightly knit fabric out of the basic motive.

1. Motive with interval filled in. Expansion through a descending sequence:

2. Motive with interval filled in. Expansion through a descending sequence coupled with inversion (turning the motive upside-down):

3. Expansion through repetition. This passage leads into the Recapitulation:

No less characteristic of Beethoven's style are the powerful crescendos and the abrupt contrasts between soft and loud. The transition back to the home key culminates in a fortissimo proclamation of the underlying rhythm by full orchestra.

The Restatement is interrupted when an oboe solo introduces a note of pathos, momentarily slackening the tension. The second theme is transposed into C major. There is an extended coda in which the basic rhythm reveals a new fund of explosive energy.

Second movement
Side 10/2 (S)
Side 12/2 (E I)

Beethovenian serenity and strength imbue the second movement, Andante con moto (at a going pace, with movement). The key is A flat; the form, a theme and variations. There are two melodic ideas. The first is a broadly spun theme sung by violas and cellos. It is followed by one of

those hymnic upward-thrusting subjects so characteristic of the master, which echoes the basic rhythm—the "three shorts and a long" of the opening movement.

In the course of the movement Beethoven brings all the procedures of variation—changes in melodic outline, harmony, rhythm, tempo, dynamics, register, key, mode, and type of accompaniment—to bear upon his two themes. Here is how the first theme is embellished with running sixteenth notes in Variation 1:

In Variation 2 this melody is presented in thirty-second-note rhythm:

In the next Variation the melody is divided up among the various wood-wind instruments:

Finally the melody is shifted into the minor:

The second theme undergoes analogous transformations, gathering strength until it is proclaimed by the full orchestra. The coda, marked Più mosso (faster), opens with a motive on the bassoon derived from Theme 1 against syncopated chords in the strings. A dynamic crescendo rounds off the movement.

Third movement
Side 10/3 (S)
Side 12/3 (E I)

Third in the cycle of movements is the Scherzo, which returns to the somber C minor that is the home key of the work. From the depths of the bass rises a characteristic subject, a rocket theme introduced by cellos and double basses.

The basic rhythm of the first movement reappears fortissimo in the horns. Nourished by dynamic changes and a crescendo, the movement steadily accumulates force and drive. The Trio shifts to C major. It is based on a gruffly humorous motive of running eighth notes stated by cellos and double basses and imitated in turn, in ever higher register, by violas, second violins, and first violins. The motive of the double basses

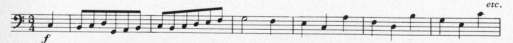

was described by Berlioz in a celebrated phrase as the "gambols of a frolicsome elephant." Here the term scherzo is applicable in its original meaning of "jest." Beethoven's cosmic laughter resounds through these measures: a laughter that shakes—and builds—a world.

This motive is expanded through repetition and sequence:

The Scherzo (section A) returns in a modified version, with changed orchestration. It is followed by a mysterious transitional passage that is spun out of the Scherzo theme and the basic rhythm, which is presented by various instruments and finally tapped out mysteriously by the kettle-drums:

pp

The Scherzo theme is developed through motivic expansion of its last three notes:

There is a steady accumulation of tension until the orchestra, in a blaze of light, surges into the triumphal Allegro in C major.

Beethoven achieves dramatic contrasts of color through his changes of mode. The first movement is in a somber minor. The second, with its Classical serenity, is in major. The third, save for the jovial Trio, returns to minor. Then the dark C minor is dispelled for good with the upsurge of the finale. At this point three instruments make their appearance for the first time in the symphonies of the Classical Viennese school—piccolo, double bassoon, and trombone, lending brilliance and body to the orchestral sound.

Fourth movement
Side 10/3, cont. (S)
Side 12/3, cont. (E I)

The fourth movement is a monumental sonata form in which Beethoven overcomes what would seem to be an insuperable difficulty: to fashion an ending that will sustain the tension of what has gone before. Rhythmic energy, bigness of conception, and orchestral sonority carry the work to its overpowering conclusion. Two themes in C major are opposed to one in G. The opening idea is based on a chord-and-scale

pattern. This is followed by a theme that serves as a bridge from C to

G major. The contrasting key of G major is represented by a vigorous theme containing triplets:

There follows a closing theme (codetta) played by clarinets and violas. It rounds off the Exposition with a decisive gesture:

The Development is marked by dynamic rhythm and free modulation. Then—an amazing stroke!—Beethoven brings back the "three shorts and a long" as they appeared in the third movement. This bringing back of material from an earlier movement gives the symphony its cyclical form. He deliberately allows the momentum to slacken so that he may build up tension against the upsurge of the Recapitulation, which is followed by an extensive coda fashioned from materials already heard. The pace accelerates steadily up to the concluding Presto. There is a final outcropping of the basic rhythm. The symphonic stream at the very end becomes an overwhelming torrent as the Tonic chord—source and goal of all activity—is hurled forth by the orchestra again and again.

The Pathétique Sonata

As in the case of the *Moonlight* and the *Appassionata,* the title of the *Piano Sonata in C minor,* Opus 13—*Pathétique*—was not Beethoven's. Such fanciful names were frequently added by music publishers in order to stimulate sales. If they caught on as they did, it was because they expressed something of what this music meant to those who heard it.

First movement
Side 9/1 (S)
Side 11/1 (E I)

Certainly the quality of Beethovenian pathos is manifest from the first chords of the slow introduction. Marked Grave (solemn), this celebrated opening has something fantasy-like about it, as if Beethoven had captured here the passionate intensity that so affected his listeners when he improvised at the keyboard. Notice the dotted rhythm that contributes to the solemnity of these measures, and the contrary motion: when the melody ascends in the first measure, the bass line descends—and vice versa. The chord pattern is repeated at a higher level in measures 2 and 3 (ascending sequence):

Striking, too, are the contrasts between forte and piano. This type of contrast, an essential feature of Beethoven's dynamism, is used with maximum effectiveness a little further on when it is combined with a change of register: fortissimo chords in the bass are contrasted with a softly expressive melody in the treble. All in all this introduction, written on the threshold of the nineteenth century (1799), speaks a powerful language new to piano music. It ends with a descending chromatic scale and the instruction "attacca subito il Allegro" (attack the Allegro immediately).

The movement proper, marked Allegro di molto e con brio (very fast and with vigor), opens in the home key—C minor—with an impetuous idea that climbs to its peak and descends, while the left hand maintains the rumble of a sustained tremolo in the bass.

A bridge passage modulates, leading to the second theme in E-flat minor, whose gentle lyricism offers an effective contrast to the first. This is a supplicating melody that leaps from the bass register to the treble, which involves crossing the hands.

A third theme in E flat, the relative major key, moves steadily upward in a gradual crescendo; a codetta rounds off the Exposition. Before proceeding with the next section Beethoven brings back the dramatic theme of the introduction, like a fleeting reminiscence. In the Development he skillfully combines the first theme of the Allegro with the theme of the introduction:

For a while the two hands reverse their roles as the left hand carries the melody while the right takes over the tremolo. A transitional passage that descends from high F to a low C leads back to the home key of C minor. In the Recapitulation the material is restated. The second theme is transposed not to the home key but to F minor. This makes possible an effective return to the home key when the third theme appears in C minor. Very dramatic, just before the end of the movement, is a brief reminder of the slow introduction, followed by a precipitous cadence in the home key.

Throughout Beethoven uses the resources of the instrument most imaginatively. In addition to the contrasts we have mentioned between higher and lower register, as well as between soft and loud, he exploits the somber coloring of the bass, the rich sound of full chords, the brilliance of rapid scale passages, the excitement of a sustained tremolo, and the power of a slowly gathering crescendo allied with a gradual climb in pitch.

Second movement
Side 9/2 (S)
Side 11/2 (E I)

The second movement is the famous Adagio cantabile (slow and song-ful) which shows off the piano's ability to sing. A lyric melody is introduced in the middle register over a simple accompaniment. Here is the combination of inwardness and strength that impelled nineteenth-century writers to describe the Beethovenian slow movement as a "hymnic adagio":

This melody alternates with two contrasting sections, giving an A-B-A-C-A structure. Urgency is added to the third idea (C) by triplet rhythm, sudden accents, crescendos, and dramatic arpeggios deep in the bass. The principal melody is repeated with more elaborate figuration. A beautiful coda leads to the pianissimo ending.

Third movement
Side 9/3 (S)
Side 11/3 (E I)

Beethoven in this sonata abandons the usual four-movement scheme; the third is the final movement. This is a rondo, to whose principal theme the C-minor tonality imparts a darker coloring that sets it apart from the usually cheerful rondo-finales of Haydn and Mozart. With such a point

of departure Beethoven constructs a movement with more drama to it than had been customary in the rondo. The principal theme alternates with two other ideas in the pattern A-B-A-C-A-B-A, with a codetta after the B section and a coda at the end. The frame is spacious; within it, lyric episodes alternate with dramatic.

The *Pathétique* has been a favorite for generations. In the hands of a great artist it stands revealed as one of Beethoven's most personal sonatas.

Chronologically Beethoven's life fell in almost equal parts in the eighteenth and nineteenth centuries. His career bridged the transition from the old society to the new. The sum of his message was freedom. By freedom, though, he understood not romantic revolt but the inner discipline that alone constitutes freedom. His music stems from a Promethean struggle for self-realization. It is the expression of a titanic force, the affirmation of an all-conquering will.

45 Classical Chamber Music

> "No other form of music can delight our senses with such exquisite beauty of sound, or display so clearly to our intelligence the intricacies and adventures of its design."
>
> — HENRY HADOW

By *chamber music* is meant ensemble music for from two to about eight or nine instruments with one player to the part, as distinct from orchestral music, in which a single instrumental part is presented by anywhere from two to eighteen players. The essential trait of chamber music is its intimacy and refinement; its natural setting is the home. In this domain we find neither the surge and thunder of the symphony nor the grand gesture of the operatic stage. The drama is of an inward kind. Each instrument is expected to assert itself to the full, but the style of playing differs from that of the solo virtuoso. Where the virtuoso is encouraged to exalt his own personality, the chamber-music player functions as part of a team.

The Classical era saw the golden age of chamber music. Haydn and Mozart, Beethoven, and Schubert established the true chamber-music style, which is in the nature of a friendly conversation among equals. The central

Chamber music is in the nature of a friendly conversation among equals. A painting by Jack Levine (b. 1915), **String Quartette.** *(The Metropolitan Museum of Art; Arthur H. Hearn Fund, 1942.)*

Instrumental combinations

position in Classical chamber music was held by the string quartet. Consisting of first and second violins, viola, and cello, this group came to represent the ideal type of happy comradeship among instruments, lending itself to music of exquisite detail and purity of style. Other favored combinations were the duo sonata—piano and violin or piano and cello; the trio—piano, violin, and cello; and the quintet, usually consisting of a combination of string or wind instruments, or a string quartet and solo instrument such as the piano or clarinet. The age produced, too, some memorable examples of chamber music for larger groups—sextet, septet, and octet.

Schubert: *The* Trout Quintet

One of the most popular of Schubert's chamber works, the *Trout Quintet* dates from 1819, when the composer was twenty-two. He had just completed a happy journey through upper Austria, whose landscape pervades this music. In the course of the trip he was asked to make his song *Die Forelle* (The Trout) available to players of chamber music. Schubert responded with the *Quintet in A major* for piano and strings, whose fourth movement consists of a set of variations on the melody of the song.

In a quintet for piano and strings, a natural opposition ensues between the piano sound and that of the string mass. Schubert, significantly, strengthened the string group. Instead of writing for the usual quartet he employed a violin, viola, cello, and double bass.

IV: Theme and Variations
Side 9/4 (S)
Side 2/3 (E II)

The most popular movement is the set of variations on *Die Forelle*. The theme is announced in D major by the first violin, against a background of the other string instruments:

Variation 1 assigns the melody to the piano against arpeggios in the strings. In Variation 2 the viola sings the tune against exciting arabesques in the upper register of the violin. Variation 3 shifts the melody to the double bass against elaborate running passages on the piano. In these three variations the melody remains unchanged. The next two variations present it with changes of register, dynamics, harmony, melodic outline, rhythm, and type of accompaniment. Variation 4 shifts to D minor and triplet rhythm, and is marked by some bewitching modulations, as is Variation 5, which begins in B-flat major. In the sixth and final variation Schubert returns to the mood of *Die Forelle* by using the rippling figure of the original piano accompaniment to the song.

Remaining movements

The other movements raise no issues that we have not already touched upon. The opening Allegro vivace in A, a cheerful movement in ⁴⁄₄ time, is followed by an Andante in ¾ in F that looks back to the quietude of the eighteenth-century slow movement and shows striking changes of key. The Scherzo is a Presto in A, in ¾ time; it makes an effective contrast with the Theme and Variations that follow. The fifth movement is an Allegro giusto (fast, in strict time) in ²⁄₄, in the home key of A: a beautiful rondo in Hungarian style. The prevailing optimism of Schubert's early twenties is reflected throughout the work.

Chamber music holds out to the listener a very special musical experience. It offers him delights that no other branch of music can duplicate.

FIVE

Medieval, Renaissance, and Baroque Music

"Music was originally discreet, seemly, simple, masculine, and of good morals. Have not the moderns rendered it lascivious beyond measure?" — JACOB OF LIÈGE (*fourteenth century*)

46 Harmony and Counterpoint: Musical Texture

"Ours is an age of texture." — GEORGE DYSON

In writings on music we encounter frequent references to the fabric or texture. Such comparisons between music and cloth are not as unreasonable as may at first appear, since the melodic lines may be thought of as so many threads that make up the musical fabric. This fabric may be one of several types.

Monophonic Texture

The simplest is *monophonic* or single-voice texture. ("Voice" refers to an individual part or line even when we speak of instrumental music, a reminder of the fact that all music stems from vocal origins.) Here the melody is heard without either a harmonic accompaniment or other vocal lines. Attention is focused on the single line. All music up to about a thousand years ago, of which we have any knowledge, was monophonic.

To this day the music of the Oriental world—of China, Japan, India, Java, Bali, and the Arab nations—is largely monophonic. The melody may be accompanied by a variety of rhythm and percussion instruments that embellish it, but there is no third dimension of depth or perspective such as harmony alone confers upon a melody. To make up for this lack the single line, being the sole bearer of musical meaning, takes on great complexity and finesse. The monophonic music of the Orient boasts subtleties of pitch and refinements of rhythm unknown in our music.

Polyphonic Texture

When two or more melodic lines are combined we have a *polyphonic* or many-voiced texture. Here the music derives its expressive power and its interest from the interplay of the several lines. Polyphonic texture is based on counterpoint. This term comes from the Latin *punctus contra punctum,* "point against point" or "note against note"—that is to say, one musi-

Counterpoint cal line against the other. *Counterpoint* is the art and science of combining in a single texture two or more simultaneous melodic lines, each with a rhythmic life of its own.

It was a little over a thousand years ago that European musicians hit upon the device of combining two or more lines simultaneously. At this point Western art music parted company from the monophonic Orient. There ensued a magnificent flowering of polyphonic art that came to its high point in the fifteenth and sixteenth centuries. This development of counterpoint took place at a time when composers were mainly preoccupied with religious choral music, which by its very nature is many-voiced.

Homophonic Texture

In the third type of texture a single voice takes over the melodic interest while the accompanying voices surrender their individuality and become blocks of harmony, the chords that support, color, and enhance the principal part. Here we have a single-melody-with-chords or *homophonic* texture. Again the listener's interest is directed to a single line; but this line, unlike that of Oriental music, is conceived in relation to a harmonic background. Homophonic texture is familiar to all; we hear it when the pianist plays the melody with his right hand while the left sounds the chords, or when the singer or violinist carries the tune against a harmonic accompaniment on the piano. Homophonic texture, then, is based on harmony, just as polyphonic texture is based on counterpoint.

We have said that melody is the horizontal aspect of music while harmony is the vertical. The comparison with the warp and woof of a fabric consequently has real validity. The horizontal threads, the melodies, are held together by the vertical threads, the harmonies. Out of their interaction comes a weave that may be light or heavy, coarse or fine.

The three types of texture are apparent from the look of the music on the page:

A composition need not use one texture or another exclusively. For example, a symphonic movement may present a theme against a homophonic texture. In the development section, however, the texture is apt to become increasingly contrapuntal. So, too, in a homophonic piece the composer may enhance the effect of the principal melody through an interesting play of counterthemes and counterrhythms in the accompanying parts. This is the case in the best orchestral and piano music of the Classic-Romantic period.

The problem of texture is related too to the general style of an era. There was a great shifting of interest from polyphonic to homophonic music around the year 1600. Contrapuntal and harmonic texture existed side by side, the one influencing the other. After 1750 and throughout the Classic-Romantic period, composers emphasized the homophonic aspect of music over the contrapuntal. A reaction set in with the twentieth century, which turned back to independent part writing. We may sum up the various periods of music history, from the standpoint of texture, as follows:

Before the tenth century A.D.	monophonic
From around 1000 to 1600	polyphonic (contrapuntal)
1600–1750	polyphonic-homophonic
1750–1900	homophonic; contrapuntal procedures absorbed into orchestral and chamber music
Since 1900	revival of interest in polyphonic texture

We have studied the sonata-symphony and other forms that stemmed out of the homophonic-harmonic period. In subsequent chapters we will examine the great forms of polyphonic music.

Devices of Counterpoint

Imitation

When several independent lines are combined, composers try to give unity and shape to the texture. A basic procedure for achieving this end is *imitation,* in which a subject or motive is presented in one voice and then restated in another. While the imitating voice restates the theme, the first voice continues with counterpoint. This continuing repetition of an idea by all the voices is musically most effective. It is of the essence in contrapuntal thinking. We have spoken of the vertical and horizontal threads in musical texture. To these imitation adds a third, the diagonal, as is apparent from the following example:

How long is the statement that is to be imitated? This varies considerably. It may be the entire length of a melodic line that runs from the beginning to end of a piece. Or the imitation may occur intermittently. When the whole length of a melodic line is imitated, we have a strict type *Canon.* of composition known as a *canon.* The name comes from the Greek word for "law" or "order." Each phrase heard in the leading voice is repeated almost immediately in an imitating voice throughout the length of the work. The most popular form of canon is the round, in which each voice enters in succession with the same melody. A *round,* therefore, is a canon for voices at the unison or octave. Composers do not often cast an entire piece or movement in the shape of a canon. What they do is to use canonic devices as effects in all sorts of pieces. The example of diagonal texture just given shows canonic imitation as it occurs in the final movement of César Franck's *Sonata for Violin and Piano.* Since this canon is supported by harmonies in the piano part, it is obvious that Franck here combines contrapuntal and harmonic texture.

Contrapuntal writing is marked by a number of devices that have *Inversion* flourished for centuries. *Inversion* is a species of treatment in which the melody is turned upside down; that is, it follows the same intervals but in the opposite direction. Where the melody originally moved up by a third, the inversion moves down a third. Where it descended by a fourth, it now ascends a fourth. Thus, D–F–C (up a third, down a fourth), inverted

Augmentation becomes D–B–E (down a third, up a fourth). *Augmentation* consists of presenting a theme in longer time values. A quarter note may become a half, a half note a whole, and so on. In consequence, if the tempo remains the same, the theme in its new version sounds slower. *Diminution* consists of presenting a theme in shorter time values. A whole note may become a half, a half note a quarter, which, at the same tempo, makes the theme sound faster. *Retrograde,* also known as *cancrizans* or *crab motion,* means to state the melody backwards. If the original sequence of notes reads B–D–G–F, the imitation reads F–G–D–B. Retrograde-and-inversion imitates the theme by turning it upside down and backwards at the same time. It should be added that, while imitation is an important element in contrapuntal writing, not all counterpoint is imitative.

Diminution

Retrograde

Musical Texture and the Listener

The different types of texture require different types of listening. Homophonic music poses no special problem to music lovers of today. They are able to differentiate between the principal melody and its attendant harmonies, and to follow the interrelation of the two. They are helped in this by the fact that most of the music they have heard since their childhood consists of melody and chords.

The case is different with polyphonic music, which is not apt to appeal to those who listen with half an ear. Here we must be aware of the independent lines as they flow alongside each other, each in its own rhythm. This requires much greater concentration on our part. Only by dint of repeated hearings do we learn to follow the individual voices and to separate each within the contrapuntal web.

As an exercise in listening contrapuntally let us take a simple example: the fourth movement of Bach's cantata *Wachet auf, ruft uns die Stimme* (Awake, a Voice Is Calling). The tenors are singing the chorale melody, mostly in quarter notes. Above them the violins are playing a florid counterpoint of a livelier nature. Below them the cellos and double basses are carrying the bass line, mostly in quarter and eighth notes. Thus the three lines are distinct not only in register but also in rhythm and color. It is well to listen to the piece several times, concentrating first on each voice alone, then on any two, finally on all three. One becomes aware, in following the three planes of movement, of the illusion of space which it is the unique capacity of counterpoint to create; of the fascinating tensions, both musical and psychological, brought into being by the simultaneous unfolding of several lines.

Side 14/2 (S)
Side 5/3 (E I)

Contrapuntal music does not yield its secrets as readily as do the less complex kinds. By the same token it challenges our attention and holds our interest. With each rehearing we seem to discover another of its facets.

47 The Remote Past

"Nothing is more characteristic of human nature than to be soothed by sweet modes and stirred up by their opposites. Infants, youths, and old people as well are so naturally attuned to musical modes by a kind of spontaneous feeling that no age is without delight in sweet song." — BOETHIUS (c. 480–524)

The relics of the ancient civilizations—Sumer, Babylonia, Egypt—bear witness to a flourishing musical art. In the antique world, religious myth and tradition ascribed divine powers to music. The walls of Thebes rose and those of Jericho fell to the sound of music. David played his lyre to cure the melancholy of Saul. In the temple at Jerusalem the Levites, who were the musicians, "being arrayed in fine linen, having cymbals and psalteries and harps, stood at the east end of the altar, and with them an hundred and twenty priests sounding with trumpets."

Only a few fragments have descended to us of the music of antiquity. The centuries have forever silenced the sounds that echoed through the Athenian amphitheater and the Roman circus. Those sounds and the attitudes they reflected, in Greece and throughout the Mediterranean world, formed the subsoil out of which flowered the music of later ages. They became part of the heritage of the West.

Gregorian Chant

Music functioned in the Christian Church from its earliest days. St. Paul exhorted the Ephesians to be filled with the Spirit by "speaking to yourselves in psalms and hymns and spiritual songs, singing and making melody in your heart to the Lord." The music of the Church absorbed Greek, Hebrew, and Syrian influences. It became necessary in time to assemble the ever growing body of chants into an organized liturgy. The task extended over several generations but is traditionally associated with the name of Pope Gregory the Great, who reigned from 590 to 604.

Melody   Like the music of the Greeks and Hebrews from which it descended, *Gregorian chant* (also known as *plainchant* or *plainsong*) consists of a single-line melody. In other words, it is monophonic in texture and does not know the third dimension of harmony and counterpoint. Its freely flowing vocal line is subtly attuned to the inflections of the Latin text. Gregorian melody is free from regular accent. It embodies what may be called prose rhythm in music, or free-verse rhythm, as distinguished from metrical-poetry rhythm such as we find in the regularly accented measures of duple or triple meter.

The Gregorian melodies, numbering more than three thousand, were worked over in the course of generations until they took on their tradi-

The undulating line of Gregorian chant parallels the curvilinear movement which animates early Romanesque art. A miniature from the Echternach Gospels, c. 700 A.D., showing the Symbol of St. Mark.

tional shape. They formed a body of anonymous melody whose roots reached deep into the spiritual life of the folk; a treasure of religious song which, as someone well said, relates to "Everyman rather than Me." Gregorian chant avoids the excitement of wide leaps and dynamic contrasts. Its gentle rise and fall constitute a kind of disembodied musical speech, "a prayer on pitch." Free from the shackles of regular phrase structure, the continuous, undulating vocal line is the counterpart in sound of the sinuous traceries of Romanesque art and architecture.

At first the Gregorian chants were handed down orally from one generation to the next. As the number of chants increased, singers needed to

Neumes

be reminded of the general outlines of the different melodies. Thus came into being the *neumes* (see p. 217), little ascending and descending signs that were written above the words to suggest the course of the melody.

Text settings

As far as the setting of text is concerned, the melodies fall into three main classes: *syllabic,* that is, one note to each syllable; *neumatic,* generally with groups of two to four notes to a syllable, each group represented by a single neume in the original notation; and *melismatic,* with a single syllable extending over longer groups of notes, as in the setting of the word *Alleluia.* The melismatic style, descended from the rhapsodic improvisations of the Orient, became a prominent feature of Gregorian chant and exerted a strong influence on Western music.

The Medieval Modes

The melody patterns of Gregorian chant were classified according to modes. (A mode, it will be recalled, is a specific pattern of whole and half steps.) The Medieval or church modes were groups of eight tones, each of which had its central tone. There were eight modes, four *authentic* ("original") and four *plagal* ("derived"). The central or *final* tone, indicated in the following examples by a whole note with vertical lines on either side, was the first tone of the authentic modes, the fourth tone in the plagal. In addition, each mode had a *dominant,* a secondary tonal center, indicated in the examples by an ordinary whole note:

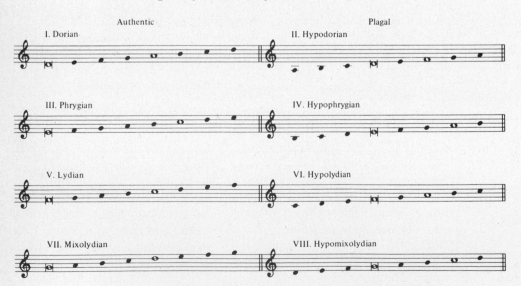

It will be noticed that if Mode I, the Dorian, is sung with a B flat it corresponds to the natural minor scale, while Mode V, the Lydian, with a B flat corresponds to the major. Thus modal harmony bore within it the seeds of the major-minor harmony that ultimately supplanted it. Notice, too, that the authentic modes can be played on the white keys of the piano, whereas to build the major or minor scales from the same starting points we would have to use sharps or flats.

The church modes served as the basis for European art music for a thousand years. With the development of polyphony, or many-voiced music, a harmonic system evolved based on the modes. The adjective *modal* consequently refers to the type of melody and harmony that prevailed in the early and later Middle Ages. It is frequently used in opposition to *tonal,* which refers to the harmony based on the major-minor tonality that supplanted the modes.

A Gregorian Melody

Side 11/3 (S)
Side 1/1 (E 1)

A beautiful example of Gregorian style is the Introit from the prayers for the Feast of the Assumption. (*Introit,* related to the Latin word for "entrance," was originally a chant accompanying the entrance of the priest to the altar.) The text consists of two statements (stanzas), each four lines long:

Gaudeamus omnes in Domino,	Let us all rejoice in the Lord,
diem festum celebrantes sub honore Mariae Virginis:	Celebrating a feast-day in honor of the Blessed Virgin Mary,
des cujus Assumptione gaudent Angeli,	For whose Assumption the angels rejoice
et collaudant Filium Dei.	And give praise to the Son of God.
Eructavit cor meum verbum bonum:	My heart hath uttered a good word:
dico ego opera mea regi.	I speak my words to the King.
Gloria Patri, et Filio, et Spiritu Sancto.	Glory be to the Father, Son, and Holy Ghost.
Sicut erat in principio, et nunc et semper,	As it was in the beginning, now, and forever,
et in saecula saeculorum. Amen.	World without end. Amen.

The evolution of notation in Western music

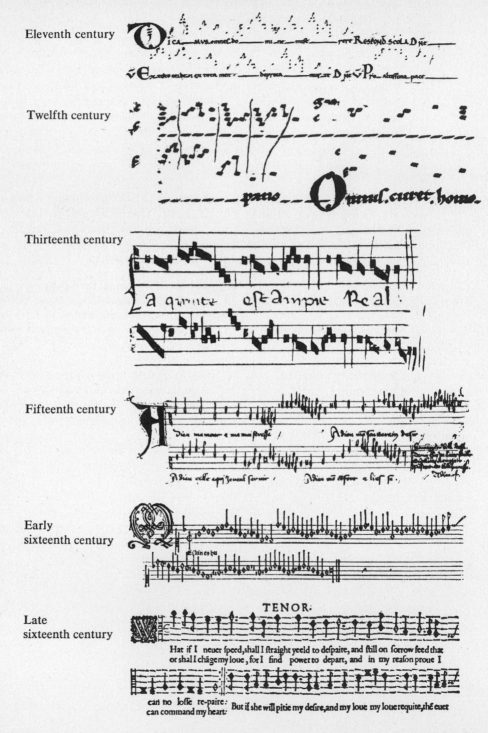

Eleventh century

Twelfth century

Thirteenth century

Fifteenth century

Early
sixteenth century

Late
sixteenth century

Dorian mode   The melody is in Mode I (Dorian), corresponding to the eight white keys on the piano from D to D. Yet in the first stanza a B flat is used instead of a B natural. This anticipates the natural minor scale that was to come into use many centuries later.

The melody lies within a narrow range and moves by step or narrow leap. It is more highly organized than is apparent at a first hearing, consisting of melodic cells that are repeated either exactly or somewhat *Motivic* varied. For example, the motive under the bracket (A) recurs in various *shape* guises on the words "Domino," "honore," and several others. As a result, the upward leap of a fourth common to all these becomes a distinguishing feature that imparts unity to the melodic line. Here is how this plainchant looks in Gregorian notation:

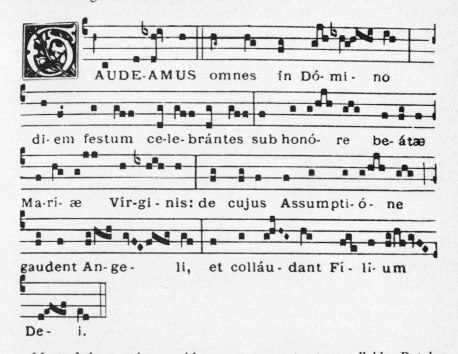

Most of the text is set with one or two notes to a syllable. But key words are extended for several notes—for example, "Domino" (Lord), "Angeli" (angels) and "Filium Dei" (Son of God)—which serves to *Melismas* bring them into prominence. This melismatic treatment is a feature of the first section. The second, by contrast, is set syllabically—that is, mostly one note to a syllable. The melody of the second section consequently sounds less ornate, more direct. After the second section we hear again the first, which gives the piece an A–B–A shape. This return of the first melody rounds out the form, achieving an effect of symmetry and balance. *Unmeasured* Throughout, the rhythm is unmeasured; it follows the natural flow of the *rhythm* Latin and might be described as free rhythm, distinguished from metrical rhythm as prose is from poetry. We do not normally think of prose as rhythmic; yet in the hands of a master, poetic prose takes on a rhythmic life of its own. This is what we find in Gregorian chant.

Cadences   The note at the end of each text line is especially important since it serves as a resting-place or cadence. The four lines of the first stanza end, respectively, on A, A, F, and D. The four lines of the second stanza end on A, D, A, and F. These are the principal tones of this mode, and they also outline what we know as the D-minor chord. We can thus identify in Gregorian chant the beginnings of concepts about harmony and form that were not to mature until centuries later.

The Gregorian melodies are remarkable for their unhurried flow, their organic unity, and the way they mold themselves to the natural inflections of the text. Our richest legacy from the period of pure monophonic texture, they nourished fifteen hundred years of European folk, popular, and art music. They bring us as close as we shall ever come to the lost musical art of the ancient Mediterranean culture—the art of Greece, Syria, and Palestine.

48 The Later Middle Ages

"There are many new things in music that will appear altogether plausible to our descendants." — JEAN DE MURIS (1319)

The Rise of Polyphony

Romanesque period   Within the Romanesque period (c. 850–1150) took place the single most important development in the history of Western music: the emergence of polyphony as a stylistic factor of prime importance. This occurred at about the same time that European painting was developing the science of perspective. Thus hearing and seeing in depth came into European culture together, and must be accounted among its most significant products.

Once several melodic lines proceeded side by side, there could no longer be the flexible prose rhythms of single-line music. Polyphony brought about the emergence of regular meters that enabled the different voices to keep together. This music had to be written down in a way that would indicate precisely the rhythm and the pitch. In this way evolved our modern staff,

Exact notation   whose lines and spaces made it possible to indicate the exact pitch, and whose notes, by their appearance, could indicate the duration of each sound.

With the development of exact notation, music took a long step from being an art of improvisation and oral tradition to one that was carefully planned and that could be preserved accurately. Henceforth a musical

Minstrels were welcome at the court of Alfonso X of Castile, provided they lived up to the king's high artistic expectations. A Spanish book painting from the thirteenth century depicting two flutists.

work could be studied by many musicians; the creative experience of one could nourish all the others. The period of anonymous creation characteristic of folk art drew to a close. The individual composer appeared upon the scene.

Gothic era   This development took shape during the Gothic era (c. 1150–1450). The period saw a flourishing secular music in the art of the minstrels and troubadours of the feudal courts. More important, it witnessed the rise of the cathedrals with their choirs and organs. The mastery of construction that made possible the building of those mighty edifices had its counterpart in music. The new science of counterpoint was brought to heights of virtuosity. The learned musicians, for the most part monks and priests, mastered the art of constructing extended musical works through the various devices of counterpoint. Their prime interest at this point was in the structural combining of musical elements, which explains the derivation of the word "composer" from the Latin *componere,* "to put together." The creative musician of the late Gothic period thought of himself primarily as a master builder.

The Notre Dame School

Organum   The earliest kind of polyphonic music was called *organum*. This developed when the custom arose of adding to the Gregorian melody a second or organal voice that ran parallel to the plainchant at the interval of a fifth or a fourth above or below. When these lines were duplicated an octave above, there resulted a piece of four voices that moved in parallel octaves, fifths, and fourths, as in the following example of ninth-century organum:

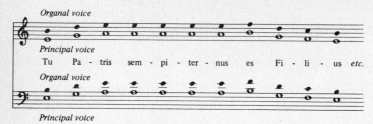

The way was now open for the development of a polyphonic art in which the individual voices moved with ever greater independence, not only in parallel but also in contrary motion. Leaders in this development were the composers whose center was the Cathedral of Notre Dame in Paris during the twelfth and thirteenth centuries. The two outstanding members of the Notre Dame school are the first composers of polyphonic music whose names are known to us: Leonin, who lived in the latter part of the twelfth century, and his disciple Perotin, who was active somewhere between 1180 and 1230.

It was self-evident to the Medieval mind that the new must be founded on the old. Therefore the composer of organum based his piece on a pre-existing Gregorian chant. While the tenor sang the melody in enormously *Leonin*   long notes, the upper voice moved freely above it. Here, for example, is an extensive melisma by Leonin over the first note of a Gregorian melody:

In both architecture and music, the Gothic period saw advances in techniques of construction. The Cathedral of Notre Dame, Paris.

Naturally, in this long-drawn-out version the Gregorian chant was no longer recognizable as a melody. Its presence was symbolic, anchoring the new in the old, inspiring and guiding the added voice.

Perotin

While Leonin limited himself to counterpoint in two parts, Perotin extended the technique by writing for three and four voices. His music shows a tendency toward shorter melodic phrases, clear-cut rhythms, at times even a vaguely "major" feeling (comparable to the "minor" atmosphere we noted in our example of Gregorian chant). His larger compositions take on a spacious resonance that evokes the echoing vaults of the Gothic cathedral. He is remembered today as the foremost member of a school that laid the foundation for a magnificent flowering of polyphonic art.

The Motet

The *motet* emerged as the most important form of early polyphonic music. This term is applied loosely to a choral composition, sacred or secular, with or without instrumental accompaniment.

The early motet illustrates how the Medieval composer based his own work on what had been handed down from the past. He selected a passage of Gregorian chant and, keeping the notes intact, rearranged them in a recognizable rhythmic pattern. He thus fashioned two or three phrases,

Cantus firmus

separated by rests, that he could repeat as many times as he needed to fill out the length of the piece, while above it he added one, two, or three countermelodies of his own. The basic theme, sung by the tenor, was known as *cantus firmus* (fixed melody), and served as a point of departure for his own creativity. The second, third, and fourth voices were known, respectively, as *duplum, triplum,* and *quadruplum.*

"Motet" derives from the French *mot* (word), referring to the words that were joined to the added parts. Duplum and triplum might sing two different Latin texts at the same time; or one might sing Latin words while another sang French. In this way a sacred text might be combined with a quite secular—even racy—one. The basic Gregorian theme, hidden

European painting moved from the flat surface to perspective as music passed from monophonic to polyphonic texture. A painting by Petrus Crescentius, **World of Sports in the Later Middle Ages,** from the *Book of Rural Profits. (Courtesy of The Trustees, Pierpont Morgan Library.)*

among the voices and repeated over and over (like an ostinato in later music) fused these disparate elements into a unity—if not in the listener's ear, at least in the composer's mind.

The Mass

The Mass is the most solemn ritual of the Roman Catholic Church. It constitutes a re-enactment of the sacrifice of Christ. The name is derived from the Latin *missa,* "dismissal" (of the congregation at the end of the service).

The aggregation of prayers that make up the Mass falls into two categories: those that vary from day to day throughout the church year, the *Proper;* and those that remain the same in every Mass, the *Ordinary.* The liturgy, which reached its present form about nine hundred years ago, provides Gregorian melodies for each item of the ceremony. With the rise of polyphony composers began to weave additional voices around the plainchant. They concentrated on the prayers that were an invariable part of the service rather than on the variable items that were heard only once during the liturgical year. Thus came into prominence the five sections that the public knows as the musical setting of the Mass: Kyrie, Gloria, Credo, Sanctus, and Agnus Dei. (Today these sections of the Mass are recited or sung in the language of the country.) The opening section, the Kyrie—a prayer for mercy—dates from the early centuries of Christianity, as its original Greek text attests. It is an A-B-A form that consists of nine invocations: three "Kyrie eleison" (Lord, have mercy), three "Christe eleison" (Christ, have mercy), and again three "Kyrie eleison." There follows the "Gloria in excelsis Deo" (Glory to God in the highest). This is a joyful hymn of praise which is omitted in the penitential seasons, Advent and Lent. The third movement is the confession of faith, "Credo in unum Deum, Patrem omnipotentem" (I believe in one God, the Father Almighty). It includes also the "Et incarnatus est" (And He became flesh), the "Crucifixus" (He was crucified), and the "Et resurrexit" (And He rose again). Fourth is "Sanctus, Sanctus, Sanctus" (Holy, Holy, Holy), which concludes with the "Hosanna in excelsis" (Hosanna in the highest) and the "Benedictus qui venit in nomine Domini" (Blessed is He who comes in the name of the Lord), after which the "Hosanna in excelsis" is repeated as a kind of refrain. The fifth and last part, "Agnus Dei, qui tollis peccata mundi" (Lamb of God, who takes away the sins of the world), is sung three times. Twice it concludes with "Miserere nobis" (Have mercy on us), and the third time with the prayer "Dona nobis pacem" (Grant us peace).

Sections of the Mass

Like the motet, the polyphonic setting of the Mass was usually based on a fragment of Gregorian chant. This became the cantus firmus that served as the foundation of the work, supporting the florid patterns that the other voices wove around it. When used in all the movements of a Mass,

Cantus firmus

the Gregorian cantus firmus helped to weld the work into a unity. As we noted in our discussion of organum and the motet, the combining of a composer's original creation with a pre-existing melody appealed to the Medieval mind. It provided him with the fixed element that he could embellish with all the resources of his artistry, somewhat as, centuries later, did the theme and variations.

Requiem   Of the Masses for special services the most important is the Mass for the Dead, the Requiem, which is sung at funeral and memorial services. We discussed Verdi's magnificent setting in Chapter 34. The name, you will recall, comes from the opening verse "Requiem aeternam dona eis, Domine" (Rest eternal grant unto them, O Lord). Included are prayers in keeping with the solemnity of the occasion, among them the awesome evocation of the Last Judgment, "Dies irae" (That Day of Wrath).

The history of the Mass as an art form extends over the better part of eight hundred years. In that time it garnered for itself some of the greatest music ever written.

Machaut: *Kyrie from the* Messe de Notre Dame

The breakup of the feudal social structure brought with it new concepts of life, art, and beauty. This ferment was reflected in the musical style that made its appearance at the beginning of the fourteenth century in France and somewhat later in Italy, known as *ars nova* (new art). The music of the French *ars nova* shows greater refinement than the *ars antiqua* (old

His life   art) which it displaced. Its outstanding figure was the French composer-poet Guillaume de Machaut (c. 1300–77). He took holy orders at an early age, became secretary to John of Luxemburg, King of Bohemia, and was active at the court of Jean, Duke of Normandy, who subsequently became king of France. He spent his old age as a canon of Rheims, admired as the greatest musician of the time.

Machaut's double career as cleric and courtier impelled him to both religious and secular music. His poetic ballads reveal him as a proponent of the ideals of medieval chivalry—a romantic who, like Sir Thomas Mallory in his lament for King Arthur, exalted the moral and social code of an age that was finished. He was the first known composer to write a complete Mass. It is his most famous work: the *Messe de Notre Dame* (Mass of Our Lady), which tradition associates with the coronation of Charles V at Rheims in 1364. Actually, it was composed years earlier.

The Mass   The work is set for four voices rather than (like the motet discussed in the previous chapter) for three. By this time the two lower voices have moved down to the bass register, where they stand out much more clearly against the upper ones. As a result, the harmonic space has been broadened. The cantus firmus, drawn from a Gregorian chant, is in the tenor part. Notice how Machaut rearranges the chant in a four-note rhythm that is repeated throughout the sections.

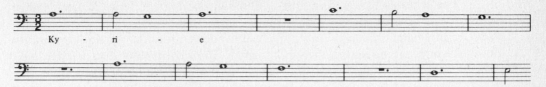

In its new guise the chant is certainly not perceptible to the ear, especially as it is buried in the counterpoint. Its importance lies in its use as a symbolic bond between the composer's work and the sacred chant. In a more practical way, it served as a form-building element in the construction of the piece.

Side 11/4 (S)
Side 1/2 (E 1)

As is customary, the movement is in three sections: "Kyrie eleison," "Christe eleison," and "Kyrie eleison." The third section is not a repetition of the first, as might have been the case in the Classic-Romantic era. There are only two words of text in each section, the final "e" of "Kyrie" or "Christe" being sustained in an extended melisma until the word "eleison" enters at the cadence. The opening "Kyrie" begins with a strong rhythmic stride in triple meter. (Incidentally, the Medieval mind— with its love of symbols—regarded triple meter as more perfect than duple because the number three represented the Holy Trinity.) Machaut here makes no attempt to mirror the mood of supplication in the text. This is not so much a plea for mercy as a demand. The impression of power is strengthened by harsh dissonances, which may be reinforced by the clangor of accompanying instruments, such as shawms, sackbuts, and bells.

Accompaniment

It was believed for many years that the religious music of the Middle Ages was sung without instrumental accompaniment. Modern scholarship, however, has recognized the prominent role of instruments in this music. Of course, composers did not begin to indicate which instruments they had in mind until centuries later. The choice at any given performance depended largely on what was available. However, the ancient instruments used in modern recordings of Machaut's Mass give us a fairly accurate idea of the sound he heard in the Cathedral at Rheims.

Cantus firmus

Before each section we hear that portion of Gregorian chant on which its cantus firmus is based. In this way we can savor to the full the contrast between the original chant and the composition that grew out of it:

Gregorian Chant	*Kyrie of the Mass*
monophonic	polyphonic
soft (*p* or *pp*)	loud (*f* or *ff*)
prose rhythm (unmeasured)	metrical rhythm (triple meter)
unaccented	decisive accents
without instrumental background	with instrumental background

The second and third sections are less rhythmic than the first and move at a more moderate pace. The texture is more contrapuntal, unfolding in flowing lines that constantly interweave. In these sections the cantus firmus is arranged in longer units. The final section unites voices and instruments in a powerful sound, almost in a mood of triumph. The cadences at the end of each section consist of the same four notes—D, A, D, A (open fifths and octaves). They strike the ear with a kind of primitive splendor, conjuring up an era that seems much closer to us now than it once did.

Music in the twentieth century has moved steadily away from the major-minor tonality that dominated the Classic-Romantic period. More and more people have come to rediscover this older music, with its austere modal harmonies, its rugged vitality, and its lean, open sound.

The Burgundian School

At the waning of the Middle Ages stands the Burgundian school that flourished in the fifteenth century in the duchy of Charles the Bold. The Burgundian masters abandoned the complexities of Gothic counterpoint in favor of a simpler and more appealing style. They established the practice of basing all movements of the Mass on the same melody, thereby achieving unity within a large-scale architecture. They used the voices in high register along with a mixture of contrasting instruments—double reeds, recorders, viols, trombones—to attain a bright, lustrous tone. Under their influence the intervals of a fifth and fourth—hitherto the basic

Guillaume Dufay (left) and Gilles Binchois. Miniature from a fifteenth-century manuscript.

consonances—were supplemented with the more euphonious third (as from *do* to *mi* or C–E) and sixth (as from *mi* up to *do* or E–C). The Burgundians spearheaded the movement to replace the meandering vocal lines of the past with well-defined melodies and clear-cut rhythms. Their harmony grew ever simpler and more direct, foreshadowing a language based on triads, tonic-dominant relationships, and a sense of key.

Dufay: Alma redemptoris mater

His life

Chief figure of the Burgundian school was Guillaume Dufay (c. 1400–74). Sprung from the peasantry, he brought into art music the charm of folksong. Dufay was a master of intimate lyric forms. He bridged the gap between the late Gothic in France and the Renaissance in Italy, where he lived for nine years. He has been "discovered" by the twentieth century and is much admired by contemporary musicians.

Side 11/5 (S)
Side 1/4 (E 1)

Dufay's style is well exemplified by his *Alma redemptoris mater,* for three voices and instruments. Several important characteristics distinguish this piece from Machaut's. Most important, the cantus firmus based on Gregorian chant has been elevated to the soprano part, where the listener can hear it. Instead of being a mystical symbol, it is now a graceful melody that delights the ear. As a result, this voice dominates the others. Also, instead of following the sacred chant slavishly, Dufay adapts it both rhythmically and melodically to his own expressive purpose, so that it takes on the quality of a popular tune. Compare his version with the original chant:

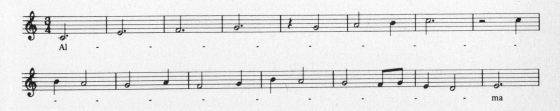

Harmonic change

Equally significant, the open fifths and octaves that impart so harsh a clang to Medieval harmony have been replaced in Dufay's music by more euphonious thirds and sixths, reflecting the humanizing influence of Italy on the rougher style of northern France. As a result, Dufay's harmony impresses us as having moved a considerable distance away from the archaic sound of Machaut's.

Alma redemptoris mater,	Gracious mother of the Redeemer,
quae pervia caeli porta manes,	Abiding at the doors of Heaven,
et stella maris, succurre cadenti,	Star of the sea, aid the falling,
surgere qui curat populo.	Rescue the people who struggle.
Tu quae genuisti, natura mirante,	Thou who, astonishing nature,
tuum sanctum genitorem:	Hast borne thy holy Creator:
Virgo prius ac posterius,	Virgin before and after,
Gabrielis ab ore sumens illud Ave,	Who heard the Ave from the mouth of Gabriel,
peccatorum miserere.	Be merciful to sinners.

The motet opens with an extended melisma on the first vowel of "Alma." Throughout the piece, single words are sustained for series of notes. When words are dissolved in music in this way, the composer is obviously using the text merely as a scaffolding. Dufay's prime concern is the flow of the vocal line.

Textural characteristics The motet is in triple meter and in three sections. The first consists of a single melody, at first unaccompanied, repeated over supporting chords— that is, homophonic texture. The cadences fall on C- and G-major chords, giving the music—despite its modal inflection—a majorlike ring. The second section has a fuller sound. The texture here is contrapuntal, with arresting imitations on the first lines of the second stanza. The third section, beginning with the word "Virgo," returns to the chordal texture of the first. Sustained chords, beginning with "sumens illud Ave," serve as a kind of codetta. The fact that this codetta begins in the middle of a sentence shows how much more preoccupied Dufay is with the music than with the text. The chords have three tones each, but the final ones have four. They look ahead across the centuries to the chords of major-minor harmony.

Accompaniment The motet is accompanied by three old instruments: a *cornett* (not to be confused with the cornet, to which it is not related), a woodwind instrument with a cup-shaped mouthpiece; a *crumhorn,* a woodwind instrument with a double reed enclosed not in the mouthpiece but near its top end; and a *sackbut,* which is an early trombone with an exceedingly narrow bore.

Characteristic are the sweet harmonies and the radiant sonority of the interweaving voices. Dufay introduced a euphony that was new to music. It was one of the signal achievements of his serene art, an art that lies between the twilight of the Middle Ages and the dawn of the Renaissance.

The span from Gregorian chant to Dufay measured almost a thousand years. This was the Gothic age, during which the heritage of the ancient Mediterranean culture was fused with the genius of the rude northern tribes. Out of this union came a new thing into the world: the European tradition.

49 The Renaissance

"I am not pleased with the Courtier if he be not also a musician, and besides his understanding and cunning [in singing] upon the book, have skill in like manner on sundry instruments." — BALDASSARE CASTIGLIONE: *The Courtier* (1528)

The Renaissance (c. 1450–1600) is one of the beautiful if misleading names in the history of culture: beautiful because it implies an awakening of intellectual awareness, misleading because it suggests a sudden rebirth of learning and art after the presumed stagnation of the Middle Ages. History moves continuously rather than by leaps and bounds. The Renaissance was the next phase of a cultural process that, under the leadership of the universities and princely courts, had begun long before.

What the Renaissance does mark is the passing of European society from an exclusively religious orientation to a secular; from an age of unquestioning faith and mysticism to one of belief in reason and scientific inquiry. The focus of man's destiny was seen to be his life on earth rather than in the hereafter. There was a new reliance on the evidence of the senses rather than on tradition and authority. Implied was a new confidence in man's

Philosophical developments

The human form, denied for centuries, was revealed in the Renaissance as a thing of beauty. A statue by Donatello (c. 1386–1466), **David.**

ability to solve his problems and rationally order his world. This awakening found its symbol in the culture of Greek and Roman antiquity. The men of the Renaissance discovered the summit of human wisdom not only in the Church fathers and saints, as their ancestors had done, but also in Homer and Vergil and the ancient philosophers.

Historical developments

Historians used to date the Renaissance from the fall of Constantinople to the Turks in 1453 and the emigration of Greek scholars to the West. It might be better, if a date is needed, to pick that of the invention of printing and paper around the year 1440. Several momentous events set off the new era from the old. The introduction of gunpowder brought to an end the age of knighthood. The development of the compass made possible the voyages of discovery that opened up a new world and demolished old superstitions. The revival of ancient letters was associated with the humanists. This revival had its counterpart in architecture, painting, and sculpture. If the Romanesque found its grand architectural form in the monastery and the Gothic in the cathedral, the Renaissance lavished its constructive energy upon palace and château. The gloomy fortified castles of the Medieval barons gave way to spacious edifices that displayed the harmonious proportions of the classical style. In effect, Renaissance architecture embodied the striving for a gracious and reasoned existence that was the great gesture of the age.

Artistic developments

So, too, the elongated saints and martyrs of medieval painting and sculpture were replaced by the Venus of Botticelli and the Athenian sages of Raphael. Even where artists retained a religious atmosphere, the Mother of Sorrow and the symbols of grief gave way to smiling madonnas —often posed for by very secular ladies—and dimpled cherubs. The human form, denied for centuries, was revealed as a thing of beauty; also as an object of anatomical study. Nature entered painting along with the nude, and with it an intense preoccupation with the laws of perspective and composition. Medieval painting had presented life as an allegory; the Renaissance preferred realism. The Medieval painters posed their figures frontally, impersonally; the Renaissance developed psychological characterization and the art of portraiture. Medieval painting dealt in types; the Renaissance concerned itself with individuals. Space in Medieval painting was organized in a succession of planes over which the eye traveled as over a series of episodes. The Renaissance created unified space and the simultaneous seeing of the whole. It discovered the landscape, created the illusion of distance, and opened up endless vistas upon the physical loveliness of the world.

The Renaissance came to flower in the nation that stood closest to the classical Roman culture. Understandably the great names we associate with its painting and sculpture are predominantly Italian: Donatello (c. 1386–1466), Masaccio (1401–28), Botticelli (1444–1510), Leonardo da Vinci (1452–1519), Michelangelo (1475–1564), Raphael (1483–1520), and Titian (1488–1576). With the masters who lived in the second half

The Renaissance created unified space and the simultaneous seeing of the whole. A painting by Sandro Botticelli (1444–1510), **The Adoration of the Magi.** *(National Gallery of Art, Washington, D.C.)*

of the century, such as Tintoretto (1518–94) and Veronese (1528–88), we approach the world of the early Baroque.

Intellectual developments   The Renaissance achieved a heightened awareness of the human personality. Its turbulence and dynamic force were in marked contrast to the static nature of Medieval society. It gave impetus to the twin currents of rationalism and realism that have prevailed in European culture ever since. Granted that its love of art and beauty existed side by side with tyranny, ignorance, superstition; that its humanism took shape in a scene dominated by treachery and lust. It is the noble usage of history to judge an age by its finest. By that measure this period ranks high. From the multicolored tapestry of Renaissance life emerge figures that have captured the imagination of the world: Lorenzo de' Medici and Ludovico Sforza, Benvenuto Cellini and Machiavelli, Pope Alexander VI and Sir Thomas More, Lucrezia Borgia and Beatrice d'Este. Few centuries can match the sixteenth for its galaxy of great names. The list includes Erasmus (1466–1536) and Martin Luther (1483–1546), Rabelais (1494?–1553) and Cervantes (1547–1616), Marlowe (1564–93) and Shakespeare (1564–1616).

With these men we find ourselves in a world that speaks our language. The Renaissance marks the birth of the modern European temper and of

The painting and poetry of the Renaissance abound in references to music. A painting by Jacopo Tintoretto (1518–94), **Ladies Making Music.**

Western man as we have come to know him. In that turbulent time was shaped the moral and cultural climate we still inhabit.

Sixteenth-Century Music

The painting and poetry of the Renaissance abound in references to music. Nothing more clearly attests to the vast importance of the art in the cultural life of the time. The pageantry of the Renaissance unfolded to a momentous musical accompaniment. Throwing off its Medieval mysticism, music moved toward clarity, simplicity, and a frankly sensuous appeal.

A cappella music

The age achieved an exquisite appreciation of *a cappella* music. (Literally, "for the chapel." This term denotes a vocal work without instrumental accompaniment.) The sixteenth century has come to be regarded as the golden age of the a cappella style. Its polyphony was based on a principle called *continuous imitation*. The motives wandered from vocal line to vocal line within the texture, the voices imitating one another so that the same theme or motive was heard now in the soprano or alto, now in the tenor or bass. There resulted an extremely close-knit musical fabric that was capable of the most subtle and varied effects.

The composers of the Flemish school were pre-eminent in European music from around 1450 to the end of the sixteenth century. They came from the southern Lowlands, which is now Belgium, and from the adjoining provinces of northern France and Burgundy. In their number were several who wrote their names large in the history of music.

50 Josquin des Prez

"He is the master of the notes. They have to do as he bids them; other composers have to do as the notes will." — MARTIN LUTHER

With the Flemish master Josquin des Prez (c. 1450–1521), the transition is complete from the anonymous composer of the Middle Ages, through the shadowy figures of the late Gothic, to the highly individual artist of the Renaissance. He is the first composer who emerges from the mists of history as a fully rounded personality; the first musician, as one historian put it, "who impresses us as having genius."

His life   Josquin studied with the Flemish master Johannes Ockeghem, who exerted a powerful influence on several generations of composers. (We will discuss Josquin's *Lament on the Death of Ockeghem.*) His checkered career led him to Italy, where he served at several ducal courts—especially those of Galeazzo Sforza, Duke of Milan, and Ercole d'Este, Duke of Ferrara—as well as at the Sistine Chapel in Rome. During his stay in Italy his Northern art absorbed the classical virtues of balance and moderation, the sense of harmonious proportion and lucid form that found their archetype in the radiant art of Raphael. After leaving the Papal Chapel he appears to have been active for several years at the court of Louis XII of France. His last appointment was as a canon at the collegiate church of Conde; he was buried in the choir of this church.

His music   The older generation of musicians had been preoccupied with solving the technical problems of counterpoint—problems that fit the intellectual cli-

Josquin des Prez.

JOSQVINVS PRATENSIS.

mate of the waning Middle Ages. Josquin appeared at a time when the humanizing influences of the Renaissance were wafting through Europe. The contrapuntal ingenuity that he inherited from Ockeghem he was able to harness to a higher end—the expression of emotion. The early years of his career were spent in achieving consummate mastery of canonic devices. Thenceforth he was able to advance to a free, continuous imitation of themes that left room for the imaginative development of musical ideas. His music is rich in feeling, in serenely beautiful melody and expressive harmony. Its clarity of structure and humanism bespeak the man of the Renaissance.

Déploration sur la mort de Johan Okeghem

Side 12/1 (S)
Side 1/7 (E 1)

Artists through the ages have created works lamenting the death of a colleague. From the elegy that the Greek poet Bion wrote for his fellow-poet Moschus to Ben Jonson's lines on Shakespeare, from Shelley's lament for Keats in *Adonaïs* to Auden's elegy for Yeats and Stravinsky's *In Memoriam Dylan Thomas,* such works have formed a special genre in the annals of art. Josquin's *Déploration sur la mort de Johan Okeghem* (Lament on the Death of Johannes Ockeghem) is a beautiful tribute to his mentor. Notice that in the second stanza the French poet Jean Molinet mentions, along with Josquin, three other disciples of the Flemish master.

Nymphes des bois, déesses des fontaines,
   Chantres expers de toutes nations,
Changez voz voix fort clères et haultaines
   En cris tranchantz et lamentations,
Car d'Atropos les molestations
   Vostr'Okeghem par sa rigeur attrape,
Le vray trésoir de musicque et chief
     d'oeuvre,
   Qui de trépas désormais plus n'éschappe,
Dont grant doumaige est que la terre
     coeuvre.

Nymphs of the woods, goddesses of the streams,
   Fine singers of every nation,
Change your bright and lofty voices
   To piercing wails and lamentations.
For Atropos with cruel shears
   Your Ockeghem has taken,
Music's very treasure and true master

   From death can now no more escape,
And, great pity, in earth lies buried.

Acoutres vous d'abitz de deuil:
   Josquin, Brumel, Pierchon, Compère.
Et plorez grosses larmes d'oeil:
   Perdu avez vostre bon père.
Requiescat in pace. Amen.

Clothe yourself in deepest mourning,
   Josquin, Brumel, Pierchon, Compère.
And from your eyes shed a flood of tears:
   For your good father now is lost.
May he rest in peace. Amen.

Cantus firmus

Requiem aeternam dona eis Domine,
   et lux perpetua luceat eis.

Eternal rest grant them, O Lord,
   And may your everlasting light shine on
     them.

Josquin's *Lament,* for five voices, falls into two sections. In the first he pays homage to Ockeghem's style by imitating the seamless flow of the older master's counterpoint, a counterpoint marked by soaring asymmetrical lines, the extension of single syllables over a succession of notes, and overlapping cadences. Into this earlier style Josquin injects a mood of mournful lyricism. Characteristic is the drooping vocal line at the end of a phrase—the downward movement by a tone or semitone that was to become a much-used musical symbol of sorrow. We find this effect at the end of the first phrase. Notice, incidentally, the shapely curve of the melody as it rises to a peak and falls:

Throughout this section the sad mood is underlined by the fact that the voices move within an extremely narrow range (a psychologically sound coupling of sorrow with the kind of lassitude that inhibits movement). The use of a cantus firmus in Latin against the French text derives, of course, from an earlier time. This cantus firmus, drawn from the Mass for the Dead, is sung in the Phrygian mode, which was associated with mourning in the same way that, centuries later, the minor mode came to be regarded as "sadder" than the major.

The second stanza, which apostrophizes Josquin and his contemporaries, is set in what was then the modern manner, with short phrases, clear-cut cadences, and verbal clarity based on a single syllable to each note. Josquin here contrasts the new expressive humanism of the Renaissance with the antique style of the first stanza. Noteworthy is the symmetrical phrase structure of this section: two strophes of sixteen measures each, in which a seven-measure phrase is answered by a phrase of nine measures. These are followed by an eight-measure statement and an eight-measure cadence. Most touching is the ending, with all the voices joining in solemn chords on the words "Requiescat in pace. Amen."

Scaramella

Scaramella, a delightful nonsense song, shows Josquin's response to Italian popular melody. Rooted in the rhythms of folk dance, this style led the composer away from the undulating lines of late-medieval music toward regular meters, symmetrical phrases, and clear-cut cadences. This trend was strengthened by the text, which consists of two regular four-line stanzas:

Scaramella va alla guerra	Scaramouche goes to war
Colla lancia et la rotella	With his lance and his shield,
La zombero boro borombetta,	With a rum-tum and a rum-tum-tum,
La zombero boro borombo.	A rum-tum, rum-tum-tum.
Scaramella fa la gala	Scaramouche plays the gallant
Colla scarpa et la stivala,	With his shoe and his boot,
La zombero boro borombetta,	With a rum-tum and a rum-tum-tum,
La zombero boro borombo.	A rum-tum, rum-tum-tum.

The music underlines this regularity. In the first stanza a phrase of four measures is followed by one of five, a phrase of five measures by one of four. In the second stanza two phrases of five measures are followed by two of four. Thus we see music moving toward the symmetries that will take over at a later time. In *Scaramella* the master of canonic device wears his learning ever so lightly. Imitation among the voices there is aplenty, but this is never allowed to interfere with the zest and gayety of the song. The result is utterly charming.

Josquin brought to his art a new vision of beauty. His age justly named him "the Prince of Music." He was forgotten for centuries, but our time has restored him to his rightful place as one of the masters.

51 Other Sixteenth-Century Masters

"It is impossible to find a man who is truly a musician and is vicious."

— VINCENZO GALILEI (father of the astronomer; 1581)

Palestrina and the Catholic Reform

After the revolt of Martin Luther the desire for a return to true Christian piety brought about a reform movement within the Catholic Church. This movement became part of the Counter-Reformation whereby the Church strove to recapture the minds of men. Among its manifestations were the activities of Franciscans and Dominicans among the poor; the founding of the Society of Jesus (Jesuits) by St. Ignatius Loyola (1491–1556); and the deliberations of the Council of Trent, which extended—with some interruptions—from 1545 to 1563.

In its desire to regulate every aspect of religious discipline, the Council took up the matter of church music. The cardinals were much concerned over the corruption of the traditional chant by the singers, who added all manner of embellishments to the Gregorian melodies. They objected to the use of instruments other than the organ in the religious service, to the practice of incorporating popular songs in Masses, to the secular spirit that

Giovanni Pierluigi da Palestrina.

was invading sacred music, and to the general irreverent attitude of church musicians. They pointed out that in polyphonic settings of the Mass the sacred text was made unintelligible by the overelaborate contrapuntal texture. Certain zealots advocated abolishing counterpoint altogether and returning to Gregorian chant, but there were many music lovers among the cardinals who opposed so drastic a step. The committee assigned to deal with the problem contented itself with issuing general recommendations for a more dignified service. The authorities favored a pure vocal style that would respect the integrity of the sacred texts, that would avoid virtuosity and encourage piety.

His life   Giovanni Pierluigi, called da Palestrina after his birthplace (c. 1525–94), met the need for a reformed church music in so exemplary a fashion that for posterity he has remained *the* Catholic composer. He served as organist and choirmaster at various churches including that of St. Peter's in Rome. His patron, Pope Julius III, appointed him a member of the Sistine Chapel choir even though, as a married man, he was ineligible for the semi-ecclesiastical post. He was dismissed by a later Pope but ultimately returned to St. Peter's, where he spent the last twenty-three years of his life. Palestrina's music gives voice to the religiosity of the Counter-Reformation, its transports and its visions. He created a universal type of expression ideally suited to moods of mystic exaltation. The contemplative beauty of his music does not exclude intense emotion; but this is emotion directed to an act of faith.

    A true Italian, Palestrina was surpassingly sensitive to the needs of the human voice. It was from this vantage point that he viewed his function as a church composer: "I have held nothing more desirable than that what is

An engraving from the late sixteenth century depicting the celebration of the Mass. **A Religious Service,** by Philippe Galle after Johannes Stradanus.

sung throughout the year, according to the season, should be agreeable to the ear by virtue of its vocal beauty." It was his good fortune to live not only at a time when the art of music had progressed far enough for him to achieve this goal, but also within a historical situation that made it necessary for him to do so.

Typical of his style is the *Mass Ascendo ad Patrem* (I ascend to the Father), so called because its basic motive was drawn from an earlier motet of that name. The idea of ascent is dramatized in the music by an upward leap of an octave, which is used in various ways at the beginning of each movement. The work is for five voices—soprano, alto, two tenors, and bass—that interweave mellifluously. In the Sanctus each voice enters in turn with the ascending octave:

Mass excerpts
Side 12/2 (S)
Side 2/1 (E I)

San - ctus, San - ctus, San - ctus, San - - - ctus

The key word "Sanctus" (Holy) is expanded throughout the opening statement, which proceeds at a measured pace. From C as a central tone the music moves to a cadence on G—an anticipation of the Tonic-Dominant relationship that will become so important later on. At the words "Dominus Deus Sabaoth" (Lord God of Hosts), the rate of movement quickens. The music grows in fullness to illustrate the idea "Pleni sunt coeli et terra gloria tua" (Heavens and earth are full of Thy glory). A brief faster section, with a change to triple meter on the words "Hosanna in excelsis" (Praise in the Highest), serves as a codetta that ends affirmatively on what we think of today as a C-major chord.

In the Benedictus two sopranos and an alto are combined with a tenor. The soloistic writing creates a texture of utter transparency. Palestrina bases the opening measures on the sensuous beauty of the women's voices. The vocal lines, lying close together, frequently crisscross as they weave their contrapuntal web. The music flows gently on the words "Benedictus qui venit" (Blessed is He who comes), leading to what sounds like a cadence in A. Palestrina sustains the contemplative mood through the second half of the sentence, "in nomine Domine" (in the name of the Lord). The Hosanna is repeated in an expanded version, giving a well-rounded form (A-B-C-B), and the movement ends vigorously on the same C-major cadence as before.

Palestrina's style incarnates the pure a cappella ideal of vocal polyphony, in which the individual voice fulfills its destiny through submergence in the group. His music remains an apt symbol of the greatness art can aspire to when it subserves a profound moral conviction.

The Renaissance Madrigal

In the madrigal the Renaissance found one of its chief forms of secular music. The sixteenth-century *madrigal* was an aristocratic form of poetry-and-music that came to flower at the small Italian courts, where it was a favorite diversion of cultivated amateurs. The text was a short poem of lyric or reflective character, rarely longer than twelve lines, marked by elegance of diction and refinement of sentiment. Conspicuous in it were the affecting words for weeping, sighing, trembling, dying that the Italian madrigalists learned to set with such a wealth of expression. Love and unsatisfied desire were by no means the only topics of the madrigal. Included, too, were humor and satire, political themes, scenes and incidents of city and country life, with the result that the Italian madrigal literature of the sixteenth century presents a vivid panorama of Renaissance thought and feeling.

Instruments participated, duplicating or even substituting for the voices. Sometimes only the top part was sung while the other lines were played on instruments. During the first period of the Renaissance madrigal—the second quarter of the sixteenth century—the composer's chief concern is to give pleasure to the performers, without much thought to an audience. In the middle phase (c. 1550–80), the Renaissance madrigal becomes a conscious art form directed toward the listener. It takes on the elaborateness of concert music, with much contrapuntal imitation and development of musical ideas. Also, there is a closer relationship between words and music.

The final phase of the Italian madrigal (1580–1620) extends beyond the late Renaissance into the world of the Baroque. The form achieves the height of sophistication both in poetry and music. It becomes the direct expression of the composer's personality and feelings. Certain traits are carried to the point of mannerism: rich chromatic harmony, dramatic declamation, vocal virtuosity, and vivid depiction in music of emotional words.

The madrigal was an aristocratic form that flowered at the Italian courts, where it was a favorite diversion of cultivated amateurs. A painting by Sebastiano Florigerio, **Divertissement musical** (c. 1540).

Weelkes: As Vesta Was Descending

As in the case of the sonnet, England took over the madrigal from Italy and developed it into a native art form. All the brilliance of the Elizabethan age is reflected in the school of madrigalists who flourished in the late sixteenth century and on into the reign of James I. The English madrigal soon developed a character all its own.

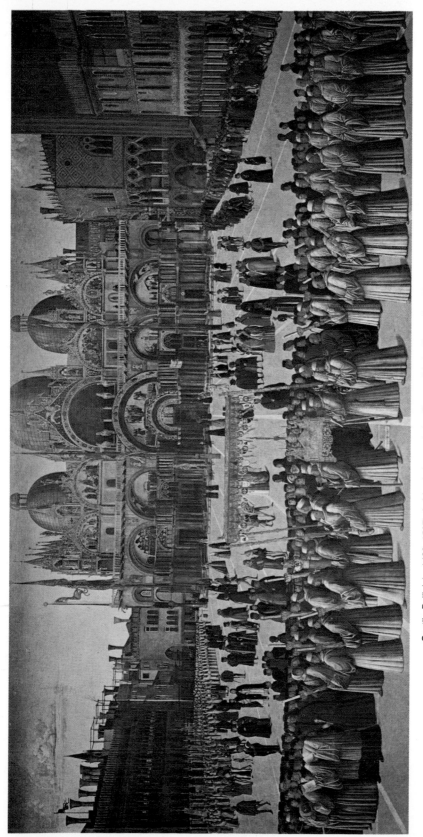

Gentile Bellini (c. 1429–1507), in his glorious painting **Procession in Piazza San Marco,** captured the splendid pageantry of the city. *(Accademia, Venice; Photo Scala New York.)*

The Renaissance painter preferred realism to allegory, psychological characterizations to stylized stereotypes, unified space to a succession of planes. All of these characteristics are exemplified in the **School of Athens,** by Raphael (1483–1520). *(Raphael Stanze, Vatican; Scala New York/Florence.)*

Best-known among the first generation of Elizabethan madrigalists is Thomas Morley (1557–1603). The second generation included such masters as Thomas Weelkes (c. 1575–1623), John Wilbye (1574–1638), and Orlando Gibbons (1583–1625). Weelkes, one of the greatest of the madrigalists, was organist of Chichester Cathedral. He also wrote church music, anthems, and some instrumental works. Weelkes was closely associated with Morley, upon whose death he composed a "remembrance" that began with the verse "Death hath deprived me of my dearest friend."

In 1601 Morley edited a collection of madrigals in honor of Queen Elizabeth, with the common refrain "Long live fair Oriana." The work, called *The Triumph of Oriana,* was not published until 1603, by which time the Queen was dead. In the last two madrigals the refrain, accordingly, was changed to "In Heaven lives Oriana."

Side 12/3 (S)
Side 2/4 (E 1)

Weelkes's *As Vesta Was Descending* is one of the finest madrigals in the collection. It was written for six voices—two sopranos and alto, two tenors and bass. The poem, probably by the composer, is a far cry from Shakespeare's beautiful tribute to the Queen:

> And the imperial votaress passed on,
> In maiden meditation, fancy-free.

But it does have the merit of lending itself to music, whereas Shakespeare's lines would resist the composer since they already are music.

> As Vesta was from Latmos hill descending,
> She spied a maiden Queen the same ascending,
> Attended only by all the shepherds swain,
> To whom Diana's darlings came running down amain:
>
> First two by two, then three by three together,
> Leaving their Goddess all alone, hasted thither,
> And mingling with the shepherds of her train,
> With mirthful tunes her presence entertain.
>
> Then sang the shepherds and nymphs of Diana,
> Long live fair Oriana.

Word painting

Weelkes takes every opportunity to indulge in the Renaissance fondness for word painting; he makes the music reflect every shade of thought and action in the words. The opening statement—"As Vesta was from Latmos hill descending"—is sung by four of the six voices, with the notes moving downward on "descending." At the first action—"She spied" —the voice parts become individualized, with much imitation among them. On the word "ascending," at the end of the second line, there is upward movement in all the parts. "Attended by all" in the next line brings in the other two voices, Tenor II and Bass.

"Came running down amain" inspires vivacious eighth notes tripping down the scale. "First two by two, then three by three" is illustrated first by two voices, then by three. At "all alone" we hear a brief solo. On the words "And mingling with the shepherds of her train," the six voices mingle very happily. So too, "With mirthful tunes her presence entertain" introduces a mood of jollity. The setting, up to this point, is mostly syllabic —that is, a single syllable to a note—with three important exceptions: the action verbs—"descending," "ascending," and "entertain"—are expanded over several notes. The writing throughout is brilliant, the voices moving over a wide range and frequently crisscrossing. The rhythm has the plasticity we noted in Renaissance music, accommodating itself in the most natural manner to the inflections of our language.

All the voices, fortissimo, announce "Then sang the shepherds and nymphs of Diana." This serves to introduce the refrain, which is the most important line. "Long live fair Oriana" enters on a melodious motive that is imitated by each voice in quick succession:

The rest of the madrigal is an extended fantasy on these four words. Weelkes handles the imitative counterpoint like a virtuoso, the result being a headlong interplay in which all the voices join on an equal basis. Excitement mounts steadily until the basic motive is announced fortissimo in augmentation (longer note values) in the bass:

This leads into the final measures, which make a powerful effect at the final cadence. One hopes that Elizabeth at some point heard this brave sound raised in her honor. By all accounts she was musician enough (like her father) to have enjoyed its fine points.

England's madrigals remain a rich legacy of her golden age. Their enchanting strains still echo through the choral pieces of English composers today.

52 The Baroque

"I do not know what I may appear to the world; but to myself I seem to have been only like a boy playing on the seashore, and diverting myself in now and then finding a smoother pebble or a prettier shell than ordinary, whilst the great ocean of truth lay all undiscovered before me." — SIR ISAAC NEWTON (1642–1727)

The period of the Baroque stretched across a turbulent century and a half of European history. It opened shortly before the year 1600, a convenient signpost that need not be taken too literally; and may be regarded as having come to a close with the death of Bach in 1750.

The term "baroque" was probably derived from the Portuguese *barroco,* a pearl of irregular shape much used in the jewelry of the time. The century and a half of Baroque art divides itself into three fifty-year periods; early, middle, and late Baroque. Since public interest until recently concentrated on the late phase, many came to think of Bach and Handel as the first great composers. Viewed against the total panorama of their era, these masters are seen rather to have been the heirs of an old and surpassingly rich tradition.

The period 1600–1750 was a time of change and adventure. The conquest of the New World stirred the imagination and filled the coffers of the Old. The middle classes gathered wealth and power in their struggle against the aristocracy. Empires clashed for mastery of the world. Appalling poverty and wasteful luxury, magnificent idealism and savage oppression—against contradictions such as these unfolded the pomp and

The emergence of the Baroque style—bold, vigorous, decorative—may be seen in this monumental masterpiece. A fresco painting by Michelangelo (1475–1564), **Creation of the Sun and the Moon,** in the Sistine Chapel, Vatican City.

The court of Louis XIV provided a model for the rest of Europe. An anonymous seventeenth-century painting of the chateau at Versailles.

splendor of Baroque art: an art bold of gesture and conception; vigorous, decorative, monumental.

Baroque art   The transition from the classically minded Renaissance to the Baroque was foreshadowed by Michelangelo (1475–1564). His turbulent figures, their torsos twisted in struggle, reflect the Baroque love of the dramatic. In like fashion the Venetian school of painters—Titian, Tintoretto, Veronese—captured the dynamic spirit of the new age. Their crowded canvases are ablaze with color and movement. They glory in the tension of opposing masses. They dramatize the diagonal.

Politics   The Baroque was the era of absolute monarchy. Princes throughout Europe took as their model the splendor of Versailles. Louis XIV's famous "I am the State!" summed up a way of life in which all art and culture served the cult of the ruler. Courts large and small maintained elaborate musical establishments including opera troupes, chapel choirs, and orchestras. Baroque opera, the favorite diversion of the aristocracy, aimed at a lofty pathos that left no room for the frailties of ordinary men. It centered about the gods and heroes of antiquity, in whom the occupant of the royal box and his courtiers found a flattering likeness of themselves.

Scientific frontiers

The Baroque was also an age of reason. Adventurers more bold than the conquistadors set forth upon the uncharted sea of knowledge. The findings of Kepler, Galileo, and Copernicus in physics and astronomy, of Descartes in mathematics and Spinoza in philosophy were so many milestones in the intellectual history of Europe. Harvey discovered the circulation of the blood. Locke laid the foundation for a scientific study of the workings of the mind. Newton's theory of gravitation revealed a universe based upon law and order. Descartes expressed the confidence of a brave new age when he wrote, "Provided only that we abstain from receiving anything as true which is not so, there can be nothing so remote that we cannot reach it, nor so obscure that we cannot discover it."

The new bourgeois culture

Excluded from the salons of the aristocracy, the middle classes created a culture of their own. Their music making centered about the home, the church, and the university group (known as *collegium musicum*). For them came into being the comic opera which, like the prose novel, was filled with keen and witty observation of life. For them painting forsook its grandiose themes and turned to intimate scenes of bourgeois life. The leaders of the Dutch school—Vermeer, Frans Hals, Ruysdael—embodied the vitality of a new burgher art that reached its high point in Rembrandt (1609–69), a master whose insights penetrated the recesses of the soul. Under the leadership of merchant princes and financiers, the culture of the city came to rival that of the palace. These new connoisseurs vied with the court in their love of splendor, responding to the opulence of

The leaders of the Dutch school embodied the vitality of a new burgher art that reached its high point in the work of Rembrandt (1606–69). **The Night Watch.**

Baroque art, to the sensuous beauty of brocade and velvet, marble and jewels and precious metals. This aspect of the Baroque finds expression in the art of Peter Paul Rubens (1577–1640), whose canvases exude a driving energy, a reveling in life. His voluptuous nudes incarnate the seventeenth-century ideal of feminine beauty. He himself was a symbol of the rising order: rugged individualist, dreamer, and man of action; entrepreneur and conqueror all in one.

The role of religion   The Baroque was an intensely devout period. Religion was a rallying cry on some of the bloodiest battlefields in history. The Protestant camp included England, Scandinavia, Holland, and the north German cities, all citadels of the rising middle class. On the Catholic side were the two powerful dynasties, Hapsburg and Bourbon, who fought one another no less fiercely than they did their Protestant foes. After decades of struggle, the might of the Spanish-Hapsburg empire was broken. France emerged as the leading state on the continent; Germany was in ruins; England rose to world power. Europe was ready to advance to the stage of modern industrial society.

Protestant culture was rooted in the Bible. Its emphasis upon the individual promoted a personal tone and strengthened the romantic tendency in the Baroque. Milton (1608–74) in *Paradise Lost* produced the poetic epic of the Protestant world view, even as Dante three and a half centuries earlier had produced that of the Catholic in *The Divine Comedy*. The heroic hymn tunes of the Reformation nourished the profoundly spiritual art of Bach. The oratorios of Handel harnessed Baroque splendor to an ethical ideal. The two composers mark the supreme musical achievement of the Protestant spirit.

The Counter-Reformation   The Catholic world for its part tried to retrieve the losses inflicted by Luther's secession. The Counter-Reformation mobilized all the forces of the church militant. The Jesuits, recognizing faith to be a matter of the whole personality, strove to fire the hearts and minds and senses of the faithful. They made music, sculpture, architecture, painting, and even the theater arts tributary to their purpose. The rapturous mysticism of the Counter-Reformation found expression in the canvases of El Greco (c. 1542–1614). His elongated ash-gray figures, bathed in an unearthly light, are creatures of a visionary mind that distorts the real in its search for a reality beyond. Baroque theatricalism and pathos came to fullness in the sculptor Gianlorenzo Bernini (1598–1680). His famous *Apollo and Daphne* captures in marble all the restlessness and dramatic quality of the

Between the conflicting currents of absolute monarchy and rising bourgeois power, Reformation and Counter-Reformation, the Baroque fashioned its grandiose art. Alien to its spirit were restraint and detachment. Rather it achieved its ends through violent opposition of forces, lavish creativity, and abandon. With these went the capacity to organize a thousand details into a monumental, overpowering whole.

The theatricality of the Baroque is brilliantly manifested in this sculpture by Gianlorenzo Bernini (1598–1680), **Apollo and Daphne.**

The role of the artist   The artist played a variety of roles in Baroque society. He might be an ambassador and intimate of princes, as were Rubens and Van Dyck; or a priest, as was Vivaldi; or a political leader, like Milton. He functioned under royal or princely patronage, as did Corneille and Racine; or, like Bach, was in the employ of a church or free city. To the aristocrats whom he served he might be little more than a purveyor of elegant entertainment. Yet, beneath the obsequious manner and fawning dedications demanded by the age, there was often to be found a spirit that dared to probe all existing knowledge and shape new worlds; a voice addressing itself to those who truly listened—a voice that was indeed "the trumpet of a prophecy."

53 Main Currents in Baroque Music

"The end of all good music is to affect the soul." — CLAUDIO MONTEVERDI

The Emergence of Opera

With the transition from Renaissance to Baroque came a momentous change: the shifting of interest from a texture of several independent parts of equal importance to music in which a single melody predominated; that

Monody

is, from polyphonic to homophonic texture. The new style, which originated in vocal music, was named *monody*—literally, "one song," music
for one singer with instrumental accompaniment. (Monody is not to be
confused with monophony; see p. 207.) The year 1600 is associated with
the emergence of the monodic style. Like many such milestones, the date
merely indicates the coming to light of a process that was long preparing.

*The
Camerata*

The victory of the monodic style was achieved by a group of Florentine
writers, artists, and musicians known as the Camerata, a name derived
from the Italian word for "salon." Among their numbers were Vincenzo
Galilei, father of the astronomer Galileo, and the composers Jacopo Peri
and Giulio Caccini. The men of the Camerata were aristocratic humanists.
Their aim was to resurrect the musical-dramatic art of ancient Greece.
Since almost nothing was known of the music of the Athenian tragedy,
they imagined it in terms of their own needs and desires. Instead of
resurrecting something dead the Camerata came forth with an idea that was
very much alive.

This idea was that music must heighten the emotional power of the
text. The Florentine humanists dreamed of bringing their music into close
relationship with poetry, and through poetry with life itself. "I endeav-
ored," wrote Caccini in 1602, "the imitation of the conceit of the words,
seeking out the chords more or less passionate according to the meaning."

*The stile rap-
presentativo*

Thus came into being what its inventors regarded as the *stile rappresenta-
tivo* (representational style), consisting of a recitative that moved freely
over a foundation of simple chords.

*The origins
of opera*

The Camerata soon realized that the representational style could be applied not only to a poem but to an entire drama. In this way they were
led to the invention of opera, considered by many to be the single most
important achievement of Baroque music. The first complete opera that has
come down to us, *Euridice,* was presented in 1600 at the marriage of
Henry IV of France to Maria de' Medici. The libretto was by Ottavio
Rinuccini, the music by Peri (with the addition of some passages by
Caccini).

The Camerata appeared at a time when it became necessary for music
to free itself from the complexities of counterpoint. The year 1600, like the
year 1900, bristled with discussions about *le nuove musiche*—"the new
music" and what its adherents proudly named "the expressive style." As
sometimes happens with inventors, the noble amateurs of the Florentine
salon touched off more than they realized.

The Figured Bass

The melody-and-chords of the new music was far removed from the
intricate interweaving of voices in the old. Since musicians were soon
familiar with the basic harmony, it became unnecessary to write the chords
out in full. Instead the composer put a numeral, indicating the harmony

The importance of the thorough-bass instrument in Baroque performance is graphically demonstrated in this wash drawing by Giuseppe Zocchi (1711–67).

required, above or below the bass note. For example, the figure 6 under a bass note indicated a chord whose root lay a sixth above the note. Thus, a 6 below the note A called for the F-major or F-minor triad. The application of this principle on a large scale resulted in "the most successful system of musical shorthand ever devised"—the *figured bass* or *thorough-bass* (from *basso continuo,* a continuous bass, "thorough" being the old form of "through.") The actual filling in and elaboration of the harmony was left to the performer. A similar practice obtains in jazz music today, where the player elaborates on the harmonies from the skeletal version on the page.

Thorough-bass instruments

So important was this practice for a century and a half that the Baroque is often referred to as the period of thorough-bass. The figured bass required at least two players: one to perform the bass line on a bass instrument—cello, double bass, or bassoon—and the other to fill in or "realize" the chords on an instrument capable of harmony, such as a harpsichord or organ, a guitar or lute. (The sixteenth-century *lute,* extremely popular in Spain, Italy, France, and England, was a plucked-string instrument with a round body, a flat neck, one single and five double strings, and a pegbox bent back at an angle. A modern descendant is the mandolin.)

The shorthand of figured-bass writing was particularly valuable at a time when printing was an involved and costly process. Since most works

A painting by the Master of the Half-Length Figure, **Young Girl Playing the Lute** (c. 1550).

were intended for a single occasion or season they were left in manuscript, the parts being copied out by hand. It was a boon to composers to be able to present their music in abbreviated fashion, knowing that the performers would fill in the necessary details. When we read of an old master producing hundreds of cantatas and dozens of operas, we may be sure that "there were giants in the earth in those days." But the thorough-bass helped.

Keyboard Instruments

Baroque organ

The three important keyboard instruments of the Baroque were the organ, the harpsichord, and the clavichord. The Baroque organ had a pure, transparent tone. Its stops did not blend the colors into a symphonic cloudburst, as is the case with the twentieth-century organ, but let the voices stand out clearly so that the ear could follow the counterpoint. The colors of the various stops contrasted sharply; but, although the tone was penetrating, it was not harsh because the wind pressure was low. Through the use of two keyboards it was possible to achieve even levels of soft and loud.

Harpsichord

The *harpsichord* too was capable of producing different sonorities because of its two keyboards. The instrument differed from the piano in two important respects. First, its strings were plucked by quills instead of being struck with hammers. The resultant tone was bright and silvery, but it could not be sustained like the tone of the piano. There had to be continual movement in the sound: trills, embellishments of all kinds, chords broken up into arpeggio patterns, and the like. Second, the pressure of the fingers on the keys varied the tone only slightly on the harpsichord, whereas the piano has a wide range of dynamics. The harpsichord was therefore incapable of the crescendo and decrescendo that became so essential a feature of Classic-Romantic music. But it was an ideal medium for contrapuntal music, for it brought out the inner voices with luminous clarity. It lent itself to a grand manner of playing that on the one hand was elevated and dramatic, on the other, rhythmically precise, refined, and playful. It was immensely popular during the Baroque as a solo instrument. In addition, the harpsichord was indispensable in the realization of the thorough-bass, and was the mainstay of the ensemble in chamber music and at the opera house.

Clavichord   The *clavichord* consisted of a wooden oblong box, from two to five feet long, that rested on legs or on a table. The strings were set vibrating

The Compenius organ at Fredericksborg Castle, Denmark, dates from about 1610.

by small brass wedges known as tangents. Dynamic gradations were possible, within a limited range, through pressure on the keys. Clavichord tone was tender, subtle, intimate. It was, however, a small tone. By the end of the eighteenth century both clavichord and harpsichord had been supplanted in public favor by the piano.

The word *clavier* (or *klavier*) was used in Germany as the general term for keyboard instruments, including harpsichord, clavichord, and

A late seventeenth-century Italian harpsichord.

A German clavichord by John Christopher Jesse, dated 1765.

organ. Whether a certain piece was intended for one rather than the other must often be gathered from the style rather than the title. In any event, the rendering of Bach's *Wohltemperiertes Clavier* as *Well-Tempered Clavichord* is misleading. Closer to the mark is *Well-Tempered Clavier*.

The Major-Minor System

The Baroque witnessed one of the most significant changes in all music history: the transition from the medieval church modes to major-minor tonality. As music turned from vocal counterpoint to instrumental harmony, it demanded a simplification of the harmonic system. The various church modes gave way to two standard scales: major and minor. With the establishment of major-minor tonality, the thrust to the keynote or *do* became the most powerful force in music.

Now each chord could assume its function in relation to the key center. Composers of the Baroque soon learned to exploit the opposition between the chord of rest, the I (Tonic), and the active chord, the V (Dominant). So, too, the movement from home key to contrasting key and back became an important element in the shaping of musical structure. Composers developed larger forms of instrumental music than had ever been known before.

Important in this transition was a major technical advance. Due to a curious quirk of nature, keyboard instruments tuned according to the scientific laws of acoustics (first discovered by the ancient Greek philosopher Pythagoras) give a pure sound for keys with signatures of up to three flats or sharps, but the intervals become increasingly out-of-tune as more sharps or flats are added. As instrumental music acquired greater prominence, it became more and more important to be able to play in all the keys. In the seventeenth century, a discovery was made: by slightly mistuning the intervals within the octave—and thereby spreading the discrepancy evenly among all keys—it became possible to play in every major and minor key without unpleasant results. This adjustment is known *Equal* as *equal temperament*. It increased the range of harmonic possibilities *temperament* available to the composer, as Johann Sebastian Bach demonstrated in *The Well-Tempered Clavier,* whose two volumes each contain a prelude and fugue in every one of the twelve major and twelve minor keys. Equal temperament transformed the major-minor system at last into a completely flexible medium of expression.

Use of The growing harmonic sense brought about a freer handling of dis-
dissonance sonance. Baroque musicians used dissonant chords for emotional intensity and color. In the setting of poetry the composer heightened the impact of an expressive word through dissonance. Such harmonic freedom could not fail to shock the conservatives. The Italian theorist Artusi, writing in 1600 *On the Imperfections of Modern Music*—an attack on Monteverdi and his fellow innovators—rails against those musicians who "are harsh to the

ear, offending rather than delighting it," and who "think it within their power to corrupt, spoil, and ruin the good old rules."

The major-minor system emphasized the distinction between the tones included in the key, that is, the diatonic tones, and the five foreign or chromatic tones. Baroque composers associated moods of well-being with diatonic harmony, anguish with chromatic.

The major-minor system was the collective achievement of several generations of musicians. It expressed a new dynamic culture. By dividing the world of sound into definite areas and regulating the movement from one to the other, it enabled the composer to mirror the exciting interplay of forces in the world about him.

54 Further Aspects of Baroque Music

"Musick hath 2 ends, first to pleas the sence, & that is done by the pure Dulcor of Harmony, & secondly to move ye affections or excite passion."

— ROGER NORTH: *The Musicall Grammarian* (1728)

The Doctrine of the Affections

Now that man was become the measure of all things, there was much speculation concerning the passions and affections, by which were meant the deep-lying forces that determine our emotional life. It was realized that these are peculiarly responsive to music. The *doctrine of the affections* related primarily to the union of music and poetry, where the mental state was made explicit by the text. The Baroque developed an impressive technique of what is known as tone painting, in which the music vividly mirrored the words. Ideas of movement and direction—stepping, running, leaping, ascending, descending—were represented graphically through the movement of the melody and rhythm. Bach exhorted his pupils to "play the chorale according to the meaning of the words." He associated the idea of resurrection with a rising line. The sorrow of the Crucifixion was symbolized by a bass line that might descend stepwise along the chromatic scale. Temptation was allied to a sinuous theme that suggests the serpent. Once the musical figure is brought into being, it abandons its picture quality and becomes abstract musical material to be developed according to purely musical procedures. In short, the imagination of the pure musician takes over.

Tone painting

This supremacy of music shows itself in two traits that strike the listener when he hears the vocal literature of the Baroque. We have already encountered both. In the first place, lines, phrases, and individual words are repeated over and over again in order to allow room for the necessary musical expansion. This practice springs from the realization that music

Word repetition and melisma

Rhythm in Baroque music produces the same effect of turbulent, yet controlled motion that animates Baroque painting. Nicolas Poussin (1594–1665), **The Rape of the Sabine Women.** *(The Metropolitan Museum of Art, Harris Brisbane Dick Fund, 1946.)*

communicates more slowly than words and needs more time in which to establish its meaning. In the second place, a single syllable will be extended to accommodate all the notes of an expressive melodic line, so that the word is stretched beyond recognition (the style of setting known as melismatic). Thus, the music born of words ends by swallowing up the element that gave it birth.

In instrumental music the practice took root of building a piece on a single mood—the basic "affection." This was established at the outset by a striking musical subject out of which grew the entire composition. In this way composers discovered the imperious gesture that opens a piece of Baroque music, of a tension and pathos that pervade the whole movement.

Rhythm in Baroque Music

The Baroque, with its fondness for energetic movement, demanded a dynamic rhythm based on the regular recurrence of accent. The bass part became the carrier of the new rhythm. Its relentless beat is an arresting trait in many compositions of the Baroque. This steady pulsation, once under way, never slackens or deviates until the goal is reached. It imparts to Baroque music its unflagging drive, producing the same effect of turbulent yet controlled motion that animates Baroque painting, sculpture, and architecture.

Dance forms   Composers became ever more aware of the capacity of the instruments for rhythm. They found that a striking dance rhythm could serve as the basis for an extended piece, vocal or instrumental. Popular and court dances furnished an invigorating element to musical art. Nor, in that stately age, were the rhythms necessarily lively. Idealized dance rhythms served as the basis for tragic arias and great polyphonic works. In a time when courtiers listened to music primarily for entertainment, composers dressed up a good part of their material in dance rhythms. Many a dance piece served to make palatable a profounder discourse. In effect, rhythm pervaded the musical conception of the Baroque and helped it capture the movement and drive of a vibrant era.

Continuous Melody

The elaborate scrollwork of Baroque architecture bears witness to an abundance of energy that would not leave an inch of space unornamented. Its musical counterpart is to be found in one of the main elements of Baroque style—the principle of continuous expansion. A movement based on a single affection will start off with a striking musical figure that unfolds through a process of ceaseless spinning out. In this regard the music of the Baroque differs from that of the Classical era, with its balanced phrases and cadences. It is constantly in motion, in the act of becoming. When its energy is spent, the work comes to an end.

In vocal music the melody of the Baroque was imbued with the desire always to heighten the impact of the words. Wide leaps and the use of chromatic tones served to emphasize the affections. There resulted a noble melody whose spacious curves outlined a style of grand expressiveness and pathos.

Terraced Dynamics

Baroque music does not know the constant fluctuation of volume that marks the Classic-Romantic style. The music moves at a fairly constant level of sonority. A passage uniformly loud will be followed by one uniformly soft, creating the effect of light and shade. The shift from one level to the other has come to be known as *terraced dynamics* and is a characteristic feature of the Baroque style.

The composer of the Classic-Romantic era who desired greater volume of tone directed each instrument to play louder. The Baroque composer wrote instead for a larger number of players. The Classic-Romantic

The elaborate scrollwork of Baroque architecture finds its musical counterpart in continuous melody. The High Altar of the Theatine Church, Munich.

musician used the crescendo as a means of expression within a passage. The Baroque composer found his main source of expression in the contrast between a soft passage and a loud—that is, between the two terraces of sound. Each passage became an area of solid color set off against the next. This conception shapes the structure of the music, endowing it with a monumental simplicity. (Probably, in performance, singers and players used the crescendo and decrescendo more than we think.)

It follows that Baroque composers were much more sparing of expression marks than those who came after. The music of the period carries little else than an occasional forte or piano, leaving it to the player to supply whatever else may be necessary.

Two-Part Form

Two-part or binary (A-B) form played an important role in Baroque music. This is the question-and-answer type of structure found, in its simplest form, in a tune such as *London Bridge*. The principle gave rise to a tightly knit structure in which the A part moved from home to contrasting key while the B part made the corresponding move back. Both parts used closely related or even identical material. The form was made apparent to the ear by the modulation and a full stop at the end of the first part. As a rule each part was repeated, giving an A-A-B-B structure.

In three-part form contrast is injected by the middle section. Binary form, on the other hand, is all of a piece in texture and mood. It embodies a single affection—that is, a single mood for which reason it was favored by a musical style based on continuous expansion. Binary form prevailed in the short harpsichord pieces of dance character that were produced in quantities during the seventeenth and early eighteenth centuries. It was a standard type in the suite, one of the favorite instrumental forms of the Baroque.

The Ground Bass

The principle of unity in variety expressed itself in an important procedure of Baroque music, the *ground bass* or *basso ostinato* (literally, "obstinate bass"). This consisted of a short phrase that was repeated over and over in the bass while the upper voices pursued their independent courses. With each repetition of the bass, some aspect of melody, harmony, and/or rhythm would be changed. The upper voices were frequently improvised. Thus the ostinato supplied a fixed framework within which the composer's imagination disported itself. Baroque musicians developed a masterful technique of variation and embellishment over the ground bass.

The ostinato is extremely effective both as a unifying device and as a means of building tension. Later we shall find it playing an important part in twentieth-century music.

Instrumental Color

The Baroque was the first period in history in which instrumental music was comparable in importance to vocal. The interest in this branch of the art stimulated the development of new instruments and the perfecting of old. The spirit of the age demanded increased brilliancy of tone. The gentle lute was ousted by the less subtle guitar. The reserved viol with its "still music," as Shakespeare called it, was supplanted by the more resonant violin. Baroque music made generous use of trumpet, trombone, flute, oboe, and bassoon. On the whole, composers thought in terms of line, so that a string instrument, a woodwind, and a brass might be assigned to play the same line in the counterpoint. Besides, since a movement was based on a single affection, the same instrumental color might be allowed to prevail throughout, as opposed to the practice of the Classical and Romantic periods when color was constantly changed. Much music was still performed by whatever instruments happened to be available at a particular time and place. At the same time composers—especially in the late Baroque—chose instruments more and more for their color. They specified ever more clearly what instruments were to play a particular work, with the result that music moved steadily toward an art of orchestration.

Virtuosity and Improvisation

The interest in instruments went hand in hand with a desire to master their technique. Virtuosity on the organ and harpsichord, violin and trumpet had its counterpart in the opera house in a phenomenal vocal technique that has never been surpassed.

Technical mastery brought a growing awareness of what each instrument could do best, and with it a heightened sense of style. Composers differentiated ever more clearly among the various styles: vocal and instrumental; church, theater, chamber; keyboard, string, woodwind, brass. At the same time they were given to mixing the styles. It was part of the Baroque straining for effect to cause one medium to take over the qualities of another: to make Dresden china imitate the daintiness of lace, wrought iron the curl of leaves and flowers. In like fashion instrumental music copied the brilliant coloratura of the voice, while vocal music emulated the arabesques of the instruments. Church music used to advantage the dramatic style of opera and the rhythms of the dance. The delicate ornamentation of harpsichord music influenced the writing for strings. Organ sonority affected the style of the orchestra. Each nourished the other, to the enrichment of all.

Improvisation played a prominent part in the musical practice of the Baroque. The realizing of the thorough-bass would have been impossible if musicians of the period had not been ready to "think with their fingers."

Baroque opera embodied the splendor and monumentality of Baroque art. Stage design by Giuseppe Galli-Bibiena for an opera by Johann Joseph Fux presented in Vienna in 1716.

A church organist was expected as a matter of course to be able to improvise an intricate contrapuntal piece. The ability in this regard of great organists such as Bach and Handel was legendary. This abandonment to the inspiration of the moment suited the rhapsodic temper of the Baroque, and even influenced the art of composition. Many passages in the fantasias and toccatas of the time, with their abrupt changes of mood, bear the mark of extemporaneous speech.

Improvisation functioned in Baroque music also in another way. The singer or player was expected to add his own embellishments to what was written down (as is the custom today in jazz). This was his creative contribution to the work. The practice was so widespread that Baroque music sounded altogether different in performance from what it looked like on paper.

Baroque Opera

The formal or serious opera of the Baroque, the *opera seria,* was attuned to the social order that ended with the French Revolution. This was an opera for princely courts, the favorite diversion of Hapsburgs, Bourbons, Medici, and the rest, embodying the world view of a feudal caste whose gaze was directed to the past, to an imaginary realm where heroes torn between love and honor declaimed to noble music while time stood still in an enchanted grotto out of antiquity or the medieval age.

Baroque opera was a vital force whose influence extended far beyond the theater. It created the great forms of the lyric drama—recitative and aria, ensemble and chorus—that served as models to every branch of the art. The *da capo aria,* in which the first part is repeated after the middle section, established the ternary form (A-B-A) as a basic pattern of musical structure. Within its own conventions, Baroque opera taught composers to depict the passions and the affections, the lyric contemplation of nature, the quintessence of love, hate, fear, jealousy, exaltation. In sum, the opera house of the Baroque was the center for new trends and experiments, through which music attained a dramatic-expressive power such as it had never possessed before.

55 Claudio Monteverdi

"The modern composer builds upon the foundation of truth."

The innovations of the Florentine Camerata awaited the composer who would infuse life into them and enrich them with the resources of the

Claudio Monteverdi. *(Collection André Meyer.)*

past. That composer was Claudio Monteverdi (1567–1643), in whom the dramatic spirit of the Baroque found its first spokesman.

His Life and Music

Monteverdi spent twelve fruitful years at the court of the Duke of Mantua. In 1613 he was appointed choirmaster of St. Mark's in Venice, and retained the post until his death thirty years later. Into his operas and ballets, madrigals and religious works he injected an emotional intensity that was new to music. He aspired above all to make his music express the emotional content of poetry. "The text," he declared, "should be the master of the music, not the servant." There resulted a noble art, full of pathos and rooted in the truths of human nature.

Scene from Orfeo

Side 12/4 (S)
Side 2/6 (E I)

The qualities of Monteverdi's art are well exemplified in the recitative from *Orfeo* (Orpheus; 1607), *Tu se' morta*. Orfeo, the poet-singer of antiquity whose music charmed rocks, trees, and savage beasts, having learned of his wife Eurydice's death, decides to follow her to the nether regions:

Tu se' morta, se' morta, mia vita,   You are dead, dead, my darling,
ed io respiro; tu se' da me partita,   And I live; you have left me,

se' da me partita per mai più,	Left me forevermore,
mai più non tornare, ed io rimango—	Never to return, yet I remain—
no, no, che se i versi alcuna cosa ponno,	No, no, if verses have any power,
n'andrò sicuro al più profondi abissi,	I shall go boldly to the deepest abysses,
e intenerito il cor del re dell'ombre,	And having softened the heart of the king of shadows,
meco trarotti a riverder le stelle,	Will take you with me to see again the stars,
o se ciò negherammi empio destino,	Or if cruel fate will deny me this,
rimarrò teco in compagnia di morte!	I will remain with you in the presence of death!
Addio terra, addio cielo, e sole, addio.	Farewell earth, farewell sky, and sun, farewell.

Recitative   The recitative is accompanied by a small organ and a bass lute that realizes the harmonies. With what economy of means Monteverdi transforms the text into a grandly pathetic declamation! The vocal line is the epitome of simplicity, yet it floods the words with emotion. Notice how the

Tu___ se' mor - ta, se' mor - ta, mia vi - ta

repetition of key words and phrases heightens the pathos; how the voice descends on the words "profondi abissi" (deepest abysses), and rises again on the phrase "meco trarotti a riverder le stelle" (will take you with me to see again the stars). The harmony is for the most part composed of simple triads, with dissonances used sparingly to generate tension. Chromatic intervals and an occasional wide leap project the tragic mood. Wholly Italian is the sensitivity to the beauty and affective power of the voice. Wholly Monteverdian is the poignancy of the emotion conveyed, a poignancy that music henceforth was never to forget.

Chorus   The chorus offers a majestic commentary on Eurydice's death, addressing itself to the cruelty of fate:

Ahi, caso acerbo, ahi, fat'empio e crudele,	Ah, bitter chance, ah, fate wicked and cruel,
ahi, stelle ingiuriose, ahi, cielo avaro.	Ah, stars of ill omen, ah, heaven avaricious.
Non si fidi uom mortale di ben caduco e frale,	Let not mortal man trust good fortune, short-lived and frail,
che tosto fugge, e spesso a gran salita il precipizio è presso.	Which soon disappears, for often to a bold ascent the precipice is near.

Monteverdi achieves extraordinarily rich sound based on a succession of chords moving at a stately pace. There is a sudden piano as the text reminds mortal man that Fortune is a capricious goddess. The words "che tosto fugge" (which soon disappears), in true madrigal style, bring a quickening of pace and lively imitation among the contrapuntal lines. On the final line, "a gran salita il precipizio è presso" (to a bold ascent the precipice is near), the music returns to the stately chords of the opening.

When an art form genuinely reflects the soul of a nation, its history manifests a striking unity of outlook and achievement. From Monteverdi the heritage descends through two hundred and fifty years of Italian opera to Giuseppe Verdi. In the plaint of Orfeo we hear the throb of passion, the profoundly human quality that echoes in more familiar guise through the measures of *Aïda* and *Otello*.

56 Henry Purcell

"As Poetry is the harmony of Words, so Musick is that of Notes; and as Poetry is a Rise above Prose and Oratory, so is Musick the exaltation of Poetry."

His Life and Music

Henry Purcell (c. 1659–95) occupies a special niche in the annals of his country. He was last in the illustrious line that, stretching back to pre-Tudor times, won for England a foremost position among the musically creative nations. With his death the ascendancy came to an end. Until the rise of a native school of composers almost two hundred years later, he remained for his countrymen the symbol of an eminence they had lost.

Purcell's brief career unfolded at the court of Charles II, extending through the turbulent reign of James II into the period of William and

Henry Purcell.

Mary. He held various posts as singer, organist, and composer. Purcell's works cover a wide range, from the massive contrapuntal choruses of the religious anthems and the odes in honor of his royal masters, to patriotic songs like *Britons, Strike Home,* which stir his countrymen even as do the patriotic speeches that ring through the histories of Shakespeare.

Yet this national artist realized that England's music must be part of the European tradition. It was his historic role to assimilate the achievements of the Continent—the dynamic instrumental style, the movement toward major-minor tonality, the recitative and aria of Italian opera, and the pointed rhythms of the French—and to acclimate these to his native land.

Purcell's odes and anthems hit off the tone of solemn ceremonial in an open-air music of great breadth and power. His instrumental music ranks with the finest achievements of the middle Baroque. His songs display the charm of his lyricism no less than his gift for setting our language. In the domain of the theater he produced, besides a quantity of music for plays, what many of his countrymen still regard as the peak of English opera.

Dido and Aeneas

Presented in 1689 "at Mr. Josias Priest's boarding-school at Chelsy by young Gentlewomen . . . to a select audience of their parents and friends," *Dido and Aeneas* achieved a level of pathos for which there was no precedent in England. A school production imposed obvious limitations, to which Purcell's genius adapted itself in extraordinary fashion. Each character is projected in a few telling strokes. The mood of each scene is established with the utmost economy. The libretto by Nahum Tate, one of the drearier poets laureate of England, provided Purcell—despite some execrable rhymes—with a serviceable framework. As in all school productions, this one had to present ample opportunities for choral singing and dancing. The opera took about an hour. Within that span Purcell created a work of incredible concentration and power. Both he and his librettist could assume that their audience was familiar with Vergil's classic. They could therefore compress the plot and suggest rather than fill in the details.

Aeneas and his followers, fleeing from the ruins of Troy, are shipwrecked on the shores of Carthage. There he wins the love of Queen Dido. He returns her love, but the gods desire him to continue his journey in order to found a new Troy—Rome—on the shores of Italy. In Vergil's epic this is his manifest destiny. In Purcell's opera a malicious Sorceress fakes a message from Jove that sends the hero on his way. Dido, overcome with grief,

Side 12/5 (S)
Side 3/1 (E I)

mounts the funeral pyre whose flames light the way for Aeneas's ships as they sail out of the harbor.

The culminating point of the opera is Dido's lament after Aeneas's departure: *When I am laid in earth.* This majestic threnody, scored for soprano and strings, unfolds over a ground bass that descends along the chromatic scale.

The aria builds in a continuous line to the searing high G on "Remember me"—one of those strokes of genius that, once heard, is never forgotten. In Vergil's poem the Queen mounts the funeral pyre whose flames light the way for Aeneas's ships as they sail out of the harbor. In Purcell's opera the chorus sings a final lament: *With drooping wings, ye Cupids, come, And scatter roses on her tomb.*

Purcell in this work struck the true tone of lyric drama. He might have established opera in England had he lived twenty years longer. As it was, his masterpiece had no progeny. It remained as unique a phenomenon in history as the wonderful musician whom his contemporaries called "the British Orpheus."

57 Johann Sebastian Bach

"The aim and final reason of all music should be nothing else but the Glory of God and the refreshment of the spirit."

Johann Sebastian Bach (1685–1750) was heir to the polyphonic art of the past. This he vitalized with the passion and humanity of his own spirit. He is the culminating figure of Baroque music and one of the titans in the history of art.

His Life

He was born at Eisenach in Germany, of a family that had supplied musicians to the churches and town bands of the region for upwards of a century and a half. Left an orphan at the age of ten, he was raised in the town of Ohrdruf by an older brother, an organist who prepared him for the family vocation. From the first he displayed inexhaustible curiosity concerning every aspect of his art. "I had to work hard," he reported in later years, adding with considerably less accuracy, "Anyone who works as hard will get just as far."

Johann Sebastian Bach.

Early years

His professional career began when he was eighteen with his appointment as organist at a church in Arnstadt. At twenty-three he received his first important post: court organist and chamber musician to the Duke of Weimar. His nine years at the ducal court (1708–17) were spent in the service of a ruler whose leaning toward religious music accorded with his own. The Weimar period saw the rise of his fame as an organ virtuoso and the production of many of his most important works for that instrument.

The Weimar period

The Cöthen period

Disappointed because the Duke had failed to advance him, Bach decided to accept an offer from the Prince of Anhalt-Cöthen. At Cöthen, Bach served a prince partial to chamber music. In his five years there (1717–23) he produced suites, concertos, sonatas for various instruments, and a wealth of clavier music; also the six concerti grossi dedicated to the Margrave of Brandenburg. The Cöthen period was saddened by the death of Maria Barbara in 1720. The composer subsequently married Anna Magdalena, a young singer in whom he found a loyal and understanding mate. Of his twenty children—seven of the first marriage and thirteen of the second—half did not survive infancy. One son died in his twenties, another was mentally deficient. Four others became leading composers of the next generation: Wilhelm Friedemann and Carl Philipp Emanuel, sons of Maria Barbara; and Anna Magdalena's sons Johann Christoph and Johann Christian.

The Leipzig years

Bach was thirty-eight when he was appointed to one of the most important posts in Germany, that of Cantor of St. Thomas's in Leipzig. The cantor taught at the choir school of that name, which trained the choristers of the city's principal churches (he was responsible for nonmusical subjects too); and served as music director, composer, choirmaster and organist of St. Thomas's Church. Bach's twenty-seven years in Leipzig (1723–50) saw the production of stupendous works. The clue to his inner life must be sought in his music. It had no counterpart in an outwardly uneventful existence divided between the cares of a large family, the pleasures of a sober circle of friends, the chores of a busy professional life, and the endless squabbles with a host of officials of town, school, and church who never conceded that they were dealing with anything more than a competent choirmaster. With the years the Council learned to put up with their obstinate cantor. After all, he was the greatest organist in Germany.

The routine of his life was enlivened by frequent professional journeys, when he was asked to test and inaugurate new organs. His last and most interesting expedition, in 1747, was to the court of Frederick the Great at Potsdam, where his son Carl Philipp Emanuel served as accompanist to the flute-playing monarch. Frederick on the memorable evening announced to his courtiers with some excitement, "Gentlemen, old Bach has arrived." He led the composer through the palace showing him the new pianos that were beginning to replace the harpsichord. Upon Bach's invitation the King gave him a theme on which he improvised one of his astonishing fugues. After his return to Leipzig he further elaborated on the royal theme, added a trio sonata, and dispatched *The Musical Offering* to "a Monarch whose greatness and power, as in all the sciences of war and peace, so especially in music everyone must admire and revere."

The prodigious labors of a lifetime took their toll; his eyesight failed. After an apoplectic stroke he was stricken with blindness. He persisted in his final task, the revising of eighteen chorale preludes for the organ. The dying master dictated to a son-in-law the last of these, *Before Thy Throne, My God, I Stand.*

His Music

The artist in Bach was driven to conquer all realms of musical thought. His position in history is that of one who consummated existing forms rather than one who originated new ones. Whatever form he touched he brought to its ultimate development. He cut across boundaries, fusing the three great national traditions of his time—German, Italian, French—into

St. Thomas's Church in Leipzig. From a contemporary engraving.

a convincing unity. His sheer mastery of the techniques of composition has never been equaled. With this went incomparable profundity of thought and feeling and the capacity to realize to the full all the possibilities inherent in a given musical situation.

Organ music

Bach was the last of the great religious artists. He considered music to be "a harmonious euphony to the Glory of God." And the glory of God was the central issue of man's existence. The prime medium for Bach's poetry was the organ. His imagery was rooted in its keyboard and pedals, his inspiration molded to its majestic sonorities. He created for the instrument what is still the high point of its literature. In his own lifetime he was known primarily as a virtuoso organist, only Handel being placed in his class. When complimented on his playing he would answer disarmingly, "There is nothing remarkable about it. All you have to do is hit the right notes at the right time and the instrument plays itself."

Keyboard music

In the field of keyboard music his most important work is the *Well-Tempered Clavier*. The forty-eight preludes and fugues in these two volumes (1722, 1744) have been called the pianist's Old Testament (the New, it will be recalled, being Beethoven's sonatas).

Chamber and orchestral music

Of the sonatas for various instruments, a special interest attaches to the six for unaccompanied violin (c. 1720). The master creates for the four strings an intricate polyphonic structure and wrests from the instrument forms and textures of which one would never have suspected it capable. *The Brandenburg Concertos* (1721) present various instrumental combinations pitted against one another. The four *Suites for Orchestra* contain dance forms of appealing lyricism. We will discuss in detail the *Suite No. 3* and the *Brandenburg Concerto No. 2*.

Religious works

The two-hundred-odd cantatas that have come down to us form the centerpiece of Bach's religious music. They constitute a personal document of transcendent spirituality; they project his vision of life and death. The drama of the Crucifixion inspired Bach to plenary eloquence. His Passions are epics of the Protestant faith. That according to St. John (1723) depicts the final events in the life of Christ with almost violent intensity. *The Passion According to St. Matthew* (1729) is more contemplative in tone.

B-minor Mass

The *Mass in B minor* occupied Bach for a good part of the Leipzig period. The first two movements, the Kyrie and Gloria, were written in 1733, and were dedicated to Friedrich Augustus, Elector of Saxony. The greatest of Protestant composers turned to a Catholic monarch in the hope of being named composer to the Saxon court, a title that would strengthen him in his squabbles with the Leipzig authorities. The honorary title was eventually granted. To the Kyrie and Gloria originally sent to the Elector "as an insignificant example of that knowledge which I have achieved in musique" he later added the other three movements required by Catholic usage, the Credo, Sanctus, and Agnus Dei. The dimensions of this mightiest of Masses make it unfit for liturgical use. In its mingling of Catholic and Protestant elements the work symbolically unites the two factions of Christendom. It has found a home in the concert hall, a place of worship to whose creed all that come may subscribe.

The Fugue

From the art and science of counterpoint issued one of the most exciting types of Baroque music, the fugue. The name is derived from *fuga,* the Latin for "flight," implying a flight of fancy, possibly the flight of the theme from one voice to the other. A *fugue* is a contrapuntal composition in which a theme or subject of strongly marked character pervades the entire fabric, entering now in one voice, now in another. The fugue consequently is based on the principle of imitation. The subject constitutes the unifying idea, the focal point of interest in the contrapuntal web.

Fugal voices

A fugue may be written for a group of instruments; for a solo instrument such as organ, harpsichord, or even violin; for several solo voices or for full chorus. Whether the fugue is vocal or instrumental, the several lines are called voices, which indicates the origin of the type. In vocal and orchestral fugues each line is articulated by another performer or group of performers. In fugues for keyboard instruments the ten fingers—on the organ, the feet as well—manage the complex interweaving of the voices.

Subject

Answer

Counter-subject

Episodes

Key relationships

Stretto

Pedal point

The *subject* or theme is stated alone at the outset in one of the voices—soprano, alto, tenor, or bass. It is then imitated in another voice—this is the *answer*—while the first continues with a *countersubject* or countertheme. Depending on the number of voices in the fugue, the subject will then appear in a third voice and be answered in the fourth, with the other voices usually weaving a free contrapuntal texture against these. (If a fugue is in three voices there is, naturally, no second answer.) When the theme has been presented in each voice once, the first section of the fugue, the Exposition, is at an end. The Exposition may be restated, in which case the voices will enter in a different order. From there on the fugue alternates between exposition sections that feature the entrance of the subject and less weighty interludes known as *episodes,* which serve as areas of relaxation.

The subject of the fugue is stated in the home key, the Tonic. The answer is given in a related key, that of the Dominant, which lies five tones above the Tonic. There may be modulation to foreign keys in the course of the fugue, which builds up tension against the return home. The Baroque fugue thus embodied the contrast between home and contrasting keys that was one of the basic principles of the new major-minor system.

As the fugue unfolds there must be not only a sustaining of interest but the sense of mounting urgency that is proper to an extended art work. The composer throughout strives for continuity and a sense of organic growth. Each recurrence of the theme reveals new facets of its nature. The composer manipulates the subject as pure musical material in the same way that the sculptor molds his clay. Especially effective is the *stretto* (from the Italian *stringere,* "to tighten"), in which the theme is imitated in close succession, with the subject entering in one voice before it has been completed in another. The effect is one of voices crowding upon each other, creating a heightening of tension that brings the fugue to its climax. A frequent feature of the fugue—generally toward the end—is the *pedal point,* by which we mean one tone, usually the Dominant or Tonic, that is sustained in the bass while the harmonies change in the other parts. (The pedal point sometimes occurs in the treble register.) The final statement of the subject, generally in a decisive manner, brings the fugue to an end.

The fugue is based on a single affection, or mood—the subject that dominates the piece. Episodes and transitional passages are usually woven from its motives or from those of the countersubject. There results a remarkable unity of texture and atmosphere. Another factor for unity is the unfaltering rhythmic beat (against which, however, the composer may weave a diversity of counterrhythms). The only section of the fugue that follows a set order is the Exposition. Once that is done with, the further course of the fugue is bound only by the composer's fancy. Caprice, exuberance, surprise—all receive free play within the supple framework of this form.

Fugal technique reached unsurpassable heights at the hands of Bach and Handel. In the Classic-Romantic period the fugue was somewhat neglected, although fugal writing became an integral part of the composer's technique. Passages in fugal style occur in many a symphony, quartet, and sonata, often in the Development section. Such an imitative passage inserted in a nonfugal piece is known as a *fugato*. It affords the composer the excitement of fugal writing without the responsibilities.

Fugato

The fugue, then, is a rather free form based on imitative counterpoint, that combined the composer's technical skill with imagination, feeling, and exuberant ornamentation. There resulted a type of musical art that may well be accounted one of the supreme achievements of the Baroque.

Organ Fugue in G minor

Side 13/1 (S)
Side 4/1 (E I)

The *G-minor Fugue* known as "the Little," to distinguish it from a longer fugue in the same key called "the Great," is one of the most popular of Bach's works in this form. This organ fugue is in four voices. The subject is announced in the soprano and is answered in the alto. Next it enters in the tenor and is answered in the bass. In accordance with fugal procedure these entries alternate between the home key (G minor) and the contrasting key (D minor). The subject is a sturdy melody that begins by outlining the Tonic chord and flowers into fanciful arabesques.

The Exposition completed, an episode appears in which a striking motive is heard in imitation between alto and soprano. This motive takes on increasing significance as the fugue proceeds.

The piece is marked by compactness of structure and directness of speech. The subject, as is customary in fugues in the minor mode, is presently shifted to the major. After a climactic expansion of the material the theme makes its final appearance on the pedals, in the home key. The work ends brilliantly with a major chord.

The Suite

The *suite* consisted mainly of a series of dance movements, all in the same key. It presented an international galaxy of dance types: the German *allemande,* in duple meter at a moderate tempo; the French *courante,* in triple meter at a moderate tempo; the Spanish *sarabande,* a stately dance in triple meter; and the English *jig (gigue),* in a lively ⁶⁄₈ or ⁶⁄₄. These had begun as popular dances, but by the time of the late Baroque they had left the ballroom far behind and become abstract types of art music. Between the slow sarabande and fast gigue might be inserted a variety of optional numbers of a graceful song or dance type such as the minuet, the *gavotte,* the lively *bourrée* or *passepied.* These dances of peasant origin introduced a refreshing earthiness into their more formal surroundings. The suite sometimes also incorporated the operatic overture, as well as a variety of short pieces with attractive titles. In short, once a composer passed the formal prelude or overture he had wide choice in the organization of the suite, whether it was for solo instrument or orchestra.

The standard form of the pieces in the suite was the binary structure (A-B) consisting of two sections of approximately equal length, each being rounded off by a cadence. The first part, you will recall, usually moved from the home key (Tonic) to a contrasting key (Dominant), while the B part made the corresponding move back. Composers might have demurred, a century later, at writing a group of five, six, or seven pieces all in the same key; but at a time when major-minor tonality was still a novelty, the assertion of the home key over and over again had a reassuring effect.

The essential element of the suite was dance rhythm, with its imagery of physical movement. The form met the needs of the age for elegant entertainment music. At the same time it offered composers a wealth of popular rhythms that could be transmuted into art.

Suite No. 3 in D major

Bach wrote four orchestral suites. The first two are supposed to have been written during the Cöthen period (1717–23), the last two at Leipzig.

Titian (c. 1477–1576) captured the dynamic spirit of the Baroque age in his canvases, ablaze with color and movement. In **Bacchanale** we sense the tension of opposing masses and the dramatization of the diagonal. *(Prado, Madrid; Scala, New York/Florence.)*

The paintings of Peter Paul Rubens (1577–1640) exude a driving energy, a reveling in life. His voluptuous nudes incarnate the seventeenth-century ideal of feminine beauty. **The Rape of the Daughters of Leucippus.** *(Alte Pinakothek, Munich; Scala, New York/Florence.)*

The *Suite No. 3* is scored for two oboes, three trumpets, drums, first and second violins, violas, and basso continuo; we will consider two movements.

Second movement
Side 13/2 (S)
Side 4/2 (E I)

2. Air. Modeled on the operatic aria, this lyric type of movement was introduced into the suite for greater contrast. The Air from Bach's *Suite No. 3,* for strings only, won universal popularity in an arrangement for the violin by the nineteenth-century virtuoso August Wilhelmj, under the title *Air for the G String.* The seamless melody unfolds in a continuous flow,

presented by the first violins over the steady beat of the cellos. The Air is a two-part form. The first part, which is repeated, modulates from the Tonic, D major, to the Dominant, A major. The second part, twice as long as the first, leads back to D major, ending with a strong cadence. This part too is repeated.

Fifth movement
Side 13/3 (S)
Side 4/3 (E I)

5. Gigue. A sprightly dance piece to which the 6/8 time imparts a most attractive lilt. The formal scheme is similar to that of the other dance numbers: a two-part structure in which each part is repeated. As has been pointed out, not all the repeat signs are likely to be observed in performance. Once again, the first part modulates from D to A major; the second part returns to D. The piece is noteworthy for Bach's use of melodic patterns in sequence.

This *Suite in D,* like its companions, shows the lighter side of Bach's genius. Its courtly gestures and ornate charm evoke a vanished world.

The Concerto Grosso

No less important than the principle of unity in Baroque music was that of contrast. This found expression in the *concerto grosso,* a form based on the opposition between two dissimilar masses of sound. (The Latin verb *concertare* means "to contend with," "to vie with." The *concertante* style is based on this principle.) A small group of instruments known as the *concertino* was pitted against the large group, the concerto grosso or *tutti* (all). The contrast was one of color and dynamics, a uniform level of soft sound being set off against loud. In other words, the orchestra here took over the terraced dynamics of organ and harpsichord.

The concertino, or solo group, might consist of a string trio such as two violins and a cello, or any combination that caught the composer's fancy. The large group as a rule was based on the string choir, but might be supplemented by winds. The harpsichord furnished harmonic support for both groups. The composer was able to write more difficult music for the solo group than for the full ensemble. This was a signal advantage in an age when expert players were none too plentiful.

The concerto grosso embodied what one writer of the time called "the fire and fury of the Italian style." Two Italian masters were outstanding in this field, Arcangelo Corelli and Antonio Vivaldi. Corelli influenced Handel; Vivaldi supplied the model for Bach.

Brandenburg Concerto No. 2

In 1719 Bach had occasion to play before the Margrave Christian Ludwig of Brandenburg, son of the Great Elector. The prince was so impressed that he asked the composer to write some works for his orchestra: Two years later Bach sent him the six pieces that have become known as the *Brandenburg Concertos,* with a dedication in flowery French that beseeched His Royal Highness "not to judge their imperfection by the strictness of that fine and delicate taste which all the world knows You have for musical works; but rather to take into consideration the profound respect and the most humble obedience to which they are meant to bear witness." It is not known how the Margrave responded to the works that have immortalized his name.

In these pieces Bach captured the spirit of the concerto grosso, in which two groups vie with each other, one stimulating the other to sonorous flights of fancy. The second of the set, in F major, has long been a favorite, probably because of the brilliant trumpet part. The solo group—the concertino—consists of trumpet, flute, oboe, and violin, all of them instruments in the high register. The accompanying group—the tutti—includes first and second violins, violas, and double basses. The basso continuo is played by cello and harpsichord.

First movement
Side 13/4 (S)
Side 4/4 (E I)

The opening movement is a sturdy Allegro, bright and assertive. The broad, simple outlines of its architecture depend on well-defined areas of light and shade—the alternation of the tutti and the solo group. The virile tone of the opening derives from the disposition of the parts. Flute, oboe, and violin play the theme in unison with the first violin of the ac-

companying group, while the trumpet outlines the Tonic triad. The contrapuntal lines unfold in a continuous, seamless texture, powered by a rhythmic drive that never flags from beginning to end. The movement modulates freely from the home key of F major to the neighboring major and minor keys. When its energies have been fully expended it returns to F for a vigorous cadence.

Second movement
Side 13/5 (S)
Side 4/5 (E I)

The slow movement is an Andante in D minor, a soulful colloquy among solo violin, oboe, and flute. Each in turn enters with the theme:

The continuo instruments articulate the affective harmonies of the ac-
companiment, while the solo instruments trace serenely melodious lines.
This moving Andante is informed with all the noble pathos of the Baroque.
Third
movement
     Third and last is an Allegro assai (very fast). Trumpet, oboe, violin,
Side 13/6 (S)
Side 4/6 (E I) and flute enter in turn with the jaunty subject of a four-voiced fugue.

The contrapuntal lines are tightly drawn, with much crisscrossing of parts.
The lively interchange is in the nature of a gay conversation among four
equals, abetted in frothiest fashion by the members of the tutti. The movement reaches its destination with the final pronouncement of the subject
by the trumpet.

Chorale and Cantata

A *chorale,* we saw, is a hymn tune, specifically one associated with German
Protestantism. The chorales served as the battle hymns of the Reformation.
Their sturdy contours bear the stamp of an heroic age.
Martin
Luther   As one of his reforms, Martin Luther (1483–1546) established that the
congregation participate in the service. To this end, he inaugurated services
in German rather than Latin, and allotted an important role to congrega-
tional singing. "I wish," he wrote, "to make German psalms for the people,
that is to say sacred hymns, so that the word of God may dwell among the
people also by means of song."

Luther and his aides created the first chorales. They adapted a number
of tunes from Gregorian chant, others from popular sources and from secular art music. Appropriate texts and melodies were drawn, too, from Latin
hymns and psalms. In the course of generations there grew up a body of religious folk song that was in the highest sense a national heritage. Originally
sung in unison, these hymns soon were written in four-part harmony to be
sung by the choir. The melody was put in the soprano, where all could hear
it and join in singing it. In this way, the chorales greatly strengthened the
trend to clear-cut melody supported by chords (homophonic texture).

In the elaborate vocal works that appeared in the Protestant church service, the chorale served as a unifying thread. When at the close of an extended work the chorale unfolded in simple four-part harmony, its granitic strength reflected the faith of a nation. One may imagine the impact upon a congregation attuned to its message. The chorale nourished centuries of German music and came to full flower in the art of Bach.

A cantata (from the Italian *cantare,* "to sing"—that is, a piece to be sung) is a work for vocalists, chorus, and instrumentalists based on a poetic text of a lyric or dramatic nature, either sacred or secular. By the time of Bach, the cantata in Germany had absorbed the recitative, aria, and duet of the opera; the pomp of the French operatic overture; and the dynamic instrumental style of the Italians. These elements were cemented into a unity by the all-embracing presence of the Lutheran chorale.

Cantata No. 140: Wachet auf, ruft uns die Stimme

Wachet auf, which dates from the Leipzig period (1731), is one of the finest examples of the chorale cantata as Bach perfected it. By that time the cantata in Germany had absorbed the recitative, aria, and duet of the opera; the pomp of the French operatic overture; and the dynamic instrumental style of the Italians. These elements were cemented into a unity by the all-embracing presence of the Lutheran chorale.

The sacred cantata was an integral part of the service. It was related, along with the sermon and prayers that followed it, to the Gospel for the day. Every Sunday of the church year required another. What with some extra works for holidays and special occasions, an annual cycle came to about sixty cantatas. Cantors of Lutheran churches were expected to furnish such cycles. Bach composed four or five cycles—approximately two hundred and forty to three hundred cantatas, of which only about two hundred have come down to us.

Wachet auf was composed for the twenty-seventh Sunday after Trinity. The Gospel for the day (Matthew 25:1–13) tells the parable of the five wise and the five foolish virgins, who went forth at midnight to meet the Bridegroom. Bach appropriately based the cantata on the chorale *Wachet auf, ruft uns die Stimme* (Awake, a Voice Is Calling) by the mystic poet-composer Philipp Nicolai (1556–1608), who wrote both the words and music of the famous hymn. The three verses of the chorale form the supporting pillars of Bach's structure. They occur at the beginning, middle, and end of the cantata. (Between these are two recitatives and two duets. It is not known who wrote the text for these.) The image of Christ as Heavenly Bridegroom stirred Bach's imagination to a work of poetic mysticism.

1. Chorale Fantasia. E-flat major, ¾ time.

Wachet auf, ruft uns die Stimme,	Awake, a voice is calling—
der Wächter sehr hoch auf der Zinne,	The watchman high on the tower,
wach' auf, du Stadt Jerusalem!	Awake, city of Jerusalem!

An illustration from J. G. Walther's *Music Dictionary* (1732) showing details of the orchestra used in a cantata performance.

Mitternacht heisst diese Stunde;	This is the hour of midnight;
sie rufen uns mit hellem Munde:	They call us with bright voices:
wo seid ihr klugen Jungfrauen?	Where are you, wise Virgins?
Wohl auf, der Bräut'gam kommt,	Cheer up, the Bridegroom cometh.
steht auf, die Lampen nehmt! Alleluja!	Arise, take your lamps! Alleluia!
Macht euch bereit zu der Hochzeit,	Make yourselves ready for the wedding,
ihr müsset ihm entgegen gehn.	You must go forth to greet him.

First movement
Side 14/1 (S)
Side 5/1 (E I)

A majestic dotted rhythm, established at the outset, derives from the French overture (see p. 288) and evokes the image of a stately procession. This is counterposed to the syncopated figure introduced in the fifth measure by the violins and imitated in the oboes:

Some commentators see in these two motives the approach of the Bridegroom's procession and the impatience of the Virgins. Be that as it may, the instrumental introduction establishes the proper mood of expectancy. The music is scored for two oboes and a tenor oboe; *violino piccolo* (a small violin tuned a minor third higher than the ordinary violin); first and second violins, violas, and the figured bass, whose harmonies—in sacred music—are generally realized on the organ.

The chorus is in the usual four parts, with a horn playing along with the sopranos. The chorale is sung by the sopranos in notes of equal value, with a few intermediate notes omitted. Heard in this skeletal version, the melody

stands apart from the other voices, which sing the same text in livelier rhythms. This distinction between the soprano and the three other voices is maintained throughout the movement.

A similar distinction is drawn between the material entrusted to the instruments and that presented by the voices. Besides maintaining the basic dotted rhythm, the instruments present a more florid counterpoint. The two streams of sound, vocal and instrumental, advance side by side, the instrumental coming to the fore during the interludes that separate the lines of the chorale. There are fine examples of the tone painting dear to the Baroque. The word "hoch" (high) in line 2, for example, occurs on the highest note of the phrase. So too the lower voices generate excitement by leaping upward on such words as "wach' auf" (awake); "wo, wo, wo seid ihr" (where, where are you?); "wohl auf" (cheer up) and "steht auf" (arise). The word "Alleluja!" is treated melismatically, with the voices executing exuberant roulades on a single syllable. The altos enter first, the tenors in imitation, then the basses, in a fugal passage that serves as interlude between two lines of the chorale. Now the sopranos enter with the "Alleluja," still maintaining their steady, unvarying rhythm.

The music for the first three lines of the poem is repeated for the next three. From then on the movement proceeds by the process of continuous expansion that is so characteristic of the Baroque. The key scheme underlines the architecture: the music modulates from the home key of E flat to the Dominant, B flat; from E flat to the relative minor, C minor, and finally back to E flat. The instrumental introduction is repeated da capo at the end, enclosing the spacious design within a frame. This fantasia is unrivaled for richness of detail within a highly coordinated scheme.

4. Chorale. E-flat major, ¾ time.

Zion hört die Wächter singen,	Zion hears the watchmen singing,
das Herz tut ihr vor Freuden springen,	Her heart leaps for joy,
sie wacht und steht eilend auf.	She awakes and quickly rises.

Ihr Freund kommt von Himmel prächtig,	Her friend comes from heaven, resplendent,
von Gnaden stark, von Wahrheit mächtig,	Strong in grace, powerful in truth;
ihr Licht wird hell, ihr Stern geht auf.	Her light shines bright, her star rises.
Nun komm, du werte Kron,	Now come, thou precious crown,
Herr Jesu, Gottes Sohn. Hosianna!	Lord Jesus, Son of God, Hosanna!
Wir folgen all' zum Freudensaal	We follow to the hall of joy
und halten mit das Abendmahl.	To partake of the Lord's Supper.

Fourth movement
Side 14/2 (S)
Side 5/3 (E I)

The second verse of the chorale is sung by the tenors in a more melodious version than was heard before; it is based on shorter note values; and the intermediate notes are included, giving the full outline of the tune. The chorale is presented in combination with a most arresting countermelody, which is played by violins and violas.

This movement, essentially, is a trio for tenor voices, strings, and basso continuo. It is the best-known movement of the cantata.

7. Chorale. E-flat major, 4/4 time.

Gloria sei dir gesungen	May Gloria be sung to Thee
mit Menschen- und englischen Zungen,	With the tongues of men and angels,
mit Harfen und mit Cymbeln schon.	With lovely harps and cymbals.
Von zwölf Perlen sind die Pforten	Of twelve pearls are wrought the gates
an deiner Stadt; wir sind Konsorten	Of Thy city; we are companions
der Engel hoch um deinen Thron.	Of the angel high above Thy throne.
Kein Aug' hat je gespürt,	No eye has ever beheld,
kein Ohr hat je gehört solche Frende.	No ear has ever heard such joy
Des sind wir froh, io, io!	As we fell, ee-o, ee-o,
ewig in dulci jubilo.	Forever *in dulci jubilo* (in sweet jubilation).

Seventh movement
Side 14/3 (S)
Side 5/5 (E I)

The chorale is now sung in the four-part harmonization of Bach. Each voice is supported by instruments of the full ensemble. Thus, at the climax of the cantata, the melody stands revealed in all its simplicity and grandeur.

The notion may be dismissed that Bach was unappreciated in his life-time. He could not have continued to write cantatas for thirty-five years if he had not reached his public. He was known and admired by his generation even if his greatness was not realized in full. It was the following generations that neglected him. The Lutheran world out of which he stemmed ceased to be a living force even while he was immortalizing its spirit. To the musical public of the 1760s the name Bach meant his four sons, whose success as composers far exceeded his. Even they considered his music old-fashioned. One of them, with an engaging lack of filial piety, referred to him as "the old Wig."

Yet the memory of him did not wholly die. It was kept alive in the decades after his death by his sons, his pupils, and by those who had heard him play. Then the revival began, tentatively at first but with increasing force until it had become a veritable renascence. The Romantic age felt akin to his fevor, his chromatic harmonies, his vaulting architecture, the surge and splendor of his polyphony. The *St. Matthew Passion,* forgotten for more than three-quarters of a century, was resurrected by the twenty-year-old Mendelssohn in an epochal performance in 1829. Chopin practiced Bach before his concerts. Liszt transcribed some of the organ works for the piano. Schumann was one of the founders of the Bach Society, an organization that undertook the monumental task of publishing a complete edition of the master's works.

Bach's spirit animated not only the nineteenth century but, in even more fruitful manner, the twentieth. We see him today not only as a consummate artist who brought new meanings to music, but as one of the gigantic figures of Western culture.

58 George Frideric Handel

"Milord, I should be sorry if I only entertained them. I wished to make them better."

If Bach represents the subjective mysticism of the late Baroque, Handel incarnates its worldly pomp. Born in the same year, the two giants of the age never met. The Cantor of Leipzig had little point of contact with a composer who from the first was cut out for an international career. Handel's natural habitat was the opera house. He was at home amid the intrigues of court life. A magnificent adventurer, he gambled for fame and fortune in a feverish struggle to impose his will upon the world, and dominated the musical life of a nation for a century after his death.

His Life

He was born in 1685 at Halle in Germany, in what was then the kingdom of Saxony, the son of a prosperous barber-surgeon who did not regard music as a suitable profession for a young man of the middle class. His father's death left him free to follow his bent. After a year at the University of Halle the ambitious youth went to Hamburg, where he gravitated to the opera house and entered the orchestra as second violinist. He soon absorbed the Italian operatic style that reigned in Hamburg. His first opera, *Almira,* was written when he was twenty and created a furor.

The early operas

Handel's thoughts turned to Italy. Only there, he felt, would he master the operatic art. He reached Rome shortly before his twenty-second birthday; the three years he spent in Italy unfolded against a splendid background peopled by music-loving princes and cardinals. His opera *Rodrigo* was produced in Florence under the patronage of Prince Ferdinand de' Medici. The libretto of his opera *Agrippina* was written by the Viceroy of Naples, Cardinal Grimani. Presented at Venice in 1709, the work sent the Italians into transports of delight. The theater resounded with cries of "Long live the dear Saxon!"

At the age of twenty-five Handel was appointed conductor to the Elector of Hanover. He received the equivalent of fifteen hundred dollars a year at a time when Bach at Weimar was paid eighty. A visit to London in the autumn of 1710 brought him for the first time to the city that was to be his home for well-nigh fifty turbulent years. *Rinaldo,* written in a fortnight,

The move to London

George Frideric Handel.

conquered the English public with its fresh, tender melodies. A year later Handel obtained another leave and returned to London, this time for good. With the *Birthday Ode for Queen Anne* and the *Te Deum* (hymn of thanksgiving) for the Peace of Utrecht he entered upon the writing of large-scale works for great public occasions, following in the footsteps of Purcell. Anne rewarded him with a pension, whereupon nothing would make him go back to his Hanoverian master. By an unforeseen turn of events his master came to him. Anne died and the Elector ascended the throne of England as George I. The monarch was vexed with his truant composer; but he loved music more than protocol, and soon restored him to favor.

Opera in London

Handel's opportunity came with the founding in 1720 of the Royal Academy of Music. The enterprise, launched for the purpose of presenting Italian opera, was backed by a group of wealthy peers headed by the King. Handel was appointed one of the musical directors and at thirty-five found himself occupying a key position in the artistic life of England. For the next eight years he was active in producing and directing his operas as well as writing them. His crowded life passed at a far remove from the solitude we have come to associate with the creative process. He produced his works in bursts of inspiration that kept him chained to his desk for days at a time. He would turn out an opera in from two to three weeks.

The rise of ballad opera

Despite his productivity the Royal Academy tottered to its ruin, its treasury depleted by the extravagance of the peers, its morale sapped by mismanagement and dissension. The final blow was administered in 1728 by the sensational success of John Gay's *The Beggar's Opera*. Sung in English, its tunes related to the experience of the audience, this humorous ballad opera was the answer of middle-class England to the gods and heroes of the aristocratic opera seria. Ironically, even a bit of Handel's *Rinaldo* found its way into the score.

It should have been apparent to the composer-impresario that a new era had dawned; but, refusing to read the omens, he invested thousands in the New Royal Academy of Music. Again a succession of operas rolled from his pen, among them *Orlando Furioso* (1733), "the boldest of his works." But not even Handel's colossal powers could indefinitely sustain the pace. He was fifty-two when he crashed. "This infernal flesh," as he called it, succumbed to a paralytic stroke. Desperate and grievously ill, he acknowledged defeat and went abroad to recover his health. His enemies gloated: the giant was finished.

They underestimated his powers of recovery. He came back to resume the battle. It needed five more expensive failures to make him realize that opera seria in London was finished. At this lowest point in his fortunes there opened, by chance, the road that was to lead him from opera in Italian to oratorio in English, from ruin to immortality. Many years before, in 1720, he had written a masque entitled *Haman and Mordecai,* on a text by Pope adapted from Racine's *Esther*. He subsequently decided to bring

Canaletto (1697–1768), **View of London,** c. 1750. *(Crown Collections, Copyright reserved to Her Majesty the Queen.)*

The Handel-ian oratorio

this "sacred opera" before the public. When the Bishop of London forbade the representation of biblical characters in a theater, Handel hit upon a way out. "There will be no acting upon the Stage," he announced in the advertisement, "but the house will be fitted up in a decent manner, for the audience." In this way London heard its first Handelian oratorio.

He could not remain indifferent to the advantages of a type of entertainment that dispensed with costly foreign singers and lavish scenery. *Deborah* and *Athalia* had been composed in 1733. The next six years witnessed his final struggle on behalf of opera seria. Then, in 1739, there followed two of his greatest oratorios, *Saul* and *Israel in Egypt,* both composed within the space of a little over three months. Many dark moments still lay ahead. He had to find his way to a new middle-class public. That indomitable will never faltered. *Messiah, Samson, Semele, Joseph and His Brethren, Hercules, Belshazzar* (1742–45), although they did not conquer at once, were received sufficiently well to encourage him to continue on his course. Finally, with *Judas Maccabaeus* (1746), the tide turned. The British public responded to the imagery of the Old Testament. The suppression of the last Stuart rebellion created the proper atmosphere for Handel's heroic tone. He kept largely to biblical subjects in the final group of oratorios (1748–52)—*Alexander Balus, Joshua, Susanna, Solomon, Jephtha*—an astonishing list for a man in his sixties. With these the master brought his work to a close.

There remained to face the final enemy—blindness. But even this blow

Final years   did not reduce him to inactivity. Like Milton and Bach, he dictated his last works, which were mainly revisions of earlier ones. He continued to appear in public, conducting the oratorios and displaying his legendary powers on the organ.

In 1759, shortly after his seventy-fourth birthday, Handel began his usual oratorio season, conducting ten major works in little over a month to packed houses. *Messiah* closed the series. He collapsed in the theater at the end of the performance and died some days later. The nation he had served for half a century accorded him its highest honor. "Last night about Eight O'clock the remains of the late great Mr Handel were deposited at the foot of the Duke of Argyll's Monument in Westminster Abbey. . . . There was almost the greatest Concourse of People of all Ranks ever seen upon such, or indeed upon any other Occasion."

His Music

Himself sprung from the middle class, Handel made his career in the land where the middle class first came to power. A vast social change is symbolized by his turning from court opera to oratorio. In so doing he became one of the architects of the new bourgeois culture and a creator of the modern mass public.

An *oratorio* is a large-scale musical work for solo voices, chorus, and orchestra, set to a libretto of sacred or serious character. It took its name from the Italian word for a place for prayer, and was performed in a church or hall, without scenery, costumes, or acting. Based as a rule on a biblical story and imbued with religious feeling, the action unfolded, often with the help of a Narrator, in a series of recitatives and arias, ensemble numbers such as duets, trios, and the like, and choruses. The oratorio was not part of a religious service. It was longer than the cantata and, because of the larger forces used, considerably more ambitious in scope.

The oratorios   The oratorios of Handel are choral dramas of overpowering vitality and grandeur. Vast murals, they are conceived in epic style. Their soaring arias and dramatic recitatives, stupendous fugues and double choruses consummate the splendor of the Baroque. With the instinct of the born leader he gauged the need of his adopted country, and created in · the oratorio an art form steeped in the atmosphere of the Old Testament, ideally suited to the taste of England's middle class. In the command of Jehovah to the Chosen People to go forth and conquer the land of Canaan they recognized a clear mandate to go forth and secure the British Empire.

Handel made the chorus—the people—the center of the drama. Freed from the rapid pace imposed by stage action, he expanded to vast dimensions each scene and emotion. The chorus now touches off the action, now reflects upon it. As in Greek tragedy it serves both as protagonist and ideal spectator. The characters are drawn larger than life-size. Saul,

Joshua, Deborah, Judas Maccabaeus, Samson are archetypes of human nature; creatures of destiny, majestic in defeat as in victory.

Handel's rhythm has the powerful drive of the Baroque. One must hear one of his choruses to realize what momentum can be achieved with a simple ¼ time. His wonderful sense of sound comes out in the pieces intended for outdoor performance, the *Water Music* and *Royal Fireworks Music.* The operas contain some of the composer's finest measures. Among the master's vocal pieces are odes, cantatas, church compositions, and big choral pieces written to celebrate occasions of national rejoicing. Best-known are the *Coronation Anthems* for the accession of George II, one of which—*Zadok the Priest*—has helped crown every subsequent ruler of England. He also produced an impressive amount of instrumental music. Best known in this category are the twelve Concerti Grossi, Opus 6, which with Bach's *Brandenburg Concertos* represent the peak of Baroque orchestral music.

Messiah

"For the Relief of the Prisoners in the several Gaols, and for the Support of Mercer's Hospital in Stephen's-street and of the Charitable Infirmary on the Inn's Quay, on Monday the 12th of April, will be performed at the Musick Hall in Fishamble-Street, *Mr. Handel's new Grand Oratorio, called the Messiah,* in which the Gentlemen of the Choirs of both Cathedrals will assist, with some Concertos on the Organ, by Mr. Handel." In this fashion Dublin was apprised in the spring of 1742 of the launching of one of the world's most widely loved works.

The music was written down in twenty-four days, Handel working as one possessed. His servant found him, after the completion of the *Hallelujah Chorus,* with tears streaming from his eyes. "I did think I did see all Heaven before me, and the Great God Himself!" Upon finishing *Messiah,* the master went on without a pause to *Samson,* the first part of which was ready two weeks later. Truly it was an age of giants.

With its massive choruses, tuneful recitatives, and broadly flowing arias *Messiah* has come to represent the Handelian oratorio in the public mind. Actually it is not typical of the oratorios as a whole. Those are imbued with dramatic conflict, while *Messiah* is cast in a mood of lyric contemplation.

Overture,
Part I
Side 14/4–5 (S)
Side 6/2–3 (E I)

The Overture, in the French style, opens with a Grave (slow, solemn) in dotted rhythms, in a somber E minor; this is repeated, and leads to the Allegro, a sturdy three-voiced fugue. It is followed by a recitative for tenor, *Comfort ye, my people,* in E major, Larghetto e piano (larghetto is not as slow as largo). The melodic line, midway between recitative and aria, is heard against one of those broadly flowing accompaniments of which Handel knew the secret. The "basic affection" of the music reflects the opening phrase of the text, which consists of two verses from Isaiah:

Comfort ye, comfort ye, my people, saith your God; speak ye comfortably to Jerusalem; and cry unto her, that her warfare is accomplished, that her iniquity is pardoned.
The voice of him that crieth in the wilderness, Prepare ye the way of the Lord, make straight in the desert a highway for our God.

The repetition of words and phrases is typical of Baroque music. Notice how sensitively Handel sets the text, revealing in fullest measure the music hidden in the words "Comfort ye." The final sentence is set in true recitative, in which the inflections of the language take precedence over purely musical considerations.

The next number, *Every valley shall be exalted,* is an air (aria) for tenor. It is marked Andante, but the word is to be taken in the eighteenth-century sense of "moving," implying a brisk gait. The orchestral introduction returns as interlude and postlude, imparting to the piece its spacious architecture. The text is another verse from Isaiah:

Every valley shall be exalted, and every mountain and hill made low; the crooked straight, and the rough places plain.

The opening measures establish the mood of exaltation that the words demand; this music is vigorous and affirmative. The first phrase of the tenor solo moves up along the octave and down in a broad arch:

The piece abounds in word painting. Handel extracts maximum tension from the contrast between "crooked" and "straight," "rough" and "plain," the last-named being always spread over a smoothly flowing passage. The music takes off in an unwavering rhythm whose forward thrust gives the aria its sovereign unity of thought and expression.

The climax of the work is, of course, the *Hallelujah Chorus.* This is a powerful Allegro in 4/4. The text is from Revelations:

Hallelujah. For the Lord God omnipotent reigneth.
The kingdom of this world is become the kingdom of our Lord, and of His Christ: and He shall reign for ever and ever.
King of Kings, and Lord of Lords, Hallelujah!

The musical investiture of the key word "Hallelujah!" is one of those strokes of genius that resound through the ages. In contrast is the measured tread of the next thought, "for the Lord God omnipotent reigneth," which is soon combined with the Hallelujah rhythm. "The kingdom of this world" brings a change of mood: piano instead of forte, chordal texture instead of counterpoint, flow instead of thrust. Counterpoint returns with "and He shall reign for ever and ever," the voices entering in turn, each imitating the one before. The final sentence brings the climax of the piece. This triumphal outburst has been aptly compared to the finale of Beethoven's *Fifth*

Symphony. The drums beat, the trumpets resound. This music sings of a victorious Lord, and His host is an army with banners.

Messiah today is regarded as a religious work. It was, however, in no way intended for a church service, but was meant to be an Entertainment, as its librettist described it. That is, it was intended for the commercial concert hall by a bankrupt impresario-composer eager to recoup his losses. That so exalted a conception could take shape in such circumstances testifies to the nature of the age whence it issued—and to the stature of the master of whom Beethoven said, "He was the greatest of us all."

59 From Baroque to Classical

"The state of music is quite different from what it was . . . Taste has changed astonishingly, and accordingly the former style of music no longer seems to please our ears."

— JOHANN SEBASTIAN BACH (writing in 1730)

Other Instrumental Forms

Baroque music developed a number of instrumental forms that we have not discussed. It may be helpful to describe briefly the most important of these.

The Sonata

The sonata was widely cultivated throughout the Baroque. It consisted of either a movement in several sections, or several movements that contrasted in tempo and texture. A distinction was drawn between the *sonata da camera* or *chamber sonata,* which was usually a suite of stylized dances intended for performance in the home, and the *sonata da chiesa* or *church sonata*. This was more serious in tone and more contrapuntal in texture. Its four movements were arranged in the sequence slow-fast-slow-fast. It should be noted that "sonata," to the Baroque, did not mean the highly structured, three-sectional movement it became in the Classical period.

Instrumen-
tation

Sonatas were written for from one to six or eight instruments. The favorite combination for such works was two violins and continuo. Because of the three printed staffs in the music, such compositions came to be known as *trio sonatas*. Yet the title is misleading, because it refers to the number of parts rather than to the number of players. As we saw, the basso continuo needed two performers—a cellist (or bass viol player or bassoonist) to play the bass line, and a harpsichordist or organist to realize the harmonies indicated by the figures.

Prelude

A *prelude* is a fairly short piece based on the continuous expansion of a melodic or rhythmic figure. The prelude originated in improvisation on the lute and keyboard instruments. In the late Baroque it served to introduce a group of dance pieces or a fugue. Bach's *Well-Tempered Clavier,* we saw, consists of forty-eight Preludes and Fugues.

The prelude achieved great variety and expressiveness during the Baroque. It assimilated the verve of dance rhythm, the lyricism of the aria, and the full resources of instrumental style. Since its texture was for the most part homophonic, it made an effective contrast with the contrapuntal texture of the fugue that followed it.

Toccata

The Baroque *toccata* (from the Italian *toccare,* "to touch," referring to the keys) was a composition for organ or harpsichord that exploited the resources of the keyboard in a glittering display of chords, arpeggios, and scale passages. It was free and rhapsodic in form, marked by passages in a harmonic style alternating with fugal sections. In the hands of the north German organists the toccata became a virtuoso piece of monumental proportions, either as an independent work or as companion piece to a fugue.

Chorale prelude and variations

Church organists, in announcing the chorale to be sung by the congregation, fell into the practice of embellishing the traditional melodies. In so doing they drew upon the wealth of Baroque ornamentation, harmony, and counterpoint. There grew up a magnificent body of instrumental art— *chorale prelude* and *chorale variations*—in which organ virtuosity of the highest level was imbued with the spirit of inspired improvisation.

Passacaglia

One of the most majestic forms of Baroque music is the *passacaglia,* which utilizes the principle of the ground bass. A melody is introduced alone in the bass, usually four or eight bars long, in a stately triple meter. The theme is repeated again and again, serving as the foundation for a set of continuous variations that exploit all the resources of polyphonic art. A related type is the *chaconne,* in which the variations are based

Chaconne

not on a melody but on a succession of harmonies repeated over and over. Passacaglia and chaconne exemplify the Baroque urge toward abundant variation and embellishment of a musical idea, and that desire to make much out of a little which is the essence of the creative act.

Overtures, French and Italian

The operatic overture was an important type of large-scale orchestral music. The *French overture* (of which we have discussed several examples) generally followed the pattern slow-fast-slow. Its middle section was in the loosely fugal style known as fugato. The *Italian overture* consisted of three sections too: fast-slow-fast. The opening section was not in fugal style; the middle section was lyrical; there followed a vivacious, dancelike finale. This pattern, expanded into three separate movements, was later adopted by the concerto grosso and the solo concerto. In addition, the operatic overture of the Baroque was one of the ancestors of the symphony.

Inventions and sinfonias   An *invention*—the word signifies an ingenious idea—is a short piece for the keyboard in contrapuntal style. The title is known to pianists from Bach's collection of fifteen inventions in two voices and a like number in three. Bach called the latter group *Sinfonias,* which shows how flexible was musical terminology in those days. His purpose in the inventions, he wrote, was "upright instruction wherein the lovers of the clavier, and especially those desirous of learning, are shown a clear way not alone to have good *inventiones* but to develop the same well."

The instrumental forms of the Baroque manifest great diversity and venturesomeness. In this they epitomize the spirit of the era that shaped their being.

A Comparison of Styles: Baroque and Classical

In comparing the Baroque and Classical styles, it becomes apparent that the Baroque favored a highly emotional type of expression. Its turbulence is at the opposite end from Classical poise. It had a far greater interest in religious music than did the Classical era. The Baroque gave equal importance to instrumental and vocal forms. During the Classical era the emphasis shifted steadily to the instrumental branch of the art.

The great instrumental types of the Classical era—solo and duo sonata, trio and quartet, symphony and concerto—traced their ancestry to the Baroque sonata, concerto and concerto grosso, suite and overture. But be-

Forms   tween the Baroque and Classical eras there interposed a momentous shift of interest from polyphonic to homophonic texture. Baroque music exploited the contrapuntal—that is, the linear-horizontal aspect of music, even as the Classical era developed the harmonic or chordal-vertical aspect. This basic difference affected every aspect of musical style.

In Baroque music, a movement was usually shaped by a single affection or mood. Thus, the chief instrumental form of the Baroque, the fugue, was

Texture   based on a single theme presented within a contrapuntal texture. The Classical sonata-allegro, on the other hand, centered about two contrasting themes presented in a homophonic texture. The fugue depended on theme imitation, the sonata form on theme development. The fugue theme basically retains its identity throughout; the sonata themes undergo substantial changes as the material is developed. The fugue presents a continuous texture, while the sonata form consists of three contrasting sections— Exposition, Development, and Recapitulation. As someone has well said, the sonata is sewn together, the fugue is woven together.

Color   The Baroque concept of the "single affection" influenced instrumental color. An oboe will accompany the voice throughout an entire movement of a cantata or Mass. The Classical style, on the other hand, demanded continual changes of tone color. So too, the relentless single rhythm that dominates an entire movement of Baroque music gives way in the Classical era to more flexible patterns. Composers of the Baroque did not mix timbres as the Classical composers did. They used the different instruments to trace the lines of the counterpoint; for this reason they chose single colors that would stand out against the mass.

Improvisation vs. specificity   Improvisation was of the essence in Baroque style; the performer who realized the figured bass participated in creating the music. The Classical era, on the other hand, influenced by the spirit of rationalism, tried to give the composer total control over his material. The Classical composers wrote out all the parts, limiting improvisation to the cadenza in the concerto. They specified what instruments were to be used in the performance of their scores, as well as the dynamic markings, whereas composers of the Baroque were inclined to leave such matters to the taste and discretion of the performer. Hence it was only in the Classical era that the orchestra was stabilized in the four sections that we know today. Music founded on the thorough-bass emphasized soprano and bass; the Classical composers aimed for a more equable distribution of the parts. Once the figured bass was eliminated, the harpsichord disappeared from the orchestra. Now the other instruments shared in the responsibility of filling in the harmonies, a circumstance that spurred the development of an orchestral style. The terraced dynamics of the Baroque resulted in even levels of soft and loud alternating in areas of light and shade. The Classical era exploited the crescendo and decrescendo, as well as the dramatic surprise inherent in explosive accents, sudden fortissimos and sudden rests.

The Baroque was a period of rhapsodic improvisation. Hence its music, in its massiveness and wealth of ornamentation, its tumultuous piling-up of sonorities and its rapturous outpouring, was far closer to the Romantic spirit than to the Classical. For this reason we are able to trace a certain parallelism in the history of art: from the visionary mysticism of the Middle Ages to the Classicism of the Renaissance; from the pathos and passion of the Baroque to the ordered beauty of late eighteenth-century Classicism; and from the Romanticism of the nineteenth century to the Neoclassicism of the twentieth.

SIX

The Twentieth Century

"The century of aeroplanes has a right to its own music. As there are no precedents, I must create anew." — CLAUDE DEBUSSY

60 Transition to a New Age

"I came into a very young world in a very old time." — ERIK SATIE

It became apparent toward the end of the nineteenth century that the Romantic impulse had exhausted itself. The grand style had run its course, to end in the overblown gestures that mark the decline of a tradition. The composers born in the 1860s and '70s, who reached artistic maturity in the final years of the century, could not but feel, as did Satie, that they had come into the world in a "very old time." It was their historic task to bridge the gap between a dying Romanticism and the twentieth century.

The post-Romantic era, overlapping the Romantic period, extended from around 1890 to 1910. This generation of composers included radicals, conservatives, and those in between. Some continued in the traditional

The Romantic tradition persisted in the work of many artists at the turn of the century. Arnold Böcklin (1827–1901), **The Isle of the Dead.** (The Metropolitan Museum of Art, Reisinger Fund, 1926.)

path; others struck out in new directions; still others tried to steer a middle course between the old and the new. During these years the national schools—French, Russian, Bohemian—that had ended the supremacy of German musical culture continued to flourish. This development came to a head with the First World War, when Germany and Austria were cut off from the rest of Europe. In the post-Romantic period several newcomers appeared on the musical horizon. Besides Finland these included England, Spain, and the United States. And there emerged the movement that more than any other ushered in the twentieth century—Impressionism.

Three members of this generation—Puccini (who was discussed in the section on Romanticism), Sibelius, and Strauss—were steeped in the nineteenth-century tradition. Yet their later works, such as Strauss's *Salome,* Sibelius's *Fourth Symphony,* and Puccini's *Turandot,* unquestionably belong to the new age. In any case, the decades that framed the turn of the nineteenth century are of paramount interest to music lovers. They not only brought the art from the twilight of one epoch to the dawn of another, but they also contained the seeds of much that is important to us today.

61 Mahler: *Symphony No. 4*

"To write a symphony is, for me, to construct a world."

One of the striking phenomena of the mid-century musical scene has been the upsurge of Gustav Mahler's popularity. For whatever reason, his troubled spirit seems to reach our musical public in a most persuasive way. "My time will come," he used to say. It has.

His Life

Gustav Mahler (1860–1911) was born and raised in Bohemia. His father, owner of a small distillery, was not slow in recognizing the boy's talent. Piano lessons began when Gustav was six. He was sent to Vienna and entered the Conservatory at fifteen, the University three years later. His professional career began modestly enough: at the age of twenty, he was engaged to conduct operettas at a third-rate summer theater. A dynamic conductor who found his natural habitat in the opera house, Mahler soon achieved a reputation that brought him ever more important posts, until *Royal Opera, Budapest* at twenty-eight he was director of the Royal Opera at Budapest. From Budapest Mahler went to Hamburg. Then, at thirty-seven, he was offered the most important musical position in the Austrian Empire—the director-

Gustav Mahler, in a charcoal sketch by Dolbin.
(Collection André Meyer.)

Imperial Opera, Vienna

ship, with absolute powers, of the Vienna Opera. His ten years there (1897–1907) made history. He brought to his duties a fiery temperament, unwavering devotion to ideals, and the inflexible will of the zealot. When he took over, Massenet was the chief drawing card. By the time his rule ended he had taught a frivolous public to revere Mozart, Beethoven, and Gluck, and made them listen to uncut versions of Wagner's operas.

"Humanly I make every concession, artistically—none!" Such intransigence was bound to create powerful enemies. Mahler's final years in Vienna were embittered by the intrigues against him, which flourished despite the fact that he had transformed the Imperial Opera into the premier lyric theatre of Europe. The death of a little daughter left him grief-stricken. A second disaster followed soon after: he was found to have a heart ailment. When he finally was forced to resign his post, the blow was not unexpected. Mahler, now almost forty-eight (he had only three more years to live), accepted an engagement at New York's Metropolitan Opera. He hoped to earn enough to be able to retire at fifty, so that he finally might compose with the peace of mind that had never been granted him. His three years in New York were not free of the storms that his tempestuous personality inevitably provoked. In 1909 he assumed direction of the New York Philharmonic Orchestra. When the ladies of the Board made it plain to Alma Mahler that her husband had flouted their wishes, she expostulated, "But in Vienna the Emperor himself did not dare to interfere!"

New York Philharmonic

In the middle of a taxing concert season with the Philharmonic he fell ill with a streptococcus infection. It was decided to bring him to Paris, where a new serum treatment had been developed. Arrived in Paris, he took a turn for the worse. Thus he set forth on his last journey, back to the scene of his greatest triumphs—the enchanting, exasperating Vienna he both loved and detested. On his deathbed he conducted with one finger on the quilt, uttering a single word: "Mozart. . . ."

He was buried, as he had requested, beside his daughter in a cemetery outside Vienna. At last that unquiet heart was at rest.

His Music

"The act of creation in me is so closely bound up with all my experience that when my mind and spirit are at rest I can compose nothing." In this identification of art with personal emotion Mahler was entirely the Romantic. Music for him was vision, intoxication, fulfillment: "a mysterious language from beyond." The sounds were symbols of states of mind and soul. "What is best in music," he observed, "is not to be found in the notes." In his notes resound the great themes of an age that was drawing to its close: nature, poetry, and folklore, love of man and faith in God, the sorrow of human destiny and the loneliness of death.

Symphonies

Mahler was the last in the illustrious line of Viennese symphonists that extended from Haydn, Mozart, Beethoven, and Schubert to Bruckner and Brahms. His tone imagery was permeated by the jovial spirit of Austrian popular song and dance. His nine symphonies abound in lyricism, with melodies long of line and richly expressive harmonies. (The *Tenth Symphony* was left unfinished at his death, but recently has been edited and made available for performance.) It was in the matter of texture that Mahler made his most important contribution to contemporary technique. Basing his orchestral style on counterpoint, he caused two or more melodies to unfold simultaneously, each setting off the other.

Symphony No. 4 in G major: *Fourth Movement*

Fourth movement
Side 15/2 (S)
Side 9/2 (E II)

The Fourth Symphony, completed in 1900, is one of Mahler's most appealing works. Characteristic is the fourth movement, a child's view of heaven that he transformed into an enchanting song for soprano and orchestra. He drew the text from a famous collection of German folk poetry, *Des Knaben Wunderhorn* (The Youth's Magic Horn). The anonymous poetry depicts the joys of the celestial abode in artless terms. There is much dancing and singing, encouraged by an endless supply of fresh fruit, vegetables, free wine, and bread baked by the angels. St. John furnishes the lamb, St. Luke slaughters the ox, St. Peter catches fish, St. Martha does the cooking while St. Cecilia and her band make music to which none on earth can compare. The opening clarinet melody recalls a flute theme from the first movement; and a jingling theme adorned with grace notes, as of sleighbells, is derived from the opening measures of the symphony. It serves as a refrain between the stanzas. The opening phrase of the vocal part sets the tone of childlike innocence:

Wir ge-nie-ssen die himm - - li-schen Freu-den, d'rum tun wir das Ir - di-sche mei-den.
We en-joy all the plea - - sures of Heav-en, a-void-ing all earth - ly sor-row.

The mood is sustained until the end, when the English horn plays in longer notes the jingling grace-note figure, now becalmed. The work ends in a mood of serene tenderness that is as typical of Mahler as are his more fiery moments.

Mahler engaged in a gigantic effort to breathe vitality into the Romantic world of thought and feeling that was in process of disintegration. This circumstance imparts to his music its fevered unrest, his nostalgia. His intensely personal vision of life and art has made him one of the major prophets of the twentieth century.

62 Impressionism

> For we desire above all—nuance,
> Not color but half-shades!
> Ah! nuance alone unites
> Dream with dream and flute with horn.
>
> — PAUL VERLAINE

The Impressionist Painters

In 1867 Claude Monet, rebuffed by the academic salons, exhibited under less conventional auspices a painting called *Impression: Sun Rising*. Before long "impressionism" had become a term of derision to describe the hazy, luminous paintings of this artist (1840–1926) and his school. A distinctly Parisian style, Impressionism counted among its exponents Camille Pissarro (1830–1903), Edouard Manet (1832–83), Edgar Degas (1834–1917), and Auguste Renoir (1841–1919). Discarding those elements of the Romantic tradition that had hardened into academic formulas, they strove to retain on canvas the freshness of their first impressions. They took painting out of the studio into the open air. What fascinated them was the continuous change in the appearance of things. They painted water lilies, a haystack, or clouds again and again at different hours of the day. Instead of mixing their pigments on the palette they juxtaposed brush-strokes of pure color on the canvas, leaving it to the eye of the beholder to do the mixing. An iridescent sheen bathes their painting. Outlines shimmer and melt in a luminous haze.

The Impressionists took painting out of the studio into the open air; their subject was light. Claude Monet (1840–1926), **Impression: Sun Rising.**

The Impressionists abandoned the grandiose subjects of Romanticism. The hero of their painting is not man but light. Not for them the pathos, the drama-packed themes that had inspired centuries of European art. They preferred "unimportant" material: still life, dancing girls, nudes; everyday scenes of middle-class life, picnics, boating and café scenes; nature in all her aspects, Paris in all her moods. Ridiculed at first—"Whoever saw grass that's pink and yellow and blue?"—they ended by imposing their vision upon the age.

The Symbolist Poets

A parallel revolt against traditional modes of expression took place in poetry under the leadership of the Symbolists, who strove for direct poetic experience unspoiled by intellectual elements. They sought to suggest rather than describe, to present the symbol rather than state the thing. Symbolism as a literary movement came to the fore in the work of Charles Baudelaire (1821–67), Stéphane Mallarmé (1842–98), Paul Verlaine (1844–96), and Arthur Rimbaud (1854–91). These poets were strongly influenced by Edgar Allan Poe (1809–49), whose writings were introduced into France by his admirer Baudelaire. They used a word for its color and its music rather than its proper meaning, evoking poetic images "that sooner or later would be accessible to all the senses."

The Symbolists experimented in free verse forms that opened new territories to their art. They achieved in language an indefiniteness that had hitherto been the privilege of music alone. Characteristic was Verlaine's pronouncement: "Music above all!" Like the Impressionist painters, the Symbolists discarded the grand pathos of Romanticism; they glorified the tenuous, the intimate, the subtle. They expressed the moral lassitude of their time, its longing for enchantment of the senses, its need for escape.

The essentially musical approach of the Symbolists was not lost upon the musicians. According to the composer Paul Dukas, it was the writers, not the musicians, who exerted the strongest influence on Debussy.

Impressionism in Music

When young Debussy submitted to the authorities of the Conservatory his cantata *The Blessed Damozel* they stated in their report: "It is much to be desired that he beware of this vague impressionism which is one of the most dangerous enemies of artistic truth." Therewith was transferred to the domain of music a term that was already firmly established in art criticism. Debussy himself never liked the word and expressed himself

Turning from the grandiose subjects of Romanticism, the Impressionists derived their themes from nature in all her aspects. A painting by Pierre Auguste Renoir (1843–1919), **Torso of a Young Girl in the Sun.**

Music and ballet furnished Edgar Degas (1843–1917) with many themes, as in this painting, **Degas' Father Listening to the Guitarist Pagans.** *(Museum of Fine Arts, Boston.)*

acidly concerning "what some idiots call impressionism, a term that is altogether misused, especially by the critics." But the label stuck, for it seemed to describe what most people felt about his music.

Impressionism came to the fore at a crucial moment in the history of European music. The major-minor system had served the art since the seventeenth century. Composers were beginning to feel that its possibilities had been exhausted. Debussy's highly individual tone sense was attracted to other scales, such as the medieval modes that impart an archaic flavor to his music. (The reader will recall the church modes given on p. 214). Debussy emphasized the primary intervals—octaves, fourths, and fifths—which he used in parallel motion. Notice the strong resemblance between the opening measures of *La Cathédrale engloutie* (The Sunken Cathedral)—

New sonorites

—and the following example of ninth-century organum:

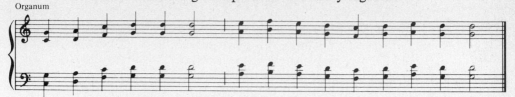

Here Debussy evokes an image of powerful austerity, old and remote things. He was also sympathetic to the novel scales introduced by the Russian and Scandinavian nationalists, and lent a willing ear to the harmonies of Borodin, Musorgsky, Grieg. He responded to the Moorish strain in Spanish music. Especially he was impressed by the Javanese and Chinese orchestras that were heard in Paris during the Exposition of 1889. In their music he found a new world of sonority: rhythms, scales, and colors that offered a bewitching contrast to the stereotyped forms of Western music.

The major-minor system, as we saw, is based on the pull of the active tones to the Tonic or rest tone. Debussy regarded this as a formula that killed spontaneity. We do not hear in his music the triumphal final cadence of the Classic-Romantic period, in which the Dominant chord is resolved to the Tonic with the greatest possible emphasis. His fastidious ear explored subtle harmonic relationships; he demanded new and delicate perceptions on the part of the listener. Classical harmony looked upon dissonance as a momentary disturbance that found its resolution in the consonance. But Debussy used dissonance as a value in itself, freeing it from the need to resolve. In the following example—the closing measures of his piano prelude *Ce qu'a vu le vent d'Ouest* (What the West Wind Saw)—he creates a type of cadence in which the final chord takes on the function of a rest chord not because it is consonant, but because it is less dissonant than what

Uses of dissonance

preceded. Through these and kindred procedures Debussy strengthened the drive toward the "emancipation of the dissonance." He thus taught his contemporaries to accept tone combinations that had hitherto been regarded as inadmissible, even as the Impressionist painters taught them to see colors in sky, grass, and water that had never been seen there before.

Whole-tone scale

Debussy is popularly associated with the *whole-tone scale*. This is a pattern built entirely of whole-tone intervals, as in the sequence C–D–E–F♯–G♯–A♯–C. The whole-tone scale avoids the semitone distances 3–4 and 7–8 (*mi-fa* and *ti-do*) of the major scale. Thereby it sidesteps the thrust of *ti* to *do* that gives the traditional scale its drive and direction. There results a fluid scale pattern whose charm can be gauged only from hearing it played. Debussy did not invent the whole-tone scale nor did he use it as frequently as many suppose. It lent itself admirably, however, to the nuances of mood and feeling that haunt his music, as in the following magical passage from the third act of *Pelléas et Mélisande:*

Parallel chords

Several other procedures have come to be associated with musical Impressionism. One of the most important is the use of parallel or "gliding" chords, in which a chord built on one tone is duplicated immediately on a higher or lower tone. Here all the voices move in parallel motion, the effect being one of blocks of sound gliding up or down. In the following measures from *Soirée dans Grenade* (Evening in Granada), the entire passage consists of a single chord structure which is duplicated on successive tones.

Such parallel motion was prohibited in the classical system of harmony; but it was precisely these forbidden progressions that fascinated Debussy.

The harmonic innovations inseparable from Impressionism led to the formation of daring new tone combinations. Characteristic was the use of the five-tone combination known as *ninth chords* (from the interval of a ninth between the lowest and highest tones of the chord). These played so prominent a part in *Pelléas* that the work came to be known as "the land of ninths." Here is a characteristic sequence of parallel ninth chords from *Pelléas:*

Ninth chords

As a result of the procedures just outlined, Impressionist music wavered between major and minor without adhering to either. In this way was abandoned one of the basic contrasts of Classical harmony. Impressionism advanced the disintegration of the major-minor system. It floated in a borderland between keys, creating elusive effects that might be compared to the misty outlines of Impressionist painting.

Orchestral color

These evanescent harmonies demanded colors no less subtle. No room here for the thunderous climaxes of the Romantic orchestra. Instead there was a veiled blending of hues, an impalpable shimmer of pictorial quality: flutes and clarinets in their dark lower register, violins in their lustrous upper range, trumpets and horns discreetly muted; and over the whole a silvery gossamer of harp, celesta, and triangle, glockenspiel, muffled drum, and cymbal brushed with a drumstick.

So too the metrical patterns of the Classic-Romantic era, marked by an accent on the first beat of the measure, were hardly appropriate for this new dreamlike style. In many a work of the Impressionist school

Rhythmic pulse

the music glides from one measure to the next in a gentle flow that discreetly veils the pulse of the rhythm.

Impressionism opened up to music a world of dream and enchantment. And it captured a vision of fragile beauty in a twilight moment of European culture.

63 Claude Debussy

"I love music passionately. And because I love it I try to free it from barren traditions that stifle it. It is a free art gushing forth, an open-air art boundless as the elements, the wind, the sky, the sea. It must never be shut in and become an academic art."

His Life

The most important French composer of the early twentieth century, Claude Debussy (1862–1918) was born near Paris in the town of St. Germain-en-Laye, where his parents kept a china shop. He entered the Paris Conservatory when he was eleven. Within a few years he shocked his professors with bizarre harmonies that defied the sacred rules. "What rules then do you observe?" inquired one of his teachers. "None—only my own pleasure!" "That's all very well," retorted the professor, "provided you're a genius." It became increasingly apparent that the daring young man was.

Prix de Rome

He was twenty-two when his cantata *L'Enfant prodigue* (The Prodigal Son) won the Prix de Rome. Like Berlioz before him, he looked upon his stay in the Italian capital as a dreary exile from the boulevards and

Claude Debussy, in a portrait by Baschet.

cafés that made up his world. Already he discerned his future bent. "The music I desire," he wrote a friend, "must be supple enough to adapt itself to the lyrical effusions of the soul and the fantasy of dreams."

Pelléas et Mélisande

The 1890s, the most productive decade of Debussy's career, culminated in the writing of *Pelléas et Mélisande*. Based on the symbolist drama by the Belgian poet Maurice Maeterlinck, this opera occupied him for the better part of ten years. He continued to revise the score up to the opening night, which took place on April 30, 1902, at the Opéra-Comique. *Pelléas* was attacked as being decadent, precious, lacking in melody, form, and substance. Nevertheless, its quiet intensity and subtlety of nuance made a profound impression upon the musical intelligentsia. It caught on and embarked on an international career.

After *Pelléas* Debussy was famous. He was the acknowledged leader of a new movement in art, the hero of a cult. In the first years of the century he exhausted the Impressionist vein and found his way to a new and tightly controlled idiom, a kind of distillation of Impressionism.

Later years

His energies sapped by the ravages of cancer, he worked on with remarkable fortitude. The outbreak of war in 1914 rendered him for a time incapable of all interest in music. France, he felt, "can neither laugh nor weep while so many of our men heroically face death." After a year of silence he realized that he must contribute to the struggle in the only way he could, "by creating to the best of my ability a little of that beauty which the enemy is attacking with such fury." He was soon able to report to his publisher that he was "writing like a madman, or like one who has to die next morning." To his perturbation over the fate of France were

To the Impressionist Édouard Manet (1832–83), light was the hero of his painting, not **Mlle. Victorine in the Costume of an Espada.** *(The Metropolitan Museum of Art, Bequest of Mrs. H. O. Havemeyer, 1929. The H. O. Havemeyer Collection.)*

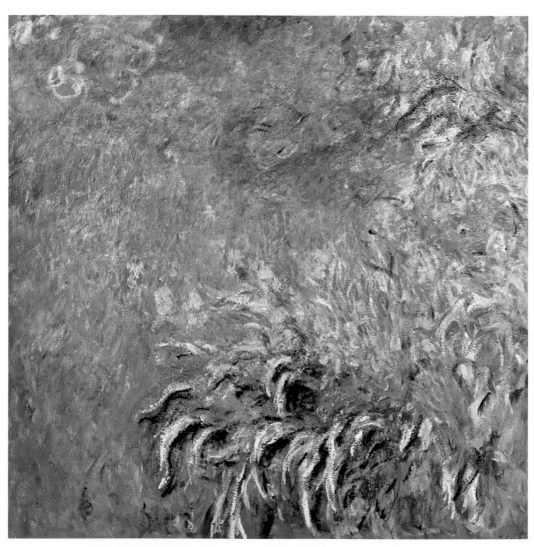

An irridescent sheen bathes Impressionist painting; outlines shimmer and melt in a luminous haze in this seductive canvas by Claude Monet (1840–1926), **Iris Beside a Pond.** *(The Art Institute of Chicago.)*

added physical torment and, finally, the realization that he was too ill to compose any longer. His last letters speak of his "life of waiting—my waiting-room existence, I might call it—for I am a poor traveler waiting for a train that will never come any more."

He died in March 1918 during the bombardment of Paris. The funeral procession took its way through deserted streets as the shells of the German guns ripped into his beloved city. It was just eight months before the victory of the nation whose culture found in him one of its most distinguished representatives.

His Music

For Debussy, as for Monet and Verlaine, art was primarily a sensuous experience. The epic themes of Romanticism were distasteful to his temperament both as man and artist. "French music," he declared, "is clearness, elegance, simple and natural declamation. French music aims first of all to give pleasure."

From the Romantic exuberance that left nothing unsaid Debussy sought refuge in an art of indirection, subtle and discreet. He substituted for the sonata structure those short flexible forms that he handled with such distinction. Mood pieces, they evoked the favorite images of Impressionist painting: gardens in the rain, sunlight through the leaves, clouds, moonlight, sea, mist.

Orchestral works

Debussy worked slowly, and his fame rests on a comparatively small output. Among the orchestral compositions the *Prélude à l'après-midi d'un faune* (Prelude to the Afternoon of a Faun) is firmly established in public favor, as are the three *Nocturnes* (1893–99): *Nuages* (Clouds), *Fêtes* (Festivals), *Sirènes* (Sirens); *La Mer* (The Sea; 1905); and *Ibéria* (1908). His handling of the orchestra has the French sensibility. He causes individual instruments to stand out against the mass. In his scores the lines are widely spaced, the texture light and airy.

Piano pieces

His piano pieces form an essential part of the modern repertory. Among the best-known are *Claire de lune* (Moonlight; 1890), the most popular piece he ever wrote; *Soirée dans Grenade* (Evening in Granada; 1903); *Reflets dans l'eau* (Reflections in the Water; 1905); and *La Cathédrale engloutie* (The Sunken Cathedral; 1910).

Vocal music

Debussy was one of the most important among the group of composers who established the French song as a national art form independent of the lied. His settings of Baudelaire, Verlaine, and Mallarmé—to mention three poets for whom he had a particular fondness—are marked by exquisite refinement. In chamber music he achieved an unqualified success with his *String Quartet in G minor* (1893). The three sonatas of his last years—for cello and piano; flute, viola, and harp; violin and piano— reveal him as moving toward a more abstract, more concentrated style.

Chamber music

Opera

Finally there is *Pelléas et Mélisande*. This "old and sad tale of the

Pencil drawing by Larionov for the ballet *L'après-midi d'un faune* (1912). The legendary Nijinsky (standing right) created a sensation in Paris dancing the principal role. *(Collection André Meyer.)*

woods" captures the ebb and flow of the interior life. The characters move in a trancelike world where a whisper is eloquence: Mélisande of the golden hair and the habit of saying everything twice; Pelléas, caught in the wonder of a love he does not understand; Golaud, who marries Mélisande but never fathoms her secret, driven by jealousy to the murder of his younger half-brother; and Arkel, the blind king of this shadowy land. Maeterlinck's drama gave Debussy his ideal libretto. The result was a unique lyric drama that justifies Romain Rolland's description of him as "this great painter of dreams."

Prélude à l'après-midi d'un faune

Side 16/1 (S)
Side 8/3 (E II)

Debussy's best-known orchestral work was inspired by a pastoral of Stéphane Mallarmé that evokes the landscape of pagan antiquity. The poem centers about the mythological creature of the forest, half man, half goat. The faun, "a simple sensuous passionate being," in Edmund Gosse's phrase, awakes in the woods and tries to remember. Was he visited by three lovely nymphs or was this but a dream? He will never know. The sun is warm, the earth fragrant. He curls himself up and falls into a wine-drugged sleep.

Debussy completed the tone poem in 1894 when he was thirty-two. His imagination was attuned to the pagan setting, and his music invokes emotions as voluptuous as they are elusive. It unfolds what he well called his "harmonious harmony."

The piece opens with a flute solo in the velvety lower register. The melody glides along the chromatic scale, narrow in the range, languorous; the tempo is "very moderate":

Glissandos on the harp usher in a brief dialogue of the horns. Of these sounds it may be said, as of the opening chords of *Tristan,* that their like had never been heard before. The dynamic scheme is discreet; pianissimo and mezzo-piano predominate. There is only one fortissimo. The whole-tone scale is heard. Notable is the limpid coloring. The strings are muted and divided. Flute and oboe, clarinet and horns are used soloistically, standing out against the orchestral texture.

Almost every fragment of melody is repeated forthwith, a trait that the composer carries to the length of mannerism. Characteristic is the relaxed rhythm which flows across the barline in a continuous stream. By weakening and even wiping out the accent Debussy achieved that dreamlike fluidity which is a prime trait of Impressionist music.

A more decisive motive emerges, marked En animant (growing lively). It is played by a solo oboe "softly and expressively," and leads into a slight crescendo. Its wider range and more active rhythm contrast with the opening melody:

The third theme is marked Même mouvement et très soutenu (same tempo and very sustained). Played in unison first by woodwinds, then by the strings, it is an ardent melody that carries the composition to its emotional crest.

The first melody returns in altered guise. At the close, antique cymbals are heard, *ppp*. (*Antique cymbals* are small discs of brass, held by the player one in each hand; the rims are struck together gently and allowed to vibrate.) "Blue" chords sound on the muted horns and violins, infinitely remote. The work dissolves in silence. It takes nine minutes to play. Rarely has so much been said so briefly.

A sensitive tone poet who was relentlessly exacting with himself, Debussy looms as the first major composer of our era. He bridges the gap between Romanticism and the twentieth century. His is a domain limited in scope but replete with beauty. Every note he set down justifies the proud title he assumed in the time of his country's peril: Claude Debussy, *musicien français*.

64 Main Currents in Twentieth-Century Music

"The entire history of modern music may be said to be a history of the gradual pull-away from the German musical tradition of the past century." — AARON COPLAND

The Reaction Against Romanticism

"Epochs which immediately precede our own," writes Stravinsky, "are temporarily farther away from us than others more remote in time." The first quarter of the twentieth century was impelled before all else to throw off the oppressive heritage of the nineteenth. Composers of the new gen-

The transition from nineteenth-century Romanticism to twentieth-century fantasy was epitomized in the last great painting of Henri Rousseau (1844–1910), entitled **The Dream.** *(Collection, The Museum of Modern Art, New York. Gift of Nelson A. Rockefeller.)*

The splendid abstraction of African sculpture provided inspiration for European art. Guardian figure of the Ijo people from Southern Nigeria. *(Courtesy of the Museum of Primitive Art, New York.)*

eration were fighting not only the Romantic past but the Romanticism within themselves.

The turning away from the nineteenth-century spirit was manifest everywhere. Away from the subjective and the grandiose; from pathos and heaven-storming passion; from the Romantic landscape and its picture-book loveliness; from the profound musings on man and fate; from the quest for sensuous beauty of tone—"that accursed euphony," as Richard Strauss called it. The rising generation viewed the Romantic agony as Wagnerian histrionics. It considered itself to be made of sterner stuff. Its goal was a sweeping reversal of values. It aimed for nothing less than "To root out private feelings from art."

Non-Western Influences

The new attitudes took shape just before the First World War. The spiritual exhaustion of Western culture showed itself in an indefinable restlessness. European art sought to escape its overrefinement, to renew itself in a fresh and unspoiled stream of feeling. There was a desire to capture the spontaneity, the freedom from inhibition that was supposed to characterize primitive life. People idealized brute strength and the basic impulses that seemed to have been tamed by an effete civilization. Even as the fine arts discovered the splendid abstraction of African sculpture, music turned to the dynamism of non-Western rhythm. Composers ranged from Africa to Asia and eastern Europe in their search for fresh rhythmic concepts. Out of the unspoiled, vigorous folk music in these areas came powerful rhythms of an elemental fury that tapped fresh sources of feeling and imagination, as in Bartók's *Allegro barbaro* (1911), Stravinsky's *The Rite of Spring* (1913), and Prokofiev's *Scythian Suite* (1914).

The New Classicism

One way of rejecting the nineteenth century was to return to the eighteenth. The movement "back to Bach" assumed impressive proportions in the early twenties. There was no question here of duplicating the accents of the Leipzig master; the slogan implied rather a reviving of certain principles that appeared to have been best understood in his time. Instead of worshiping at the shrine of Beethoven and Wagner, as the Romantics had done, composers began to emulate the great musicians of the eighteenth century—Handel, Scarlatti, Couperin, Vivaldi—and the detached, objective style that was supposed to characterize their music.

There was a misconception here. Only the social music of the eighteenth century, the concerti grossi, harpsichord pieces, serenades and divertimenti, may be said to embody sweet reasonableness and detachment. In their great works Bach and Handel marshaled all the expressive power of which music in their time was capable. But each age recreates the past in its own image. To the nineteenth century, Bach was a visionary and mystic. For the twentieth he became the model for an amiable counterpoint that jogged along as crisply as ever did a piece of dinner music for a German prince. All this implied a rejection of the intensely personal quality of Romantic art. Where the nineteenth-century artist was

The New Classicism exalted the virtues of order, balance, and proportion. **The Nostalgia of the Infinite**, a painting by Giorgio de Chirico (b. 1888). *(Collection, The Museum of Modern Art, New York.)*

as subjective as possible, his twentieth-century counterpart tried to see the world objectively.

Basic to the new esthetic was the notion that the composer's function is not to express emotions but to manipulate abstract combinations of sound. This view found its spokesman in Stravinsky. "I evoke neither human joy nor human sadness," he declared. "I move toward a greater abstraction." Neoclassicism spelled the end of the symphonic poem and of the Romantic attempt to bring music closer to the other arts. It led composers from programmatic to absolute music.

Neoclassicism focused attention on craftsmanship, elegance, taste. Future generations will find it significant that in a period of social, political, and artistic upheaval there should have been affirmed so positively the Classical virtues of objectivity, serenity, and balance.

The New Nationalism

In the twentieth century nationalism pursued different aims than in the nineteenth. The Romantic composers had idealized the life of the people. They fastened on those elements of local color and atmosphere that were picturesque and exportable. The new nationalism went deeper. It approached folk song in the spirit of scientific research, separating genuine peasant music from the watered-down versions of the café musicians. It sought the primeval soul of the nation and encouraged the trend toward authenticity. We find this point of view very much to the fore in the works of such men as Béla Bartók, Manuel de Falla, and Ralph Vaughan Williams. In addition, a new type of nationalism came into being that emanated from the culture of cities rather than the countryside and sought to capture the pulse of modern urban life.

Twentieth-century nationalism uncovered the harsh dissonances, percussive rhythms, and archaic modes that became elements of a new tonal language. Its discoveries enriched the resources of music and encouraged the breaking away from nineteenth-century ideals.

Expressionism

If Paris was the center of the New Classicism, Vienna remained the stronghold of dying Romanticism. From the city of Freud emanated the attempt to capture for art the shadowy terrain of the subconscious.

Expressionism was the German answer to French Impressionism. Whereas the Latin genius rejoiced in luminous impressions of the outer world, the Germanic temperament preferred digging down to the subterranean regions of the soul. Expressionism set up inner experience as the only reality. It enthroned the irrational. Through the symbolism of dreams it released the primitive impulses suppressed by the intellect. "There is only one greatest goal toward which the artist strives," declared Arnold

The images on the canvases of Expressionist painters issued from the realm of the unconscious: hallucinated visions that defied traditional notions of beauty in order to express the artist's inner self. Wassily Kandinsky (1866–1944), **Painting (Autumn).** *(The Solomon R. Guggenheim Museum.)*

Schoenberg: *"To express himself."* But expression, for the Expressionists, had to take place at the deepest levels of awareness.

As with Impressionism, the impulse for the movement came from painting. Wassily Kandinsky (1866–1944), Paul Klee (1879–1940), Oskar Kokoschka (1886–), and Franz Marc (1880–1916) influenced Schoenberg and his disciples even as the Impressionist painters influenced Debussy. The distorted images of their canvases issued from the realm of the unconscious—hallucinated visions that defied conventional notions of beauty in order to achieve the most powerful expression of the artist's inner self. Yet, within a twentieth-century framework, Expressionism retained certain nineteenth-century attitudes. It inherited the Romantic love of overwhelming effect and intensity, of the strange, the macabre,

Expressionist painters

the grotesque. It took over the Romantic interest in the demonic forces hidden deep within the human personality. Like the Romantic movement itself, Expressionism in music triumphed first in the central European area that lies within the orbit of Germanic culture. The movement reached its peak in the period of the Weimar Republic. It is familiar to Americans through the paintings of Kandinsky and Klee, the writings of Franz Kafka (1883–1924), the dancing of Mary Wigman (made familiar in the United States through the art of Martha Graham), the acting of Conrad Veidt, and through such films as *The Cabinet of Dr. Caligari.* Expressionist tendencies entered European opera through Richard Strauss's *Salome* and *Elektra,* and reached their full tide in the dramatic works of Schoenberg and his disciple Alban Berg. Within the orbit of our own culture, Expressionistic elements are to be discerned in the work of such dissimilar artists as James Joyce, William Faulkner, and Tennessee Williams.

In its preoccupation with states of soul, Expressionist music sought ever more powerful means of communicating emotion, and soon reached the boundaries of what was possible within the major-minor system. Inevitably, it had to push beyond.

65 New Elements of Style

"Music is now so foolish that I am amazed. Everything that is wrong is permitted, and no attention is paid to what the old generation wrote as composition." — SAMUEL SCHEIDT (1651)

The Revitalization of Rhythm

Europe after the First World War found surcease for its shattered nerves in athletics and sports. The body itself came to be viewed as a rhythmic machine. Thus ballet came to provide an important platform for the new music, and some of the foremost composers of the twentieth century won success in this field.

This physicality—along with primitivism, the hectic pace of urban life, the surge and clatter of a highly industrialized society—found a musical outlet in increasingly complex rhythms. Twentieth-century music turned away from the standard patterns of duple, triple, or quadruple meter. Composers explored the possibilities of nonsymmetrical patterns based on odd numbers: five, seven, eleven, thirteen beats to the measure.

In nineteenth-century music a single meter customarily prevailed through an entire movement or section. Now the metrical flow shifted constantly, sometimes with each bar, as in Stravinsky's *The Rite of Spring* (1913; see the example on p. 329). Formerly music presented to the ear one

Polyrhythm

rhythmic pattern at a time, sometimes two. Now composers turned to *polyrhythm*—the use of several rhythmic patterns simultaneously. As a result of these innovations, Western music achieved something of the complexity and suppleness of Asiatic and African rhythms. The music of Stravinsky and Bartók revealed to their contemporaries an explosive, elemental rhythm of enormous force and tension. Both men were partial to the rhythmic ostinato—the use of a striking rhythmic pattern which, by being repeated over and over again, takes on an almost hypnotic power.

The twentieth century turned away from metrical rhythms based on the regular recurrence of accent, just as it turned away from metrical poetry to free verse. The new generation of composers preferred freer rhythms. The listener will not respond to these new rhythms as he would to a Strauss waltz or a Sousa march, by tapping his foot or waving his hand with the beat. As compensation, he will find rhythms that are flexible in the highest degree, of an almost physical power and drive. Indeed, the revitalization of rhythm is one of the major achievements of early twentieth-century music.

Melody

Rhythm was not the only element in which symmetrical structure was abandoned. Melody was affected too. In the nineteenth century, melody was often based on regular phrases of four or eight measures set off by evenly spaced cadences. This expansive structure is not congenial to the modern temper.

Composers today do not develop the neatly balanced repetitions that prevailed formerly. Their ideal is a direct forward-driving melody from which all nonessentials have been cut away. They assume a quicker perception on the part of the hearer than did composers in the past. A thing is said once rather than in multiples of four. The result is a taut, angular melody of telegraphic conciseness. A splendid example is the resilient theme from the finale of Bartók's *Concerto for Orchestra* (1943):

Instrumental melody

Nineteenth-century melody was fundamentally vocal in character; composers tried to make the instruments "sing." Twentieth-century melody is based primarily on an instrumental conception. It is neither unvocal nor antivocal; it is simply not conceived in relation to the voice. It abounds in wide leaps and dissonant intervals. The second theme in the opening movement of Shostakovich's *First Symphony* (1925) illustrates the instrumental character of twentieth-century melody.

Twentieth-century composers have enormously expanded our notion of what is a melody. As a result, many a pattern is accepted as a melody today that would hardly have been considered one a century ago.

Harmony

The triads of traditional harmony, we saw, were formed by combining three tones on every other degree of the scale: 1–3–5 (for example, C–E–G), 2–4–6 (D–F–A), 3–5–7 (E–G–B), and so on. Such chords are composed of a third and a fifth. (The interval from step 1 to step 3, as from C to E, is known as a *third*—that is, a distance of three tones counting the lower, middle, and upper tone. The interval from step 1 to step 5, as from C to G, is known as a *fifth:* C–D–E–F–G). Traditional harmony also employed four-tone combinations known as *seventh chords* (steps 1–3–5–7), so-called because from the lowest to the highest tone is an interval of seven steps; and five-tone combinations known as *ninth chords* (steps 1–3–5–7–9).

New chord structures

Twentieth-century composers added another "story" or two, forming highly dissonant combinations of six and seven tones—for instance, chords based on steps 1–3–5–7–9–11 and 1–3–5–7–9–11–13 of the scale. The emergence of these complex "skyscraper" chords imparted a greater degree of tension to music than had ever existed before.

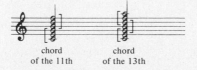

chord   chord
of the 11th   of the 13th

A chord of seven tones, such as the second one shown above, hardly possesses the unity of the Classical triad. It is composed of no less than three separate triads: the I chord (steps 1–3–5), the V chord (steps 5–7–9), and the II chord (steps 9–11–13, that is, 2–4–6). In this formation the Dominant chord is directly superimposed on the Tonic, so that the two poles of Classical harmony, Tonic and Dominant, are brought together in a kind of montage. What our forebears were in the habit of hearing in succession is thus sounded simultaneously. Such a chord, which contains all seven steps of the major scale, not only adds spice to the traditional triad, but also increases the volume of sound, an effect much prized by composers. Here is an example:

Polychords and polyharmony   A seven-tone "skyscraper" is, in effect, a *polychord*. A succession of such chords creates several planes of harmony. One of the outstanding achievements of the new age is a kind of *polyharmony* in which the composer plays two or more streams of harmony against each other, exactly as in former times single strands of melody were combined. The interplay of the several independent streams adds a new dimension to the harmonic space. The following is a famous example of polyharmony from Stravinsky's *Petrushka* (1911). The clash of the two harmonic currents produces a bright, virile sonority that typifies the twentieth-century revolt against the sweet sound of the Romantic era:

The interval of a third was associated with the music of the past. To free themselves from the sound of the eighteenth and nineteenth centuries, composers cast about for other methods of chord construction; they began to base chords on the interval of the fourth. This turning from *tertial* to *quartal harmony* constitutes one of the important differences between nineteenth- and twentieth-century music. Chords based on fourths have a pungency that is very much of our century, as the following examples demonstrate.

Quartal harmony

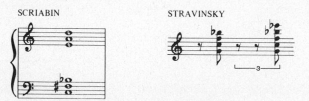

Composers also based their harmonies on other intervals. Here is a chord of piled-up fifths from Stravinsky's *Rite of Spring* (1913), and cluster chords based on seconds from Bartók's *Mikrokosmos* (1926).

The Emancipation of the Dissonance

The history of music, we have seen, has been the history of a steadily increasing tolerance on the part of the listener. Throughout this long evolution one factor remained constant. A clear distinction was drawn between dissonance, the element of tension, and consonance, the element of rest. Consonance was the norm, dissonance the temporary disturbance. Twentieth-century harmony has rejected this distinction. In many contemporary works tension tends to become the norm—a clear case of art imitating life. The difference between consonance and dissonance is considered nowadays to be only a difference in degree. "Dissonant tones," Schoenberg taught, "appear later among the overtones, for which reason the ear is less acquainted with them. Dissonances are only the remote consonances." In other words, the distinction is relative rather than absolute, which means that a chord is judged not on its intrinsic character but in relation to the chords that precede or follow it. As a result, a dissonance can serve as a final cadence, as in the example from Debussy on p. 301, because it is less dissonant than the chord that came before. In relation to the greater dissonance, it is judged to be consonant.

Twentieth-century composers emancipated the dissonance, first, by making it more familiar to the ear; second, by freeing it from the obligation to resolve to consonance. Their percussive harmonies taught our ears to accept tone combinations whose like had never been heard before.

Texture: Dissonant Counterpoint

The nineteenth century was occupied with harmony; the early twentieth emphasized counterpoint. The Romantic composer thought in terms of vertical mass; the twentieth-century composer thought largely in terms of horizontal line. Where the Romantics exalted the magic sonority of the chord, their successors stressed a neat fabric of tightly woven lines. This was part of the movement "back to Bach" and to the earlier masters of polyphony.

By adopting the contrapuntal ideal, composers substituted line for mass, thereby lightening the swollen sound of the post-Romantic period. The new style swept away both the Romantic cloudburst and the Impressionist haze. In their stead was installed a texture of widely spaced lines from whose interplay the music derived its tensions: an airy texture that fit the Neoclassic ideal of craftsmanship, order, and detachment.

Consonance unites the constituent tones of harmony or counterpoint; dissonance separates them and makes them stand out against each other. Composers began to use dissonance to set off one line against another. Instead of basing their counterpoint on the euphonious intervals of the third and sixth, they turned to the astringent seconds and sevenths, as in the following example from Hindemith's *Ludus Tonalis* (1943):

Or the independence of the voices might be heightened by putting them in different keys. Thus came into being a linear texture based on dissonant counterpoint, objective, logical, powered by driving rhythms, and marked by solid workmanship as by sober sentiment.

Orchestration

Orchestral writing followed the same anti-Romantic direction as prevailed in other departments of the art. The rich sonorities of nineteenth-century orchestration were alien to the temper of the 1920s and '30s. The trend was toward a smaller orchestra and a leaner sound, one that was hard, bright, sober. "One is tired," wrote Stravinsky, "of being saturated with timbres."

The decisive factor in the handling of the orchestra was the change to a linear texture—the texture, for example, of Stravinsky's *Symphony of Psalms* or Schoenberg's *Variations for Orchestra*. Color came to be used in the new music not so much for atmosphere or enchantment as for bringing out the lines of counterpoint and of form. Whereas the nineteenth-century orchestrator made his colors swim together, the Neoclassicist desired each to stand out against the mass. In many pieces the sound of the orchestra drew closer to the chamber-music ideal. In general, Neoclassicism rejected the Romantic use of timbre as an end in itself. Composers restored color to its Classical function, as the obedient handmaiden of idea, structure, and design.

The Popularity of Absolute Forms

The Neoclassicists took over from their Romantic predecessors the large forms of absolute music—symphony and concerto, solo sonata, string quartet and other types of chamber music—which they adapted to their own esthetic. Their attitude was summed up in Prokofiev's observation, "I want nothing better than sonata form, which contains everything necessary for my needs." In addition, they revived a number of older forms: toccata, fugue, passacaglia and chaconne, concerto grosso, theme and variations, suite, and the social forms of the Viennese period—divertimento and serenade.

Formalism   The tendency to elevate formal above expressive values is known as *formalism.* The second quarter of our century, it goes without saying, was a formalist age. The New Classicism, like the old, strove for purity of line and proportion. Characteristic of this goal was Stravinsky's emphasis on formal beauty rather than emotional expression: "One could not better define the sensation produced by music than by saying that it is identical with that evoked by contemplating the interplay of architectural forms. Goethe thoroughly understood this when he called architecture frozen music."

The Influence of Jazz

Composers through the ages have vitalized their music by the use of forms and materials drawn from popular music. In the twentieth century, a primary source for new inspiration from outside the realm of art music was American jazz, which we will consider in detail in Chapters 80 and 81.

Among the aspects of jazz that particularly interested European composers were its rhythmic excitement, its gay syncopation and polyrhythm, and its chamber-music sonority, resulting from an ensemble of soloists (woodwind and brass) playing against the rhythmic-harmonic background supplied by piano, string bass, banjo, and drums. Although the improvisational spirit of jazz remained foreign to the music written by European composers of this period, there arose a literature that clearly attempted to evoke the unconventional sound, the contrapuntal texture, and the rhythmic freedom of ragtime and blues. Among the works reflecting various aspects of jazz influence were *Golliwog's Cakewalk* by Debussy, Erik Satie's ballet *Parade,* Stravinsky's *Ragtime* for eleven instruments and *Piano-Rag-Music,* Darius Milhaud's ballets *Le Boeuf sur le toit* and *La Création du monde,* and Ernst Krenek's opera *Jonny spielt auf,* as well as the operas of Kurt Weill (*The Three-Penny Opera* and *Mahagonny*).

Jazz assumed some strange shapes as soon as it left American hands. Nevertheless, the New Classicism for a time advanced under the twin banner of Bach and jazz—a formidable combination.

66 New Conceptions of Tonality

"Every tone relationship that has been used too often must finally be regarded as exhausted. It ceases to have power to convey a thought worthy of it. Therefore every composer is obliged to invent anew, to present new tone relations." — ARNOLD SCHOENBERG

No single factor set off the music of our time more decisively from that of the past than the new conceptions of tonality that emerged in the twentieth century. These, in general, followed one of three paths: 1) expanded tonality; 2) the simultaneous employment of two or more keys, or polytonality; 3) the rejection of tonality, or atonality and twelve-tone music.

Expanded Tonality

In the major-minor system, seven tones were chosen out of the twelve to form a key. This "seven out of twelve" way of hearing music was expanded in the twentieth century to a "twelve out of twelve"—that is, the free use of twelve tones around a center. This approach, espoused by composers like Hindemith and Bartók, retained the basic principle of traditional tonality, loyalty to the Tonic; but, by considering the five chromatic tones to be as much a part of the key as the seven diatonic ones, it immeasurably expanded the borders of tonality. In other words, the chromatic scale of seven basic tones plus five visitors gave way to a twelve-tone scale in which eleven tones gravitated to the Tonic.

This use of twelve tones around a center not only did away with the distinction between diatonic and chromatic, but also wiped out the distinction between major and minor that was so important to the Classic-Romantic era. For example, traditional harmony presented two groups of seven tones with C as a center: C major and C minor. A twentieth-century piece, on the other hand, could be in the tonality of C—that is, in C major-minor, using all the twelve tones around the center C instead of dividing them into two separate groups of seven. There resulted an ambiguous tonality that suited the modern temper.

In general, the key was no longer so clearly defined an area in musical space as it used to be, and the shift from one key center to another was made with a dispatch that put to shame the most exuberant modulations of the Wagner era. Transitional passages were dispensed with. One tonality was simply displaced by another, in a way that kept both the music and the listener on the move. An excellent example is the popular theme from *Peter and the Wolf* (1936). Prokofiev was extremely fond of this kind of displacement. (The asterisk indicates change of tonality.)

In similar fashion chords utterly foreign to the tonality were included,

not even as modulations but simply as an extension of the key to a new tonal plane. As a result a passage sounded A-majorish, shall we say, rather than in A major.

Expansion of tonality was encouraged by a number of factors: interest in the exotic scales of Bali, Java, and other Far Eastern cultures; use of scales derived from the folk music of areas more or less outside the major-minor orbit, such as those of Russia, Scandinavia, Spain, Hungary and other Balkan countries; revival of interest in the medieval church modes and in composers who wrote long before the major-minor system evolved, such as the masters of fifteenth- and sixteenth-century counterpoint. The twentieth-century composer went far afield both in time and space in order to find new means of expression.

Polytonality

Tonality implied the supremacy of a single key and a single tone center. Composers in the past made the most out of the contrast between two keys heard in succession. The next step was to heighten the contrast by presenting them simultaneously.

To confront the ear with two keys at the same time meant to depart radically from the basic principle of traditional harmony. *Polytonality*— the use of two or more keys together—came to the fore in the music of Stravinsky and Milhaud, whence it entered the vocabulary of the age. Toward the end of a piece one key was generally permitted to assert itself over the others. In this way the impression was restored of orderly progression toward a central point.

Polytonality was used to bring out the different levels or planes of the harmony. By putting two or more streams of music in different keys the friction between them was immeasurably heightened. A famous example is the chord from Stravinsky's *Petrushka* that is associated with the luckless hero of this ballet: a C-major arpeggio superimposed upon one in F-sharp major.

In polytonal music the tension came from the clash of keys. Therefore each key had to be firmly established, as in the following example from Prokofiev's *Sarcasms* for piano (1912), in which right and left hand play in different keys:

So too, *Petrushka,* despite its daring harmonic combinations, has a surprisingly C-major look—that is, comparatively few sharps or flats: what used to be referred to as "white" music. The tendency toward "whiteness" was one of the characteristics of Parisian Neoclassicism.

By the same token Vienna, the center of Expressionism, inherited the fondness for chromatic harmony that was at the heart of German Romanticism.

Atonality

Although the principle of key was flexible enough in adjusting to the needs of the new music, there was bound to appear a musician who questioned whether such adjustment was at all possible. This was Arnold Schoenberg, who proclaimed that the concept of key had outlived its usefulness.

Schoenberg rebelled against the "tyranny" of the Tonic. He maintained that as long as the tones of the key, whether seven or twelve, were kept subordinate to a central tone, it was impossible to utilize all the resources of the chromatic scale. He advocated doing away with the Tonic—in other words, treating the twelve tones as of equal importance. In this way music would be freed, he maintained, from a number of procedures that had ceased to be fruitful.

To do away with the Tonic means abandoning a principle as fundamental in the musical universe as gravitation is in the physical. Schoenberg pointed out that since the major-minor system had not existed longer than three centuries, there was no reason to suppose that it could not be superseded. "Tonality is not an eternal law of music," he asserted, "but simply a means toward the achievement of musical form." The time had come, according to him, to seek new means.

To the music of Schoenberg and his school there attached itself the label *atonality.* He disliked the term as strongly as Debussy did Impressionism. "I regard the expression atonal as meaningless. Atonal can only signify something that does not correspond to the nature of tone." However, the name persisted.

Atonal music was much more of an innovation than polytonal music, for it rejected the framework of key. It excluded consonance which, according to Schoenberg, was no longer capable of making an impression. Its starting point was dissonance; it moved from one level of dissonance to another. There resulted a music that functioned always at maximum tension, without areas of relaxation. Dissonance resolving to consonance had been, symbolically, an optimistic act, affirming the triumph of rest over tension, of order over chaos. Atonal music, significantly, appeared at a time in European culture when belief in that triumph was sorely shaken.

Having accepted the necessity of moving beyond the existing tonal system, Schoenberg sought a unifying principle that would take the place of the key. He found this in a strict technique that he had worked out by the early 1920s. He named it "the method of composing with twelve tones."

The Twelve-Tone Method

"I was always occupied," Schoenberg declared, "with the desire to base the structure of my music *consciously* on a unifying idea." The twelve-tone technique made it possible for him to achieve coherence and unity in a musical composition without recourse to traditional procedures such as tonal organization, harmonic relationships, and expansion and development of themes. Each composition that uses Schoenberg's method is based on an arbitrary arrangement of the twelve chromatic tones that is called a *tone row*—or, as he terms it, a basic *set*. This row or set is the unifying idea that is the basis of that particular composition, and serves as the source of all the musical events that take place in it. The term
Serial *serial technique* is often used in this connection, an allusion to the series
technique of twelve tones. European writers prefer the expression *dodecaphonic,* which is the Greek equivalent of *twelve-tone.*

The twelve-tone row differs from a scale in one important respect. A scale is a traditional pattern that serves as the basic series for hundreds of composers and thousands of compositions. It soon becomes familiar to the listener; any departure from the pattern is at once perceptible to the
The tone row ear. The tone row, on the other hand, is the basic series of a particular composition, constituting a unique configuration of the twelve tones not to be found in any other piece. Since the twelve tones of the row are regarded as equally important, no one of them is allowed to appear more than once in the series lest it take on the prominence of a Tonic. (A tone may be repeated immediately, but this is regarded as an extension, not a new appearance.) When the basic set has unfolded it is repeated throughout the work, with the twelve tones always in the same order. Consequently the row determines the choice and succession of the intervals, shaping the overall sound of the piece. The row may be turned upside

down (inversion); it may be presented backward (retrograde); or upside down and backward (retrograde of the inversion). Each of these four versions—the original row and its three variants—may begin on any one of the twelve tones of the scale, giving forty-eight possibilities. The movement from one row form to another is loosely analogous to the passing from one key to another (modulation) in the old tonal architecture. The tone row, in fine, pervades the entire fabric of the composition, engendering not only the melody but the contrapuntal lines that unfold against it; also the harmony, since segments of the row may appear in vertical formation as chords. Thus, the unifying idea—the row—creates all the other ideas within the piece.

Texture   The basic set, of course, establishes not only a series of pitches but—even more important—a series of interval relationships. The persistence of this series of intervals in the melodies, harmonies, and counterpoints of an extended composition cannot but result in the closest possible relationship among these three dimensions of the musical tissue. The old distinction between melody and accompaniment is thereby done away with, the result being a texture of unparalleled homogeneity. Twelve-tone music, in short, seeks the utmost variety within the most stringent unity.

The following example shows the four versions of the basic set of Schoenberg's *Piano Concerto,* Opus 42. O stands for the original form, R for retrograde, I for inversion, and RI for the retrograde of the inversion.

All this, you will object, is quite arbitrary. To which your Schoenbergian will retort that all art is arbitrary. Precisely its artifice makes it art. Musical composition has always had its "rules of the game." If they seem to be more in evidence here, it is only because the system is new and its procedures are unfamiliar. The only valid criterion is: are Schoenberg's rules such as to enable a creative musician to express his thoughts, his feelings, and his time? Schoenberg's followers answer with an emphatic yes.

Dodeca-phonic melody   Dodecaphonic melody differs from the traditional kind in one important respect. Melody as we have come to know it generally lies in one register. However, in their desire for maximum intensity of expression, twelve-tone composers developed a jagged type of melody marked by enormous leaps from one octave to another. This poses severe problems for the performer, especially in vocal music, as in the following excerpt from Anton Webern's *Cantata No. 1,* Opus 29 (1939):

Hel - le stei - gen, bald__ im Him - mel

This angularity of line disappears if we rewrite Webern's melody so that the tones fall within the same octave:

In addition, the gravitational pull attaching to tones in the traditional harmonic system is weakened or wholly destroyed. For example, the strongest drive in tonal music is that of the seventh tone of the scale to the Tonic (*ti* to *do;* for example, B ascending to C). This drive is circumvented in twelve-tone music if the B ascends a ninth to the C of the octave above, or descends a seventh to the C below. As a matter of fact, intervals of the seventh and ninth are extremely prominent in twelve-tone music.

Contrapuntal techniques   Twelve-tone thinking is essentially contrapuntal thinking. It represents a horizontal-linear conception of music, with emphasis on melodic line rather than on the harmonic mass. This conception is implemented by the devices of counterpoint: canonic and fugal imitation; augmentation and diminution (the duplication of a motive in longer or shorter note values); inversion and retrograde. The twelve-tone method eliminates the repetitions and sequences, the balanced phrases and cadences of the older style. It embodies Schoenberg's doctrine of "perpetual variation." The dynamic of this music requires that no thought ever be repeated or duplicated save in some new form. As Schoenberg advised his students: "Never do what a copyist can do instead."

The tone row is not to be regarded as the theme of the piece. By the time a dodecaphonic composer has presented it in inverted and retrograde forms, and derived from it all his melodies, harmonies, and contrapuntal lines, in constantly varied rhythms, the row will have lost its identity as far as the ordinary ear is concerned. You will hardly be able to follow its wanderings as you can follow the course of a theme in a symphony. However, since the row determines the choice and succession of the intervals, its all-embracing presence governs every aspect of the music. More important, it pervades the thinking of the composer, providing him with the framework for his piece, even if that framework is no more visible to the beholder than is the steel skeleton that holds up a building.

The first masters of the dodecaphonic style display all the logic of this rigidly organized system; yet over their music brood the troubled visions that agonized the consciousness of Europe in the aftermath of the First

World War. However, the twelve-tone method is not equivalent to any particular style of composition. In recent years, as Schoenberg's method has been adopted and developed by many composers of different esthetic persuasions, it has become clear that twelve-tone music can be written in many styles.

The adherents of the twelve-tone method gained world-wide influence in the years following the Second World War. In the 1950s and '60s, dodecaphonic thinking emerged as the most advanced line of thought in musical esthetics and profoundly influenced the course of contemporary music.

67 Igor Stravinsky

"I hold that it was a mistake to consider me a revolutionary. If one only need break habit in order to be labeled a revolutionary, then every artist who has something to say and who in order to say it steps outside the bounds of established convention could be considered revolutionary."

It is granted to certain artists to embody the most significant impulses of their time and to affect its artistic life in the most powerful fashion. Such an artist was Igor Stravinsky (1882–1971), the Russian composer who for half a century gave impetus to the main currents in twentieth-century music.

Igor Stravinsky, by Picasso.

His Life

Stravinsky was born in Oranienbaum, a summer resort not far from St. Petersburg (Leningrad), where his parents lived. He grew up in a musical environment; his father was the leading bass at the Imperial Opera. Although he was taught to play the piano, his musical education was kept on the amateur level; his parents wanted him to study law. He matriculated at the University of St. Petersburg and embarked on a legal career, meanwhile continuing his musical studies. At twenty he submitted his work to Rimsky-Korsakov, with whom he subsequently worked for three years.

Diaghilev

Success came early to Stravinsky. His music attracted the notice of Serge Diaghilev, the legendary impresario of the Russian Ballet, who commissioned Stravinsky to write the music for *L'Oiseau de feu* (The Firebird), which was produced in 1910. Stravinsky was twenty-eight when he arrived in Paris to attend the rehearsals. Diaghilev pointed him out to the ballerina Tamara Karsavina with the words, "Mark him well—he is a man on the eve of fame."

The Firebird was followed, a year later, by *Petrushka*. Presented with Nijinsky and Karsavina in the leading roles, this production secured Stravinsky's position in the forefront of the modern movement in art. In the spring of 1913 was presented the third and most spectacular of the ballets Stravinsky wrote for Diaghilev, *Le Sacre du printemps* (The Rite of Spring). The opening night was one of the most scandalous in modern musical history; the revolutionary score touched off a near riot. People hooted, screamed, slapped each other, and were persuaded that what they were hearing "constituted a blasphemous attempt to destroy music as an art." A year later the composer was vindicated when the *Sacre,* presented at a symphony concert under Pierre Monteux, was received with enthusiasm and established itself as a masterpiece of new music.

The outbreak of war in 1914 brought to an end the whole way of life on which Diaghilev's sumptuous dance spectacles depended. Stravinsky, with his wife and children, took refuge in Switzerland, their home for the next six years. The difficulty of assembling large bodies 'of performers during the war worked hand in hand with his inner evolution as an artist: he moved away from the grand scale of the first three ballets to works more intimate in spirit and modest in dimension.

The Russian Revolution had severed Stravinsky's ties with his homeland. In 1920 he settled in France, where he remained until 1939. During these years Stravinsky concertized extensively throughout Europe, performing his own music as pianist and conductor. He also paid two visits to the United States. In 1939 he was invited to deliver the Charles Eliot Norton lectures at Harvard University. He was there when the Second World War broke out, and decided to live in this country. He settled in California,

Later years

outside Los Angeles, and in 1945 became an American citizen. In his later years, Stravinsky's worldwide concert tours made him the most celebrated figure in twentieth-century music, and his caustically witty books of "conversations" with his disciple Robert Craft are full of musical wisdom and footnotes to history. He died in New York on April 6, 1971.

His Music

Stravinsky showed a continuous development throughout his career. With inexhaustible avidity he has tackled new problems and pressed for new solutions. This evolution led from the post-Impressionism of *The Firebird* and the audacities of *The Rite of Spring* to the austerely controlled classicism of his maturity. In the course of it he laid ever greater emphasis upon tradition and discipline. "The more art is controlled, limited, worked over, the more it is free." He consistently extolled the element of construction as a safeguard against excess of feeling. "Composing for me is putting into an order a certain number of sounds according to certain interval relationships." A piece of music was for him first and foremost a problem. "I cannot compose until I have decided what problem I must solve." The problem was esthetic, not personal. As one of his biographers points out, "We find his musical personality in his works but not his personal joys or sorrows."

Early works

The national element predominates in his early works, as in *The Firebird, Petrushka,* and *Le Sacre du printemps,* which recreates the rites of pagan Russia. The Neoclassical period was ushered in by the *Symphonies of Wind Instruments* (1920), dedicated to the memory of Debussy. This period culminated in several major compositions. *Oedipus Rex* (1927) is an "opera-oratorio"; the text is a translation into Latin of Cocteau's adaptation of the Greek tragedy. From the shattering impact of the opening chords, *Oedipus Rex* is an unforgettable experience in the theater. The archaic Greek influence is manifest too in several ballets, of which the most important is *Apollon Musagète* (Apollo, Leader of the Muses; 1928), which marked the beginning of his collaboration with the choreographer George Balanchine.

Neoclassical period

The *Symphony of Psalms* (1930) is regarded by many as the chief work of Stravinsky's maturity. In 1950 he completed *The Rake's Progress,* an opera on a libretto by W. H. Auden and Chester Kallman, after Hogarth's celebrated series of engravings. Written as the composer was approaching seventy, this radiantly melodious score, which uses the set forms of the Mozartean opera, is the quintessence of Neoclassicism.

Stravinsky, imperturbably pursuing his own growth as an artist, had still another surprise in store for his public. In the works written after he was seventy, he showed himself increasingly receptive to the serial procedures of the twelve-tone style, which in earlier years he had opposed. This preoccupation came to the fore in a number of works dating from the middle fifties, of which the most important are the ballet *Agon* (1957) and *Threni—id est Lamentationes Jeremiae Prophetae* (Threnodies: Lamentations of the Prophet Jeremiah; completed 1958).

Twelve-tone works

Stravinsky's aphorisms display his gift for trenchant expression. "We have a duty to music, namely, to invent it. . . . Instinct is infallible. If it leads us astray it is no longer instinct. . . ." When asked to define the difference between *The Rite of Spring* and *Symphony of Psalms:* "The difference is twenty years." Of the innumerable anecdotes to which his ready tongue has given rise it will suffice to quote one. After the out-of-town opening of *Seven Lively Arts,* which included a ballet by Stravinsky, the managers of the show, apprehensive as to how the music would be received on Broadway, wired him: "Great success. Could be sensational if you authorize arranger Mr. X to add some details to orchestration. Mr. X arranges even the works of Cole Porter." To which Stravinsky wired back: "Am satisfied with great success."

Le Sacre du printemps

Le Sacre du printemps (The Rite of Spring; 1913)—"Scenes of Pagan Russia"—not only embodies the cult of primitivism that so startled its first-night audience; it also sets forth the lineaments of a new tonal language—the percussive use of dissonance, polyrhythms, and polytonality. The work is scored for a large orchestra, including an exceptionally varied percussion group.

Part I
Side 15/3 (S)
Side 9/3 (E II)

Part I. *Adoration of the Earth.* The Introduction is intended to evoke the birth of spring. A long-limbed melody is introduced by the bassoon, taking on a curious remoteness from the circumstance that it lies in the instrument's uppermost register. The narrow range and repetition of fragments gives this theme a primitive character:

The awakening of the earth is suggested in the orchestra. On stage, a group of young girls is discovered before the sacred mound, holding a long garland. The Sage appears and leads them toward the mound. The orchestra erupts into a climax, after which the bassoon melody returns.

Dance of the Adolescents. Dissonant chords in the lower register of the strings exemplify Stravinsky's "elemental pounding"; their percussive quality is heightened by the use of polytonal harmonies. A physical excitement attends the dislocation of the accent, which is underlined by syncopated chords hurled out by eight horns. The ostinato—a favorite rhythmic device of Stravinsky—is repeated with hypnotic insistence. A theme emerges on the bassoons, moving within a narrow range around a central tone, with a suggestion of elemental power.

Valentine Hugo's sketches of the *Danse sacrale* from the original ballet *Le Sacre du printemps* (1913), choreographed by Nijinsky. *(Collection André Meyer.)*

The main theme of the movement, a more endearing melody in folk style, is introduced by the horns. Stravinsky expands this idea by means of the repetition technique so characteristic of the Russian school.

Game of Abduction. The youths and maidens on the stage form into two phalanxes which in turn approach and withdraw from one another. Fanfares on the woodwinds and brass add a luminous quality to the sound.

Side 15/4 (S)
Side 9/4 (E II)
The climax of the ballet comes with the final number, *Sacrificial Dance of the Chosen Virgin,* in which the sacrifice is fulfilled. The music mounts in fury while the chosen maiden dances until she falls dead. The men in wild excitement bear her body to the foot of the mound. There is the scraping sound of the *guiro* (a Latin-American instrument consisting of a serrated gourd scraped with a wooden stick); an ascending run on the flutes and piccolos; and with a fortissimo growl in the orchestra this luminous score comes to an end.

More than half a century has passed since *Le Sacre* was written. It is still an amazing work.

Symphony of Psalms

The *Symphony of Psalms* (1930) was among the works commissioned by the Boston Symphony Orchestra to celebrate its fiftieth anniversary. There resulted one of Stravinsky's grandest works, "composed for the glory of God" and "dedicated to the Boston Symphony Orchestra."

The choice of instruments is unusual. The score omits clarinets, violins, and violas, and calls for two pianos and a mixed chorus.

Psalm XXXVIII (Vulgate)
Verses 13–14

Exaudi orationem meam, Domine,
  et deprecationem meam:
  auribus percipe lacrimas meas.
Ne sileas, quoniam advena ego sum apud te,
  et peregrinus, sicut omnes patres mei.
Remitte mihi,
  ut refrigerer prius quam abeam,
  et amplius non ero.

Hear my prayer, O Lord,
  and my supplication;
  give ear to my tears.
Be not silent; for I am a stranger with Thee,
  and a sojourner, as all my fathers were.
O forgive me,
  that I may be refreshed,
  before I go hence, and be no more.

*First
movement*

*Side 5/3 (S)
Side 10/1 (E II)*

The symphony opens with a prelude-like section in which flowing arabesques are traced by oboe and bassoon. These are punctuated by an urgent E-minor chord which, spread out across the orchestral gamut, asserts the principal tonality. The altos enter with a chantlike theme consisting of two adjacent notes—the interval of a minor second (semitone) that plays an important role throughout the work.

This idea alternates with the fuller sound of choral passages as the movement builds to its climactic point on the words "Remitte mihi" (O forgive me) over a strong pedal point on E. The modal harmony creates an archaic atmosphere and leans towards the Phrygian (the mode that matches the pattern of the white keys on the piano from E to E). Tension is created by the fact that the music seems again and again to be climbing toward the key of C without ever reaching it.

In upholding the Apollonian discipline in art Stravinsky reveals the age to itself. His spirit was one with the spirit of our time. This is made plain in the closing lines of his *Autobiography:* "I live neither in the past nor in the future. I am in the present. I cannot know what tomorrow may bring forth. I can only know what the truth is for me today. This is what I am called upon to serve, and I serve it in all lucidity."

68 Béla Bartók

"What is the best way for a composer to reap the full benefits of his studies in peasant music? It is to assimilate the idiom of peasant music so completely that he is able to forget all about it and use it as his musical mother tongue."

It was the mission of Béla Bartók (1881–1945) to reconcile the folk melody of his native Hungary with the main currents of European music. In the process he created an entirely personal language and revealed himself as one of the major artists of our century.

His Life

*Early contact
with folk
music*

Bartók was born in a small Hungarian town where his father was director of an agricultural school. He studied at the Royal Academy in Budapest, where he came in contact with the nationalist movement that aimed to shake off the domination of German musical culture. His interest in folklore led him to realize that what passed for Hungarian in the eyes of the world

Béla Bartók. *(Photo copyright by G. D. Hackett, New York.)*

—the idiom romanticized by Liszt and Brahms and kept alive by café musicians—was really the music of the Gypsies. The true Hungarian folk idiom, he decided, was to be found only among the peasants. In company with his fellow composer Zoltán Kodály he toured the remote villages of the country, determined to collect the native songs before they died out forever. Personal contact with peasant life brought to the surface the profound humanity that is the essential element of Bartók's art. "Those days I spent in the villages among the peasants were the happiest of my life. In order really to feel the vitality of this music one must, so to speak, have lived it. And this is possible only when one comes to know it by direct contact with the peasants."

Bartók became a leading figure in the musical life of his country. The alliance between Admiral Horthy's regime and Nazi Germany on the eve of the Second World War confronted him with issues that he faced squarely. He protested the performance of his music on the Berlin radio and at every opportunity took an anti-Fascist stand. To go into exile meant surrendering the position he enjoyed in Hungary. But he would not compromise. "He who stays on when he could leave may be said to acquiesce tacitly in everything that is happening here." Bartók's friends, fearing for his safety, prevailed upon him to leave the country while there was still time. He came to the United States in 1940 and settled in New York City.

Emigration to the U.S.

The last five years of his life yielded little in the way of happiness. Sensitive and retiring, he felt uprooted, isolated in his new surroundings. He made some public appearances, playing his music for two pianos with his wife and onetime pupil, Ditta Pásztory-Bartók. These did not suffice to relieve his financial straits. To his son he wrote in the fall of 1941, "Concerts are few and far between. If we had to live on those we would really be at the end of our tether."

Last years In his last years he suffered from leukemia and was no longer able to appear in public. Friends appealed for aid to ASCAP (American Society of Composers, Authors, and Publishers). Funds were made available that provided the composer with proper care in nursing homes and enabled him to continue writing to the end. A series of commissions from various sources spurred him to the composition of his last works. They rank among his finest. He worked feverishly to complete the *Third Piano Concerto* and a concerto for viola and orchestra that had been commissioned by William Primrose. When he realized that he was dying he concentrated on the piano concerto in order to leave his wife "the only inheritance within his power." In his race against time he wishfully wrote *vége*—The End—on his working sketch a few days before he actually finished the piece. The *Viola Concerto,* left unfinished, was brought to completion from his sketches by his friend and disciple Tibor Serly. "The trouble is," he remarked to his doctor shortly before the end, "that I have to go with so much still to say." He died in the West Side Hospital in New York City.

The tale of the composer who spends his last days in poverty and embitterment only to be acclaimed after his death would seem to belong to the past, to the legend of Mozart and Schubert. Yet it happened in our time. Bartók had to die in order to make his success in the United States. Almost immediately there was an upsurge of interest in his music that soon assumed the proportions of a boom. As though impelled by a sense of guilt for their previous neglect of his works, conductors, performers, record companies, broadcasting stations, and even his publishers rushed to pay him the homage that might have brought him comfort had it come in time.

His Music

Like Stravinsky, Bartók was careful to disclaim the role of revolutionary. "In art there are only fast or slow developments. Essentially it is a matter of evolution, not revolution." Despite the newness of his language he was rooted in the Classical heritage. He adhered to the logic and beauty of Classical form, and to Beethoven's vision of music as an embodiment of human emotion.

Bartók found authentic Hungarian folk music to be based on ancient modes, unfamiliar scales, and nonsymmetrical rhythms. These freed him from what he called "the tyrannical rule of the major and minor keys," and brought him to new concepts of melody, harmony, and rhythm. "What we had to do," he wrote, "was to divine the spirit of this unknown music and to make this spirit, so difficult to describe in words, the basis of our works."

Bartók recording folk songs in Transylvania. *(Photo copyright by G. D. Hackett, New York.)*

Rhythmic innovation   Bartók's is one of the great rhythmic imaginations of modern times. His pounding, stabbing rhythms constitute the primitive aspect of his art. Passages in his scores have a Stravinskyan look, the meter changing almost at every bar. Like the Russian master, he is fond of syncopation and repeated patterns (ostinatos). Bartók played a major role in the revitalization of European rhythm, infusing it with early vitality, with kinetic force and tension. He is best known to the public by the three major works of his last period. The *Music for Strings, Percussion, and Celesta,* written in 1936, is regarded by many as his masterpiece. Tonal opulence and warmth characterize the *Concerto for Orchestra* (1943), a favorite with American audiences. The master's final statement, the *Third Piano Concerto* (1945), is an impassioned and broadly conceived work, its three movements by turn dramatic, contemplative, satanic. The last-named quality connects him with the Hungarian master of the Romantic period, Franz Liszt.

Bartók's music encompasses the diverse trends of his time: polytonality and atonality, Expressionism, Neoclassicism, and folk dance. It reaches from the primitive to the intellectual, from program music to abstract, from the local-national to the universal. Into all these he infused the high aim of a former age: to touch the heart.

Music for Strings, Percussion, and Celesta: *First Movement*

This work (1936) was a landmark in the twentieth-century cultivation of chamber-music textures. Bartók's conception called for two string groups to frame the percussion and celesta. He carefully specified the arrangement of the players on the stage:

	Double Bass I	Double Bass II	
Cello I	Timpani	Bass Drum	Cello II
Viola I	Side Drums	Cymbals	Viola II
Violin II	Celesta	Xylophone	Violin IV
Violin I	Piano	Harp	Violin III

*First
movement*
Side 16/2 (S)
Side 10/2 (E II)

Andante tranquillo. The movement is based on a single crescendo that grows inexorably from *pp* to a fortissimo climax and then works back to a *ppp*. We hear a fugue based on an undulating chromatic theme that moves within the range of a fifth, from A to E, and includes all the semitones between. This subject is introduced by the muted violas. Each time the subject enters it appears alternately a fifth higher and lower, fanning out from

the central tone A—first on E (a fifth above A), then on D (a fifth below A); on B (a fifth above E), G (a fifth below D), F sharp (a fifth above B), and so on—growing steadily in power until the climactic point is reached on E flat. Thereupon the theme is inverted and the movement returns to the central A. Thus, the crescendo-decrescendo pattern is combined with a sequence of tonal centers that are a fifth apart in an ascending-descending motion. Since the entire movement is woven out of the generating theme, this Andante achieves an extraordinary concentration of thought and consistency of texture.

Bartók's prime characteristic both as musician and man was the uncompromising integrity that informed his every act—what a compatriot of his has called "the proud morality of the mind." He was one of the great spirits of our time.

69 Arnold Schoenberg

"I personally hate to be called a revolutionist, which I am not. What I did was neither revolution nor anarchy."

It is worthy of note that, like Stravinsky and Bartók, the other great innovator of our time disclaimed revolutionary intent. Quite the contrary, his disciples regard him as having brought to its culmination the thousand-year-old tradition of European polyphony.

The images on the canvases of Expressionist painters issued from the realm of the unconscious: hallucinated visions that defied the traditional notion of beauty in order to express more powerfully the artist's inner self. This is exemplified in **Panel (3)** by Wassily Kandinsky (1866–1944). *(Collection, The Museum of Modern Art, New York. Mrs. Simon Guggenheim Fund.)*

This late work by the painter Paul Klee (1879–1940), **Heroic Strokes of the Bow,** expresses the artist's intensely personal reactions to music through simple, yet symbolic forms. *(Collection of Nelson A. Rockefeller; photo by Charles Uht.)*

His Life

Arnold Schoenberg (1874–1951) was born in Vienna. He began to study the violin at the age of eight, and soon afterward made his initial attempts at composing. Having decided to devote his life to music, he left school while in his teens. Presently he became acquainted with a young musician, Alexander von Zemlinsky, who for a few months gave him lessons in counterpoint. This was the only musical instruction he ever had. In 1899, when he was twenty-five, Schoenberg wrote the string sextet *Verklärte*

Early years   *Nacht* (Transfigured Night). The following year several of his songs were performed in Vienna and precipitated a scene. "And ever since that day," he once remarked with a smile, "the scandal has never ceased."

In 1901, after his marriage to Zemlinsky's sister, he moved to Berlin and obtained a post in a theater, conducting operettas and music-hall songs. Schoenberg's early music already displayed certain traits of his later style. A publisher to whom he brought a quartet observed, "You must think that if the second theme is a retrograde inversion of the first theme, that automatically makes it good!"

Arnold Schoenberg,
by Oskar Kokoschka
(b. 1886).

With each new work Schoenberg moved closer to as bold a step as any artist has ever taken—the rejection of tonality. The First World War interrupted his creative activity. Although he was past forty, he was called up for military service in the Vienna garrison. He had reached a critical point in his development. There followed a silence of seven years, between 1915 and 1923, during which he clarified his position in his own mind, and evolved a set of structural procedures to replace tonality. The goal once set, Schoenberg pursued it with that tenacity of purpose without which no prophet can prevail. His "method of composing with twelve tones" caused great bewilderment in the musical world. All the same, he was now firmly established as a leader of contemporary musical thought. In 1925, he was appointed to succeed Ferruccio Busoni as professor of composition at the Berlin Academy of Arts. The uniquely favorable attitude of the Weimar Republic toward experimental art had made it possible for one of the most iconoclastic musicians in history to carry on his work from the vantage point of an official post.

Move to the United States

This period in Schoenberg's life ended with the coming to power of Hitler in 1933. He arrived in the United States in the fall of 1933. After a short period of teaching in Boston, he joined the faculty of the University of Southern California, and shortly afterward was appointed professor of composition at the University of California in Los Angeles. In 1940 he became an American citizen. He taught until his retirement at the age of seventy, and continued his musical activities till his death in 1951. A seeker after truth until the end, to no one more than to himself could be applied the injunction he had written in the text of his cantata *Die Jakobsleiter* (Jacob's Ladder; 1913): "One must go on without asking what lies before or behind."

His Music

Post-Wagnerian Romanticism

Schoenberg's first period may be described as one of post-Wagnerian Romanticism; he still used key signatures and remained within the boundaries of tonality. The best-known work of this period is *Verklärte Nacht,* Opus 4, which poses no problems to anyone who has listened to *Tristan.* Indeed, the work became something of a popular hit after it was used by Antony Tudor as the accompaniment for his Expressionist ballet *Pillar of Fire.* Schoenberg's second period, the atonal-Expressionist, got under way with the *Three Piano Pieces,* Opus 11 (1909), in which he abolished the distinction between consonance and dissonance as well as the sense of a home key. Concentrated and intense, these short pieces point the way to his later development.

Atonal Expressionism

Twelve-tone period

Schoenberg's third period, that of the twelve-tone method, reached its climax in the *Variations for Orchestra,* Opus 31 (1927–28). This is the first twelve-tone composition for orchestra and one of Schoenberg's most powerful works. In the fourth and last period of his career—the American phase—he carried the twelve-tone technique to further stages of refinement. He also modified his doctrine sufficiently to allow tonal elements to coexist with the twelve-tone style, and on occasion wrote "old-fashioned" music with key signatures.

Schoenberg was a tireless propagandist for his ideas, a role for which his verbal gifts and his passion for polemics eminently fitted him. Essays and articles flowed from his pen, conveying his views in a trenchant, aphoristic style which, late in life, he transferred from German to English. The following observations are characteristic: "Genius learns only from itself, talent chiefly from others. . . . Creation to an artist should be as natural and inescapable as the growth of apples to an apple tree. . . . The twelve tones will not invent for you. . . . It is said of many an author that he has indeed technique, but no invention. That is wrong: either he also lacks technique or he also has invention. . . ."

Five Pieces for Orchestra, *Opus 16: Nos. 1 and 2*

The *Five Pieces for Orchestra* (1909) constitu e one of the key works of Schoenberg's second period, when his language became atonal. In order to solve the problems of the new idiom, he concentrated on the short lyric forms. In line with the Expressionist point of view, he connected the *Five Orchestral Pieces* with specific emotions and moods and gave them descriptive titles. Forty years later—in 1949—he revised the *Five Pieces,* rescoring them for an orchestra of the usual size instead of the huge ensemble required in the original version.

First piece

Side 16/3 (S)
Side 10/3 (E II)

I. *Vorgefühle* (Premonitions). The first piece, marked "very fast," shows how well the atonal idiom lends itself to the expression of fear and anxiety. This music evokes a hallucinatory world where agony of soul reigns unrelieved. The basic theme is an ascending motive that is announced at the outset by muted cellos, against descending parallel fifths on clarinets:

This theme reappears throughout the piece in manifold guises, with changes of rhythm (augmentation and diminution) and variation in the size of its intervals. The climb to the final note underlines the continuous sense of climax. Schoenberg exploits striking instrumental effects, such as the frightening rasp of muted horn and trombone, and *fluttertonguing* (a rolling of the tongue, as if pronouncing d-r-r-r, used in playing wind instruments) on the muted trumpet. He intrigues the ear with unwonted contrasts of high and low registers, achieves a remarkable luminosity of texture, and keeps the sound mass in a state of dynamic impulsion.

II. *Vergangenes* (Yesteryears). Andante. A lyrical meditation, in-

Second piece
Side 16/4 (S)
Side 10/4 (E II)

tensely Romantic in character. The opening harmonies are composites of colors as well as tones: each note of the chord is played by a different instrument. The bare look of the notes on the page shows the line of descent from the fervidly chromatic idiom of *Tristan* (see p. 130). The introductory motive on the cello sets the mood for a music that seems to be suspended in time.

A new section is ushered in by an expressive idea on the muted viola, which emerges as the principal theme of the piece. There enters a hopping figure on the bassoon, against a flowing ostinato on the celesta, which becomes a counter-subject for the principal idea. The climax is a whisper: sixteenth-note figures derived from the bassoon motive build up—to a *ppp!* The chief motive dominates the closing pages. The final sounds are extremely rarefied: a splash of color on the celesta, harmonics on strings and harp, against sustained harmonies in woodwinds and muted brass.

A Survivor From Warsaw

The cantata *A Survivor from Warsaw* sprang out of one of the most profound experiences of Schoenberg's life. Like many Austrian-Jewish intellectuals of his generation, he had grown away from his Jewish origins and ultimately became a Catholic. The rise of Hitlerism reminded him that he was a Jew. After he left Germany he found it spiritually necessary to return to the Hebrew faith. He was deeply shaken when, at the end of the war, the world learned how the Nazis had transported millions of Jews from all over Europe into the Warsaw Ghetto and then herded them into the gas chambers of Dachau, Buchenwald, Auschwitz. The world learned too how the final remnant of Jews in the Ghetto decided to die fighting rather than be slaughtered, and organized the first uprising in Occupied Europe. Emotionally involved as he was in these historic events, Schoenberg in *A Survivor from Warsaw* (1947) produced one of his most dramatic works.

We pointed out how well the atonal idiom lent itself to the moods of fear and suspense that were native to German Expressionism. These moods predominate in *A Survivor,* a six-minute cantata marked by the same emotional intensity that we noted in the first of the *Five Pieces for Orchestra (Premonitions)*. Here the fear and suspense are brought into dramatic focus through the text, which was written by Schoenberg himself in English. He was no literary craftsman, and he was writing in a language that he had learned late in life; yet the blazing sincerity out of which he wrote more than makes up for a certain crudity of style.

The plot

A narrator recounts how a group of Jews were conducted to their death by a detachment of Nazi soldiers. The Germans order the Jews out of the camp and line them up for the final march. They urge them on with blows and curses, shooting those that fall behind. Finally the order comes to count off, so that the sergeant may know how many to deliver to the gas chamber. They begin to count, first slowly, then faster. Finally, as by a common impulse, they begin to sing the *Shema Yisroel*—the ancient prayer that is the central creed of the Hebrew faith.

The grim tale is told by one who survived because he was left among the dead. At two points narration gives way to action. First, when the narrator quotes the sergeant, imitating his brutal manner of barking commands. Here Schoenberg uses the percussion instruments—bass drum, snare drum, xylophone, cymbals—to underscore the text. Second, at the dramatic climax of the piece, the grandiose moment, as Schoenberg called it, when in the face of death the Jews begin to sing. At this point, when the narrator is replaced by male chorus, the full orchestra enters for the first time. (Hitherto the orchestra has played only in groups.)

The music

Side 18/1 (S)
Side 10/5 (E II)

From the suspenseful fanfare of the trumpets at the outset, the score abounds in remarkable strokes. For example, the high trill on the trombones in the orchestral introduction. Or the unusual effects on the string instruments, produced by tapping the strings with the stick of the bow or by scratching the strings with the stick. In the same category are the high trills on the woodwinds, fluttertonguing on the muted brass, and the snarling sound produced by forcing the tone of muted trumpets and horns. Extraordinary too is the crescendo, accelerando, and breathless intensification of rhythm (based on a pattern of two against three) when the Jews count off, faster and faster, until "it finally sounded like a stampede of wild horses."

The cantata belongs to the final period of Schoenberg's career, when he was using the fully developed twelve-tone method. A few examples will suffice to show how this technique nurtured his sense of logical structure. The piece opens with two urgent trumpet fanfares, each accompanied by a two-note chord in the strings:

The row   Although the twelve-tone row on which the cantata is based does not
appear in melodic form until the entrance of the chorus, all the previous
material is derived from it. Thus, the four notes of Trumpet I are the first
four notes of the row, and the two violin notes are the next two.

The fanfare, in Trumpet II, and its accompanying notes comprise the beginning of the row's inversion (remember that in twelve-tone composition
a pitch may appear in any octave).

Schoenberg uses the elements of the row in diverse ways. It will suffice
to cite one further example. When the narrator speaks of "the old prayer
they had neglected for so many years," a melody is heard in the muted
horn, pianissimo:

This melody consists of the first six notes of the row, transposed to begin
on B flat:

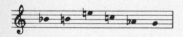

Later, this melody returns at the climax, as the opening phrase of the *Shema
Yisroel.*

Despite the formal intricacies of his method, Schoenberg maintained
again and again that the prime function of a composer was to move the
listener. "I write what I feel in my heart—and what finally comes on paper
is what first coursed through every fibre of my body. A work of art can
achieve no finer effect than when it transmits to the beholder the emotions that raged in the creator, in such a way that they rage and storm
also in him." In *A Survivor from Warsaw* Schoenberg fashioned a work of
art that fully transmits to us the emotions that raged in him.

His belief in the necessity and rightness of his method sustained him and
gave him the strength to carry through his revolution. His doctrines focused
attention on basic compositional problems, and decisively affected the
course of musical thought in the twentieth century.

70 Alban Berg

"When I decided to write an opera, my only intention was to give to the theater what belongs to the theater. The music was to be so formed that at each moment it would fulfill its duty of serving the action."

It was the unique achievement of Alban Berg (1885–1935) to humanize the abstract procedures of the Schoenbergian technique, and to reconcile them with the expression of feeling. Upon a new and difficult idiom he imprinted the stamp of a lyric imagination of the first order.

His Life

Berg was born in Vienna. He came of a well-to-do family and grew up in an environment that fostered his artistic proclivities. At nineteen he made the acquaintance of Arnold Schoenberg, who was sufficiently impressed with the youth's manuscripts to accept him as a pupil. During his six years with Schoenberg (1904–10) he acquired the consummate mastery of technique that characterizes his later work. Schoenberg was not only an exacting master, but also a devoted friend and mentor who shaped Berg's whole outlook on art.

The outbreak of war in 1914 hurled Berg into a period of depression. "The urge 'to be in it,' " he wrote to Schoenberg, "the feeling of helplessness at being unable to serve my country, prevented any concentration on work." A few months later he was called up for military service, despite his uncertain health (he suffered from asthma and attacks of nervous debility). He was presently transferred to the War Ministry in Vienna. Already *Wozzeck* occupied his thoughts; but he could not begin writing the music until the war was over. In December 1925 *Wozzeck* was presented at the Berlin State Opera. At one stroke Berg was lifted from comparative obscurity to international fame.

In the decade that remained to him he produced only a handful of works; but each was a significant contribution to his total output. During these years he was active as a teacher. He also wrote about music, propagandizing tirelessly on behalf of Schoenberg and his school. With the coming to power of Hitler, the works of the twelve-tone composers were banned in Germany as alien to the spirit of the Third Reich. The resulting loss of income was a source of worry to Berg, as was, to a far greater degree, the rapid Nazification of Austria. Schoenberg's enforced emigration to the United States was a bitter blow.

Exhausted and ailing after the completion of the *Violin Concerto,* Berg went to the country for a short rest before resuming work on his opera

Alban Berg. Wash drawing by G. Stekel, 1935. *(Collection André Meyer.)*

Lulu. An insect bite brought on an abscess that caused infection. Upon his return to Vienna he was stricken with blood poisoning and died on Christmas Eve 1935, seven weeks before his fifty-first birthday.

His Music

Berg's art issued from the world of German Romanticism—the world of Schumann, Brahms, Wagner, Richard Strauss, and Mahler. The Romantic streak in his temperament bound him to this heritage even after he had embraced the twelve-tone style. Berg's was the imagination of the musical dramatist. For him the musical gesture was bound up with character and action, mood and atmosphere. Yet, like his teacher, he leaned toward the formal patterns of the past—fugue and invention, passacaglia, variations, sonata, and suite.

Berg's most widely known composition, after *Wozzeck,* is the *Lyric Suite,* written in 1925–26. The work is in six movements. The first and last follow strictly "the method of composing with twelve tones." Originally written for string quartet, the *Lyric Suite* achieved such popularity that in 1928 the composer arranged the three middle movements for string orchestra.

Alban Berg is probably the most widely admired master of the twelve-tone school. His premature death robbed contemporary music of a major figure.

Wozzeck

In 1914 Berg saw the play that impelled him to the composition of *Wozzeck.* He finished the draft of the libretto by the summer of 1917. Most of the music was written from 1918 to 1920 and orchestrated the following year. The vocal score was published in 1923 with the financial help of Alma Mahler, to whom *Wozzeck* was dedicated.

The author of the play, Georg Büchner (1813–37), belonged to the generation of intellectuals who were stifled by the political repressions of Metternich's Europe. His socialist leanings brought him into conflict with the authorities. After his death at twenty-four, the manuscripts of *Danton's Tod* (The Death of Danton) and the unfinished *Woyzeck* (this was the original spelling) were found among his papers. In the stolid infantryman Wozzeck he created an archetype of "the insulted and injured" of the earth.

Libretto   Berg's libretto tightened the original play. He shaped the material into three acts, each containing five scenes. These are linked by brief orchestral interludes whose motivic facture serves to round off what has preceded as well as to introduce what follows. As a result, Berg's "opera of protest and compassion" has astonishing unity of texture and mood.

The action centers around Wozzeck's unhappy love for Marie, by whom he has had an illegitimate child. Wozzeck is the victim of the sadistic Captain and of the Doctor, a coldly scientific gentleman who uses Wozzeck for his experiments—to which the soldier submits because he needs the money. (Wozzeck is given to hallucinations. The Doctor is bent on proving his theory that mental disorder is related to diet.) Marie cannot resist her infatuation with the handsome Drum Major. Wozzeck slowly realizes that she has been unfaithful to him. Ultimately he kills her. Driven back to the death-scene by guilt and remorse, he drowns himself. The tragedy unfolds in three acts. The first is the exposition of the theme: "Wozzeck in relation to his environment." The second is the development of the theme: "Wozzeck becomes more and more convinced of Marie's infidelity." The third act is the catastrophe: "Wozzeck murders Marie and atones by suicide."

The vocal line sensitively portrays characters and situations. Harmonically, the greater part of the opera is cast in an atonal-Expressionist idiom. Berg anticipates certain twelve-tone procedures; he also looks back to the tonal tradition, puts a number of passages in major and minor keys, and uses leitmotifs in the Wagnerian manner. The snatches of popular song in the score create an effective contrast to their atonal surroundings. Appearing in so special a context, they take on a strange wistfulness.

Act III,   Profoundly moving is the scene in which Wozzeck, haunted by remorse,
Scene 4   returns to the pond (Act III, Scene 4). How poignant is his "Marie! Was
Side 17/1 (S) hast Du für eine rote Schnur um den Hals?" (Marie, what is that red string
Side 11/1 (E II) around your neck?) His last words as he drowns, "Ich wasche mich mit Blut . . ." (I wash myself in blood—the water is blood . . . blood . . .), usher in a series of ascending chromatic scales that pass in a ghostly pianissimo from the strings to the woodwinds and brass.

There follows a symphonic meditation in D minor, a passionate lament for the life and death of Wozzeck. This inspired fantasy indicates how richly Berg's art was nourished by the Romanticism of Mahler. The final

Wozzeck, Act II, Scene 3: Wozzeck (Peter Glossop) raises his hand to strike Marie (Janis Martin), in the Metropolitan Opera production. *(Photo copyright by Beth Bergman.)*

scene takes place in the morning in front of Marie's house. Children are playing. Marie's little boy rides a hobbyhorse. Other children rush in with news of the murder, but Marie's son does not understand. The children run off. The little boy continues to ride and sing. Then, noticing that he has been left alone, he calls "Hopp, hopp" and rides off on his hobbyhorse, to the sound of clarinet, drum, xylophone, and strings *ppp.* For sheer heartbreak the final curtain has few to equal it in the contemporary lyric theater.

Wozzeck envelops the listener in a hallucinated world in which the hunters are as driven as the hunted. It could have come only out of central Europe in the 1920s. But its characters reach out beyond time and place to become eternal symbols of the human condition.

71 Anton Webern

"With me, things never turn out as I wish, but only as is ordained for me—as I must."

Anton Webern (1883–1945) is still not very well known to the public at large. All the same his works have shaped the musical thinking of our time in a most decisive fashion.

His Life

Anton von Webern (he dropped the prefix of nobility in later life) was born in Vienna. His musical gifts asserted themselves at an early age. He was twenty-one when he met Schoenberg and, with Alban Berg, formed the nucleus of the band of disciples who gathered around the master.

After the First World War he settled in Mödling, a suburb of Vienna, where he lived quietly, devoting himself to composition and teaching. He suffered great hardship after Austria became part of the Third Reich. The Nazis regarded his music as *Kulturbolshevismus* (cultural bolshevism), forbade its performance, and burned his writings. He was permitted to teach only a few pupils, and had to give his lectures—in which he expounded the Schoenbergian point of view—in secret. In order to avoid forced labor during the war, he worked as proofreader for a Viennese publisher. To escape the Allied bombings of Vienna, Webern and his wife sought refuge at the home of their son-in-law in Mittersill, a small town near Salzburg. But fate awaited him there. On September 15, 1945, as he stepped out of his house in the evening to smoke a cigarette (the war had ended five months before, but Mittersill was still under a curfew), he failed to understand an order to halt and was shot by a trigger-happy sentry of the American occupying forces. "The day of Anton Webern's death," wrote his most celebrated admirer, Igor Stravinsky, "should be a day of mourning for any receptive musician. We must hail not only this great composer but also a real hero. Doomed to total failure in a deaf world of ignorance and indifference, he

Anton Webern. Lithograph by Hildegarde Jone, 1946. *(Collection André Meyer.)*

inexorably kept on cutting out his diamonds, his dazzling diamonds, of whose mines he had such a perfect knowledge."

His Music

Webern responded to the radical portion of Schoenbergian doctrine, just as Berg exploited its more conservative elements. Of the three masters of the modern Viennese school, he was the one who cut himself off most completely from the tonal past. The Schoenbergians, we saw, favored the short forms. Webern carried this urge for brevity much further than either of his comrades, as is clear from his *Five Orchestral Pieces*. Such conciseness seems to nullify the very notion of time as we have come to understand it in music. Hardly less novel is the musical fabric in which he clothed his ideas. His scores call for the most unusual combinations of instruments. Each tone is assigned its specific function in the overall scheme. The instruments are often used in their extreme registers; they not infrequently play one at a time, and very little. This technique confers upon the individual sound an importance it never had before.

With his *Symphony*, Opus 21 (1928) Webern came into his fully matured style. In this and the works that followed, the twelve-tone technique is used with unprecedented strictness. Schoenberg had contented himself with an organization based upon fixed series of pitches. Webern extended this concept to include timbres and rhythms. Therewith he moved toward complete control of the sonorous material—in other words, total serialization.

Five Pieces for Orchestra, *Opus 10: Nos. 3 and 4*

The *Five Pieces for Orchestra* (1911–13) bring to the fore what Webern called "the almost exclusively lyrical nature" of his music. The concentrated lyricism here makes for unprecedented brevity: the set of five numbers lasts about five minutes. The work is scored for an orchestral group in which each player is a soloist. Webern includes mandoline and guitar, instruments that have been favored by the Viennese composers because of their bright pointed sound. The pieces belong to the composer's atonal—that is to say, pre-twelve-tone—period, and come out of the Expressionist atmosphere that prevailed in central Europe at that time. As in the case of *Wozzeck,* the score shows an occasional foreshadowing of the twelve-tone technique.

Third piece
Side 16/5 (S)
Side 10/6 (E II)

The third piece is marked Sehr langsam und äusserst ruhig (very slow and extremely calm). A true son of Austria, Webern loved the mountains of his native land and their bell sounds. This slow movement is almost a study in bell sonorities, evoking as it does the clear open spaces of a mountain scene. It is eleven and one-half measures in length, in $\frac{6}{4}$ time (except for a measure of $\frac{3}{4}$ and one of $\frac{2}{4}$). Harmonium, mandoline, guitar, celesta, harp, glockenspiel, and cowbells play trills and repeated notes against gentle trills on the drums, while clarinet, muted horn and trombone, violin, muted viola and cello trace their brief, tenuous motives.

Fourth piece
Side 16/6 (S)
Side 10/7 (E II)

The fourth is the shortest piece in the entire orchestral literature, six and one-third bars that take less than half a minute to play. It is marked Fliessend, äusserst zart (flowing, extremely soft), in ¾ time. Clarinet, muted violin and viola unfold their traceries in a delicate mosaic. The first twelve tones are all different ones—in other words, a tone row. Nothing is scored below middle C. A figure on the mandoline, with a chord on the harp, is answered by one on the muted trumpet. The violin finishes with five notes played *ppp, wie ein Hauch* (like a whisper).

The creator of this remarkable music was content to go his way, an obscure figure in the musical circles of his time, overshadowed by those who made a bigger noise in the world. He had no way of knowing that little over a decade after his death, many avant-garde musicians in Europe and America would think of themselves as belonging to "the age of Webern."

72 Other Composers of the Twentieth Century

Milhaud

France produced several figures who had an impact upon the music of our time. Darius Milhaud (1892–1975) explored in greater detail than almost any of his confreres the possibilities of several keys sounding at the same time. *La Création du monde* (The Creation of the World; 1923) is a delightful ballet whose score shows Milhaud's strong response to American jazz.

Honegger

Arthur Honegger (1892–1955) was Swiss, but spent the greater part of his professional life in Paris. His music shows a richly romantic strain. Best-known among his large output is *Pacific 231,* a "machine music" depiction of a locomotive, and the *Symphony No. 5,* his finest achievement.

Poulenc

Francis Poulenc (1899–1963) ranged from Parisian elegance to a deeply felt lyricism. He was one of the finest song composers of our time. His opera *Dialogues des Carmelites* (Dialogues of the Carmelites, on a libretto by Georges Bernanos; 1953–55), about a group of nuns in the French Revolution, illustrates the romantic orientation of his later style.

Messiaen

Olivier Messiaen (b. 1908) has tried to revive the religious ideal in art; he has placed his music, as he says, "at the service of the dogmas of Catholic theology." His *Quartet for the End of Time* (1941) was written during the Second World War after he was captured by the Germans and transferred to a prisoner-of-war camp, Stalag VIIIA, in Saxony. Its eight movements glow with religious fervor and hope.

Prokofiev

The modern Russian school produced a world figure in Serge Prokofiev

(1891–1953), whose athletic rhythms, pungent harmonies, and soaring melodies have made him one of the most popular among twentieth-century composers. More of his works have established themselves as "classics" with the international public than those of any of his contemporaries save Stravinsky. Listen to the *Third Piano Concerto* (1921), *Lieutenant Kije Suite* (1934), *Peter and the Wolf* (1936), the *Piano Sonata No. 7* (1942), and the *Fifth Symphony* (1944).

Shostakovich   Dmitri Shostakovich (1906–75) was the first Russian composer of international repute who was wholly a product of Soviet musical culture. His *First Symphony* (1925), written for his graduation from the Leningrad Conservatory when he was nineteen, remained his best; but you will derive much pleasure from the *Fifth Symphony* (1937) and the *Concerto for Piano, Trumpet, and Strings* (1933).

Hindemith   Paul Hindemith (1895–1963) was the most important German composer of this generation. He left Germany when Hitler came to power and had a great vogue in this country in the 1940s, when he taught composition at Yale. The symphony he derived from his opera *Mathis der Maler* (Mathis the Painter; 1934) is his best-known work. Also popular is his *Symphonic Metamorphosis on Themes of Weber* (1943).

Kodály   Zoltán Kodály (1882–1967) was associated with Béla Bartók in the collection and study of peasant songs. *Háry János* (1926), a folk play with music centering about a retired soldier of exuberant imagination, won an international success.

Orff   Carl Orff, born in Munich in 1895, took his point of departure from the clear-cut melody, simple harmonic structure, and vigorous rhythm of Bavarian popular song. His best-known work is the "dramatic cantata" *Carmina burana* (Songs of Beuren; 1936).

Krenek   Ernest Krenek (b. 1900) won fame with his jazz opera *Jonny spielt auf* (Johnny Plays!; 1927). He is a prolific composer of operas, ballets, piano sonatas, symphonies, four piano concertos, and eight string quartets.

Weill   Kurt Weill (1900–50) was one of the most arresting figures to emerge in Germany in the Twenties. To the international public his name is indissolubly linked with *Die Dreigroschenoper* (The Three-Penny Opera), which he and the poet Bertolt Brecht adapted from John Gay's celebrated *Beggar's Opera*. Upon the lusty antics of Gay's work Weill and Brecht superimposed the despair, the agonized outcry of a Germany in the aftermath of the First World War. It remains his masterpiece.

de Falla   Manuel de Falla (1876–1946) tried to base a twentieth-century art on authentic Spanish folklore. He is remembered chiefly for the ballets *El Amor brujo* (Love the Magician; 1915) and *The Three-Cornered Hat* (1919).

Bloch   Ernest Bloch (1880–1959) differs from other composers of Jewish extraction such as Mendelssohn, Meyerbeer, Saint-Saëns, or Mahler, who were assimilated into the musical culture of the country in which they lived. He tried to create a Hebraic style based on his response to the Old Testament. *Schelomo,* a Rhapsody for cello and orchestra (1915)—the title is the Hebrew name of the poet-king Solomon—evokes a biblical landscape with all the force of a temperament given to sensuous abandon and mystical exaltation.

Walton   William Walton (b. 1902) was the outstanding representative of the modern English school in the second quarter of the century. He is best known in this country for his oratorio *Belshazzar's Feast* (1931). He is also appreciated here as a film composer. Among his most successful scores were those for Sir Laurence Olivier's *Henry V* (1944) and *Hamlet* (1947).

Britten   Benjamin Britten (1913–1976) was a musician of great invention, technical mastery, and charm. Besides a quantity of orchestral, choral, and chamber music, Britten wrote a number of operas, of which the most important is *Peter Grimes* (1945). He was the most important English composer of his generation.

SEVEN
The American Scene

"What we must arrive at is the youthful optimistic vitality and the undaunted tenacity of spirit that characterize the American man. That is what I hope to see echoed in American music." — EDWARD MACDOWELL

73 The Past

"Music . . . the favorite passion of my soul." — THOMAS JEFFERSON

The Beginnings

The first publication to appear in British North America was the *Bay Psalm Book,* which was published in Cambridge in 1640. Its appearance underlines what was the chief function of music in early New England: the singing of psalms and hymns.

Jefferson

In Virginia, on the other hand, there evolved a society of planters who adhered to the social amenities of Cavalier England. As in the aristocratic circles of Europe, music served for polite and elegant entertainment. Jefferson was an amateur violinist, played string quartets at the weekly musicales of Governor Fauquier, and invented an ingenious violin stand which when folded did duty as an end table. Years later, in planning Monticello, he inquired of a friend in France whether there might not be found a gardener, weaver, cabinetmaker, and stone cutter who could double on French horn, clarinet, oboe, and bassoon. "The bounds of an American fortune," he writes, "will not admit the indulgence of a domestic band of musicians, yet I have thought that a passion for music might be reconciled with that economy which we are obliged to observe."

In the absence of an aristocracy to act as patrons, music in colonial America found an outlet in public concerts, which were first given in such cities as Boston and Charleston in the 1730s. Ballad opera, too, found favor with the public. The ordinance against theater in Boston stated that such entertainments discouraged industry, frugality, and piety (in that order). To get around the law, stage shows masqueraded as "moral lectures" and "readings." By the end of the century the Bostonians had succumbed to several dozen ballad operas.

Hopkinson

The best-known of our early composers was an aristocratic amateur. Francis Hopkinson (1737–91) came from the same stratum of society in Philadelphia as did his friend Jefferson in Virginia. Composing was but one of the many interests of this jurist, writer, statesman, signer of the Declaration of Independence and framer of the Constitution. His love of music impelled him to poetic effusions such as the following, a description of his emotional response to the sound of the organ:

Hail heav'n born music! by thy pow'r we raise
Th'uplifted soul to arts of highest praise:
Oh! I would die with music melting round,
And float to bliss upon a sea of sound.

In 1788 Hopkinson published a collection of songs "in an easy, familiar style, intended for young practitioners on the harpsichord or fortepiano"; he was responsible also for the texts. The work was dedicated to Washington, to whom he wrote, "However small the Reputation may be that I shall derive from this work, I cannot, I believe, be refused the Credit of being the first Native of the United States who has produced a Musical Composition." To which Washington replied, "I can neither sing one of the songs, nor raise a single note on any instrument to convince the unbelieving. But I have, however, one argument which will prevail with persons of true estate (at least in America)—I can tell them that *it is the production of Mr. Hopkinson.*"

Rooted in the English song style of the eighteenth century, Hopkinson's

The subject of this anonymous eighteenth-century drawing, **Grand Rehearsal of the Anniversary Ode**, was probably the piece set to music by a Mr. Selby and performed in Boston on July 4, 1787. (*Research Center for Musical Iconography, CUNY.*)

melodies have an artless charm. Typical is this lilting refrain from *My Gen'rous Heart Disdains:*

The First New England School

Hymn and psalm tunes

Apart from the church service, the singing of hymns and psalms was a diversion that occupied an important place in the social life of the community. There was a continual need for new tunes and texts, as well as a growing desire for higher standards of performance. This need was met by a talented group of native composers, mostly self-taught, whose home base was New England, whence their activities spilled over into the neighboring colonies. True pioneers, they functioned as singing masters who traveled through the countryside, holding classes wherever they could—in churches, schools, taverns—and organizing "singing assemblies." They not only composed their own tunes but also compiled the melodies of their fellow composers and were active in getting those published. As a result of their efforts, several hundred tunebooks appeared in the final decades of the eighteenth century.

Of the numerous composers of the First New England School—among them were Daniel Reed (1757–1836), Timothy Swan (1785–1842), and Supply Belcher (1751–1836)—only one is known to the public today. He may be regarded as the central figure of the movement.

William Billings

William Billings (1746–1800), a native of Boston, was a man of remarkable energy and exuberant temperament. A tanner by trade, he was optimistic enough to believe that he could make his living as a composer. Thereupon he gave up tanning and devoted himself tirelessly to a multifaceted activity as teacher, conductor, composer, publisher, and promoter of music. "Great art thou, O Music!" he wrote with youthful enthusiasm, "and with thee there is no competitor." As with many another musician, there were moments later on when he may have regretted his choice.

Fuging

Like most of the Yankee tunesmiths, Billings was vastly fond of the *fuging piece* (the word was probably pronounced *fudging*), in which a psalm or hymn tune was treated contrapuntally. The typical fuging (or fuguing) piece of the New England school began with the tune harmonized in traditional four-part fashion. There followed a section in which each voice entered with the melody in turn, in a contrapuntal texture that lasted for a few measures. The "fuge" was then repeated, giving the piece a compact A-B-B form. In the preface to his last collection, *The Continental Harmony* (1794), Billings maintained with characteristic ebullience that there was more variety in one piece of fuging music than in twenty pieces of plain song. "The audience are most luxuriously entertained and exceedingly delighted . . . Now the solemn bass demands their attention, now the manly tenor, now the lofty counter [alto], now the volatile treble [soprano], now here, now there, now here again! O enchanting! O ecstatic! Push on, push on, ye sons of harmony!"

Anthem

Billings was also associated with the canon (round) and anthem. The *anthem* was longer than the psalm or hymn tune. Its text could be either religious or secular; Billings described it as "divine song, generally in prose." The anthem, in effect, was an extended composition in several sections, marked by contrasts in meter and tempo, texture and mood, in which brief solo passages for any or all of the four voices alternated with the full chorus.

Chester
Side 17/2 (S)
Side 11/2 (E II)

Billings reached the peak of his success in the period of the Revolutionary War, when his psalms, anthems, humorous pieces, and fuging tunes were widely sung. His hymn *Chester* became a marching song of the Continental Army. The militant words and granitelike tune perfectly captured the spirit of that fiery time:

Let tyrants shake their iron rod,
And Slav'ry clank her galling chains,
We fear them not, We trust in God,
New England's God forever reigns.

The Foe comes on with haughty stride,
Our troops advance with martial noise,
Their Vet'rans flee before our Youth,
And Gen'rals yield to beardless Boys.

What grateful Off'ring shall we bring?
What shall we render to this Lord?
Loud Hallelujah let us sing,
And praise His name on Ev'ry Chord.

Last years   Then his vogue passed. He spent his last years in dire poverty, and was rewarded for his life's efforts with a pauper's grave in Boston Common. His memory lived on, however, to inspire some twentieth-century Americans. Otto Luening's *Prelude on a Hymn Tune by William Billings,* Henry Cowell's *Hymns and Fuguing Tunes,* and William Schuman's *New England Triptych* pay homage to this extraordinary American primitive.

74 The Nineteenth Century: Emergence of an American School

"Men profess to be lovers of music, but for the most part they give no evidence in their opinions and lives that they have heard it. It would not leave them narrow-minded and bigoted." — HENRY THOREAU: *Journal,* 1851

A Century of Growth

The young republic attracted an influx of musicians from England, France, and Germany, who brought with them a tradition and a level of technique beyond any that existed here. In consequence, the new generation of American musicians was better equipped than their predecessors. A typical fig-
The Masons   ure was Lowell Mason (Medfield, Massachusetts, 1792–Orange, New Jersey, 1872), who wrote *Nearer, My God to Thee* and other standard hymns. His son William Mason (Boston, 1829–New York, 1905) studied with Liszt at Weimar and became one of the foremost pianists and teachers of his day. The circle was now complete—Europeans had come to the New World to live, Americans were returning to Europe to study.

The vogue of the visiting virtuoso began. The Norwegian violinist Ole Bull was followed, in 1850, by Jenny Lind. What with her gift for song and P. T. Barnum's genius for publicity, Jenny was a sensation. Toward the middle of the century, America produced its own virtuoso in Louis
Gottschalk   Moreau Gottschalk (1829–69). Born in New Orleans, the son of an English Jew and a Creole, Gottschalk was one of the adored pianists of the Romantic period. Handsome and magnetic, he was a Lisztian figure who left his white gloves on the piano to be torn to shreds by overwrought ladies in need of a little something to press between the pages of a book. Gottschalk left behind some salon pieces such as *The Last Hope* and *The Dying Poet* that nourished several generations of pupils and parents. More important were the exotic miniatures he wrote during the 1840s—*Bamboula, Le Bananier, The Banjo*—which, by exploiting the New Orleans locale, pointed the way to an awakening nationalism. He died of yellow fever, while touring in Brazil. Gottschalk has been rediscovered in our time, and hailed as one of the first Americanists.

Edward Hicks (1780-1849) was one of America's important "primitives." A painting by the Quaker artist, **The Peaceable Kingdom**. (*Abby Aldrich Rockefeller Folk Art Collection, Williamsburg, Virginia.*)

Orchestral and choral societies

The organization of musical life proceeded apace. Early in the century Boston had a Philo-Harmonic Society that presented symphonies of Haydn and others, as well as a Haydn and Handel Society for the performance of choral works. Both were organized by Gottlieb Graupner, who had played in the orchestra under Haydn when the master visited London in the 1790s. Graupner was thus in a position to transmit to his fellow Bostonians the traditions of the Viennese Classical school. Philadelphia had a similar organization in the Musical Fund Society, which was organized in 1820. Our oldest permanent orchestra, the New York Philharmonic, began its career in 1842. The European revolutions of 1848 caused thousands of liberals to emigrate from central Europe. German musicians came over in large numbers and ultimately formed the backbone of the symphony orchestras, singing societies, and chamber-music groups that were springing up throughout the country. In this way the traditions of Weimar and Leipzig, Munich and Vienna were established in our midst and became a decisive factor in shaping our musical taste.

Opera companies

Opera kept pace with symphony. New Orleans had a permanent opera company by 1810, which toured widely with a varied repertory. Manuel Garcia's company came to New York in 1825 and was followed by others that presented the newest works of Rossini, Bellini, and Donizetti along with the operas of Mozart. Many of these were presented in English. This was an age that looked upon opera as an exciting form of theater, so it seemed logical that the drama unfold in the language of the audience.

Concert halls

A burgeoning concert life needed auditoriums. New York City's Academy of Music was built before the Civil War, as was Philadelphia's. These were followed by the Music Hall in Cincinnati (1878), the Metropolitan Opera House (1883), the Auditorium in Chicago (1889), Carnegie Hall in New York (1891), and Symphony Hall in Boston (1900). Music education

Music schools

too moved forward rapidly. It was the great achievement of Lowell Mason to establish music in the public-school curriculum. This important step was taken in the second quarter of the century. Equally important was the founding of music schools: the Peabody Institute in Baltimore in 1860, Oberlin Conservatory in Ohio in 1865, and—all in 1867—the New England Conservatory in Boston, Cincinnati Conservatory, and Chicago Musical College.

Mid-century saw the emergence of native professional composers. The first Americans to handle the traditional forms of European music—sym-

Bristow

phony and opera—were George Frederick Bristow (Brooklyn, 1825–1898,

Under P.T. Barnum's management, the Swedish soprano Jenny Lind took American audiences by storm. A contemporary engraving depicting her first appearance in America, at Castle Garden, on September 11, 1850.

Fry

New York) and William Henry Fry (Philadelphia, 1815–1864, Santa Cruz, West Indies).

Foster

But the great American composer of the pre-Civil War period did not come from the tradition of Haydn and Mozart or Donizetti and Bellini. He came out of the humbler realm of the minstrel show. Stephen Foster (1826–64) was born in Lawrenceville, Pennsylvania. His was a substantial middle-class environment in which music was not even remotely considered to be a suitable career for a man. His parents took note of his talent but did nothing to encourage or train it. Foster's lyric gift, unassimilated to any musical culture, found its natural outlet in the sphere of popular song.

Foster's was a temperament unable to accommodate itself to the bourgeois ideal of success. He was, as his biographer John Tasker Howard has written, "a dreamer, thoroughly impractical and . . . never businessman enough to realize the commercial value of his best songs." His course led with tragic inevitability from the initial flurries of good fortune, through the failure of his marriage, to the hall bedroom on the Bowery and the alcoholic's lonely death at the age of thirty-eight. In that time he managed to write some two hundred songs, a half dozen of which have imprinted themselves on the American soul.

Seen in the perspective of history this lovable weakling, the despair of his parents, his wife, and his brothers, emerges as one of our great artists. He stands among the very few musicians whose personal vision created the songs of a nation.

The Second New England School

The decades following the Civil War witnessed an impressive expansion of musical life throughout the country. Most important, there appeared a native school of well-trained composers. First to achieve more than ephemeral fame was John Knowles Paine (Portland, Maine, 1839–Cambridge, Massachusetts, 1906), who was mentor of the so-called Boston or New England group that was active at the turn of the century. Among them were Arthur Foote (Salem, Massachusetts, 1853–1937, Boston), George Chadwick (Lowell, Massachusetts, 1854–1931, Boston), Arthur Whiting (Cambridge, Massachusetts, 1861–1936, Beverly, Massachusetts), Horatio Parker (Auburndale, Massachusetts, 1863–1919, Cedarhurst, Long Island), Amy Marcy Cheney (Mrs. H. H. A.) Beach (Henniker, New Hampshire, 1867–1944, New York), and Daniel Gregory Mason (Brookline, Massachusetts, 1873–1953, Greenwich, Connecticut). These composers, working within the traditional forms of European music, achieved a higher level of accomplishment than had ever existed in this country before.

Paine and his followers

The time had come for music to take its place (although not without opposition) in the curricula of our leading universities. Paine was the first professor of music at Harvard, Parker taught at Yale, and Daniel Gregory

The romantic adventurousness associated with the westward expansion of the United States is expressed in this atmospheric painting by George Caleb Bingham (1811-79), **Fur Traders on the Missouri**. (*The Metropolitan Museum of Art; Morris K. Jesup Fund, 1933.*)

Mason at Columbia. Thus began a development whereby our colleges and universities offered American composers an increasingly important platform for the dissemination of their music and ideas.

The composers just mentioned were oriented toward the German tradition of Schumann, Mendelssohn, and Brahms, or that of Wagner and Liszt. It was their historic mission to raise the level of American music to the standards of Europe. But their music, weakened by their genteel outlook on art and life, bore only a limited relationship to their milieu and thus has not survived. On the comparatively rare occasions when their works are performed, one is astonished to discover how much—within their limitations—they did achieve.

MacDowell and Loeffler

MacDowell   A more striking personality was Edward MacDowell (New York, 1860–1908, New York), the first American composer to achieve a reputation abroad. He studied composition in Germany and came to the notice of Liszt, who secured performances of his works. MacDowell settled in Germany and taught there for several years. In 1888 he returned to the United States.

The four piano sonatas and two concertos for piano and orchestra reveal MacDowell to have been at home in the large forms. He was at his best, however, in the small lyric pieces that are still favorites with young pianists, such as the *Woodland Sketches* (including *To a Wild Rose*), *Fireside*

Tales, and *New England Idyls.* MacDowell was the first professor of composition at Columbia University, but resigned his post in bitterness because the university did not accord to music the importance he felt it deserved. After his death his wife founded the MacDowell Colony on their property at Peterborough, New Hampshire, where musicians, painters, and writers are given the opportunity to do their work undisturbed by the cares of daily living. There could be no more fitting memorial to this lyric poet whose Romantic sensibility delighted several generations.

Loeffler Alsatian-born Charles Martin Loeffler (1861–1935, Medfield, Massachusetts), came to this country when he was twenty. He is remembered chiefly for *A Pagan Poem* (1901), a chamber work he later rewrote for piano and orchestra. Loeffler was a recluse and a mystic. His was a music of shadowy visions. It showed his affinity for Gregorian chant, Medieval modes, and Impressionist harmonies. His works bear some resemblance to the style that came to be associated with Debussy, yet he found his way to it in the 1890s, before he could have heard much of the Frenchman's music.

Loeffler anticipated one of the most significant developments in American musical life—the turning from German to French influence. The enormous popularity of Impressionism in this country during the first quarter of our century broke the grip of the German conservatory. Increasingly, new generations of American musicians went to Paris, even as their predecessors had gone to Leipzig, Munich, or Weimar. This trend was strengthened by the boycott of all things German during the First World War, and created a significant new orientation in the 1920s.

The composers we have mentioned in this chapter, although they lived in the post-Romantic era, were really Romanticists who had arrived too late. In the world arena they have been overshadowed by their European contemporaries, compared to whom they take second place. Yet comparisons are hardly in order. The European post-Romantics were the heirs of a rich past. The Americans were building for a rich future. They were pioneers dedicated to a lofty vision. We have every reason to remember them with pride.

75 Twentieth-Century Americans (I)

"The best way to write American music is simple. All you have to do is to be an American and then write any kind of music you wish." — VIRGIL THOMSON

Toward an American Music

During the first quarter of our century the serious American composer was something of a stepchild in his own country. His music faced a two-fold handicap: it was modern, and it lacked the made-in-Europe label that carries such weight with our public. He had no powerful publishers to champion his cause, no system of grants and fellowships to give him the leisure to compose, no famous conductors to bring him the performances he needed. He had to function, in effect, in a scene that was not quite ready for him.

Despite this handicap, American composers forged ahead to master the techniques of modern musical speech. As they become more sure of themselves, they aspired in ever greater measure to give expression to the life about them. At first they concentrated on those features of the home scene that were not to be found in Europe: the lore of the Indian, the Negro, and the cowboy. They became increasingly aware of a wealth of native material that was waiting to be used: the songs of the southern mountaineers, which preserved intact the melodies brought over from England three hundred years ago; the hymns and religious tunes that had such vivid associations for Americans everywhere; the patriotic songs of the Revolutionary period and the Civil War, many of which had become folk songs; the tunes of the minstrel shows that had reached their high

By the end of the nineteenth century, artists began to draw their inspiration from the American scene. A painting by Grant Wood (1892-1942), **American Gothic.** *(The Art Institute of Chicago.)*

point in the songs of Foster. There were, in addition, the work songs from various parts of the country—songs of sharecroppers, lumberjacks, miners, river men; songs of prairie and railroad, chain gang and frontier. Then there was the folklore of the city dwellers—commercialized ballads, musical-comedy songs, and jazz: a world of melody, rhythm, and mood.

Certain composers, on the other hand, resisted this kind of local color. They preferred the international idioms of twentieth-century music that had been stripped of folk elements: Impressionism, Neoclassicism, atonality, and twelve-tone music. Others managed to reconcile the two attitudes. They revealed themselves as internationally minded in certain of their works, but employed folklore elements in others. It was gradually realized that Americanism in music was a much broader concept than had at first been supposed: American music could not but be as many-faceted as America itself. A work did not have to quote a Negro spiritual, an Indian harvest song, or a dirge of the prairie in order to qualify for citizenship.

The music of the modern American school follows no single formula. Rather, it reflects the contradictory tendencies in our national character: our jaunty humor, and our sentimentality; our idealism, and our worship of material success; our rugged individualism, and our wish to look and think like everybody else; our visionary daring, and our practicality; our ready emotionalism, and our capacity for intellectual pursuits. All of these and more are abundantly present in a music that has bigness of gesture, vitality, and all the exuberance of youth.

The First Generation (Composers Born 1870–1890)

The drive to shake off the domination of German traditions gathered momentum through the early years of the century. One of its first spokes-

Farwell man was Arthur Farwell (St. Paul, Minnesota, 1872–1951, New York), who spent the usual apprenticeship in Germany, followed by what was then not so usual—a term of study in Paris. After his return from Europe Farwell taught at Cornell University and became a tireless propagandist for a new esthetic. "The first correction we must bring to our musical vision," he wrote in 1903, "is to cease to see everything through German spectacles . . ." He advocated a musical expression rooted in "ragtime, Negro songs, Indian songs, Cowboy songs, and, of the utmost importance, new and daring expressions of our own composers, sound-speech previously unheard." Farwell studied the Indian melodies of the Southwest and tried to assimilate those in works like *From Mesa and Plain* (1905), whence the *Navajo War Dance* that was a well-known piano piece in its day.

Gilbert Henry F. Gilbert (Somerville, Massachusetts, 1868–1928, Cambridge, Massachusetts), shared Farwell's preoccupation with Americana. "More than the music of any individual composer," he wrote, "more than the music of any particular school, the folk tunes of the world, of all nationalities, races and peoples have been to me a never-failing source of delight, wonder and inspiration. In them I can hear the spirit of all great music. Through them I can feel the very heartbeat of humanity." *The Dance in Place Congo,* a symphonic poem (1906), evoked the picturesque "bamboula" rhythm of New Orleans that had intrigued Louis Gottschalk a half century earlier. The work was presented as a ballet at the Metropolitan Opera House in 1918. Gilbert is remembered also for the *Comedy Overture on Negro Themes* (1905) and *Negro Rhapsody* (1913).

Powell

Regionalism now entered into American music, as it already had into our literature. Virginia-born John Powell (Richmond, Virginia, 1882–1963, Charlottesville, Virginia) became "the composer of the South." He turned for inspiration to our Anglo-American folk songs, as in his *Sonata Virginianesque* for violin and piano (1919). His greatest success, however, came with the *Negro Rhapsody* for piano and orchestra (1918).

While these composers and their fellows were proclaiming a new esthetic, an unknown New Englander was working in isolation to find a vital way of expressing the American spirit in music. We turn now to Charles Ives, whom the perspective of history reveals as the first major prophet of our musical coming of age.

76 Charles Ives

"Beauty in music is too often confused with something that lets the ears lie back in an easy chair. Many sounds that we are used to do not bother us, and for that reason we are inclined to call them beautiful. Frequently, when a new or unfamiliar work is accepted as beautiful on its first hearing, its fundamental quality is one that tends to put the mind to sleep."

Charles Edward Ives (1874–1954) waited many years for recognition. Today he stands revealed as the first great American composer of the twentieth century, and one of the most original spirits of his time.

His Life

Ives was born in Danbury, Connecticut. His father had been a bandmaster in the Civil War, and continued his calling in civilian life. Charles at thirteen held a job as church organist and already was arranging music for the various ensembles conducted by his father. At twenty he entered Yale, where he studied composition with Horatio Parker. Ives's talent for music asserted itself throughout his four years at Yale; yet when he had to choose a career he decided against a professional life in music. He suspected that society would not pay him for the kind of music he wanted to compose. He was right.

Business life   He therefore entered the business world. Two decades later he was head of the largest insurance agency in the country. The years it took him to achieve this success—roughly from the time he was twenty-two to forty-two—were the years when he wrote his music. He composed at night, on weekends, and during vacations, working in isolation, concerned only to set down the sounds he heard in his head.

The few conductors and performers whom he tried to interest in his works pronounced them unplayable. After a number of these rebuffs Ives gave up showing his manuscripts. When he felt the need to hear how his music sounded, he hired a few musicians to run through a work. Save for these rare and quite inadequate performances, Ives heard his music only in his imagination. He pursued his way undeflected and alone, piling up one score after another in his barn in Connecticut. When well-meaning friends suggested that he try to write music that people would like, he could only retort, "I can't do it—I hear something else!"

Ives's double life as a business executive by day and composer by night finally took its toll. In 1918, when he was forty-four, he suffered a physical breakdown that left his heart damaged. The years of unrewarded effort had taken more out of him emotionally than he had suspected. Although he lived almost forty years longer, he produced nothing further of importance.

Charles Ives.

The demands of abstract form and color are beginning to overcome representational elements in this painting by Willem de Kooning (b. 1904), entitled **Woman, I.** *(Collection, The Museum of Modern Art, New York.)*

The "drip painting" of Jackson Pollock (1912–56) paralleled the interest in chance as an element of musical composition. **Number 1, 1948.** *(Collection, The Museum of Modern Art, New York.)*

Musical life
When he recovered he faced the realization that the world of professional musicians was irrevocably closed to his ideas. He felt that he owed it to his music to make it available to those who might be less hidebound. He therefore had the *Concord Sonata* for piano privately printed, also the *Essays Before a Sonata*—a kind of elaborate program note that presented the essence of his views on life and art. These were followed by the *114 Songs*. The three volumes, which were distributed free of charge to libraries, music critics, and whoever else asked for them, caused not a ripple as far as the public was concerned. But they gained Ives the support of other experimental composers who were struggling to make their way in an unheeding world. The tide finally turned in this country when the American pianist John Kirkpatrick, at a recital in Town Hall in January, 1939, played the *Concord Sonata*. Ives was then sixty-five. The piece was repeated several weeks later by Kirkpatrick and scored a triumph. The next morning Lawrence Gilman hailed the *Concord Sonata* as "the greatest music composed by an American."

Performances
Ives had already begun to exert a salutary influence upon the younger generation of composers, who found in his art a realization of their own ideals. Now he was "discovered" by the general public and hailed as the grand old man of American music. In 1947 his *Third Symphony* achieved performance, and won a Pulitzer Prize. This story of belated recognition was an item to capture the imagination, and was carried by newspapers throughout the country. Ives awoke at seventy-three to find himself famous. Four years later the *Second Symphony* was presented to the public by the New York Philharmonic, exactly half a century after it had been composed. The prospect of finally hearing the work agitated the old man; he attended neither the rehearsals nor the performances. He was, however, one of millions who listened to the radio broadcast.

He died in New York City three years later, at the age of eighty.

His Music

Charles Ives, both as man and artist, was rooted in the New England heritage, in the tradition of plain living and high thinking that came to flower in the idealism of Hawthorne and the Alcotts, Emerson and Thoreau. The sources of his tone imagery are to be found in the living music of his childhood: hymn tunes and popular songs, the town band at holiday parades, the fiddlers at Saturday night dances, patriotic songs and sentimental parlor ballads, the melodies of Stephen Foster, and the medleys heard at country fairs and in small theaters.

This wealth of American music had attracted other musicians besides Ives. But they, subservient to European canons of taste, had proceeded to smooth out and "correct" these popular tunes according to the rules they had absorbed in Leipzig or Munich. Ives was as free from subservience to the European tradition as Walt Whitman. His keen ear caught the sound of untutored voices singing a hymn together, some in their eagerness straining and sharpening the pitch, others just missing it and flatting; so that in place of the single tone there was a cluster of tones that made a deliciously dissonant chord. Some were a trifle ahead of the beat, others lagged behind; consequently the rhythm sagged and turned into a welter of polyrhythms. He heard the pungent clash of dissonance *Ives's poly-* when two bands in a parade, each playing a different tune in a different *tonality and* key, came close enough together to overlap; he heard the effect of quarter *polyrhythms* tones when fiddlers at a country dance brought excitement into their playing by going a mite off pitch. He remembered the wheezy harmonium at church accompanying the hymns a trifle out of tune. All these, he realized, were not departures from the norm. They *were* the norm of popular American musical speech. Thus he found his way to such conceptions as polytonality, atonality, polyharmony, cluster chords based on intervals of a second, and polyrhythms. All this in the last years of the nineteenth century, when Schoenberg was still writing in a post-Wagner idiom, when neither Stravinsky nor Bartók had yet begun their careers, when Hindemith had just been born. All the more honor, then, to this singular musician who, isolated alike from the public and his fellow composers, was so advanced in his conceptions and so accurate in his forecast of the paths that twentieth-century music would follow.

Orchestral The central position in his orchestral music is held by the four sym-
works phonies (1896–1916). Among his other orchestral works are *Three Places in New England,* which we will discuss; *Three Outdoor Scenes* (1898–1911), consisting of *Hallowe'en, The Pond,* and *Central Park in the Dark,* the last-named for chamber orchestra; and *The Unanswered Question* (1908). The *Sonata No. 2* for piano—"Concord, Mass., 1840–1860"—which occupied him from 1909 to 1915, reflects various aspects of the flowering of New England; its four movements are entitled *Emerson, Hawthorne, The Alcotts,* and *Thoreau.* Ives also wrote a variety of songs, as well as chamber, choral, and piano compositions.

Three Places in New England

In this work (1903–14) Ives evokes three place-names rich in associa-
Putnam's tions for a New Englander. The second movement, *Putnam's Camp, Red-*
Camp *ding, Connecticut* is rooted in our history. It is marked Allegro (Quick-
Side 17/3 (S) Step Time). "Near Redding Center," Ives wrote, "is a small park preserved
Side 11/3 (E II) as a Revolutionary Memorial; for here General Israel Putnam's soldiers had their winter quarters in 1778–9. Long rows of stone camp fireplaces still remain to stir a child's imagination." The scene is a "4th of July" picnic held under the auspices of the First Church and the Village Cornet Band. The child wanders into the woods and dreams of the old soldiers, of the hardships they endured, their desire to break camp and abandon their cause, and of how they returned when Putnam came over the hills to lead

them. "The little boy awakes, he hears the children's songs and runs down past the monument to 'listen to the band' and join in the games and dances."

In this vivid tone-painting Ives conjures up the frenetic business of having a good time on a holiday picnic in a small American town: the hubbub, the sweating faces, the parade with its two bands that overlap, their harmonies clashing. This section abounds in polytonal, atonal, and polyrhythmic effects. Its main theme is a marching song:

Characteristic is Ives's way of quoting a popular tune and then "dissolving" it in another idea. For example, a fragment of *Yankee Doodle* is "dissolved" into something else, but the four notes of the famous tune have sufficed to release a flood of associations in the listener:

This is followed by a melody, presented as a violin solo, that has all the characteristics of a folk song without being one:

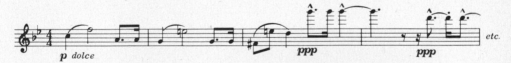

Following is the marching song from the middle section (the dream sequence):

Another marchlike melody in this section illustrates Ives's singular ability to create themes that capture the accents of American popular song:

A deep love of all things American lies at the heart of this movement. There is an exciting passage where two march rhythms clash, four measures of the one equalling three of the other. The intricate polyrhythms in the final measures lead to a daringly dissonant ending, *ffff*. This is one of those works that spring from the soil and soul of a particular place, and could have been conceived nowhere else.

The music of Charles Ives is now firmly established in our concert halls. Like the writers he admired most, he has become an American classic.

77 Edgard Varèse

"I refuse to submit myself only to sounds that have already been heard."

Edgard Varèse was one of the truly original spirits in the music of our time. The innovations of Stravinsky, Schoenberg, and Bartók unfolded within the frame of the traditional elements of their art, but Varèse went a step further: he rejected certain of those elements altogether.

His Life

Varèse was born in Paris in 1883, of Italian-French parentage. He studied mathematics and science at school, since his father intended him for an engineering career. But at eighteen he entered the Schola Cantorum, and subsequently studied at the Paris Conservatoire. With the outbreak of war in 1914 Varèse was mobilized into the French army, but was discharged

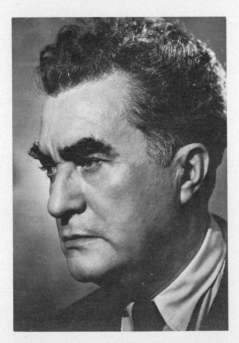

Edgard Varèse. (*Robin Carson photograph.*)

Life in the big city became an important subject in twentieth-century American art. A painting by John Marin (1870-1953), **Lower Manhattan.** (*Collection, The Museum of Modern Art, New York, the Philip L. Goodwin Collection.*)

the following year after a serious illness. He came to the United States in December, 1915, when he was thirty-two, and lost no time in making a place for himself in the musical life of his adopted land.

The greater part of Varèse's music was written during the Twenties and early Thirties. He found a champion in Leopold Stokowski, who performed his scores despite the violent opposition they aroused in conventionally minded concertgoers. Then, like his colleague Ives, Varèse fell silent when he should have been at the height of his powers. During the next twenty years he followed the new scientific developments in the field of electronic instruments, and resumed composing in 1949, when he began to work on *Déserts*.

By that time the scene had changed; there existed a public receptive to experimental music. When an enterprising record company made available four of his works, Varèse was enabled to reach an audience that had never before heard his music. He was invited by the State Department to conduct master classes in composition in Darmstadt, Germany. The younger generation of European composers who were experimenting with tape-recorded music suddenly discovered him as one whose work had been prophetic of theirs. The long-neglected master finally came into his own. He died in New York City in 1965.

His Music

The abstract images that brood over Varèse's music are derived from the life of the big city: the rumble of motors, the clang of hammers, the shriek and hiss and shrilling of factory whistles, turbines, steam drills. His stabbing, pounding rhythms conjure up the throb and hum of the metropolis. It follows that his attention is focused on the percussion, which he handles with inexhaustible invention. His music unfolds in geometrical patterns based on the opposition of sonorous planes and volumes—patterns which, in their abstraction, are the counterpart in sound of the designs of cubist painting. Varèse's music was utterly revolutionary in its day. It sounded like nothing that had ever been heard before.

"Speed and synthesis are characteristic of our epoch. We need twentieth-century instruments to help us realize those in music." With *Déserts* (1954) Varèse entered the world of electronic sound. The piece is written for orchestra; but at three points in the score there are interpolations of what Varèse called "organized sound"—music on tape. There followed, in 1958, *Poème électronique,* which was commissioned by the Philips Radio Corporation to be played in a pavilion designed by Le Corbusier at the Brussels Fair. This was intended as "a poem of the electronic age." Thus, at the age of seventy-three, the intrepid explorer was still pursuing new paths, bringing back to his less venturesome fellows the shapes and sounds of the music of the future.

Ionisation

Side 17/4 (S)
Side 11/4 (E II)

Varèse's most celebrated composition is scored for thirty-five different instruments of percussion and friction, played by thirteen performers. *Ionisation* (1931) is an imaginative study in pure sonority and rhythm, in which Varèse frees percussion and bell sounds from their traditional subservience to melody and harmony.

The instruments used fall into three groups. Those of definite pitch include tubular chimes, celesta, and piano. Among those of indefinite pitch are drums of various kinds, cymbals, tam-tam (gong), triangle, slapstick, Chinese blocks, sleighbells, castanets, tambourine, and two anviles. Also a number of exotic instruments, such as *bongos* (West Indian twin drums with parchment heads, played either with small wooden sticks or with the fingers); a *guiro* (a Cuban dried gourd, serrated on the surface and scratched with a wooden stick); *maracas* (Cuban rattles); *claves* (Cuban sticks of hardwood); and a *cencerro* (a cowbell without a clapper, struck with a drumstick). The instruments of continuous pitch include two sirens and a string drum known as a *lion's-roar,* consisting of a medium-size wooden barrel with a parchment head through which a rosined string is drawn, the sound being produced by rubbing the string with a piece of cloth or leather. Varèse directed that a *theremin*—one of the first electronic instruments—might be substituted for the sirens.

The score displays the characteristic traits of Varèse's style, especially his uncanny ability to project masses of tensile sound that generate a sense of space. The ear is teased by complex rhythmic patterns whose subtle texture recalls the rhythms of African and Asian music. Varèse deploys his array of noisemakers on interlocking planes, analogous to the soprano, alto, tenor, and bass levels of the orchestra and choir. Used in this fashion, the percussion instruments create a harmony and counterpoint all their own. The sirens set up a continuous pitch. Their protracted wail, with its mounting sense of urgency, takes shape as a vast shadowy image of our Age of Anxiety. Most adroitly managed is the relaxation that comes toward the end of the piece with the entrance of the chimes and the tone clusters in the low register of the piano. The energy stored up in these sonorous "ions" has been released; the machine comes gently to rest.

Varèse's emphasis on sheer sonority presaged one of the most important trends of our era. In the light of what is happening today, *Ionisation* stands revealed as one of the prophetic scores of the twentieth century.

78 Twentieth-Century Americans (II)

"Music is immediate, it goes on to become." — W. H. AUDEN

The second generation of twentieth-century American composers had an easier time than their predecessors. The gradual victory of musical modernism in Europe could not but have repercussions here. Besides, the emergence of a strong native school became a matter of national pride and found support in various quarters. The era of prosperity in the 1920s encouraged private patronage in the form of grants and fellowships. The conservatories too, which had hitherto concentrated on the training of instrumentalists and singers, began to turn their attention to the needs of young composers. The decade before the Second World War saw this country emerge as the musical center of the world. The presence here of Stravinsky, Schoenberg, Bartók, Hindemith, Milhaud, Krenek, and their confreres had a tremendous impact on our musical life. Many of our younger musicians studied with these masters and came directly under their influence.

The Second Generation (Composers Born 1890–1910)

Moore   Douglas Moore (Cutchogue, Long Island, 1893–1969 Greenport, Long Island) taught at Columbia University, where he was Edward MacDowell

Paintings such as **Visa**, by Stuart Davis (1894-1964), are bold commentaries on the modern American scene. (*Museum of Modern Art, New York. Gift of Mrs. Gertrud A. Mellon.*)

Professor of Music. He had his greatest success in his sixties, with the production of his opera *The Ballad of Baby Doe* (1956), on a dramatically compelling libretto by John LaTouche.

Piston   Walter Piston (Rockland, Maine, 1894–1976, Belmont, Massachusetts) was a leading representative of the international outlook among American composers. He was a Neoclassicist; his music is urbane, polished, witty. Characteristic of his style are the *Concertino for Piano and Chamber Orchestra* (1937) and the *Fourth Symphony* (1950).

Thomson   The art of Virgil Thomson (Kansas City, Missouri, 1896–) is rooted in the homespun hymns and songs, many of Civil War vintage, that were the natural inheritance of a boy growing up in the Middle West. He came into prominence with the production in 1934 of his opera *Four Saints in Three Acts* on a libretto by Gertrude Stein. Among Thomson's varied list of works are several notable film scores, of which the best-known is *Louisiana Story* (1948).

Sessions   The music of Roger Sessions (Brooklyn, New York, 1896–) presents distinguished musical ideas in a distinguished way. Romantic and Neoclassical elements intermingle, in his mature style, with Expressionist and twelve-tone influences. His eight symphonies bear the imprint of profound thought and concentrated emotion so characteristic of this composer.

Harris   The music of Roy Harris (Lincoln County, Oklahoma, 1898–) is American in its buoyancy and momentum. Twelve symphonies form the core of
his output; the *Third* (1938) has remained his finest achievement.

Hanson   Howard Hanson (Wahoo, Nebraska, 1896–) played a crucial role
during the 1920s when the battle for American music had still to be won.
As director of the Eastman School of Music and conductor of the Rochester Symphony Orchestra, he organized annual festivals of American
music at which some of the most important works of the period received
their first performance. Of his five symphonies the most important is the
Second, the *Romantic* (1930).

George Gershwin

"Jazz I regard as an American folk music; not the only one, but a very powerful one, which
is probably in the blood and feeling of the American people more than any other style of
folk music. I believe that it can be made the basis of serious symphonic works of lasting
value."

In terms of native endowment, George Gershwin (1898–1937) was without question one of the most gifted musicians that this country has produced. He was born in Brooklyn of Russian-Jewish parents who had
immigrated some years before, and grew up on the teeming East Side of
New York City. The dynamic, extrovert youngster was about ten when he
began to study the piano. Given his intensity and his eagerness to learn,
he might have gone on to a conservatory, but his future direction was

George Gershwin before his painting
of Arnold Schoenberg.

already clear to him. The sixteen-year-old boy, discussing jazz with his teacher, said, "This is American music. This is the kind of music I want to write."

Musical comedy

Gershwin took the three ingredients that went into the folk song of the streets of New York—jazz, ragtime, and the blues—and out of these wove a characteristic popular art. He was able to do this because of his spontaneous lyric gift. His first hit, *Swanee,* was brought to fame by Al Jolson. His success in musical comedy made him all the more determined to bridge the distance between "popular" and "classical." He achieved this aim in the *Rhapsody in Blue* (1924). The following year he crossed the hitherto impassable barrier between Tin Pan Alley and Carnegie Hall when he

The original poster for the concert at which Gershwin's *Rhapsody in Blue* was first performed. (*Research Center for Musical Iconography, CUNY.*)

PAUL WHITEMAN
AND HIS
Palais Royal Orchestra
WILL OFFER
An Experiment in Modern Music

Zez Confrey
and
George Gershwin

New Typically American Compositions by Victor Herbert, George Gershwin and Zez Confrey will be played for the first time.

AEOLIAN CONCERT HALL
Tuesday, Feb. 12th (LINCOLN'S BIRTHDAY) at 3 P.M.

Tickets now on Sale, 55c. to $2.20

Victor Records   Chickering Pianos   Buescher Instruments

played his *Concerto in F* with Walter Damrosch and the New York Symphony Orchestra. He next tackled the Lisztian tone poem and produced *An American in Paris* (1928). *Porgy and Bess* followed in 1935. With the

Opera

years, this "folk opera" has taken on the character of a unique work. Gershwin here was guided by the instinct of the musical dramatist. He had, besides, tenderness and compassion, the lyrics of his brother Ira, and the wonderful tunes to go with them. And so he captured, as Lawrence Gilman put it, "the wildness and the pathos and tragic fervor that can so strangely agitate the souls of men."

Film music

The last year and a half of his life was spent in Hollywood, where he wrote the music for two Fred Astaire movies—*Shall We Dance?* and *A Damsel in Distress.* He was not happy working in pictures, for the conventions of Hollywood were even less tractable than those of Broadway; besides, he missed the excitement of New York. But he never returned. After a brief illness, he was found to have a brain tumor. He did not survive the operation.

George Gershwin, dead at thirty-nine—when he was on the threshold of important advances in his art—has remained something of a legend among us. Because he was so close to us we are inclined to view him within the Broadway frame. It is well to remember that so severe a judge as Arnold Schoenberg said of him, "I grieve over the deplorable loss to music, for there is no doubt that he was a great composer."

Aaron Copland

"I no longer feel the need of seeking out conscious Americanisms. Because we live here and work here, we can be certain that when our music is mature it will also be American in quality."

Aaron Copland (1900–) is generally recognized as the representative figure among present-day American composers. He manifests the serenity, clarity, and sense of balance that we regard as the essence of the Classical temper.

Jazz idiom

In his growth as a composer Copland has mirrored the dominant trends of his time. Like Gershwin, he turned to the jazz idiom. This culminated in his brilliant *Piano Concerto* (1927). There followed a period during which

Neoclassic period

the Neoclassicist experimented with the abstract materials of his art; he produced his *Piano Variations* (1930), *Short Symphony* (1933), and *Statements for Orchestra* (1933–35). "During these years I began to feel an increasing dissatisfaction with the relations of the music-loving public and the living composer. It seemed to me that we composers were in danger of working in a vacuum." He realized that a new public for contempory music was being created by the radio, phonograph, and film scores. "It made no sense to ignore them and to continue writing as if they did not exist. I felt that it was worth the effort to see if I couldn't say what I had to say in the simplest possible terms."

Aaron Copland. *(Photo John Ardoin.)*

The "new" music   The decade that followed saw the production of the scores that established Copland's popularity. *El Salón México* (1936) is an orchestral piece based on Mexican melodies and rhythms. The three ballets are *Billy the Kid* (1938), *Rodeo* (1942), and *Appalachian Spring* (1944). Copland wrote two works for high-school students—the "play-opera" *Second Hurricane* (1937) and *Outdoor Overture* (1938). Among his film scores are *The Red Pony* (1948) and *The Heiress* (1949), which brought him an Academy Award. Two important works written in time of war are *A Lincoln Portrait* (1942), for speaker and chorus, on a text drawn from the Great Emancipator's speeches; and the *Third Symphony* (1944–46).

Copland: Billy the Kid

For the ballet based on the saga of Billy the Kid, Copland produced one of his freshest scores. In it are embedded either in whole or in part such cowboy classics as *I Ride an Old Paint, Great Grand-Dad,* and *The Dying Cowboy.* They are not quoted literally. What Copland does is to use these melodies as a point of departure for his own; they flavor the music but are assimilated to his personal style.

Billy the Kid—the Brooklyn-born William Bonney—had a brief but intense career as desperado and lover, in the course of which he became one of the legends of the Southwest. The ballet touches on the chief episodes of his life. We see him first as a boy of twelve when, his mother having been killed by a stray bullet in a street brawl, he stabs the man responsible for her death. Later, during a card game with his cronies, he is accused of cheating and kills the accuser. Captured after a running gun-battle, he is put in jail. He murders his jailer and gets away. A romantic interlude ensues when he rejoins his Mexican sweetheart in the desert. But the menacing shadows close in on him. This time there is no escaping. At the close we hear a lament for the death of the dashing outlaw.

Prologue
Side 17/5 (S)
Side 11/5 (E II)
The concert suite contains about two-thirds of the music of the ballet. *The Open Prairie,* which serves as a Prologue, evokes a spacious landscape. The theme, announced by oboe, then clarinet, creates an outdoor

A scene from *Billy the Kid*, in the American Ballet Theater production. (*Photograph by Fred Fehl.*)

atmosphere, while modal harmonies in parallel motion give a sense of space and remoteness:

This prelude unfolds in free form, woven out of the opening theme through a process of repetition and expansion. It reaches a fortissimo climax, and is followed by a scene that conjures up "a street in a frontier town." A theme, derived from the cowboy song *Great Grand-Dad,* is presented by piccolo "nonchalantly." Copland slightly changes the melody and gives it a sophisticated harmonic background:

The A-flat major tonality of this melody persists while a contrasting tune, in the key of F, is thrust against its last note. There results a striking polytonal effect:

The contrasting melody takes over. The following example shows how Copland sets it off through the use of dissonant harmony:

Polyrhythm results when the melody, in ⁴⁄₄ time, is presented against an accompaniment in 3/4. In this prairie music the physical landscape is transformed into a poetic symbol of all that is vast and immutable. It is in passages such as these that Aaron Copland shows himself to be, as he has often been described, the most American of our composers.

Crawford: String Quartet 1931

Ruth Crawford was born in East Liverpool, Ohio in 1901 and grew up "in that traditional cradle of Americanism, a minister's household." She composed along traditional lines until, in her late twenties, she came to New York. There she studied with her future husband, the musicologist Charles Seeger, who along wtih Henry Cowell and others, was active in what was then the avant-garde. Crawford's writing took a boldly experimental turn, and she produced a series of strikingly original works. She was the first woman to hold a Guggenheim fellowship in composition,

Ruth Crawford. (*Harris and Ewing photograph.*)

which made possible a year in Berlin. It was during this year that she wrote her most important work, the *String Quartet 1931.*

There was, however, no audience in America for what she had to say. Like Ives and Ruggles, she gave up composing when she should have been at the height of her creativity. After her marriage to Seeger she collaborated with him in editing collections of American folk songs. This activity played its part in determining the career of her stepson, the talented folk singer Pete Seeger. She died in Chevy Chase, Maryland in 1953, her music practically forgotten. It is only in recent years that she has been recognized as belonging to that small group of innovative American composers who in remarkable fashion anticipated developments that became current only several decades later.

Third movement

Side 17/6 (S)
Side 11/6 (E II)

String Quartet 1931 is a concise, arresting work that displays Crawford's style at its best. Characteristic is the third movement, an Andante in ¼. Charles Seeger called it "an experiment in dynamic counterpoint. Each part has a different alternation of crescendo and diminuendo, or else the same alternation but beginning and ending at different times." The instruments unite in a continuous flow of sound, so smooth that we do not hear where each instrument enters or drops out. The composer specified that "the bowing should be as little audible as possible throughout. The crescendi and decrescendi should be equally gradual." The result is an almost static continuum that seems to exist beyond time. The movement traces a very broad dynamic arch, from a mysterious *ppp* in low register to an *fff* climax in high, then back to low and a *pppp* ending. The four lines are spaced very close together at the beginning, forming tone-clusters of seconds and thirds.

They are extremely wide apart at the climax, whose power rests on the dissonance tension inherent in such intervals as major sevenths and minor ninths.

In this work Ruth Crawford foreshadowed in remarkable fashion what became a major preoccupation of composers after the Second World War. One can only conjecture how she might have developed if the time and place had been ready for her.

79 Twentieth-Century Americans (III)

"If music could be translated into human speech, it would no longer need to exist."

— NED ROREM

The Third Generation (Composers Born 1910–1930)

The American composers born in the first quarter of the twentieth century had a much firmer foundation on which to build their careers. Most of them were not only native-born but also native-trained; it was no longer necessary to go to Europe to obtain a superior musical education. The cause of American music was helped too by the rise of radio, long-playing

American painters contributed substantially to the creation of a new movement called Abstract Expressionism. Robert Motherwell (b. 1915), **The Voyage.** (*Museum of Modern Art, New York. Gift of Mrs. John D. Rockefeller, 3rd.*)

records, and television, which created a much broader audience for music than had ever existed before. Within this new public there were significant minorities who were interested in modern music and, more specifically, in modern American music. A sizable number of works by the new American school found their way onto recordings, thereby taking on a much more viable existence than that afforded by an occasional performance in a concert hall or on the air. From this extremely active generation we name a few representative figures:

Schuman   William Schuman (New York City, 1910–) has shown an affinity for the large forms of instrumental music. His nine symphonies form the central item in his output; best-known is the *Third* (1941).

Barber   Samuel Barber (West Chester, Pennsylvania, 1910–) is an avowed romantic. Several of his works have achieved wide popularity, among them the light-hearted Overture to *The School for Scandal* (1932), *Adagio for Strings* (1936), and *Essay for Orchestra, No. 1* (1937).

Menotti   Gian Carlo Menotti, born in Cadegliano, Italy, in 1911, is the most successful opera composer of our day. His list of works includes *The Medium* (1946), *The Consul* (1950), and *Amahl and the Night Visitors* (1951).

Diamond   David Diamond (Rochester, New York, 1915–) is a prolific composer; eight symphonies occupy the central position on his list. *Rounds for String Orchestra* (1944) has been widely played, as has his suite *Romeo and Juliet* (1947).

Bernstein   Leonard Bernstein (Boston, 1918–) was the first American-born musical director of the New York Philharmonic. His serious works include the *Jeremiah Symphony* (1942) and *The Age of Anxiety,* for piano and orchestra (1949). Among his scores for Broadway musicals are *On the Town,* a full-length version of his ballet *Fancy Free* (1944), *Candide* (1956), and the spectacularly successful *West Side Story* (1957).

Mennin   Peter Mennin (Erie, Pennsylvania, 1923–) is head of the Juilliard School of Music in New York City. His eight symphonies show his steady growth in the manipulation of ideas.

Rorem   Ned Rorem (Richmond, Indiana, 1923–) is one of the most gifted song writers of his generation. Such songs as *The Lordly Hudson* and *Lullaby of the Mountain Woman* are in the line of descent from the great French art song of the post-Romantic period. Among Rorem's works are three symphonies (1951, 1956, 1958), three piano concertos (1950, 1951, 1969); *Sun,* a suite for soprano and orchestra (1967).

The United States differs from European countries in one important respect: our people do not come from a single stock. On the contrary, ours is a melting-pot culture in which many national and racial groups are represented. This diversity is reflected in the backgrounds of our composers. For example, Walter Piston, Gian Carlo Menotti, and Peter Mennin are of Italian origin. A number of composers are Jewish, among them George Gershwin, Aaron Copland, William Schuman, David Diamond, and Leonard Bernstein. Varèse came of French-Italian, Howard Hanson of

Swedish stock. Among the Black composers of the modern American school
may be mentioned William Grant Still (Woodville, Mississippi, 1895–);
Ulysses Kay (Tucson, Arizona, 1917–); Howard Swanson (Atlanta,
Georgia, 1909–); Julia Perry (Lexington, Kentucky, 1924–), and David
Baker (Indianapolis, 1931–).

We have mentioned only a handful among three generations of composers whose works reflect important currents in twentieth-century musical thought. To give anywhere near a full account of their work would
carry us beyond the limits of this book. Enough has been said, however,
to indicate the diversity of these composers and of the tendencies they
represent.

80   American Jazz

"Jazz is the most astounding spontaneous musical event to take place anywhere since the
Reformation." — VIRGIL THOMSON

Jazz, by a rough definition-of-thumb, is an improvisational, Afro-American
musical idiom. It makes use of elements of rhythm, melody, and harmony
from Africa, and of melody and harmony from the European musical tradition. The influence of jazz, and of closely associated Afro-American
idioms, has been so pervasive that by now most of our popular music is in
an Afro-American idiom, and elements of jazz have permeated a good
deal of our concert music as well. (It is only in this latter sense that a
composer such as George Gershwin can be called a "jazz composer.")

If we know anything at all about jazz music, we are likely to know that
it is, first of all, a player's art and that, at least in part, the player may
make it up for us as he goes along. (An important consequence of this
fact is that recordings are the only meaningful way to preserve jazz; unlike Western concert music, it is not reproduced from a written score, but
freshly invented for every performance.) Improvisation, we saw, was not
unknown in some periods of European music—indeed, the ability to
extemporize was once a fundamental part of the equipment of every
accomplished musician. (For example, Bach, Handel, Mozart, and Beethoven were all famous for their keyboard improvisations.) But in practice,
European music generally confined improvisation to one performer at a
time. In jazz, certain things being agreed upon (a harmonic sequence, a
tempo, and the roles of the instruments), as many as eight players may
improvise at once—and this occurred even at the earliest stages of its
history.

Jazz was, first of all, a secular music of Blacks in this country. The word

A photograph taken in 1916 of one of the first Dixieland jazz combinations.

was first applied, in about 1917, to a style that evolved in New Orleans around the turn of the century. Jazz has changed continuously since then; it has not remained static like some European popular idioms (that of Spanish flamenco music, for example). But changes in jazz are not matters of caprice or fashion, as they often are in other popular American idioms. Jazz music has developed and refined itself, learning from its own past and building on it, rather in the manner of an art music. And it has gained, in the process, the high respect of musicians of all persuasions throughout the world.

The Origins: New Orleans

Ragtime

In the immediate background of New Orleans jazz were two idioms: ragtime and the blues. *Ragtime,* a sprightly, optimistic music, was basically a keyboard style, and a kind of Afro-American version of the polka or the march. The most famous of rags, Scott Joplin's *Maple Leaf Rag* (1899) * is made up of four sections, four melodies in the form A-B-A-C-D. Ragtime continued to develop parallel to early jazz, and by the time the earli-

* Unless otherwise noted, the major recorded performances cited in this chapter are included in *The Smithsonian Collection of Classic Jazz,* educational distribution by W. W. Norton & Co., Inc.

est jazz recordings were made, it had clearly influenced the New Orleans idiom. Rag music itself has often been hopelessly vulgarized almost from its beginnings, played with a stiff, inflexible rhythm on pianos deliberately made to jangle, or more recently with a touch and a rubato more appropriate to the European tradition than to ragtime.

Blues

The *blues* is an American musical and verse form, with no direct European and African antecedents that we know of. It probably began as an irregular, lamentatory chant, but by the time it was written down it had a three-line stanza in which the first two lines were identical—for example:

> The moon looks lonesome when it's shining through the trees;
> The moon looks lonesome when it's shining through the trees.
> The way a man looks lonesome when his woman packs up to leave.

Musically, the blues form is twelve measures, four measures for each line of text, harmonized simply:

	line 1	line 2		line 3	
harmony:	I	IV	I	V	I
measures:	4	2	2	2	2

In practice, various intermediate chords, and even some substitute chord patterns, have been used, at least since the second decade of this century.

The blues was not sung according to European ideas of "correct" pitch, but with a free use of "bent," "quavered," "glided," and otherwise emotionally inflected vocal sounds of various kinds. When the music was

Blue notes

written down, these effects were imitated by the so-called *blues scale,* in which the third, the seventh, and sometimes the fifth scale degrees were lowered a semitone, producing a scale resembling the minor scale. But the *blue notes* are not really minor notes in a major context. In practice they

● = a blue note, which may be as much as a half tone above or below the written pitch.

may come almost anywhere. One can say, however, that in instrumental music the blue notes tend to gravitate to the third, fifth, and seventh steps. By the mid-1920s, instrumental blues in a variety of tempos and moods were common, and "playing the blues" for the instrumentalist could mean extemporizing a melody within a blues harmonic sequence; brass, reed, and string players, particularly, were able to reproduce the interpretive vocal sounds of the blues singers on their instruments. (It should be pointed out that many pieces with the word "blues" in their titles are not really in blues form. Indeed, the word "blues" is sometimes used as loosely and carelessly as the word "jazz." There are, however, eight-bar blues, a sort of shortened version of the twelve-measure form, and there are sixteen-measure blues that borrow European folk forms for their outlines.)

The blues is a fundamental form in jazz, accounting for perhaps forty per cent of the music. And blues practices are applied to other forms. The blues tradition itself has continued, meanwhile, to become the so-called "rhythm and blues" of more recent times, and it is, of course, the direct progenitor of rock and roll as well. Thus the blues has become an international popular musical language of the twentieth century.

Song form   Another common form that we will encounter in jazz performances is of European origin—the thirty-two-bar *song form,* which is usually made up of four eight-bar phrases in the pattern A-A-B-A. (The B section is often called the *bridge* or *release.*) Typical examples of this form are *I Got Rhythm, Body and Soul,* and *Lady Be Good.* In another type of thirty-two-bar song form sometimes found, the pattern A-B-A-B, sometimes A-B-A-C, is used, as in *Embraceable You, Pennies from Heaven,* or *Indiana.* (Most popular songs have an introductory verse as well as the thirty-two-bar refrain, but this verse is infrequently used in performance.)

In a typical jazz performance, each repetition of the twelve-bar blues form or the thirty-two-bar song form is known as a *chorus;* the succession of choruses—some for full ensemble, some assigned as solos, duets, and the like, to the individual members of the group—amounts to a series of variations on a theme, using the blues or song as theme.

Jelly Roll Morton

The music of Ferdinand "Jelly Roll" Morton might be called a pianist's, composer's, and band leader's summary of Afro-American music and New Orleans jazz up to the mid-1920s. In his best recordings, Morton balances

Jelly Roll Morton.

several things beautifully: what is composed and what can be improvised, what is up to the individual and what is up to the ensemble, the effectiveness of the parts and the demands of the whole.

Dead Man Blues

Dead Man Blues (recorded in 1926) is by a seven-piece ensemble: trumpet, clarinet, trombone, piano (Morton), banjo, string bass, and drums, supplemented at one point by two additional clarinets. It is a piece built on the twelve-measure blues form, but uses, in the manner of ragtime, three themes. After a bit of comic banter, it opens with the trombonist playing a breathy version of Chopin's *Funeral March,* with a hint of humor. What follows may be schematically represented as:

section	twelve-measure chorus	content
A	1	ensemble in improvised polyphony
A^1	2	clarinet solo (Omer Simeon)
B	3	trumpet solo (George Mitchell)
B^1	4	trumpet solo continues
C	5	three clarinets in harmony
C^1	6	clarinets repeat, with trombone countermelody (Edward "Kid" Ory)
A^2	7	ensemble in improvised polyphony
Coda		two measures of section C

New Orleans style

The first chorus is in the improvised polyphony that was a feature of the New Orleans or "Dixieland" style, which, in Morton's version, dances and interweaves with an exceptional lightness and lack of stridency. The trumpeter has the lead melody, which he is free to modify and embellish, the clarinetist plays a kind of continuous counterpoint, the trombonist has a simpler basslike part, and the rhythm instruments provide a harmonic and percussive accompaniment. In the second chorus, the clarinetist breaks away for a one-chorus variation.

The B theme is stated in the trumpeter's version, conceived as a continuous two-chorus variation and not simply one chorus followed by another. The tight contrasting "trio" melody (C) is stated by the three clarinets in simple, close harmony. As they repeat, the trombone re-enters beneath them with a simple, mournful improvisation. The two-part polyphony also makes a transition to the final chorus, a new three-part polyphonic variation on the A theme that is thus both a partial recapitulation and a climax.

This is a three-minute miniature, then, made of simple materials, partly created on the spur of the moment, with a musical intelligence guiding its patterns of likeness and contrast.

One could add to the list of pieces that are among Morton's best such slower ones as *Smoke House Blues* (not a twelve-measure blues) and the quartet blues *Mournful Serenade,* and such faster "stomps" as *Black Bottom Stomp, The Chant,* and *Grandpa's Spells.*

King Oliver

Morton's best records show the high level that can be attained by a jazz composer working with skillful, carefully rehearsed players. In the other celebrated New Orleans ensemble, that of Joseph "King" Oliver, we encounter a group of improvising, blues-oriented musicians who understood each other's work so well that they could complement and even anticipate each other almost by reflex. But by 1923, when Oliver's group made its first recordings, the ensemble featured a young second cornetist whose innovative work would soon change the musical vocabulary of jazz. His name was Louis Armstrong.

Louis Armstrong

It may be difficult for some of us—particularly those who may have heard or seen him only in his later years—to realize what a great instrumentalist and important American musician Louis Armstrong was. His influence is everywhere. Anyone, anywhere in the world, in any musical idiom, who writes for trumpet is inevitably influenced by what Louis Armstrong and his progeny have shown can be done with the instrument—not only in terms of extending its range, but also in the variety of mutes, half-valve effects, and the like, that have expanded its timbral potential. All of our jazz, real and popularized, is different because of him, and our popular singers of all kinds are deeply in his debt.

Originator of "swing"

Although Armstrong was a superb, inventive melodist, and, for his time, imaginative (and wholly appropriate) in harmony as well, the essence of his contribution was rhythmic. Indeed the word "swing" was originally coined by musicians as a way of describing Louis Armstrong's unique melodic rhythm, and the term has become a part of the technical vocabulary of jazz. It has never been defined but has to do with the rhythmic momentum of the music. The so-called "swing style" of the 1930s is actually a Louis Armstrong style, in which soloists and composer-arrangers for the "big-bands" (of about fourteen pieces) undertook to adopt and explore his ideas. But the term "swing" has been applied to subsequent styles, and even been made retroactive to earlier styles, as a kind of shorthand method of indicating the rhythmic character proper to the music. As in all musics, some otherwise quite capable musicians in jazz have rhythmic problems, i.e., they don't swing.

A description can account for very little in discussing the work of a performer such as Armstrong, and even a music example is limited: in musical notation, a jazz solo is the merest sketch, lacking the nuances of attack, tone, and inflection that are all-important. One way of isolating Armstrong's contribution is to compare him with what was going on around him in his early days—for example, the King Oliver ensemble's *Weather Bird Rag* (Milestone 47022) contrasted to Armstrong's duet of

Louis Armstrong (seated at the piano) with a group of fellow performers, c. 1927.

the piece with pianist Earl Hines—or to hear him in the context of the New York ensembles with which he recorded in 1924, when he was a member of Fletcher Henderson's orchestra—as in *I Ain't Gonna Play No Second Fiddle,* with a Perry Bradford group, where he picks up the entire performance and makes it soar during his brilliant solo. Two blues performances from the mid-'20s should be cited: Armstrong's series of five, passionate descending phrases from a high B flat on *S. O. L. Blues,* and the startling stop-time chorus on the innocently titled *Potato Head Blues.*

Armstrong's improvisations

There are examples in Armstrong's recorded repertory of solos that are in highly individual embellishment styles, of solos that are entirely improvised—that is, that are harmonically oriented inventions with little or no melodic reference to a theme (and we hear these in both blues and nonblues structures). But perhaps Armstrong's greatest talent is his spontaneous ability to recompose a popular melody. He alters a note here, momentarily hurries this phrase, delays that one; he spots a cliché turn of melody and avoids it, often substituting a much superior phrase of his own invention. He can take a good popular melody like *I Gotta Right to Sing the Blues* and raise it, by an orderly simplification, into eloquence. He can take *I've Got the World on a String* and transform it by rhythmic ingenuity into something personal. (Incidentally, one must simply overlook the work of certain of Armstrong's accompanists at this period. It is partly because few players functioned on his level, of course, but it is also because Armstrong concerned himself primarily with his own improvising.)

It has been said that a great artist always suggests more things than either he or his immediate following can explore. And there are certain of Armstrong's solos with implications, particularly rhythmic implications, that jazzmen did not begin to deal with for over a decade. These include *West End Blues* (1928), *Sweethearts on Parade* (1930), *Between the Devil and the Deep Blue Sea* (the faster "take" 3, 1931), and his second version of *Basin Street Blues* (1933).

West End Blues
Side 18/2 (S)
Side 12/1 (E II)

Armstrong's portions of *West End Blues* represent a balance of striking virtuosity and eloquent simplicity—the opening, downward-then-upward phrase with its unusual change of tempo in measure 3, and the longer, descending phrase, extended by sequence and repetition to reach a resting place:

The first chorus begins calmly and simply, and then builds in a series of rising triplet arpeggios to a high B flat:

After a trombone chorus, Armstrong takes part as singer in a duet with the clarinet, the two phrases alternating back and forth. The fourth chorus is taken by Earl Hines (piano), and then Armstrong launches the final strain with a passionately held high B flat, which leads him to a series of rapid, complex ascending and descending fragments:

There is no exact precedent in Western music for such a unique combination of distillation, embellishment, and invention as one hears in Armstrong's improvising, and for it one jazz critic (André Hodeir) has borrowed the rhetorician's term "paraphrase."

We mentioned above that in 1924 Louis Armstrong played with the New York orchestra of Fletcher Henderson, and from that combination emerged the beginnings of the co-called "big-band" jazz that dominated popular music in the 1930s. But the highest achievements in that idiom belong to the composer-pianist-bandleader Edward Kennedy "Duke" Ellington—achievements that we will consider in detail in Chapter 81.

Count Basie and Lester Young

Using Armstrong's work as their guide, his most capable followers were able to work out personal styles, styles that showed the individuality of instrumental sound and interpretation of melody that are required of a jazz musician. Tenor saxophonist Coleman Hawkins, for example, built solos, like his celebrated *Body and Soul* (1937), on an adroit use of arpeggios. Trumpeter Roy Eldridge's best improvisations, like *Rockin' Chair* or *I Surrender Dear,* make only spare or even indirect use of Armstrong's *Billie Holiday* ideas. The singer Billie Holiday brought to her songs the powers of an exceptional actress, and showed an ability at melodic paraphrase comparable to Armstrong's, as can be seen from her version of *These Foolish Things* (1952) (Verve V-8808):

Lester Young (left) and Count Basie.
(*Photo Gjon Mili.*)

Pianist Art Tatum absorbed ideas of swing, and developed a largely orna-
mental style that showed a superb pianistic technique and an outstanding
harmonic imagination—one might cite recordings like *Willow, Weep for
Me; Too Marvelous for Words;* or his 1949 version of *Aunt Hagar's
Blues* (Capitol M-11028).

By 1932, the big bands had begun to absorb Armstrong's basic rhythmic
ideas and developed an ensemble swing in his manner. And in 1937,
there appeared a jazz orchestra able to build on those ideas, that of pianist

Count Basie   William "Count" Basie. The scores were relatively simple, the ensemble
was spirited, the rhythm section played with a new lightness, and the
emphasis was on the soloists.

The leader's piano is a thing of deceptive simplicity. His ideas seem
few, yet he never uses them monotonously; his touch is delicate, buoyant,
and the bane of his imitators; and his ability to improvise orderly, sequen-
tial melodies is outstanding. The Basie orchestra's most important soloist

Lester Young   was the tenor saxophonist Lester Young, whose swing was impeccable and
whose sound was light, airy, and almost vibrato-less. Young was rhythmically imaginative—there were no "strong" or "weak" beats for him. His
phrasing was asymmetrical, not confined to the traditional four- and
eight-bar units. And Young was often high-handed with the harmonic
structure of a piece. Thus his solos have a constant element of suspense
and surprise, which his abilities as a melodist ultimately resolve.

Doggin' Around (1938) gives a good introduction to both Basie and
Young. The former's piano solo (which follows a long tenor sax solo and
shorter ones on trumpet and baritone sax) is built almost entirely around

his opening idea—a little fragment which he phrases and rephrases, expands, modifies, simplifies, for thirty-two measures. Young begins with a kind of warmup or warning beneath Basie's final two bars. His opening phrase is only one note in the first measure. His next phrase begins at bar 2 and dances with a graceful complexity through bar 7. His eighth bar is silent, perhaps balancing that single note in the first bar. Bar 9 begins with a melodic link to bar 7. And so on.

Charlie Parker

In the Basie orchestra, then, we see the beginnings of change. That change culminates in the genius of alto saxophonist Charlie Parker, and was expressed, in 1945, in an innovative series of recordings done in collaboration with trumpeter John "Dizzy" Gillespie, for example, a piece such as *Shaw' Nuff*.

Parker was as harmonically exact as Coleman Hawkins, but as harmonically imaginative as Art Tatum. Rhythmically he was even more imaginative than Lester Young, and his accents might fall on any of the beats or variously in between the beats. He was a virtuoso saxophonist and an outstanding, inventive melodist. And he took up some of Louis Armstrong's most advanced ideas where the trumpeter had left them more than a decade earlier.

Embraceable You   His 1947 improvisation on *Embraceable You* ("take" 1) opens with a six-note motive that is repeated five times, although it is variously pronounced and moved around to fit the piece's chord changes. On its fifth

Charlie Parker. (*Photo Roy Whitten.*)

appearance, it is the opening to an intricate burst of melody which ultimately comes to rest with a variant of the five-note motive.

The little phrase subsequently appears and reappears in various guises (reaccented, condensed, expanded) in the solo, acting as a kind of organized reference point. Furthermore, in its general contours, the *Embraceable You* improvisation begins simply, builds to a complexity of longer phrases and shorter note values, then gradually returns to simple lyricism at its end. In jazz improvisation such as this, we hear a kind of instrumental melody considerably removed from popular song writing. Two other outstanding Parker improvisations are *Lady Be Good* (Verve V-68002; 1946) and the onomatopoetic *Klacktoveedsedstene* (Roost 2210), with drummer Max Roach.

Rhythmic evolution

Parker's and Gillespie's innovations in jazz center around innovations in rhythm, as did those of Louis Armstrong. Indeed, one might almost tell the story of Afro-American music and its evolution in rhythmic terms. The earliest music of which we have any record that shows an African influence, the so-called "Minstrel songs," have a rhythm based on a half note: for example, "*RU*fus, *RAS*tus, *JOHN*son, *BROWN*." Ragtime broke up that half-note rhythm with syncopation, and in later ragtime style the same song might go something like "*RU*fus a-*RAS*-tus a-*JOHN*son *BROWN*."

New Orleans jazz is fascinating in its rhythmic evolution, for we have phonograph records that carry it from a somewhat clipped, jerky rhythmic style, barely out of ragtime, to a style like that of clarinetist and soprano saxophonist Sidney Bechet, who came close to Louis Armstrong's rhythmic discoveries, and that of Armstrong himself. One may say, very roughly indeed, that Armstrong's rhythmic ideas are based on a quarter note, and Parker's on an eighth note.

An important aspect of the rhythmic evolution of jazz is the response of the rhythm sections to the innovations of the soloists. In the Basie orchestra, for example, the rhythm section played four evenly accented quarter notes—the full expression, perhaps, of the kind of accompaniment that Armstrong's melodic rhythm had implied. But there were further refinements. The rhythmic lead passed to the string bass, playing quarter notes pizzicato, and to the drummer's cymbals. Basie himself frequently dropped the time-keeping, "oom-pah," left-hand figures of earlier pianists. Later, "rhythm guitar" (chords struck four to the bar) was eliminated from the jazz ensemble, and drummers, carrying the basic pulse on a "ride" (suspended) cymbal with (usually) the right hand, were free to make interplaying, polyrhythmic accents on snare drum and on other cymbals with the left hand, and on the bass drum with the right foot.

Thelonious Monk

In what has preceded, it may seem that jazz has had two kinds of leadership: that of innovative, improvising soloists who periodically renew its basic vocabulary; and that of composers who give it a compositional synthesis and ensemble form. Further, the music seems to move in a kind of pendulum swing from great composer to great player—that is, from Morton to Armstrong to Ellington to Parker.

If that is a true version of the way jazz has evolved, one would expect a composer to emerge after Parker. And in the mid-1950s, jazz musicians began to turn to pianist-composer Thelonious Monk for guidance. Monk had been around earlier, making some of his best recordings, but his approach was somewhat unorthodox and had been overlooked by musicians and the public alike.

Monk is truly a hand-made artist, and his techniques are all jazz techniques. He has written several major pieces, and performed them in small ensembles, in which overall form is as important as content—and in which form itself is almost as improvisational as the solos themselves.

Misterioso

Misterioso (1948) is a Monk blues, performed by a quartet featuring the leader's piano and the vibraphone of Milt Jackson. The performance opens without an introduction, as Jackson and Monk state the theme, with the bass and drums phrasing along with them. The melody is an original version of what is essentially a traditional idea, based on what a jazz musician would call "walking" sixths—a melody made up of sixth degrees of different scales.

In the second chorus, the bass and drums begin a more conventional accompaniment and Jackson begins to improvise the blues. Monk, however, does not play standard blues-chord changes behind Jackson; he plays something that seems both related and not related to his theme. Monk plays "blue" sevenths, the next "implied" note of his theme, if you will. It is as if Monk were saying, "This is not just the blues in this key, this is my blues called *Misterioso,* and however much we make this up as we go along, something needs to make it *Misterioso* all the way through." In his own solo, Monk echos the upward, walking movement of the theme. And in the final chorus Monk lets Jackson carry the theme, while he counterpoints a kind of "spread-out" version of his previous accompaniment, in a recapitulation not only of the theme but, in effect, of the whole performance. (There is, incidentally, another version of *Misterioso* on Blue Note 81509, recorded at the same time as this one—more "regular," much less successful, but offering an interesting and instructive comparison nevertheless.)

Thelonious Monk.

Other notable Monk recordings include *Evidence, Criss Cross, Eronel, Four in One,* and his apparently simple but quite perceptive versions of such standard pieces as *Smoke Gets in Your Eyes* and *I Should Care.* There is also an outstanding quartet recording of Monk's *Trinkle Tinkle* (Milestone 47011) with saxophonist John Coltrane, on which Monk resourcefully evokes a variety of textures from his four instruments. And there is a fascinating blues improvisation by Monk on *Bags' Groove* in which he spins chorus after chorus out of his brief opening idea, and uses space, rest, and silence as expressively as notes themselves.

The vibraphonist Milt Jackson was a participant in several of Thelonious Monk's best recordings. However, he is regularly a member of the Modern Jazz Quartet; and that ensemble, in its somewhat more conservative way, has arrived at an improvisational, overall form comparable to Monk's in such pieces as *Django* and *Bluesology.*

Ornette Coleman

By the late 1950s jazz musicians had become so adroit at inventing their melodies within harmonic guidelines that it seemed time to try another approach. Trumpeter Miles Davis recorded a recital he called *Kind of Blue* that used several different approaches. On *So What?,* for example, he used A-A-B-A song form and assigned only the Dorian mode (see p. 214) to the A phrases, and the Phrygian to the B phrases, as a basis for the solos. The performance, particularly for Davis and saxophonist John Coltrane, is a classic. And one might say that Coltrane spent the rest of his life (he died in 1967) developing the implications of that single important performance.

Coincidentally a young alto saxophonist named Ornette Coleman was working on a similar approach to improvisation. The best introduc-

Lonely Woman

tion to Coleman's work is to go directly to a recording. *Lonely Woman* (1959) begins with bass and drums, each stating a different rhythm and different tempo. The trumpet (Don Cherry) and alto sax enter at an unexpected point and begin stating the theme in a third, dirgelike tempo. One thing immediately noticeable is that, even when they are playing together, the melody instruments are free to interpret a theme individually.

At certain points in Coleman's theme, the trumpet rests and the alto continues on its own. The piece is in an A-A-B-A form, with Coleman taking the B release as a solo. The main improvisation also goes to Coleman, and something that was evident from the beginning becomes even more so. *Intonation* (playing in tune) in this music is rather free and a matter of emotion and interpretation. (Coleman's own words on the matter are, "You can play sharp in tune or flat in tune"; thus a D in a context of sadness shouldn't sound the same as a D representing joy.) A writer on art music would say that Coleman uses "microtones." In jazz terms, Coleman has extended the idea of the vocally inflected blue notes to include whole phrases and episodes.

In improvising, Coleman generally stays within the key of a performance. But at certain points he does burst out of key into a momentary atonality. Since Coleman does not follow a chord pattern that would be implied by his themes, or necessarily the outline of phrases his theme sets up, he and his bass player often present a kind of freely improvised, mutually inspiring counterpoint which may momentarily clash dissonantly. This further contributes to the atmosphere of atonality in his music.

Congeniality

Such things are particularly evident in *Congeniality* (1959), which has a celebrated Coleman solo. One might assume that such free music, played with such raw emotion as his, invites a kind of melodic and harmonic chaos. But Coleman is the most orderly of players: a little idea appears, is turned and rephrased in every conceivable way until it yields a new idea which, in turn, is treated sequentially. And, above all, Coleman's melodic rhythm is fresh, traditional, and personal all at once, and freer and more varied than what had preceeded him.

Coleman's music shows that since improvised variation is, after all, the main attraction in small ensemble jazz, a solo need not be obeisant in structure or harmony to an opening theme. In performances like *The Riddle* and *Garden of Souls,* Coleman showed also that spontaneous or evolving changes of tempo, executed by the soloist and his accompaniment, can be functional aspects of a jazz musician's development of his musical ideas.

This painting, **Chicago 1955**, by the American Ben Shahn (1898–1969) reflects the improvisatory technique of its subject matter. *(Estate of Ben Shahn; Photo Scala, Florence.)*

The desire to function "in the gap between life and art" motivates Andy Warhol (b. 1930) in this Pop Art painting, **Campbell's Soup.** *(Collection, The Museum of Modern Art, New York. Philip Johnson Fund.)*

The music of Ornette Coleman is innovative, but its innovations are based on sound insight into the nature of jazz and the high accomplishments of its past. It provides a solid body of achievement on its own, and at the same time reaffirms the continuing growth of this indigenous and important American art.

81 Duke Ellington

"Not only musical genius and talent, but an unquenchable thirst, an unrequitable passion for translating the raw materials of musical sounds into his own splendid visions."

— GUNTHER SCHULLER

It has become increasingly common for the name of Duke Ellington to be numbered among the great American composers. His claim to that position rests on a huge body of music, including everything from simple tunes, theater songs, piano pieces, works for jazz septet and octet, to instrumental compositions for full jazz orchestra and, in a few instances, for jazz orchestra and symphony orchestra combined.

Duke Ellington.

His Life and Music

Edward Kennedy Ellington was born in Washington, D.C., on April 29, 1899, and he began his musical career in that city. By the mid-1920s he had established himself as an ensemble leader in New York. And by the early 1930s, he had begun to achieve international recognition as a composer. His nickname "Duke" was first conferred because of his sartorial elegance. It became his professional name and, as Albert Murray has observed, it was appropriate because Ellington was, personally and musically, a natural aristocrat. He died in New York City on May 24, 1974.

Ellington used the American dance band as his means of expression. "He plays piano," said his frequent collaborator Billy Strayhorn, "but his real instrument is the orchestra." Most of his best works are therefore instrumental miniatures conceived within the unpretentious conventions of twentieth-century dance music. But they are realized as works of high musical art.

Innovative instrumentation
In his orchestrations, and most particularly in his scoring of individual chords, Ellington proved himself to be one of the truly original musicians of our time. And through instrumental doublings by his reed players on various saxophones and clarinets, through ingenious combinations of instruments, and through the carefully crafted use of various mutes and combinations of mutes by his brass players, he achieved a rich variety of sonorities and textures from his ensemble—which in his early years numbered as few as ten musicians.

Ellington learned a great deal from his immediate predecessors and contemporaries—largely from the Fletcher Henderson orchestra—about how to transform the jazz-influenced dance band (with its reed, brass, and rhythm sections) into a true jazz orchestra. But it was when he encountered night-club "show" work, with its call for overtures, choruses, dance accompaniments, and the other demands of the miniature musical "review" which these establishments featured, that his talent began to develop. He made his dance band into a show band, and his show band a vehicle for a collaborative yet personal artistic expression.

Ellington worked with the individual talents of his musicians in the same way that dramatists of the past worked with their actors or choreographers with their dancers. Indeed, his harmonic originality was initially dictated not so much in the abstract, as by, let us say, how this particular player's A flat sounded, and how it in turn might sound when juxtaposed with that player's highly individual G in the upper register.

Blue Light *and* Subtle Lament

Side 18/3 (S)
Side 12/2 (E II)
Blue Light (1938) is a blues work of apparent simplicity, which involves only seven instruments. It is largely a succession of solos, but in its one written ensemble passage, Ellington undertakes another of his experi-

ments with muted trumpet, muted trombone, and (unexpectedly) lower-register clarinet that he began with the celebrated *Mood Indigo* (1930). The result is this strikingly original passage:

Each chorus of *Blue Light* contributes to a developing musical and emotional whole which is greater than the sum of its parts. Ellington himself sets the mood with his introduction and provides a running and unifying comment throughout, before his own contribution and summary at the end. He introduces Barney Bigard's liquid clarinet improvisation, comments further as Bigard joins the trumpet and trombone for the orchestrated chorus. His keyboard then leads trumpet and clarinet into the background as trombonist Lawrence Brown breaks away for his robust melody (a melody that later formed the basis for the 1946 Ellington piece for wordless contralto voice and orchestra, *Transblucency*). And the composer ends the piece himself with a strong and texturally varied solo piano chorus.

Side 18/4 (S)
Side 12/3 (E II)

From the same year, *Subtle Lament* is a somber five-chorus blues for the orchestra, consisting of two trumpets and a cornet, three trombones, four saxophones, guitar, string bass, piano, and drums. It begins with an introduction by piano, with the active participation of the string bass, and once again the leader's keyboard, with fills, counterpoint, and an intermittent accompaniment, seems to propel and conduct every aspect of the performance. The motive phrase of the opening chorus is:

* note doubled by muted trombone

Next is an antiphonal chorus by Ellington's pensive piano and the trombones. The trombones, then the saxophones, continue in obbligato to Rex Stewart's improvised cornet chorus, which ends on a poignant half-valve effect. In an almost optimistic mood, muted trombones return for the fourth chorus—a written variation, in effect a new theme. The final chorus finds the clarinet improvising in conversation with muted brass for eight measures and a brief recapitulation of the opening motive for the final four measures, including a broadened ending.

Blue Light is structured in contrasts. There are choruses of melodic simplicity (the clarinet solo), one of which has a density of texture (the written ensemble chorus). In contrast are the choruses of strong melody (the trombone solo and the piano solo). In *Subtle Lament* the contrasts are more complex. The two ensemble passages have melodic (horizontal) simplicity and harmonic (vertical) density. The three soloists—cornet, piano, and clarinet—all begin in more complex melodic lines, but each in its different way relinquishes the mood in favor of a contemplative simplicity for its last four measures.

Extended works

We began by calling Ellington a great miniaturist, but particularly since his death there has begun a re-evaluation of some of his extended works, including his *Reminiscing in Tempo* (1935); his four-part, thematically-integrated piece in blues forms, *Suite Thursday* (1950; the title is a pun after John Steinbeck) (Atlantic SD 2-304); *Queen's Suite* (1968), written for England's Queen Elizabeth II; and his "tone parallel" (the term is Ellington's) to the history of Blacks in this hemisphere, *Black, Brown, and Beige* (1943), the first half of which (the *Black, Brown, and Beige Suite*) was also orchestrated for symphony orchestra by Maurice Peress at the composer's suggestion.

Whether in these longer works or in his more characteristic shorter ones, Ellington's music never fails to manifest that special originality, the creativity that stimulated the French poet Blaise Cendrars to proclaim that "Such music is not only a new art form but a new reason for living."

EIGHT

The New Music

"Composers are now able as never before to satisfy the dictates of that inner ear of the imagination." — EDGARD VARÈSE

82 New Directions

"From Schoenberg I learned that tradition is a home we must love and forgo." — LUKAS FOSS

The term "new music" has been used widely throughout history, and rightly so. Has not every generation of creative musicians produced sounds and styles that had never been heard before? All the same, the years since World War II have seen such far-reaching innovations in the art that we are perhaps more justified than any previous generation in applying the label to the music of the present. In effect, we have witnessed nothing less than the birth of a new world of sound.

Mid-Century Trends in the Arts

Only rarely does an important movement in art come into being without precursors. It should therefore not surprise us that several elements of avant-garde art can be traced back to earlier developments. For example, in the years immediately before the First World War, the Italian movement

Futurism known as Futurism attracted musicians who aspired to an "art of noises" that foreshadowed the achievements of Varèse and of electronic music. Another precursor was the Dada movement, which grew up in Zurich during the war and after 1918 spread to other major art centers. The

Dadaism Dadaists, in reaction to the horrors of the bloodbath that engulfed Europe, rejected the concept of Art with a capital A—that is, something to be put on a pedestal and reverently admired; to make their point, they produced works of manifest absurdity. This nose-thumbing spirit of Dadaism was reflected in the music of many composers, especially in France, during the twenties; several decades later it was to influence the American composer John Cage. The Dada group, which included artists like Hans Arp, Marcel Duchamp, and Kurt Schwitters, subsequently merged

Surrealism into the school of Surrealists, who exploited the symbolism of dreams. The best-known Surrealists, such as the writers Guillaume Apollinaire and André Breton, the painters Giorgio de Chirico, Max Ernst, and Salvador Dali, organized the indiscipline of Dada into a visionary art based on the disassociated and distorted images of the world of dreams. Other ele-

Cubism ments entering into the family tree of contemporary art were Cubism, the Paris-based style of painting embodied in the work of Pablo Picasso,

The spirit of Dadaism is embodied in this Cubist-Surrealist painting, which scandalized the New York Armory Show of 1913. Marcel Duchamp (1887-1968), **Nude Descending a Staircase, No. 2**. (*Philadelphia Museum of Art.*)

Georges Braque, and Juan Gris, which encouraged the painter to construct a visual world in terms of geometric patterns; and Expressionism, which we discussed in Chapter 64.

Art since the Second World War has unfolded against a background of unceasing social turmoil. In this regard, of course, the 1950s and '60s have been no different from many decades that preceded them. However, there can be no question that, as the second half of the century wore on, the problems confronting civilization became steadily more severe. The knowledge that man has finally achieved the capacity to wipe himself off the face of the earth broods over our time and feeds its unease. The fixed laws and certainties of Newtonian physics have given way to a relativistic view of the universe in which chance and accident, the probable and unpredictable, are seen to have an increasingly important place. The moral imperatives that we inherited from our forebears are being questioned as never before. This restlessness of spirit is inevitably reflected in the arts, which are passing through a period of violent experimentation with new media, new materials, new techniques. Artists are freeing themselves from every vestige of the past in order to explore new areas of thought and feeling. Some even prefer to reject thought and feeling altogether.

Abstract Ex-
pressionism

Since the human eye responds more readily to fresh impressions than does the ear, contemporary painting and sculpture have reached a wider public than has contemporary music. The trend away from objective painting guaranteed the supremacy of Abstract Expressionism in this country during the 1950s and '60s. In the canvases of such men as Robert Motherwell, Jackson Pollock, Willem de Kooning, Franz Kline, and Philip Guston, space, mass, and color are freed from the need to imitate objects in the real world; they become values in the autonomous realm of painting. In other words, the Abstract Expressionists strengthened the tradition of "pure" painting—pure, that is, in its independence of external reality. The urge toward abstraction has been felt equally in contemporary sculpture, as is evident in the work of such artists as Henry Moore, Isamu Noguchi, and David Smith.

Pop Art

At the same time, a new kind of realism has come into being in the art of Jasper Johns, Robert Rauschenberg, and their fellows, who owe some of their inspiration to the Dadaists of four decades earlier. Rauschenberg's aim, as he put it, was to work "in the gap between life and art." This trend culminated in Pop Art, which draws its themes and techniques from modern urban life: machines, advertisements, comic strips, movies, commercial photography, and familiar objects connected with everyday living. The desire to function "in the gap between life and art" motivates Andy Warhol's *Four Campbell Soup Cans* and *Brillo Boxes,* Jim

In Abstract Expressionism, space and mass become independent values, liberated from the need to represent reality. A painting by Franz Kline (1910-62), **Accent Grave**. (*Private Collection, courtesy Sidney Janis Gallery, New York.*)

The urge toward abstraction has been manifested in the work of sculptors such as Henry Moore (b. 1898) in his **Lincoln Center Reclining Figure**. (© *Lincoln Center for the Performing Arts, Inc., 1965; photograph by Ezra Stoller Associates.*)

Dine's *Shovel* and *A Nice Pair of Boots,* Claes Oldenburg's monumental *Bacon, Lettuce and Tomato* and *Dual Hamburgers.* Pop Art has absorbed the literal vision of photography and the silk-screen techniques of reproducing photographs on canvas; also the Dada-like inclusion of incongruous objects into art works. For example, Rauschenberg has incorporated into his abstract oils a quilt and pillow, a radio, Coke bottles, electric clocks, and fans. These impart to his paintings the three-dimensional quality of sculpture. In this respect he is one of an influential group that is determined to expand the resources of the painter's art.

In a related vein, new styles of art have grown up because of the availability of new materials. The sculptor no longer works simply with traditional marble and bronze, but reaches out to employ wood, new types of concrete, and a variety of plastics—clear or colored, solid, foamlike, or pliable. The flexibility of new materials has suggested new forms, and there is a new genre of Environmental Art that uses all the resources of art and technology to create a world of shapes, sounds, lights, and colors into which the spectator actually steps, to be completely surrounded by the artist's vision.

Environ-mental Art

Interaction:
art and music
Developments in music have paralleled these trends. A number of composers have been strongly influenced by their painter friends. Morton Feldman, to name one, has written: "The new painting made me desirous of a sound world more direct, more immediate, more physical than anything that existed before. To me my score is my canvas, my space. What I do is try to sensitize this area—this time space." The long association between Varèse and the painter Marcel Duchamp engendered a strikingly similar point of view in both artists. A like parallelism exists between Jackson Pollock's attempt to achieve an "indeterminate" kind of painting by allowing the colors to drip freely onto the canvas, and the attempt of John Cage and his followers to achieve an indeterminate music by using procedures based on chance. Like the proponents of Pop Art, Cage has tried to expand resources; he accepts "all audible phenomena as material proper to music." When we examine the new music we find a desire for free forms in which elements of chance and randomness are permitted to operate. Many artists have chosen to loosen their control of the art work by moving away from pre-established forms. A similar desire for freedom inspired the mobiles of Alexander Calder, the component parts of which shift with each current of air to create new relationships. Artists tend more and more to look upon form as the all-pervading element in art that flows directly out of the material, so that each individual work, instead of following a set pattern, must be allowed

The themes and techniques of Pop Art are drawn from modern urban life while incorporating Dada-like incongruities into each work. A construction by Robert Rauschenberg (b. 1925) entitled **Monogram**. *(Modern Museum, Stockholm.)*

to create its own form. Significant in this respect is Cage's remark that "Form is what interests everyone and fortunately it is wherever you are and there is no place where it is not."

Dance

Other arts, too, have been subject to wide experimentation. The dance, traditionally chained to specific anecdote and gesture, found itself liberated from storytelling (in the work of George Balanchine) and from traditional patterns of movement (in the work of Martha Graham), and since the Second World War the trend toward abstraction has grown apace. The most important choreographer of the avant-garde, Merce Cunningham, has worked closely throughout his career with John Cage, introducing elements of chance and indeterminacy into his dance compositions. His objective, he states, is "to make a space in which anything can happen."

Poetry

In the field of literature, poetry has, understandably, been the most experimental genre. Many of our poets face the world of today with a profound sense of alienation. They reflect their disjointed epoch in the fragmentation of their syntax and the violence of their imagery. The utmost freedom of verse forms and a sardonic wit tinged with bitterness characterize many of the younger poets, such as the two best-known members of the so-called "New York group": Kenneth Koch and John Ashbery. Contemporary American poetry ranges from the elegant intellectualism of a John Hollander or a Richard Wilbur to the Whitmanesque exuberance of the two leading poets of the "Beat Generation," Allen Ginsberg and Gregory Corso. These poets and their colleagues reveal—as poets have always done—the most profound impulses of their time, but with an energy and passion that are in the great tradition. Even the word-oriented art of poetry, however, has given rise to strong abstract tendencies, most clearly embodied in the idea of "shaped" poems, in which words are arranged in abstract patterns on the page, the visual form taking precedence over the meaning.

Drama

Although the forms of drama and novel are by their very nature based on an imitation of life, they have not remained indifferent to the new trends. The theater has moved away from the social and psychological concerns that permeated the work of Arthur Miller and Tennessee Williams in the 1950s. It has turned instead to the "theater of the absurd," whose leading European proponents—Samuel Beckett, Eugene Ionesco, and Jean Genet—view the world with a vast disillusionment, placing metaphysical absurdity at the core of human existence. No less pervasive has been the influence of the Englishman Harold Pinter, whose plays transform the realities of human relationship into unpredictable patterns. The spirit of the absurd has also penetrated the novel—witness such works as Joseph Heller's *Catch 22* and John Barth's *Giles Goat-Boy,* to name only two of a considerable number of novels that have captured the pulse of our time.

Finally, the cinema—of all the arts the one most securely chained to

Cinema storytelling of a popular kind—has also responded to the twin impulses of experimentation and abstraction. A number of "new wave" directors have opened their films directly onto contemporary experience, mirroring with great eloquence the disjointed patterns of life about them. Among these may be mentioned Michelangelo Antonioni, Jean-Luc Godard, Federico Fellini, and Alain Resnais, in whose *Last Year at Marienbad* the Abstract-Expressionist urge found perhaps its most successful cinematic realization to date.

If the picture of artistic developments in recent decades often seems confused and contradictory, this is inevitable because of our very close vantage point. We have picked out only a few landmarks on the contemporary scene, but these are enough to indicate that art today has become increasingly intellectual, experimental, and abstract.

Toward Greater Organization

When Schoenberg based his twelve-tone method on the use of tone rows, he was obviously moving toward a much stricter organization of the sound material. This desire was even more clearly manifest in the music of Webern. However, it remained for their disciples to extend the implications of the tone-row principle to the elements of music other than pitch. The arrangement of the twelve tones in a series might be paralleled by similar groupings of twelve durations (time values), twelve dynamic values (degrees of loudness), or twelve timbres. Other factors, too, might be brought under serial organization: the disposition of registers and densities, of types of attack, or sizes of intervals. By extending the serial principle in all possible directions, a composer could achieve a totally organized fabric, every dimension of which was derived from and controlled by one basic premise: the generating power of the series.

Total This move toward *total serialism* resulted in an extremely complex,
serialism ultrarational music, marked by the utmost unity among the ideas to be expressed, the means of expressing them, and the structures through which that expression was achieved. In such a conception the series defines all the relationships that operate within a given structure; the act of composition becomes the process whereby those relationships are realized to the fullest degree. Total serialism pushed to the farthermost limits, with the thoroughness of a scientific experiment, some of the new ways of hearing and experiencing music.

Toward Greater Freedom

The urge toward a totally controlled music had its counterpart in the desire for greater—even total—freedom from all predetermined forms and procedures. Music of this type emphasizes the antirational element in artistic experience: intuition, chance, the spur of the moment. Composers who wish to avoid the rational ordering of musical sound may rely on the element of chance and allow, let us say, a throw of dice to determine the selection of their material, or may perhaps build their pieces around a series of random numbers generated by a computer. They may construct a piece from sounds selected at random; arrange it in sections but allow the performer to choose the order in which these are to be played; or indicate the general course of events in regard to pitches, durations, registers, but leave it up to the performer to fill in the details. The performer may shuffle the pages in any sequence he desires; play one fragment rather than another; or react to fellow players in one of several ways (or not at all). In any case, the performance becomes a musical "happening" in the course of which the piece is recreated afresh each time it is played.

When chance, choice, and the operation of random elements are given a free hand, the things that happen in a piece are dissociated from any pre-existing scheme. Such indeterminate music is known as *aleatory* (from *alea,* the Latin word for "dice," which from ancient times have symbolized the whims of chance). In aleatory music the overall form may be clearly indicated but the details are left to choice or chance. On the other hand, some composers will indicate the details of a composition clearly enough, but leave its overall shape to choice or chance; this type of flexible structure is known as *open form.*

Aleatory music

Open form

The mobiles of Alexander Calder (1898-1976) achieve an ideal of ever-changing form. **International Mobile**, 1949. (*Museum of Fine Arts, Houston. Gift of Dominique and John deMenil in memory of Marcel Schlumberger.*)

The composer John Cage has been the leader in this movement. "I try to arrange my composing means," he states, "so that I won't have any knowledge of what might happen." There are, naturally, limits beyond which the aleatory ideal cannot be pursued. At a certain point total freedom in music becomes either total chaos or total silence. All the same, contemporary composers have sought to create musical organisms that would take on a fresh form with each performance, just as Calder's mobiles constantly assume fresh forms. This desire for greater freedom complements the equally strong desire for the tightly organized, ultrarational structures of total serialism.

Related to these tendencies is the increased reliance on improvisation—a technique common enough in music of the Baroque and earlier eras, but so long dormant that it has had to be reintroduced, in the 1950's, and '60s, from the domain of jazz. Traditionally improvisation consists of spontaneous invention within a framework and a style that have been clearly established, so that player and listener have fairly well defined ideas of what is "good" and what is "bad." In the more extreme types of aleatory music no such criteria are envisaged, no value judgments called for: anything that happens is acceptable to the composer.

In the past, art has generally striven toward rational, highly organized forms functioning within an ideal universe in which cause gave rise to effect, in which the artist carefully selected what was essential and rigidly excluded what was not. To this ordered view of art, aleatory music and open form oppose an ideal of maximum freedom that mirrors an unpredictable, even irrational world continually in flux. Here art ceases to reflect life; it becomes a part of life, and as uncertain.

Electronic Music

"I have been waiting a long time for electronics to free music from the tempered scale and the limitations of musical instruments. Electronic instruments are the portentous first step toward the liberation of music." — EDGARD VARÈSE

Perhaps the single most important musical development of the 1950s and '60s was the emergence of electronic music. This was foreshadowed, during the earlier part of the century, by the invention of a variety of electronic instruments of limited scope. The most familiar of these is the electronic organ, which was developed primarily as a cheaper substitute for the traditional pipe organ. Others, such as the *Ondes Martenot*—an instrument producing sounds by means of an electronic oscillator and operated by a keyboard—found occasional use in concert music. Although these instruments were not sufficiently flexible to compete successfully with the traditional ones, they did point the way to future developments.

The post-war emergence of electronic music falls into three stages. The first stage came with the use of magnetic tape recording, which was much

*Musique
concrète*

more flexible as a medium for storing sounds than the flat disc recording that had been used previously. A group of technicians at the Paris radio station had already begun to experiment with what they called *musique concrète,* a music made up of natural sounds and sound effects recorded on discs and altered by changing the speed of the records. Their activities took on a new impetus when they began to use tape, which gave them a vastly wider range of possibilities in altering the sounds they used as source material, and also enabled them to cut and splice the sounds into new combinations. It was the great achievement of musique concrète to establish firmly the principle that all conceivable sounds and noises could serve as raw material for the creative musician.

There soon presented itself the possibility of using not only natural but also artificially generated sounds. A wide variety of equipment for generating and altering sounds came into use. Significant in this regard were the experiments carried on by Otto Luening and Vladimir Ussachevsky at Columbia University, and by Herbert Eimert and Karlheinz Stockhausen in Cologne. These men began their work in 1951. Within a few years there were studios for the production of tape music in many of the chief musical centers of Europe and America. With the raw sound (either naturally or electronically produced) as a starting point, the composer could isolate its components, alter its pitch, volume, or other dimensions, play it backward, add reverberation (echo), filter out some of the overtones (see Appendix V), or add additional components by splicing

The RCA Electronic Music Synthesizer at the Columbia-Princeton Music Center, New York.

The Mini Moog, a compact synthesizer admirably suited to live performances.

and overdubbing. Even though all these operations were laborious and time-consuming—it might take many hours to process only a minute of finished music—composers hastened to avail themselves of the new medium.

Synthesizers   The second step in the technical revolution came with the evolution of *synthesizers,* which are essentially devices combining sound generators and sound modifiers in one package with a unified control system. The first and most elaborate of these devices was the RCA Electronic Music Synthesizer, first unveiled in 1955; a more sophisticated model was installed four years later at the Columbia-Princeton studio in New York City. This immense and elaborate machine, which today would cost a quarter of a million dollars to build, is capable of generating any imaginable sound or combination of sounds, with an infinite variety of pitches, durations, timbres, dynamics, and rhythmic patterns far beyond the capabilities of conventional instruments. The synthesizer represented an enormous step forward, since the composer was now able to specify all the characteristics of the sound beforehand (by means of a punched paper tape), and thus could bypass most of the time-consuming "hand" techniques associated with tape-recorder music.

Because of its size and cost the RCA machine at Columbia has remained unique; but various smaller synthesizers have been devised that bring most of the resources of electronic music within the reach of a small studio. The best-known of these are the Moog and the Buchla; there is even a portable synthesizer known as the Syn-Ket, designed for the composer John Eaton. The smaller instruments can be played directly (although usually only one note at a time), thus making live performance a possibility.

Computer-generated music

The third stage of electronic development, which is still in progress, involves the use of the electronic computer as a sound generator. The basic principle here is the fact that the shape of any sound wave can be represented by a graph, and this graph can in turn be described by a series of numbers, each of which will represent a point on the graph. Such a series of numbers can be translated, by a device known as a digital-to-analog converter, into a sound tape that can be played on a tape recorder. In theory then, all that a composer has to do is to write down a series of numbers representing the sound wave he wants, feed it into the converter, and play the tape. But composers do not traditionally think in terms of the shape of sound waves, so it was necessary to devise a computer program that would translate musical specifications—pitches, durations, timbres, dynamics, and the like—into numbers. Several such programs have been prepared and are now in use. Potentially, computer sound-generation is the most flexible of all electronic media, and is likely to dominate the field in years to come.

Electronic music has two aspects of novelty. The most immediately obvious one is the creation of "new sounds," and this has impelled many musicians to use the new medium. Ultimately more important, perhaps, is the fact that the composer of electronic music is able to work directly with the sounds, and can produce a finished work without the help of an intermediary—the performer. We have seen that the serial approach demanded a totally controlled, totally specified music. This requirement found an invaluable ally in electronic music, which freed the composer from the limitations of conventional instruments and performers, leaving only the limitations of the human ear as restrictions upon his thought. An electronic work, once synthesized, was fixed forever in the form that the composer had intended; instead of "music to be performed," it was "music to be reproduced," and no longer needed the concert framework.

However, the combination of electronic sounds with live music has also proved to be a fertile field, especially since many younger composers have been working in both media. Works for soloist and recorded tape have become common, even "concertos" for tape recorder (or live-performance synthesizer) and orchestra. Electronic music has also influenced live music, challenging performers to extend themselves to produce new types of sound, and suggesting to composers new ways of thinking about conventional instruments.

We have used the term *electronic music* in the same way as we would speak of piano music or vocal music—to describe a medium, not a style. Just as piano music or vocal music may be in the Baroque, Classical, or Romantic style, so a piece using electronic sounds may be in one style or another. Naturally, when a composer writes for a particular medium he tries to take advantage of the things that it alone can do. From this point of view it does not make much sense to compose a piece of electronic music in the style of Bach or Beethoven (except, perhaps, as a stunt for the popular market). Electronic music is at its best when it says things that cannot be said in any other medium. All the same, composers of electronic music are free, just as they would be if they were writing for conventional instruments, to compose in any style that suits their fancy.

Other Aspects of the New Music

Whether it is serial or aleatory, live or electronic, most new music reflects the conviction that each composition is based upon a set of premises that are unique to it. The function of the piece is to realize fully what is implicit in these premises. Each work is regarded as a self-contained structure independent of all other structures, whose form springs from and is determined by conditions peculiar to itself. Ours obviously is no longer a time when thousands of pieces can be written in sonata, rondo,

Form   or A-B-A form. These forms ultimately had to degenerate into formulas, in spite of the infinite ingenuity with which the great masters handled them, because their rationale was based on the harmonic system of the Classic-Romantic era. The concept of predetermined form is completely alien to the spirit of the new music. The force that holds a piece together is not superimposed from without but flows directly out of the material. Since the material is unique to the piece, so is the form. It follows that today's composers have introduced infinite variety and flexibility into this aspect of music.

Pitch   Throughout the eighteenth and nineteenth centuries it was pitch—embodied in melody, harmony, and tonality—that was the dominant structural element of music. In the first half of the twentieth century rhythm in the abstract (as opposed to rhythm embodied in a theme) emerged as a form-generating principle. The new music has elevated dynamics and timbre to equal importance with pitch and rhythm, and these four dimensions may now play an equal role in determining the character of the musical discourse.

Contemporary attitudes, it need hardly be said, have liberated all the elements of music from the restrictions of the past. The concept of a music based on the twelve pitches of the chromatic (tempered) scale has obviously been left far behind. Electronic instruments make possible the use of sounds "in the cracks of the piano keys"—the microtonal intervals, such as quarter or third tones, that are smaller than the traditional semitone—and very skilled string and wind players have begun to master these novel scales. In addition, the notion of what is acceptable sonorous material has been broadened to include the domain that lies between musical and noise.

Rhythm   Rhythm, too, has been liberated from the shackles of tradition. In the past, musical time was measured according to a system of values that existed only in relation to each other: a whole note was equal to two halves, a half note equalled two quarters, and so on. These values bore no relation to absolute or physical time; they depended on the speed at which the piece was played. But electronic tape brings the composer face to face with the requirements of physical time. An inch of tape is equivalent to so many minutes and seconds. For him, therefore, musical time can no longer exist apart from physical time.

Stravinsky, Bartók, Schoenberg, and their disciples developed a musical rhythm no longer based on equal measures and the regular recurrence of accent. Their concepts have been immensely refined in the past quarter century. Music in the past gave the impression of flowing through time in an orderly fashion toward a preordained goal. Many composers today, on the other hand, try to focus the listener's attention on a texture in which each sonority or density stands almost by itself, detached from its surroundings. Their music may unfold as a series of sonorous points, each of which is momentarily suspended in time, surrounded by plenty of "air pockets" of organized silence: great static blocks of sound juxtaposed in musical space, fashioned out of tiny cell-like clusters that spin, whirl, combine, and recombine with a kind of cumulative force.

The new virtuosity

Musical styles so different from all that went before need a new breed of instrumentalists and vocalists to cope with their technical difficulties. One has only to attend a concert of avant-garde music to realize how far the art of piano playing or singing has moved from the world of Chopin and Verdi. The piano keyboard may be brushed or slammed with fingers, palm, or fist; or the player may reach inside to hit, scratch, or pluck the strings directly. A violinist may tap, stroke, and even slap his instrument. Vocal music runs the gamut from whispering to shouting, including all manner of groaning, moaning, or hissing on the way. Wind players have learned to produce a variety of double-stops, subtle changes of color, and microtonal progressions; and the percussion section has been enriched by an astonishing variety of noisemakers and special effects. True, the new performance skills have not yet filtered down to the members of our symphony orchestras. Performances of difficult new works are necessarily limited and, more often than not, unsatisfactory. When, after much effort, a contemporary composer does manage to obtain a hearing, it may be a traumatic experience for him to have his work mauled by players who are unable to cope with its technical problems. Fortunately, in each of the important musical centers groups of young players and singers are springing up who have a genuine affinity with the new music. Singers like Bethany Beardslee, Cathy Berberian, and Jan DeGaetani, pianists like David Burge, Robert Helps, Paul Jacobs, Robert Miller, Ursula Oppens, and Charles Rosen, violinists like Matthew Raimondi and Paul Zukofsky, to mention only a few, are masters of a new kind of virtuosity that cannot fail to amaze those who were brought up on the old. They are performing an invaluable service for the new music, and it is an encouraging sign that their numbers are growing.

We mentioned the impact of jazz on serious music during the second quarter of the century. The two genres have grown ever closer together. Serious composers today feel an affinity for the improvisational freedoms of jazz, as well as its cultivation of highly specialized, virtuoso styles of performance. Jazz composers, for their part, are strongly interested in certain avant-garde trends, such as electronics and serialism. The most successful example of this cross-fertilization is Gunther Schuller. He is but one of a number of gifted musicians on either side of the fence who are increasingly influenced by what is happening on the other side.

The Internationalism of the New Music

The advent of tape made it easy to take down a live performance without having to wait until it was recorded, and to send it to any part of the world. This, plus the development of the other media of communication—radio, television, recordings, and the jet plane—brought about an enormous speeding up in the dissemination of musical ideas. Composers in New York, Chicago, or Los Angeles are able to keep abreast of the latest developments in Cologne, Rome, or Paris. Many of the new composers are active on both sides of the Atlantic as performers, conductors, teachers, organizers of musical events, or participants in festivals of the new music. This inevitably has led to an internationalization of the musical scene. The new music is a language shared by European and American composers alike. In this sense music in the mid-twentieth century has recaptured something of the universality it held in the eighteenth century (and lost in the nineteenth as a result of the emphasis upon national schools).

The links between Europe and America were forged before World War II, when such leaders of European music as Stravinsky, Schoenberg, Bartók, Hindemith, and Krenek came to the United States. The war and the events leading up to it disrupted musical life on the Continent much more than in this country, with the result that the United States forged ahead in certain areas. For example, the first composer to apply serial organization to dimensions other than pitch was the American composer Milton Babbitt. The experiments of John Cage anticipated and influenced similar attempts abroad. Earle Brown was the first to use open form, Morton Feldman the first to write works that gave the performer a choice. Once the war was over the Europeans quickly made up for lost time. Intense experimentation went on in Italy, Germany, France, England, Holland, and Scandinavia. This has gradually spread eastward into the Communist world; serial and electronic music have also taken root in Japan.

In the following chapter we will discuss a group of composers——American and European—whose music is representative of the new trends. These men are pushing back boundaries and exploring frontiers;

they are actively enlarging the domain of what the rest of us can perceive, experience, and understand. Their music will bring you the excitement of discovering a new world of sound.

83 Composers of Our Time

"There is no avant-garde. There are only people who are a little late." — EDGARD VARÈSE

Crumb: Ancient Voices of Children

In recent years George Crumb (Charleston, West Virginia, 1929–) has forged ahead to a notable position among the composers of his generation. He owes this preeminence partly to the emotional character of his music, allied to a highly developed sense of the dramatic. His kind of romanticism is most unusual among the advanced composers of our time. Crumb uses contemporary technique for expressive ends that make an enormous impact in the concert hall. He has won numerous honors and awards, and is currently professor of composition at the University of Pennsylvania.

Poetry of Lorca

Crumb has shown an extraordinary affinity for the poetry of Federico García Lorca, the great poet who was killed by the Fascists during the Spanish Civil War. Besides *Ancient Voices of Children* (1970), his Lorca cycle includes four other works: *Night Music I* (1963); four books of madrigals (1965–69); *Songs, Drones, and Refrains of Death* (1968); and *Night of the Four Moons* (1969).

Ancient Voices of Children is a cycle of songs for mezzo-soprano, boy soprano, oboe, mandoline, harp, electric piano, and percussion. The texts are fragments of longer poems which Crumb grouped into a sequence so as to achieve musical continuity. There are two movements for instruments alone. These, and one of the vocal movements as well, are imbued with the spirit of dance. Indeed, the composer suggests that they can be performed by a dancer as well.

The score abounds in unusual effects. The soprano opens with a fantastic *vocalise* (a wordless melody, in this case based on purely phonetic sounds) which she directs at the strings of an electrically amplified piano, arousing a shimmering cloud of sympathetic vibrations. The pitch is "bent" to produce quarter tones. Included in the score are a toy piano, harmonica, and musical saw. The percussion players use all kinds of drums, gongs and cymbals, Tibetan prayer stones, Japanese temple bells, and tuned tom-toms (high-pitched drums of African origin); also a marimba, vibraphone, sleighbells, glockenspiel plates, and tubular bells.

George Crumb.

First song
Side 18/6 (S)
Side 12/6 (E II)

I. *El niño busca su voz.* Very free and fantastic in character. "The little boy was looking for his voice. (The king of the crickets had it.) In a drop of water the little boy was looking for his voice. I do not want it for speaking with; I will make a ring of it so that he may wear my silence on his little finger." The soprano part offers a virtuoso exhibition of what the voice can do in the way of cries, sighs, whispers, buzzings, trills, and percussive clicks (Crumb specifies *not* a clucking sound). There are even passages marked "fluttertongue"—an effect we have hitherto associated only with instruments. Throughout Crumb captures the rapturous, improvisational spirit of flamenco song. The passion is here, the sense of mystery and wonder—but in a thoroughly twentieth-century setting.

The boy soprano answers, singing offstage through a cardboard speaking tube. His "after-song" should sound "simple and unaffected, even naive." The boy's part ends *pppp,* "timidly."

In *Ancient Voices* Crumb has found the right music for the dark intimations of Lorca's poetry. The work has justly established itself as a prime example of contemporary imagination and feeling.

Carter: Eight Etudes and a Fantasy

"I like music to be beautiful, ordered, and expressive of the more important aspects of life."

Of the composers who have come into prominence in recent years, none is more widely admired by musicians than Elliott Carter (New York City, 1908–). His works are not of the kind that achieve easy popularity; but their profundity of thought and maturity of workmanship bespeak a musical intellect of the first order.

Carter started out with a musical idiom rooted in diatonic-modal harmony, but gradually assimilated a dissonant chromaticism that places him (if one must attach a label) among the Abstract Expressionists. He employs fluctuating tempo as a form-building element, through the use of a novel technique that he calls "metrical modulation," whereby the speed of the rhythmic pulse is subtly modified. When several instruments are playing together, each with its own pulse and each changing that pulse independently in a different direction, there results an original and powerful kind of texture.

Carter's impeccable craftsmanship is manifest in *Eight Etudes and a Fantasy* (1950), which offers a fine introduction to his art. The piece grew directly out of his activity as a teacher. He had asked his students to bring in examples illustrating the use of the woodwind instruments, and had invited four woodwind players to the class to perform them. Disappointed in what the class had written, he sketched some passages on the blackboard for the woodwind players to try. These later developed into the *Eight Etudes and a Fantasy,* a work that explores the possibilities of flute, oboe, clarinet, and bassoon in imaginative ways. An etude, it will be recalled, is a study piece that centers around a technical problem. As Chopin did in his etudes, Carter naturally combines the technical problem with an expressive purpose. This series of short pieces reveals an extraordinary

Elliott Carter.

command of woodwind writing and an aural imagination of the utmost originality.

Etude 4
Side 18/5 (S)
Side 12/4 (E II)

The fourth movement is a Vivace in ¾. It has been said that the essence of artistic creation is the ability to make much out of little. In this etude Carter makes much out of the littlest—a motivic cell consisting of two notes a semitone apart. This two-note kernal, tossed about among the instruments in diverse ways, flowers into melodies, harmonies, rhythms, colors, counterpoints, and dynamics. Wholly ingenious is Carter's way of having all four instruments, each playing its two tones, combine in a running scale. More important than the ingenuity is the charm of the result.

Etude 5
Side 18/5 (S)
Side 12/4 (E II)

Fifth is an Andante in 4/4. Marked cantando espressivo (singing, espressive), the fifth etude brings a change of mood. The expressive capacities of pure woodwind sound are utilized in this piece to create the kind of emotional lyricism that we generally associate with the string instruments. The music takes on an almost tragic intensity, and reveals anew how completely the vocabulary of atonality is attuned to the esthetic goals of Expressionism.

Etude 8
Side 18/5 (S)
Side 12/4 (E II)

The eighth etude is a Presto in 4/4. This is a *perpetuum mobile* (continuous motion) whose forward drive never lets up. The rapid sixteenth notes are heard against single quarter notes in high or low register that seem to comment on the main action. These quarter notes make an effective contrast, in rhythm as well as register, with the running passages.

Carter's works, oriented toward the most serious aspects of musical art, offer a continual challenge to the listener. They confirm his position as one of the most important composers in America.

Davidovsky: Synchronisms No. 1

The electronic medium all too easily can become austere and rather impersonal. It has been the signal achievement of Mario Davidovsky (Buenos Aires, Argentina, 1934–) to inject into this idiom a high order of wit and imagination. Davidovsky, who teaches composition at City College of the City University of New York and is a director of the Columbia-Princeton Electronic Center, has composed a variety of works for orchestra, ballet, and chamber groups; but he is best known for his lively electronic pieces.

Side 18/7 (S)
Side 12/7 (E II)

Among those is a series of works that combine electronic sounds with conventional instruments. Characteristic is *Synchronisms No. 1,* which opens with a single long-sustained tone on the flute that establishes the timbre of the solo instrument. When the accompaniment on tape enters, it hovers about the middle and lower registers. There is a vivacious interplay between the two bodies of sound, the opposition between them underlined through contrasts of timbre, register (high-low), dynamics (loud-soft), rhythm (fast notes-slow notes), quality (legato-staccato), type of attack

Mario Davidovsky.

and decay (percussive-melodic). The pure silvery tone of the flute sets off the guttural sounds of the tape, each maintaining its own character. As the composer expresses it, in the scientific phraseology that has attached itself to electronic composition, "Generally speaking, in the whole series of these pieces, a coherent musical continuum is sought while trying to respect the idiosyncracies of each medium." Noteworthy here is the dramatic tension that can be created through pure sound, the sense of movement and eventful activity, above all the animation, wit and fantasy that Davidovsky is able to infuse into his electronic compositions.

The second generation of electronic composers, by building on the discoveries of their predecessors, have been able greatly to expand the expressive gamut of the medium. In this development Mario Davidovsky has been and continues to be a leader.

Other Contemporaries (American)

The proponents of the new music in America include composers of several generations, representing a variety of personal styles and esthetic viewpoints.

Wolpe   Stefan Wolpe (Berlin, 1902–1972, New York), came to the United States in 1939, and his most important work has been done in this country.

Such pieces as his *Trio* (1963) for flute, cello and piano, and the *Chamber Piece No. 1* (1964) are examples of what has aptly been called "cumulative form." They are based on tiny motivic cells that generate increasing energy and tension as the music unfolds.

Cage

John Cage (Los Angeles, 1912–) is one of the daring experimenters of his generation. To the ultrarational music of the total serialists he opposed a music of total freedom based on chance and randomness. Thus he uses dice and similar procedures to produce an aleatory music that frees the performer—and the musical event—from the composer's control. Typical is *Fontana Mix* (1958), the first work on tape to establish conditions whose outcome could not be foreseen. The material consists of a set of drawings and transparent sheets, plus a graph, that can be combined in innumerable ways. Such a program allows chance to operate, so that *Fontana Mix* sounds different with each performance.

Weisgall

Hugo Weisgall (Ivančice, Czechoslovakia, 1912–), has specialized primarily in opera of a post-Expressionist cast. Among his works are *The Stronger* (after Strindberg; 1952) and *Six Characters in Search of an Author,* based on the Pirandello play (1956).

Babbitt

Milton Babbitt (Philadelphia, 1916–) has led the way toward total serialization, in which the basic row—or set, as Babbitt calls it—controls every aspect of the musical process—pitch, rhythm, dynamics, timbre. He has also been a leader in the attempt to combine live performances with electronic sound. *Philomel,* for live soprano and tape (1964), is an outstanding work in this area.

Perle

George Perle (Bayonne, New Jersey, 1915–) has sought to combine serial technique with the possibilities for harmonic direction and tension inherent in the major-minor system. This line of thought is fully explored in the eloquent *String Quartet No. 5* (1966).

Kirchner

Leon Kirchner (Brooklyn, 1919–) was a student of Schoenberg and Roger Sessions, and has assimilated many of the important traditions of the century into his expressive style. Two string quartets—*No. 1* (1949), with its Bartókian ancestry, and *No. 3* (1966), which uses electronic sounds—exemplify the range of Kirchner's resources and the development of his personal language.

Schuller

Gunther Schuller (New York, 1925–) is a leading representative of the "third stream" movement, which combines the techniques of contemporary music with those of jazz; his *Early Jazz* (1968) is one of the best books on the subject. On the other hand he has absorbed the serial techniques of the twelve-tone method. Jazz elements figure in *The Visitation* (1966), an opera on Schuller's own libretto after Franz Kafka's *The Trial,* and in his *Seven Studies on Themes of Paul Klee* for orchestra (1959).

Foss

Lukas Foss (Berlin, 1922–) developed an interest in group improvisation and aleatory procedures. *Time Cycle* (1960 version) offers a fine introduction to his style.

Martirano,   Among the many other composers who deserve mention here are: Sal-
Druckman,   vatore Martirano (1927–), whose vivid theater pieces make extensive use
Johnston, and of jazz materials and improvisation; Jacob Druckman (1928–), whose
Wuorinen   virtuoso instrumental and vocal works emphasize the theatrical as well as
the musical presence of the performers; Ben Johnston (1926–), whose
String Quartet No. 2 makes subtle and convincing use of microtonal materials; and Charles Wuorinen (1938–), the brilliant and prolific codirec-
tor of the Group for Contemporary Music. These are just a few members
of the immensely varied and talented community of composers who comprise the younger generation of American music.

Other Contemporaries (European)

Dallapiccola   Luigi Dallapiccola (Pisino, 1904–1975, Florence) united the age-old tradition of Italian vocal lyricism with the twelve-tone techniques of the Viennese school. Among his important works are *Canti di pregionia* (Songs of
Captivity; 1938–41) and the opera *Il prigioniero* (The Prisoner; 1944–
48).

Boulez   Pierre Boulez (Montbrison, 1925–) is the most important French composer of the postwar period. He is also the best known because of his widespread activities as a conductor, in which capacity he has propagandized
tirelessly in behalf of contemporary music. The emotional content of Boulez's own music extends from a gentle lyricism to a furious expressionism
that ranged him with the "angry young men" of our time. Among his chief
works are two piano sonatas (1946, 1948) and a still incomplete third; *Le
Marteau sans maître* (The Hammer without a Master; 1953–54), for contralto and six instruments; and *Pli selon pli* (Fold upon Fold; 1960), which
includes the three *Improvisions on Mallarmé*.

Stockhausen   The German counterpart of Pierre Boulez is Karlheinz Stockhausen
(Modrath, near Cologne, 1928–). He early became interested in the possibilities of electronic music, and has also explored the use of spatial dimensions, as in *Gruppen* (Groups; 1955–57), in which three orchestras, placed
on different sides of the audience, play independently, occasionally merging
in common rhythm or echoing each other.

Another approach to contemporary composition is exemplified by the
Xenakis   Greek composer Iannis Xenakis (Barila, Romania, 1922–), who was
trained as an engineer and bases his music theories on the laws of mathematics and physics. Xenakis has developed a distinctive musical idiom, as
can be heard in such works as *Pithoprakta* (1955–56)—the title means "action by probabilities"—for forty-six strings, two tenor trombones, xylophone, and wood block.

Berio   Luciano Berio (Oneglia, Italy, 1925–) is a leading figure among the
radicals of the post-Webern generation. A strong sense of theater pervades
his music, especially such works as *Circles* (1960), for soprano, harp, and

In painting, as in music, contemporary artists pursue a variety of personal styles and esthetic viewpoints. George Mathieu (b. 1921) in **Painting #7-1955** demonstrates the techniques of action painting for which he is famous. (*Courtesy Kootz Gallery, New York.*)

two percussionists; and the *Sinfonia* (1968), for vocal ensemble and orchestra.

Davies

Since World War II, the renaissance of English musical life has produced a number of gifted composers. Among the most notable is Peter Maxwell Davies (Manchester, 1934–).

Henze,
Reimann,
and Ligeti

Other important European figures include the Germans Hans Werner Henze (1926–), who began as an experimentalist of the Stockhausen stamp but has turned toward a more eclectic idiom; Aribert Reimann (1936–), composer of the opera *Melusine* and numerous skillful vocal works; and the Hungarian György Ligeti (1923–), whose choral music achieved wide attention through its use on the soundtrack of the film *2001*. There are many others, whose works prove that our time is as rich in gifted composers as was any era of the past.

Penderecki

Best-known among the younger Polish composers is Krzysztof Penderecki (1933–), who is endowed with a vivid imagination and a strong sense of dramatic effect. These qualities are apparent in his *Threnody for the Victims of Hiroshima* (1960), for fifty-two string instruments, which exploits a remarkable range of string sounds.

Postscript

We have included in these pages a variety of facts, historical, biographical, and technical, that have entered into the making of music and that must enter into an intelligent listening to music. For those who desire to explore the subject further we include a list of books that will guide the music lover in his reading. But books belong to the domain of words, and words have no power over the domain of sound. They are helpful only insofar as they lead us to the music.

The enjoyment of music depends upon perceptive listening. And perceptive listening (like perceptive anything) is something that we achieve gradually, with practice and some effort. By acquiring a knowledge of the circumstances out of which a musical work issued, we prepare ourselves for its multiple meanings; we lay ourselves open to that exercise of mind and heart, sensibility and imagination that makes listening to music so unique an experience. But in the building up of our musical perceptions —that is, of our listening enjoyment—let us always remember that the ultimate wisdom resides neither in dates nor in facts. It is to be found in one place only—the sounds themselves.

Appendices

APPENDIX I

Suggested Reading

The following list is merely a starting point, with emphasis on recent and easily available books. Those desiring to pursue the subject further will find specialized bibliographies in many of the works listed below. An asterisk (*) denotes a book available in a paperback edition.

On the Nature of Art

* Dewey, John. *Art as Experience.* New York: Putnam, 1958.
* Fleming, William. *Arts and Ideas.* New brief ed. New York: Holt, Rinehart & Winston, 1974.
* Meyer, Leonard B. *Music, the Arts and Ideas: Patterns and Predictions in 20th Century Culture.* Chicago: U. of Chicago, 1969.
* ———— *Emotion and Meaning in Music.* Chicago: U. of Chicago, 1956.
* Read, Herbert. *Art and Society.* Rev ed. New York: Schocken, 1966.

Dictionaries

Apel, Willi. *The Harvard Dictionary of Music.* 2nd rev. ed. Cambridge: Harvard, 1969.
* ————, and R. T. Daniel. *The Harvard Brief Dictionary of Music.* Cambridge: Harvard, 1960.
Baker's Biographical Dictionary of Musicians. 5th ed. (ed. Nicolas Slonimsky). New York: Schirmer, 1958, with 1971 supplement.
Grove's Dictionary of Music and Musicians. 6th ed. (ed. Stanley Sadie). New York: St. Martin's, 1977.
Scholes, Percy A. *Concise Oxford Dictionary of Music.* 2nd ed. (ed. J. O. Ward). New York: Oxford, 1964.
Thompson, Oscar. *The International Cyclopedia of Music and Musicians.* 10th rev. ed. (ed. Bruce Bohle). New York: Dodd, Mead, 1975.
Vinton, John (ed.). *Dictionary of Contemporary Music.* New York: Dutton, 1974.
Westrup, J. A., and F. Ll. Harrison. *The New College Encyclopedia of Music.* Rev. ed. (ed. Conrad Wilson). New York: Norton, 1977.

The Materials of Music

* Bekker, Paul. *The Orchestra.* New York: Norton, 1963.
* Bernstein, Leonard. *The Joy of Music.* New York: New American Library, 1967.
* Clough, John. *Scales, Intervals, Keys and Triads.* New York: Norton, 1964.
* Cooper, Grosvenor W., and Leonard Meyer. *The Rhythmic Structure of Music.* Chicago: U. of Chicago, 1960.
* Copland, Aaron. *What to Listen for in Music.* New York: Mentor, 1964.
Grove's Dictionary of Music and *Harvard Dictionary of Music:* articles on melody, harmony, rhythm, meter, tempo, timbre, etc.
* Manoff, Tom. *The Music Kit.* New York: Norton, 1976.
Ratner, Leonard G. *Music: The Listener's Art.* 2nd. ed. New York: McGraw-Hill, 1966.
* Tovey, Donald F. *The Forms of Music.* New York: Meridian, 1956.

Music History (One-Volume Works)

Borroff, Edith. *Music in Europe and the United States: A History.* Englewood Cliffs, N.J.: Prentice-Hall, 1971.
* Einstein, Alfred. *A Short History of Music.* New York: Random House, 1954.
* Gerboth, Walter, *et al.* (eds.). *An Introduction to Music: Selected Readings.* New York: Norton, 1969.

Grout, Donald. *A History of Western Music.* Rev. ed. New York: Norton, 1973.
* Janson, H. W., and Joseph Kerman. *A History of Art and Music.* New York: Abrams, 1968.
Lang, Paul Henry. *Music in Western Civilization.* New York: Norton, 1941.
* Wiora, Walter. *The Four Ages of Music* (tr. M. D. Herter Norton). New York: Norton, 1967.

Musical Instruments

Baines, Anthony (ed.). *Musical Instruments through the Ages.* New York: Walker, 1975.
* Marcuse, Sybil. *Musical Instruments: A Comprehen-*

sive Dictionary. New York: Norton, 1975.
Sachs, Curt. *History of Musical Instruments.* New York: Norton, 1940.

Styles and Periods

ANTIQUITY AND MEDIEVAL
Reese, Gustave. *Music in the Middle Ages.* New York: Norton, 1940.
Sachs, Curt. *The Rise of Music in the Ancient World.* New York: Norton, 1943.
* Seay, Albert. *Music in the Medieval World.* 2nd ed. Englewood Cliffs, N.J.: Prentice-Hall, 1975.
* Strunk, Oliver (ed.). *Source Readings in Music History: Antiquity and the Middle Ages.* New York: Norton, 1965.

RENAISSANCE AND BAROQUE
* Blume, Friedrich. *Renaissance and Baroque Music* (tr. M. D. Herter Norton). New York: Norton, 1967.
Bukofzer, Manfred F. *Music in the Baroque Era.* New York: Norton, 1947.
* Palisca, Claude V. *Baroque Music.* Englewood Cliffs, N.J.: Prentice-Hall, 1968.
Reese, Gustave. *Music in the Renaissance.* Rev. ed. New York: Norton, 1959.
* Strunk, Oliver (ed.). *Source Readings in Music History: The Baroque Era.* New York: Norton, 1965.
* ———— *Source Readings in Music History: The Renaissance.* New York: Norton, 1965.

CLASSIC AND ROMANTIC
* Blume, Friedrich. *Classic and Romantic Music* (tr. M. D. Herter Norton). New York: Norton, 1970.

Einstein, Alfred. *Music in the Romantic Era.* New York: Norton, 1947.
* Longyear, Rey M. *Nineteenth-Century Romanticism in Music.* 2nd. ed. Englewood Cliffs, N.J.: Prentice-Hall, 1973.
* Pauly, Reinhard G. *Music in the Classic Period.* 2nd. ed. Englewood Cliffs, N.J.: Prentice-Hall, 1973.
* Praz, Mario. *The Romantic Agony.* New York: Oxford, 1970.
* Rosen, Charles. *The Classical Style.* New York: Norton, 1972.
* Strunk, Oliver (ed.). *Source Readings in Music History: The Classic Era.* New York: Norton, 1965.
* ———— *Source Readings in Music History: The Romantic Era.* New York: Norton, 1965.

CONTEMPORARY
Austin, William. *Music in the Twentieth Century.* New York: Norton, 1966.
* Copland, Aaron. *The New Music, 1900–1960.* New York: Norton, 1968.
* Cowell, Henry. *American Composers on American Music.* New York: Ungar, 1962.
* Lang, Paul Henry, and Nathan Broder (eds.). *Contemporary Music in Europe: A Comprehensive Survey.* New York: Norton, 1967.
Machlis, Joseph. *Introduction to Contemporary Music.* New York: Norton, 1961.
* Salzman, Eric. *Twentieth-Century Music. An Introduction.* 2nd ed. Englewood Cliffs, N.J.: Prentice-Hall, 1974.

Jazz

* Blesh, Rudi, and Harriet Janis. *They All Played Ragtime.* Rev. ed. New York: Oak, 1966–71.
* Ellison, Ralph. "Sound and the Mainstream," in *Shadow and Act.* New York: Random House, 1972.
Feather, Leonard. *The Encyclopedia of Jazz.* Rev. ed. New York: Horizon, 1960.
Hodier, Andre. *Jazz: Its Evolution and Essence.* New York: Da Capo, 1975.

* Murray, Albert. *The Omni-Americans.* New York: Avon, 1971.
———— *The Hero and the Blues.* Columbia, Mo.: U. of Missouri, 1973.
Schuller, Gunther. *Early Jazz: Its Roots and Musical Development.* New York: Oxford, 1968.
* Shapiro, Nat, and Nat Hentoff (eds.). *Hear Me Talkin' to Ya: The Story of Jazz by the Men Who Made It.* New York: Dover, 1966.

* Spellman, A. B. *Black Music: Four Lives.* New York: Schocken, 1970.
* Stearns, Marshall. *The Story of Jazz.* New York: Oxford, 1970.
* Williams, Martin. *Where's the Melody? A Listener's*

Introduction to Jazz. Rev. ed. New York: Funk & Wagnalls, 1967.
* ——— *The Jazz Tradition.* New York: New American Library, 1971.

Genres

Cuyler, Louise. *The Symphony.* New York: Harcourt Brace Jovanovich, 1973.
Grout, Donald. *A Short History of Opera.* 2nd ed. New York: Columbia, 1965.
* Kerman, Joseph. *Opera as Drama.* New York: Vintage, 1956.

* Stevens, Denis (ed.). *A History of Song.* Rev. ed. New York: Norton, 1970.
* Ulrich, Homer. *Chamber Music.* 2nd ed. New York: Columbia, 1966.
* Weisstein, Ulrich (ed.). *The Essence of Opera.* New York: Norton, 1969.

Composers (By and On)

BACH, J. S.
* David, Hans T., and Arthur Mendel (eds.). *The Bach Reader.* Rev. ed. New York: Norton, 1966.
Geiringer, Karl, with Irene Geiringer. *Johann Sebastian Bach: The Culmination of an Era.* New York: Oxford, 1966.

BARTÓK
* Stevens, Halsey. *The Life and Music of Béla Bartók.* Rev. ed. New York: Oxford, 1967.

BEETHOVEN
* Anderson, Emily (ed. and tr.). *Selected Letters of Beethoven.* Rev. ed. New York: St. Martin's, 1967.
* Forbes, Elliot (ed.). *Thayers' Life of Beethoven.* Rev. ed. Princeton: Princeton U., 1967.
Kerman, Joseph. *The Beethoven Quartets.* New York: Knopf, 1967.
* Schindler, Anton. *Beethoven as I Knew Him.* New York: Norton, 1972.
* Sonneck, O. G. (ed.). *Beethoven: Impressions by His Contemporaries.* New York: Dover, 1967.
* Tovey, Donald F. *Beethoven.* New York: Oxford, 1965.

BERG
Adorno, Theodor W. *Alban Berg: A Biography of the Music.* New York: Grossman, 1975.

BERLIOZ
Barzun, J. *Berlioz and the Romantic Century.* 2 vols. 3rd ed. New York: Columbia, 1969.
* Berlioz, Hector. *Memoirs.* New ed. (ed. and tr. David Cairns). New York: Norton, 1975.

BOULEZ
Peyser, Joan. *Pierre Boulez.* New York: Macmillan, 1976.

BRAHMS
Burnett, James. *Brahms: A Critical Study.* New York: Praeger, 1972.
Geiringer, Karl. *Brahms: His Life and Works.* 2nd ed. New York: Oxford, 1947.

BRUCKNER
Redlich, H. F. *Bruckner and Mahler.* New York: Octagon, 1955.

BYRD
Fellowes, Edmund H. *William Byrd.* 2nd ed. London: Oxford, 1948.
Holst, Imogen. *Byrd.* New York: Praeger, 1972.

CAGE
* Cage, John. *A Year From Monday; New Lectures and Writings.* Middletown, Conn.: Wesleyan U., 1969.
* ——— *Silence.* Middletown, Conn.: Wesleyan U., 1961.

CHOPIN
Huneker, James. *Chopin: The Man and His Music* (ed. H. Weinstock). New York: Dover, 1966.
* Walker, Alan. *The Chopin Companion: Profiles of the Man and the Musician.* New York: Norton, 1973.

COPLAND
* Copland, Aaron. *Copland on Music.* New York: Norton, 1963.

COUPERIN
* Mellers, Wilfrid. *François Couperin and the French Classical Tradition.* New York: Dover, 1968.

DEBUSSY
* Debussy, Claude. "Monsieur Croche," in *Three Classics in the Esthetics of Music.* New York: Dover, 1962.
* Lockspeiser, Edward. *Debussy.* 4th ed. New York: McGraw-Hill, 1972.
* Vallas, Leon. *Claude Debussy: His Life and Works.* New York: Dover, 1973.

DVOŘÁK
Clapham, John. *Antonín Dvořák, Musician and Craftsman.* New York: St. Martin's, 1966.

GERSHWIN
Jablonski, Edward, and Lawrence Stewart. *The Gershwin Years.* New York: Doubleday, 1973.

Kimball, Robert E., and Alfred Simon. *The Gershwins.* New York: Atheneum, 1973.

GLUCK
* Einstein, Alfred. *Gluck.* New York: McGraw-Hill, 1972.

HANDEL
Abraham, Gerald (ed.). *Handel, A Symposium.* London: Oxford, 1954.
Dean, Winton. *Handel's Dramatic Oratorios and Masques.* London: Oxford, 1959.
* Lang, Paul Henry. *George Frideric Handel.* New York: Norton, 1966.

HAYDN
* Geiringer, Karl. *Haydn, a Creative Life in Music.* Rev. ed. Berkeley: U. of California, 1968.
Landon, H. C. Robbins. *The Symphonies of Joseph Haydn.* London: Barrie & Jenkins, 1955, 1961.

IVES
Ives, Charles. *Charles E. Ives Memos* (ed. John Kirkpatrick). New York: Norton, 1972.
* Perlis, Vivian. *Charles Ives Remembered: An Oral History.* New York: Norton, 1976.
Rossiter, Frank. *Charles Ives and His America.* New York: Liveright, 1975.

LISZT
Perenyi, Eleanor. *Liszt: The Artist as Romantic Hero.* New York: Little, Brown, 1974.

MACDOWELL
MacDowell, Edward. *Critical and Historical Essays.* New York: Da Capo, 1969.

MAHLER
Cardus, Neville. *Gustav Mahler: His Mind and His Music.* New York: St. Martin's, 1965.
La Grange, Henri-Louis de. *Mahler.* New York: Doubleday, 1973.
* Mahler, Alma Schindler. *Gustav Mahler: Memories and Letters* (ed. Donald Mitchell). Rev. and enlarged. Seattle: U. of Washington, 1971.
Mitchell, Donald. *Gustav Mahler: The Wunderhorn Years.* Berkeley: U. of California, 1975.

MENDELSSOHN
Werner, Eric. *Felix Mendelssohn.* New York: Free Press, 1963.

MONTEVERDI
Arnold, Denis. *Monteverdi.* New York: Octagon, 1963.
* Arnold, Denis, and Nigel Fortune (eds.). *The Monteverdi Companion.* New York: Norton, 1972.

MOZART
Anderson, Emily (ed.). *Letters of Mozart and His Family.* 2 vols. 2nd ed. (ed. A. Hyatt King and Monica Carolan). New York: St. Martin's, 1966.
* Blom, Eric. *Mozart.* New York: Macmillan, 1966.

Deutsch, Otto Erich. *Mozart: A Documentary Biography.* 2nd ed. Stanford, Cal.: Stanford U., 1966.
* Landon, H. C. Robbins, and Donald Mitchell (eds.). *The Mozart Companion.* New York: Norton, 1969.
* Lang, Paul Henry (ed.). *The Creative World of Mozart.* New York: Norton, 1963.

MUSORGSKY
* Calvocoressi, M. D. *Mussorgsky.* New York: Collier, 1962.

PROKOFIEV
Nestyev, Israel V. *Prokofiev* (tr. Florence Jonas). Stanford, Cal.: Stanford U., 1960.

PUCCINI
Ashbrook, William. *The Operas of Puccini.* New York: Oxford, 1968.

RACHMANINOFF
Bertensson, S., and J. Leyda. *Sergei Rachmaninoff: A Lifetime in Music.* New York: New York U., 1956.

RAMEAU
* Girdlestone, C. M. *Jean-Philippe Rameau: His Life and Work.* New York: Dover, 1970.

RAVEL
Orenstein, Arbie. *Ravel: Man and Musician.* New York: Columbia, 1975.

SCARLATTI, D.
* Kirkpatrick, Ralph. *Domenico Scarlatti.* New York: Apollo, 1968.

SCHOENBERG
Rosen, Charles. *Arnold Schoenberg.* New York: Viking, 1975.
Schoenberg, Arnold. *Letters* (ed. E. Stein and E. Kaiser). New York: St. Martin's, 1958.

SCHUBERT
Deutsch, Otto Erich. *Schubert: Memoirs by His Friends.* New York: Humanities, 1958.
Gál, Hans. *Franz Schubert and the Essence of Melody.* New York: Int. Pubns. Service, 1974.

SCHUMANN
* Chissell, Joan. *Schumann.* New York: Collier-Macmillan, 1962.
* Schumann, Robert. *On Music and Musicians.* New York: Norton, 1969.

SESSIONS
* Sessions, Roger. *The Musical Experience of Composer, Performer, Listener.* Princeton: Princeton U., 1971.
* ———— *Questions About Music.* New York: Norton, 1971.

SIBELIUS
Layton, Robert. *Sibelius and his World.* New York: Viking, 1970.

Tawaststjerna, Erik. *Sibelius.* Berkeley: U. of California, 1975.

STRAUSS, R.
Mann, William S. *Richard Strauss: A Critical Study of the Operas.* New York: Oxford, 1966.
Marek, George. *Richard Strauss: The Life of a Non-Hero.* New York: Simon & Schuster, 1967.

STRAVINSKY
* Lang, Paul Henry (ed.). *Stravinsky: A New Appraisal of His Work.* New York: Norton, 1963.
* Stravinsky, Igor. *An Autobiography.* New York: Norton, 1962.
* ——— *Poetics of Music.* Cambridge: Harvard, 1970.
——— , with Robert Craft. *Retrospectives and Conclusions.* New York: Knopf, 1969.
——— *Themes and Episodes.* New York: Knopf, 1966.
* Vlad, Roman. *Stravinsky.* 2nd ed. London: Oxford, 1967.
White, Eric Walter. *Stravinsky, the Composer and His Works.* Berkeley: U. of California, 1966.

TCHAIKOVSKY
* Abraham, Gerald. *The Music of Tchaikovsky.* New York: Norton, 1974.

Weinstock, Herbert. *Tchaikovsky.* New York: Knopf, 1943.

THOMSON
* Thomson, Virgil. *American Music Since 1910.* New York: Holt, Rinehart & Winston, 1971.
——— *The Art of Judging Music.* New York: Greenwood, 1969.

VERDI
Osborne, Charles. *The Complete Operas of Verdi.* New York: Knopf, 1970.

VIVALDI
* Pincherle, Marc. *Vivaldi.* New York: Norton, 1962.

WAGNER
* Gutman, Robert. *Richard Wagner: The Man, His Mind, and His Music.* New York: Harcourt Brace Jovanovich, 1974.
* Newman, Ernest. *The Life of Richard Wagner.* 4 vols. New York: Cambridge, 1976.

WEBERN
Kolneder, Walter. *Anton Webern: An Introduction to His Works* (tr. Humphrey Searle). Berkeley: U. of California Press, 1968.

APPENDIX II

Comparative Ranges of Voices and Instruments

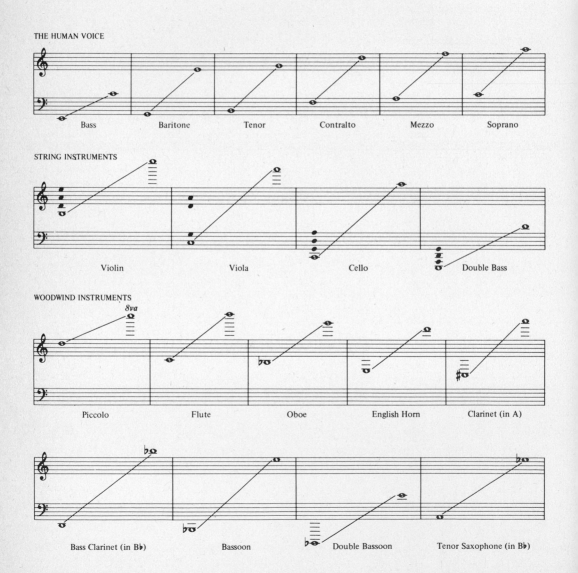

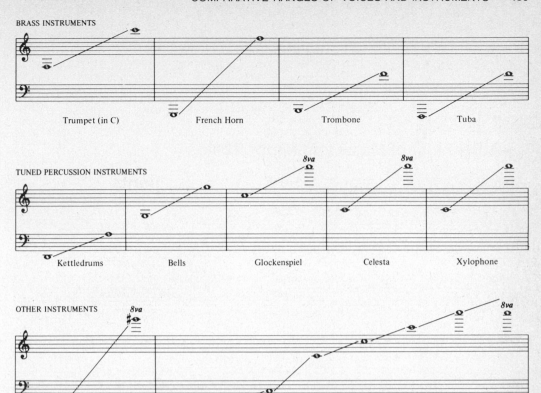

APPENDIX III

Complete List of Major and Minor Scales

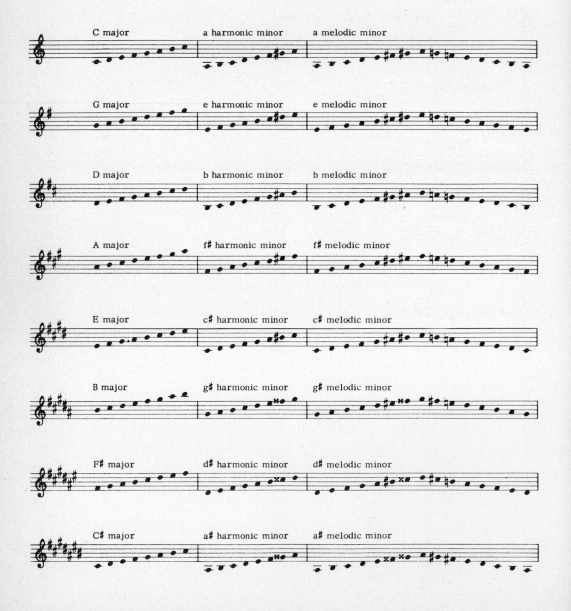

APPENDIX IV

Chronological List of Composers, World Events, and Principal Figures in Literature and the Arts 1300–1976

WORLD EVENTS	COMPOSERS	PRINCIPAL FIGURES
1307 *Dante's* Divine Comedy.	GUILLAUME DE MACHAUT (c. 1300–77)	Francesco Petrarch (1304–74)
1337 *Beginning of the Hundred Years' War between England and France.*		Giovanni Bocaccio (1313–75)
		Geoffrey Chaucer (c. 1340–1400)
1415 *John Huss burned for heresy. Henry V defeats French at Agincourt.*	GUILLAUME DUFAY (c. 1400–74) ANTOINE BUSNOIS (d. 1492) JOHANNES OCKEGHEM (c. 1420– c. 1495)	Luca della Robbia (1400–82) Giovanni Bellini (1430–1516) François Villon (1431–c. 1465) Sandro Botticelli (1447–1510)
1431 *Joan of Arc executed.*		Leonardo da Vinci (1452–1519)
1456 *Gutenberg Bible.*	JOSQUIN DES PREZ (c. 1450–1521)	Desiderius Erasmus (1466–1536) Niccolò Machiavelli (1469–1527)
1492 *Columbus discovers New World.*		Albrecht Dürer (1471–1528) Michelangelo (1475–1564)
1501 *First book of printed music published by Petrucci in Florence.*		Titian (1477–1576) Raphael (1483–1520) François Rabelais (1490–1553)
1506 *St. Peter's begun by Pope Julius II.*		Hans Holbein (1497–1543) Benvenuto Cellini (1500–71)
1509 *Henry VIII becomes King of England.*		
	THOMAS TALLIS (c. 1505–85)	
1513 *Ponce de Leon discovers Florida. Balboa reaches Pacific.*		
	JACOB ARCADELT (c. 1505– c. 1560)	
1519 *Cortez begins conquest of Mexico.*		
1534 *Henry VIII head of Church of England.*	ANDREA GABRIELI (c. 1520–86)	
1536 *Anne Boleyn beheaded.*	GIOVANNI DA PALESTRINA (c. 1525–94)	Pierre de Ronsard (1524–85) Pieter Brueghel (1525–69)
1541 *De Soto discovers the Mississippi.*		
	ROLAND DE LASSUS (c. 1532–94)	Michel de Montaigne (1533–92)
1558 *Elizabeth I becomes Queen of England.*	WILLIAM BYRD (1543–1623) GIULIO CACCINI (1545–1618)	El Greco (1542–1614) Miguel de Cervantes (1547–1616)

WORLD EVENTS	COMPOSERS	PRINCIPAL FIGURES
1572 *St. Bartholomew's Eve Massacre.*	TOMÁS LUIS DE VICTORIA (c. 1549–1611)	Edmund Spenser (1552–99)
1587 *Mary Queen of Scots executed.*	LUCA MARENZIO (c. 1553–99)	
1588 *Drake defeats Spanish Armada.*	GIOVANNI GABRIELI (c. 1557–1612)	
	THOMAS MORLEY (1557–1603)	
1590 *First three books of Spenser's* Faerie Queene *published.*	CARLO GESUALDO (1560–1613) JACOPO PERI (1561–1633)	William Shakespeare (1564–1616)
	CLAUDIO MONTEVERDI (1567–1643)	
1601 *Shakespeare,* Hamlet.		John Donne (1573–1631)
	JOHN WILBYE (1574–1638)	Ben Jonson (1573–1637)
1609 *Henry Hudson explores Hudson River.*	THOMAS WEELKES (c. 1575–1623)	Peter Paul Rubens (1577–1640)
	ORLANDO GIBBONS (1583–1625)	Frans Hals (1580?–1666)
1611 *King James Version of Bible.*	HEINRICH SCHÜTZ (1585–1672)	Gianlorenzo Bernini (1598–1680)
	GIACOMO CARISSIMI (1605–74)	Anthony Van Dyck (1599–1641)
1620 *Mayflower Compact. Plymouth settled. Francis Bacon's Novum Organum.*		Diego Velázquez (1599–1660) Rembrandt (1606–69) Pierre Corneille (1606–84)
1637 *Descartes's Discourse on Method.*		John Milton (1608–74) Molière (1622–73)
1640 The Bay Psalm Book, *first book printed in the American colonies.*	JEAN-BAPTISTE LULLY (1632–87)	John Bunyan (1628–88) John Dryden (1631–1700)
1642 *Puritan Revolution begins in England.*		Jan Vermeer (1632–75)
	DIETRICH BUXTEHUDE (1637–1707)	Sir Christopher Wren (1632–1723) Jean Baptiste Racine (1639–99)
1661 *Reign of Louis XIV begins. Absolutism.*	ARCANGELO CORELLI (1653–1713)	Daniel Defoe (1659?–1731)
1664 *New Amsterdam becomes New York.*		
1667 *Spinoza's Ethics.*	HENRY PURCELL (1659–95)	
1669 *French Academy of Music founded.*		Jonathan Swift (1667–1745)
	FRANÇOIS COUPERIN (1668–1733)	
1682 *Reign of Peter the Great begins.*		Joseph Addison (1672–1719)
	ANTONIO VIVALDI (1678–1741)	Richard Steele (1672–1729)
	GEORG TELEMANN (1681–1767)	Jean Antoine Watteau (1684–1721)
1702 *Start of War of the Spanish Succession.*	JEAN-PHILIPPE RAMEAU (1683–1764)	Alexander Pope (1688–1744)
1712 *Queen Anne succeeded by George I, Handel's patron.*	JOHANN SEBASTIAN BACH (1685–1750)	
1715 *First Opéra Comique founded.*	DOMENICO SCARLATTI (1685–1757)	
1715 *Reign of Louis XV begins.*	GEORGE FRIDERIC HANDEL (1685–1759)	Voltaire (1694–1778)
1719 *Herculaneum and Pompeii rediscovered. Classical Revival.*	GIOVANNI BATTISTA PERGOLESI (1710–36)	Giovanni Battista Tiepolo (1696–1770) William Hogarth (1697–1764)
1732 *Linnaeus's System of Nature.*	WILHELM FRIEDEMANN BACH (1710–84)	François Boucher (1703–70) Henry Fielding (1707–54)
1732 *George Washington born.*	CHRISTOPH WILLIBALD GLUCK (1714–87)	Samuel Johnson (1709–84) Jean Jacques Rousseau (1712–78)
1737 *San Carlo Opera, Naples, opened.*	CARL PHILIPP EMANUEL BACH (1714–88)	Laurence Sterne (1713–68) Thomas Gray (1716–71)
1740 *Age of Enlightened Despots begins, lasting till 1796.*	JOHANN STAMITZ (1717–57) JOSEPH HAYDN (1732–1809)	Sir Joshua Reynolds (1723–92) Thomas Gainsborough (1727–88)

WORLD EVENTS	COMPOSERS	PRINCIPAL FIGURES
1743 *Thomas Jefferson born.*	JOHANN CHRISTIAN BACH (1735–82)	Oliver Goldsmith (1728–74)
1752 *Franklin's discoveries in electricity.*		Pierre Augustin Caron de Beaumarchais (1732–99)
1756 *Opening of Seven Years' War (in America, the French and Indian War).*	WILLIAM BILLINGS (1746–1800) DOMENICO CIMAROSA (1749–1801)	Jean Honoré Fragonard (1732–1809) Edward Gibbon (1737–94) Jean Antoine Houdon (1741–1828) Francisco José de Goya (1746–1828)
1759 *Wolfe captures Quebec.*		Jacques Louis David (1748–1825) Johann Wolfgang von Goethe (1749–1832)
1763 *Canada ceded to England.*	SUPPLY BELCHER (1751–1836) MUZIO CLEMENTI (1752–1832) WOLFGANG AMADEUS MOZART (1756–91)	
1765 *Watt's steam engine.*		William Blake (1757–1827)
c. 1770 *Beginning of the factory system.*	DANIEL READ (1757–1836) MARIA LUIGI CHERUBINI (1760–1842)	Robert Burns (1759–96) Johann Christoph Friedrich von Schiller (1759–1805)
1771 *First edition,* Encyclopaedia Britannica.		
1776 *Adam Smith's* The Wealth of Nations.	LUDWIG VAN BEETHOVEN (1770–1827)	William Wordsworth (1770–1850) Sir Walter Scott (1771–1832)
1778 *La Scala Opera opened in Milan.*	GASPARO SPONTINI (1774–1851)	Samuel Taylor Coleridge (1772–1834) J. M. W. Turner (1775–1851)
1781 *Kant's* Critique of Pure Reason.		John Constable (1776–1837) Jean Dominique Ingres (1780–1867)
1787 *Constitutional Convention.*	NICCOLÒ PAGANINI (1782–1840)	
1789 *French Revolution begins.*	TIMOTHY SWAN (1785–1842)	George Gordon Lord Byron (1788–1824)
1791 *Bill of Rights.*	CARL MARIA VON WEBER (1786–1826)	
1793 *Eli Whitney's cotton gin.*		Alphonse Lamartine (1790–1869)
1796 *Jenner introduces vaccination.*	GIACOMO MEYERBEER (1791–1864)	Jean Louis Géricault (1791–1824)
1798 *Malthus's* Essay on Population.	GIOACCHINO ROSSINI (1792–1868)	Percy Bysshe Shelley (1792–1822)
1800 *Laplace's mechanistic view of universe. Volta invents voltaic pile.*	LOWELL MASON (1792–1872)	John Keats (1795–1821) Thomas Carlyle (1795–1881)
1803 *Louisiana Purchase.*		John Baptiste Camille Corot (1796–1875)
1807 *Hegel's* Phenomenology of Mind.	GAETANO DONIZETTI (1797–1848)	Alexander Pushkin (1799–1837) Honoré de Balzac (1799–1850)
1812 *Napoleon invades Russia.*	FRANZ SCHUBERT (1797–1828)	Eugène Delacroix (1799–1863) Alexandre Dumas (1802–70)
1815 *Battle of Waterloo. Congress of Vienna.*	VINCENZO BELLINI (1801–35)	Victor Hugo (1802–85)
1817 *Ricardo's* Political Economy and Taxation.	HECTOR BERLIOZ (1803–69) JOHANN STRAUSS (THE FATHER: 1804–49)	Ralph Waldo Emerson (1803–82) Nathaniel Hawthorne (1804–64) George Sand (1804–76)
1819 *First steamship to cross Atlantic.*	MICHAEL GLINKA (1804–57) FELIX MENDELSSOHN (1809–47)	Honoré Daumier (1808–79) Edgar Allan Poe (1809–49)
1823 *Monroe Doctrine.*	FRÉDÉRIC FRANÇOIS CHOPIN (1810–49) ROBERT SCHUMANN (1810–56)	Nikolai Gogol (1809–52) Alfred Lord Tennyson (1809–92) William Makepeace Thackeray (1811–63)
1824 *Bolivar liberates South America.*	FRANZ LISZT (1811–86)	Charles Dickens (1812–70)

WORLD EVENTS	COMPOSERS	PRINCIPAL FIGURES
1829 *Independence of Greece.*	RICHARD WAGNER (1813–83)	Robert Browning (1812–89)
	GIUSEPPE VERDI (1813–1901)	Charlotte Brontë (1816–55)
1830 *First railroad, Liverpool–Manchester. July Revolution in France.*	WILLIAM HENRY FRY (1815–64)	Henry David Thoreau (1817–62)
	CHARLES GOUNOD (1818–93)	Emily Brontë (1818–48)
	JACQUES OFFENBACH (1819–80)	Ivan Sergeyevich Turgenev (1818–83)
1832 *Morse invents telegraph.*		Herman Melville (1818–91)
		George Eliot (1819–80)
1833 *Slavery outlawed in British Empire.*	CÉSAR FRANCK (1822–90)	Walt Whitman (1819–92)
		John Ruskin (1819–1900)
1834 *McCormick patents mechanical reaper.*	ÉDOUARD LALO (1823–92)	Pierre Charles Baudelaire (1821–67)
		Gustave Flaubert (1821–80)
1837 *Queen Victoria ascends the throne.*	BEDŘICH SMETANA (1824–84)	Feodor Mikhailovich Dostoevsky
	ANTON BRUCKNER (1824–96)	(1821–81)
1839 *Daguerrotype invented, beginnings of photography. N.Y. Philharmonic Society and Vienna Philharmonic founded.*	JOHANN STRAUSS (THE SON: 1825–99)	Dante Gabriel Rossetti (1828–82)
	GEORGE FREDERICK BRISTOW (1825–98)	Henrik Ibsen (1828–1906)
1846 *Repeal of Corn Laws. Famine in Ireland.*	STEPHEN COLLINS FOSTER (1826–64)	George Meredith (1828–1909)
	WILLIAM MASON (1829–1905)	Leo Nikolaevich Tolstoi (1828–1910)
1848 *Revolutions throughout Europe.*	LOUIS MOREAU GOTTSCHALK (1829–69)	Emily Dickinson (1830–86)
		Camille Pissarro (1830–1903)
1848 *Gold Rush in California.* Mill's Political Economy. Marx's Communist Manifesto.	JOHANNES BRAHMS (1833–97)	Édouard Manet (1832–83)
	ALEXANDER BORODIN (1834–87)	James McNeill Whistler (1834–1903)
1852 *Second Empire under Napoleon III.* Stowe's Uncle Tom's Cabin.	CAMILLE SAINT-SAËNS (1835–1921)	Hilaire Germain Edgar Degas (1834–1917)
	LÉO DELIBES (1836–91)	Mark Twain (1835–1910)
1853 *Commodore Perry opens Japan to West. Crimean War.*		Winslow Homer (1836–1910)
	MILY BALAKIREV (1837–1910)	Algernon Charles Swinburne (1837–1909)
	GEORGES BIZET (1838–75)	
1855 *Charge of the Light Brigade.*	MODEST MUSORGSKY (1839–81)	William Dean Howells (1837–1920)
	JOHN KNOWLES PAINE (1839–1906)	H. H. Richardson (1838–86)
1857 *Dred Scott decision.*		Henry Adams (1838–1918)
		Paul Cézanne (1839–1906)
		Alphonse Daudet (1840–97)
		Auguste Rodin (1840–1917)
1858 *Covent Garden opened as opera house.*	PETER ILYICH TCHAIKOVSKY (1840–93)	Claude Monet (1840–1926)
		Thomas Hardy (1840–1928)
1859 *Darwin's* Origin of Species. *John Brown raids Harper's Ferry.*	EMMANUEL CHABRIER (1841–94)	Émile Zola (1840–1902)
		Pierre Auguste Renoir (1841–1919)
1861 *Serfs emancipated in Russia.*	ANTONÍN DVOŘÁK (1841–1904)	Stéphane Mallarmé (1842–98)
	JULES MASSENET (1842–1912)	Henry James (1843–1916)
1861 *American Civil War begins.*	EDVARD GRIEG (1843–1907)	Paul Verlaine (1844–96)
	NICHOLAS RIMSKY-KORSAKOV (1844–1908)	Friedrich Wilhelm Nietzsche (1844–1900)
1863 *Emancipation Proclamation.*		
		Anatole France (1844–1924)
1865 *Civil War ends. Lincoln assassinated.*	GABRIEL FAURÉ (1845–1924)	
	HENRI DUPARC (1848–1933)	Paul Gauguin (1848–1903)
1866 *Transatlantic cable completed.*		Augustus St. Gaudens (1848–1907)
	VINCENT D'INDY (1851–1931)	Joris Karl Huysmans (1848–1907)
1867 Marx's Das Kapital *(first vol.). Alaska purchased.*	ARTHUR FOOTE (1853–1937)	Guy de Maupassant (1850–93)
	LEOŠ JANÁČEK (1854–1928)	Robert Louis Stevenson (1850–94)

WORLD EVENTS	COMPOSERS	PRINCIPAL FIGURES
1870 *Franco-Prussian War.*		Vincent Van Gogh (1853–90)
	GEORGE CHADWICK (1854–1931)	Arthur Rimbaud (1854–91)
1871 *William I of Hohenzollern becomes German Emperor. Vatican Council proclaims papal infallibility. Paris Commune. Unification of Italy complete; Rome becomes capital. Stanley and Livingston in Africa.*	ERNEST CHAUSSON (1855–99)	Oscar Wilde (1856–1900)
	SIR EDWARD ELGAR (1857–1934)	Louis H. Sullivan (1856–1924)
		John Singer Sargent (1856–1925)
	RUGGIERO LEONCAVALLO (1858–1919)	George Bernard Shaw (1856–1950)
		Joseph Conrad (1857–1924)
1873 *Dynamo developed.*	GIACOMO PUCCINI (1858–1924)	Georges Seurat (1859–91)
		A. E. Housman (1859–1936)
1875 *New Paris Opera House opened.*	HUGO WOLF (1860–1903)	Anton Chekov (1860–1904)
	ISAAC ALBÉNIZ (1860–1909)	James M. Barrie (1860–1937)
	GUSTAV MAHLER (1860–1911)	
1876 *Telephone invented. Internal-combustion engine. Bayreuth theater opened.*	EDWARD MACDOWELL (1861–1908)	Aristide Maillol (1861–1945)
	CHARLES MARTIN LOEFFLER (1861–1935)	
1877 *Phonograph invented.*	ARTHUR WHITING (1861–1936)	
1880 *Irish Insurrection.*	CLAUDE DEBUSSY (1862–1918)	Gerhart Hauptmann (1862–1946)
	FREDERICK DELIUS (1862–1934)	Maurice Maeterlinck (1862–1949)
1881 *Tsar Alexander II assassinated. President Garfield shot.*	HORATIO PARKER (1863–1919)	Gabriele D'Annunzio (1863–1938)
	PIETRO MASCAGNI (1863–1945)	
	RICHARD STRAUSS (1864–1949)	Henri de Toulouse-Lautrec (1864–1901)
1881 *Panama Canal begun. Boston Symphony founded.*	ALEXANDER GRECHANINOV (1864–1956)	
	PAUL DUKAS (1865–1935)	Rudyard Kipling (1865–1936)
1882 *Koch discovers tuberculosis germ. Berlin Philharmonic founded.*	ALEXANDER GLAZUNOV (1865–1936)	William Butler Yeats (1865–1939)
	JEAN SIBELIUS (1865–1957)	Romain Rolland (1866–1943)
1883 *Brooklyn Bridge opened. Nietzsche's Thus Spake Zarathustra. Metropolitan Opera opened. Amsterdam Concertgebouw founded.*	FERRUCCIO BUSONI (1866–1924)	Wassily Kandinsky (1866–1944)
	ERIK SATIE (1866–1925)	H. G. Wells (1866–1946)
	ENRIQUE GRANADOS (1867–1916)	Arnold Bennett (1867–1931)
		John Galsworthy (1867–1933)
	MRS. H. H. A. BEACH (1867–1944)	Luigi Pirandello (1867–1936)
	HENRY F. GILBERT (1868–1928)	Edmond Rostand (1868–1918)
1884 *Pasteur discovers inoculation against rabies.*		Maxim Gorky (1868–1936)
	ALBERT ROUSSEL (1869–1937)	Edward Arlington Robinson (1869–1935)
1886 *Statue of Liberty unveiled in New York Harbor.*		Henri Matisse (1869–1954)
	ALEXANDER SCRIABIN (1871–1915)	Frank Lloyd Wright (1869–1959)
		André Gide (1870–1951)
1887 *Daimler patents high-speed internal-combustion engine.*	ARTHUR FARWELL (1872–1951)	John Marin (1870–1953)
	RALPH VAUGHAN WILLIAMS (1872–1958)	John M. Synge (1871–1909)
		Marcel Proust (1871–1922)
1889 *Eiffel Tower, Paris World's Fair opened. Brazil becomes republic.*		Theodore Dreiser (1871–1945)
		Georges Rouault (1871–1958)
	MAX REGER (1873–1916)	Sergei Diaghilev (1872–1929)
1890 *Journey around world completed in 72 days.*	SERGEI RACHMANINOV (1873–1943)	Piet Mondrian (1872–1946)
		Willa Cather (1873–1947)
	DANIEL GREGORY MASON (1873–1953)	
1892 *Duryea makes first American gas buggy.*	ARNOLD SCHOENBERG (1874–1951)	Robert Frost (1874–1963)
		Hugo Von Hofmannsthal (1874–1929)
1893 *World's Columbian Exposition, Chicago.*	CHARLES IVES (1874–1954)	Gertrude Stein (1874–1946)
	MAURICE RAVEL (1875–1937)	W. Somerset Maugham (1874–1965)

WORLD EVENTS	COMPOSERS	PRINCIPAL FIGURES
1894 *Nicholas II, last Tsar, ascends throne.*	MANUEL DE FALLA (1876–1946) JOHN ALDEN CARPENTER (1876–1951)	Rainer Maria Rilke (1875–1926) Thomas Mann (1875–1955) Constantine Brancusi (1876–1958)
1894 *Beginning of Dreyfus affair, lasting till 1905.*	CARL RUGGLES (1876–1971)	Isadora Duncan (1877–1927) Marsden Hartley (1877–1943)
1895 *Roentgen discovers X-rays. Marconi's wireless telegraphy.*	OTTORINO RESPIGHI (1879–1936)	John Masefield (1878–1967) Vachel Lindsay (1879–1931) Paul Klee (1879–1940)
1896 *Becquerel finds radioactivity in uranium. Olympic games revived. Gold rush in Alaska.*	ERNEST BLOCH (1880–1959) ILDEBRANDO PIZZETTI (1880–1968)	E. M. Forster (1879–1969) Raoul Dufy (1879–1953) Guillaume Apollinaire (1880–1918) Jacob Epstein (1880–1959)
1897 *Queen Victoria's Diamond Jubilee.*	BÉLA BARTÓK (1881–1945) GEORGES ENESCO (1881–1955)	Fernand Léger (1881–1955) Pablo Picasso (1881–1973)
1898 *Pierre and Marie Curie discover radium. Empress Elizabeth of Austria-Hungary assassinated. Spanish-American War.*	JOHN POWELL (1882–1963) IGOR STRAVINSKY (1882–1971) ZOLTÁN KODÁLY (1882–1967)	Georges Braque (1882–1963) James Joyce (1882–1941) Jean Giraudoux (1882–1944) Virginia Woolf (1882–1945)
1899 *Boer War. First International Peace Conference at the Hague.*	GIAN FRANCESCO MALIPIERO (1882–1973) EDGARD VARÈSE (1883–1965)	Franz Kafka (1883–1924) Maurice Utrillo (1883–1955)
1900 *Boxer Insurrection in China. Count Zeppelin tests dirigible balloon. Philadelphia Symphony founded.*	ANTON VON WEBERN (1883–1945)	Jose Ortega y Gasset (1883–1955)
1901 *Queen Victoria dies, Edward VII succeeds. De Vries's mutation theory.*	CHARLES T. GRIFFES (1884–1920) ALBAN BERG (1885–1935) JELLY ROLL MORTON (1885–1941)	Amadeo Modigliani (1884–1920) D. H. Lawrence (1885–1930) Sinclair Lewis (1885–1951) François Mauriac (1885–)
1903 *Wrights' first successful airplane flight. Ford organizes motor company.*	WALLINGFORD RIEGGER (1885–1961) HEITOR VILLA-LOBOS (1887–1959)	André Maurois (1885–1967) Diego Riviera (1886–1957) Juan Gris (1887–1927)
1904 *Opening of Russo-Japanese War. London Symphony founded. The Abbey Theatre opens in Dublin.*		Marcel Duchamp (1887–1968) William Zorach (1887–) Georgia O'Keefe (1887–) Hans Arp (1887–1966)
1905 *Sigmund Freud founds psychoanalysis. Norway separates from Sweden. First Russian Revolution.*	BOHUSLAV MARTINU (1890–1959)	Marc Chagall (1887–) Kurt Schwitters (1887–1948)
1905 *Einstein's theory of relativity first published.*	JACQUES IBERT (1890–1963) SERGE PROKOFIEV (1891–1952)	Giorgio de Chirico (1888–) T. S. Eliot (1888–1965) T. E. Lawrence (1888–1935) Thomas Hart Benton (1889–)
1906 *San Francisco earthquake and fire.*	ARTHUR HONEGGER (1892–1955)	Karel Čapek (1890–1938) Max Ernst (1891–)
1907 *Second Hague Conference. Triple Entente. William James's Pragmatism.*	DARIUS MILHAUD (1892–1974) DOUGLAS MOORE (1893–1969)	Grant Wood (1892–1944) John P. Marquand (1893–1960) Joan Miro (1893–)
1908 *Model T Ford produced.*	BESSIE SMITH (1894–1937)	Ernst Toller (1893–1939) e. e. cummings (1894–1962)
1909 *Peary reaches North Pole.*		Aldous Huxley (1894–1963) Robert Graves (1895–)
1911 *Amundsen reaches South Pole.*	WALTER PISTON (1894–76) KAROL RATHAUS (1895–1954) PAUL HINDEMITH (1895–1963)	
1912 *China becomes republic. Titanic sinks.*	WILLIAM GRANT STILL (1895–) CARL ORFF (1895–)	F. Scott Fitzgerald (1896–1940) Robert Sherwood (1896–1955) John Dos Passos (1896–)

WORLD EVENTS	COMPOSERS	PRINCIPAL FIGURES
1914 *Panama Canal completed. World War I begins.*	HOWARD HANSON (1896–) ROGER SESSIONS (1896–) VIRGIL THOMSON (1896–)	William Faulkner (1897–1962)
1915 Lusitania *sunk. Einstein presents theory of relativity.*	HENRY COWELL (1897–1965) QUINCY PORTER (1897–1966)	Louis Aragon (1897–)
1917 *U.S. enters World War I. Russian Revolution. Prohibition Amendment.*	GEORGE GERSHWIN (1898–1937)	Sergei Eisenstein (1898–1948)
1918 *Kaiser abdicates. World War I ends in armistice.*	ROY HARRIS (1898–)	Bertolt Brecht (1898–1956)
1919 *Treaty of Versailles. League of Nations formed. Mussolini founds Italian Fascist Party.*	E. K. ("DUKE") ELLINGTON (1899–1974) CARLOS CHÁVEZ (1899–)	Ernest Hemingway (1898–1961) Alexander Calder (1898–1976) Henry Moore (1898–)
1920 *Nineteenth Amendment (women's suffrage). Ireland granted home rule.*	RANDALL THOMPSON (1899–) FRANCIS POULENC (1899–1963)	Hart Crane (1899–1932) Federico García Lorca (1899–1936)
1922 *Discovery of insulin. Fascist revolution in Italy. John Dewey's* Human Nature and Conduct.	AARON COPLAND (1900–) ERNST KRENEK (1900–)	Thomas Wolfe (1900–38) Ignazio Silone (1900–)
1923 *USSR established.*	KURT WEILL (1900–50)	André Malraux (1901–76)
1924 *Lenin dies.*	LOUIS ARMSTRONG (1900–71)	John Steinbeck (1902–68)
1927 *Lindbergh's solo flight across Atlantic. Sacco and Vanzetti executed.*	RUTH CRAWFORD (1901–53)	
1928 *Graf Zeppelin crosses Atlantic. First radio broadcast of N.Y. Philharmonic Orchestra.*	SIR WILLIAM WALTON (1902–) STEFAN WOLPE (1902–72)	Langston Hughes (1902–67) George Orwell (1903–50)
1930 *Penicillin and the planet Pluto discovered.*	LUIGI DALLAPICCOLA (1904–75)	Mark Rothko (1903–70) Salvador Dali (1904–)
1931 *Japan invades Manchuria. Empire State Building completed.*	MARC BLITZSTEIN (1905–64) DMITRI SHOSTAKOVICH (1906–75)	George Balanchine (1904–) Christopher Isherwood (1904–) Willem de Kooning (1904–)
1933 *Franklin D. Roosevelt inaugurated. Hitler takes over German government.*	ELLIOTT CARTER (1908–)	Arthur Koestler (1905–) Jean-Paul Sartre (1905–)
1936 *First sit-down strike. Sulfa drugs introduced in U.S.*	OLIVIER MESSIAEN (1908–)	David Smith (1906–62) Samuel Beckett (1906–)
1937 *Japan invades China. Spanish Civil War.*	HOWARD SWANSON (1909–)	W. H. Auden (1907–73) Theodore Roethke (1908–63)
1939 *World War II starts: Germany invades Poland, Britain and France declare war on Germany, Russia invades Finland. U.S. revises neutrality stand.*	SAMUEL BARBER (1910–) WILLIAM SCHUMAN (1910–)	Richard Wright (1908–60) Stephen Spender (1900–)
1940 *Roosevelt elected to third term. Churchill becomes British prime minister.*	GIAN CARLO MENOTTI (1911–) VLADIMIR USSACHEVSKY (1911–)	Franz Kline (1910–62) Philip Guston (1912–)

WORLD EVENTS	COMPOSERS	PRINCIPAL FIGURES
1941 *U.S. attacked by Japan, declares war on Japan, Germany, Italy.*	ARTHUR BERGER (1912–)	Eugene Ionesco (1912–)
1943 *Germans defeated at Stalingrad and in North Africa. Italy surrenders.*	JOHN CAGE (1912–)	Jackson Pollock (1912–56)
1944 *D-Day. Invasion of France.*	HUGO WEISGALL (1912–)	
1945 *United Nations Conference at San Francisco. Germany surrenders. Atom bomb dropped on Hiroshima. Japan surrenders.*	BENJAMIN BRITTEN (1913–76)	Albert Camus (1913–60)
	BILLIE HOLIDAY (1915–59)	Ralph Ellison (1914–)
	DAVID DIAMOND (1915–)	Dylan Thomas (1914–53)
1946 *First meeting of U.N. General Assembly.*	GEORGE PERLE (1915–)	Tennessee Williams (1914–)
1948 *Gandhi assassinated.*	MILTON BABBITT (1916–)	Arthur Miller (1915–)
1949 *Communists defeat Chiang Kai-shek in China. USSR explodes atomic bomb.*	ALBERTO GINASTERA (1916–)	Robert Motherwell (1915–)
	ULYSSES KAY (1917–)	Robert Lowell (1917–)
1950 *North Koreans invade South Korea.*	LEONARD BERNSTEIN (1918–)	Ingmar Bergman (1918–)
1951 *Schuman Plan pools coal and steel markets of six European nations.*	GEORGE ROCHBERG (1918–)	J. D. Salinger (1919–)
1952 *George VI dies; succeeded by Elizabeth II. Eisenhower elected President.*	LEON KIRCHNER (1919–)	Federico Fellini (1920–)
	CHARLIE PARKER (1920–55)	
1954 *First atomic-powered submarine, Nautilus, launched. War in Indo-China.*	LUKAS FOSS (1922–)	Richard Wilbur (1921–)
1955 *Warsaw Pact signed. Salk serum for infantile paralysis.*	IANNIS XENAKIS (1922–)	
	GYÖRGY LIGETI (1923–)	Denise Levertov (1923–)
1957 *First underground atomic explosion.*	PETER MENNIN (1923–)	Norman Mailer (1923–)
1958 *Alaska becomes 49th state. Fifth Republic in France under De Gaulle.*	MEL POWELL (1923–)	
1959 *Castro victorious over Batista. Hawaii becomes 50th state.*	NED ROREM (1923–)	
	LUIGI NONO (1924–)	
1960 *Kennedy elected President.*	JULIA PERRY (1924–)	James Baldwin (1924–)
1962 *Cuban missile crisis. Algeria declared independent of France. Opening of Lincoln Center for the Performing Arts in New York.*	LUCIANO BERIO (1925–)	Kenneth Koch (1925–)
	PIERRE BOULEZ (1925–)	Robert Rauschenberg (1925–)
1963 *President Kennedy assassinated. Lyndon Johnson becomes 36th President.*	GUNTHER SCHULLER (1925–)	
1965 *First walk in space. White minority in Rhodesia proclaims itself independent of Britain. Alabama Civil Rights March.*	EARLE BROWNE (1926–) MORTON FELDMAN (1926–)	Allen Ginsberg (1926–)
	BEN JOHNSTON (1926–)	

WORLD EVENTS	COMPOSERS	PRINCIPAL FIGURES
1966 *France withdraws from NATO alliance.*		
1967 *Israeli-Arab "6-Day War." First successful heart transplant in South Africa.*	HANS WERNER HENZE (1926–)	
1968 *Richard M. Nixon elected President. Soviet occupation of Czechoslovakia. Martin Luther King and Robert F. Kennedy assassinated.*	SALVATORE MARTIRANO (1927–)	John Ashbery (1927–)
1969 *Apollo 11: first manned landing on the moon. De Gaulle resigns as French president.*	JACOB DRUCKMAN (1928–) KARLHEINZ STOCKHAUSEN (1928–)	John Hollander (1928–)
1970 *U.S. intervention in Cambodia. Nobel Prize in Literature to Aleksandr Solzhenitsyn.*	GEORGE CRUMB (1929–)	Claes Oldenburg (1929–)
1971 *Publication of the "Pentagon Papers." Peoples Republic of China admitted to the U.N.*	DAVID BAKER (1931–)	John Barth (1930–)
1972 *Richard Nixon re-elected. Attempted assassination of Governor George Wallace.*	KRZYSZTOF PENDERECKI (1933–)	Jean-Luc Godard (1930–) Jasper Johns (1930–)
1973 *Vietnam War ends. The "Watergate Affair" begins. Energy crisis. Vice President Agnew resigns.*	MARIO DAVIDOVSKY (1934–)	Harold Pinter (1930–)
1974 *President Nixon resigns.*	PETER MAXWELL DAVIES (1934–)	Andy Warhol (1931–) Yevgeny Yevtushenko (1933–)
1975 *Francisco Franco dies. Civil War in Angola.*		Imamu Amiri Baraka (LeRoi Jones) (1934–)
1976 *Viking spacecraft lands on Mars. U.S. celebrates its Bicentennial. Mao Tsetung dies. Jimmy Carter elected president.*	ARIBERT RIEMANN (1936–) CHARLES WUORINEN (1938–)	Frank Stella (1936–) Tom Stoppard (1937–)

APPENDIX V
The Harmonic Series

When a string or a column of air vibrates, it does so not only as a whole but also in segments —halves, thirds, fourths, fifths, sixths, sevenths, and so on. These segments produce the *overtones,* which are also known as *partials* or *harmonics.* What we hear as the single tone is really the combination of the fundamental tone and its overtones, just as what we see as white light is the combination of all the colors of the spectrum. Although we may not be conscious of the partials, they play a decisive part in our listening; for the presence or absence of overtones in the sound wave determines the timbre, the color of the tone. Following is the table of the Chord of Nature: the fundamental and its overtones or harmonics. Those marked with an asterisk are not in tune with our tempered scale.

Half the string gives the second member of the series, the octave above the fundamental. This interval is represented by the ratio 1:2; that is to say, the two tones of this interval are produced when one string is half as long as the other and is vibrating twice as fast. The one-third segment of the string produces the third member of the harmonic series, the fifth above the octave. This interval is represented by the ratio 2:3. We hear it when one string is two-thirds as long as the other and is vibrating one and a half times (³⁄₂) as fast. The one-fourth segment of the string produces the fourth member of the series, the fourth above. This interval is represented by the ratio 3:4, for its two tones are produced when one string is three-fourths as long as the other and vibrates one and a third times (⁴⁄₃) as fast. One fifth of the string produces the fifth member of the harmonic series, the major third, an interval represented by the ratio 4:5. One sixth of the string produces the sixth member of the series, the minor third, represented by the ratio 5:6; and so on. From the seventh to the eleventh partials we find approximate whole tones. Between the eleventh harmonic and its octave, 22, the semitone appears. After partial 22 we enter the realm of microtones (smaller than semitones) —third tones, quarter tones, sixth and eighth tones, and so on.

On the brass instruments, the player goes from one pitch to another not only by lengthening or shortening the column of air within the tube, which he does by means of valves, but also by splitting the column of air into its segments or partials, going from one harmonic to another by varying the pressure of his lips and breath. The bugle does not vary the length of the air column, for it has no valves. The familiar bugle calls consist simply of the different harmonics of the same fundamental.

Index

Definitions of terms appear on the pages indicated in **bold** type.